CREATIVE HOMEOWNER PRESS®

MOST POPULAR

ONE-STORY HOMES

Design V12563

470 Designs
To Suit a Range of Styles and Budgets

Contents

Note: Many of the homes featured in this book have a matching or corresponding Landscape or Deck Plan available. Some have both. These plans have an ▪L or a ▪D following their design number and square-footage notations. For information on how to order plans for landscapes and decks, see pages 370-379.

Copyright © 1994 Home Planners, Inc.

Published by Creative Homeowner Press®
A Division of Federal Marketing Corp.
24 Park Way
Upper Saddle River, NJ 07458

Printed in the United States of America.

Current Printing (last digit)
10   9   8   7   6   5   4   3   2   1

Library of Congress Number: 93-74015

ISBN: 1-880029-33-2

On The Cover: One of our favorite Cape Cod homes, Design V12563. For more information about this home, see page 313. Photo by Laszlo Regos.

The One-Story House
A Practical and Attractive Choice

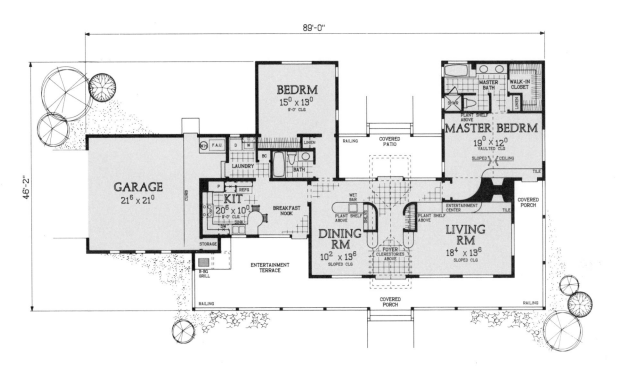

Design V13466
Square Footage: 1,800

This simple one-story rectangle contains some unique design elements that put it in a class above the norm. The bedrooms form a U-shaped area at the rear of the home that extends the patio, creating a private outdoor space. The wrapping front porch allows room off the kitchen for a summer dining area. A high-pitched roof means cathedral ceilings in the living and dining rooms and allows for triangular dormers that light up these gathering areas. Though smaller in size, the innovative design of this one-story home makes it both practical and distinctive.

A long-standing favorite, the one-story home remains a popular choice because of its low-slung, ground-hugging profile, and its easy adaptability and livability. The simplicity of its single floor plan allows for a variety of shapes—the most cost effective being the simple rectangle. With no projecting wings, bays or other protrusions—all under a straight, in-line roof—this configuration assures the most prudent use of building materials. The facility of its construction makes it less labor intensive—a penny-wise plus at the building stage.

Of course, low-cost construction is not the only consideration when making a home-plan choice. While the simple rectangle may be the most reasonable to build, an overly wide house may not be appropriate for some sites. For instance, a 100-foot-wide house may require the purchase of a large and costly lot. An equally livable arrangement with a 65-foot, L-shaped house, or a 50-foot U-shaped house, will probably result in a smaller and less expensive building site.

Consider also the energy efficiency of a square one-story over the same size rectangle. A 20' by 80' rectangular home yields a 1,600 square foot area with 200 linear feet of wall space, while a 40' by 40' home has an equal amount of square footage with only 160 feet of wall space. This results in an obvious heating and cooling savings.

For empty-nesters, the elderly or those who have physical limitations that make it impossible to climb stairs, the one-story is the clear-cut choice. Accessibility to all areas of the house and the freely adaptable floor plan mean that few if any special accommodations need to be made for adjusted living.

Remember, too, that the one-story need not be plain-Jane in its style. While added features such as bump-outs and protrusions are expensive, the amount of convenience and charm they provide and the quality of living they deliver may prove cost effective in the long run. A front-facing bay window or a kitchen greenhouse could make all the difference in an otherwise boxy design.

Basements and attics are a great investment and a provident addition to the simple one-story house. Providing square footage at a relatively low cost, these bonus areas allow for increased space with less expenditure. In many areas, building codes do not permit the location of bedrooms in typical basements. However, full or partial basements are ideal for developing recreational space, hobby areas, laundries and storage facilities. Such inexpensive space can make a one-story house significantly more livable, incorporating economy and effectual use of area. In areas of the country where basements are not practical or even possible, storage space can be allocated to garages, attics, closets and sheds.

The one-story home enjoys an advantage over multi-storied houses in providing for today's indoor/outdoor lifestyles. The one-story allows all zones—from living and sleeping areas to work spaces—direct access to patios, terraces and gardens without the expense encountered in second-floor balconies and decks. Simple amenities such as sloping ceilings, glass gable ends, skylights and sun rooms also help to open up interiors. Similarly, the U-shaped or L-shaped one-story often can enclose a pool or "outdoor room," further enhancing the economizing use of space and allowing privacy. See the plans, starting on page 13, for all the wonderful possibilities available in one-story design.

Design V13453
Square Footage: 1,442

A modified U-shaped one-story works better on a small lot than the sprawling rectangular plan. The garage at the front of the home acts as a noise buffer and provides a degree of privacy. Simple design details such as the tray ceiling in the master bedroom and the rounded glass bay in the dining room add special touches.

Design V13481B
Square Footage: 1,908

This rectangular one-story plan is an excellent choice for a narrow lot. The living areas and kitchen are to the left side, while the bedrooms hide behind the noise-dampening garage on the right. Vaulted ceilings throughout add a welcome sense of height and openness. A lovely "gazebo" extension on Design V13481B adds interest.

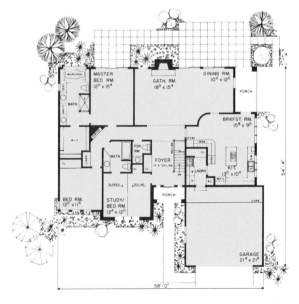

Design V13569
Square Footage: 1,981

This square one-story home compacts three bedrooms (or two and a study) into a smaller area than similarly sized rectangular plans. Amenities such as sloped ceilings, a whirlpool tub in the master bath, a covered dining porch and a warming hearth add charm and livability.

The Cost of a Mortgage

Monthly principal and interest per $1,000 of mortgage

Mortgage rate	15-year loan	20-year loan	25-year loan	30-year loan
5.000%	7.91	6.60	5.85	5.37
5.125%	7.97	6.67	5.92	5.44
5.250%	8.04	6.74	5.99	5.52
5.375%	8.10	6.81	6.07	5.60
5.500%	8.17	6.88	6.14	5.68
5.625%	8.24	6.95	6.22	5.76
5.750%	8.30	7.02	6.29	5.84
5.875%	8.37	7.09	6.37	5.92
6.000%	8.44	7.16	6.44	6.00
6.125%	8.51	7.24	6.52	6.08
6.250%	8.57	7.31	6.60	6.16
6.375%	8.64	7.38	6.67	6.24
6.500%	8.71	7.46	6.75	6.32
6.625%	8.78	7.53	6.83	6.40
6.750%	8.85	7.60	6.91	6.49
6.875%	8.92	7.68	6.99	6.57
7.000%	8.99	7.76	7.07	6.66
7.125%	9.06	7.83	7.15	6.74
7.250%	9.13	7.91	7.23	6.83
7.375%	9.20	7.98	7.31	6.91
7.500%	9.28	8.06	7.39	7.00
7.625%	9.35	8.14	7.48	7.08
7.750%	9.42	8.21	7.56	7.17
7.875%	9.49	8.29	7.64	7.26
8.000%	9.56	8.37	7.72	7.34
8.125%	9.63	8.45	7.81	7.43
8.250%	9.71	8.53	7.89	7.52
8.375%	9.78	8.60	7.97	7.61
8.500%	9.85	8.68	8.06	7.69
8.625%	9.93	8.76	8.14	7.78
8.750%	10.00	8.84	8.23	7.87
8.875%	10.07	8.92	8.31	7.96
9.000%	10.15	9.00	8.40	8.05
9.125%	10.22	9.08	8.48	8.14
9.250%	10.30	9.16	8.57	8.23
9.375%	10.37	9.24	8.66	8.32
9.500%	10.45	9.33	8.74	8.41
9.625%	10.52	9.41	8.83	8.50
9.750%	10.60	9.49	8.92	8.60
9.875%	10.67	9.57	9.00	8.69
10.000%	10.75	9.66	9.09	8.78
10.125%	10.83	9.74	9.18	8.87
10.250%	10.90	9.82	9.27	8.97
10.375%	10.98	9.90	9.36	9.06
10.500%	11.06	9.99	9.45	9.15
10.625%	11.14	10.07	9.54	9.25
10.750%	11.21	10.16	9.63	9.34
10.875%	11.29	10.24	9.72	9.43
11.000%	11.37	10.33	9.81	9.53
11.125%	11.45	10.41	9.90	9.62
11.250%	11.53	10.50	9.99	9.72
11.375%	11.61	10.58	10.08	9.81
11.500%	11.69	10.67	10.17	9.91
11.625%	11.77	10.76	10.26	10.00
11.750%	11.85	10.84	10.35	10.10
11.875%	11.93	10.93	10.44	10.20
12.000%	12.01	11.02	10.54	10.29
12.125%	12.09	11.10	10.63	10.39
12.250%	12.17	11.19	10.72	10.48
12.375%	12.25	11.28	10.82	10.58
12.500%	12.33	11.37	10.91	10.68
12.625%	12.41	11.45	11.00	10.77
12.750%	12.49	11.54	11.10	10.87
12.875%	12.58	11.63	11.19	10.97
13.000%	12.66	11.72	11.28	11.07

Note: Multiply the cost per $1,000 by the size of the mortgage (in thousands). The result is the monthly payment, including principal and interest. For example, for an $80,000 mortgage for 30 years at 10 percent, multiply 80 x 8.78 = $702.40.

A Checklist
For Plan Selection

Developing an architectural plan from the various wants and needs of an individual or family that fits into lifestyle demands and design elegance is the most efficient way to assure a livable plan. It is not only possible but highly desirable to design a plan around such requirements as separate bedrooms for each member of the family, guest suites, a quiet study area, an oversized entertainment area, a two-car garage, a completely private master suite, and a living room fireplace. Incorporated into this can be such wants as Tudor styling, 1½-stories, a large entry hall, decks and balconies, and a basement.

While it is obviously best to begin with wants and needs and then design a home to fit these criteria, this is not always practical or even possible. A very effective way around this problem is to select a professionally prepared home plan which meets all needs and incorporates as many wants as possible. With careful selection, it will be possible to modify sizes and make other design adjustments to make the home as close to custom as can be. It is important to remember that some wants may have to be compromised in the interest of meeting budgetary limitations. The trick is to build the best possible home for the available money while satisfying all absolute needs.

Following are some cost-controlling ideas that can make a big difference in the overall price of a home:

1. Square or rectangular homes are less expensive to build than irregularly shaped homes.
2. It is less expensive to build on a flat lot than on a sloping or hillside lot.
3. The use of locally manufactured or produced materials cuts costs greatly.
4. Using stock materials and stock sizes of components takes advantage of mass production cost reductions.
5. The use of materials that can be quickly installed cuts labor costs. Prefabricating large sections or panels eliminates much time on the site.
6. The use of prefinished materials saves significantly on labor costs.
7. Investigating existing building codes before beginning construction eliminates unnecessary changes as construction proceeds.
8. Refraining from changing the design or any aspect of the plan after construction begins will help to hold down cost escalation.
9. Minimizing special jobs or custom-built items keeps costs from increasing.
10. Designing the house for short plumbing lines saves on piping and other materials.
11. Proper insulation saves heating and cooling costs.
12. Utilizing passive solar features, such as correct orientation, reduces future maintenance costs.

To help you consider all the important factors in evaluating a plan, the following checklist should be reviewed carefully. By comparing its various points to any plan and a wants-and-needs list, it will be possible to easily recognize the deficiencies of a plan or determine its appropriateness. Be sure to include family members in the decision-making process. Their ideas and desires will help in finding exactly the right plan.

CHECKLIST

The Neighborhood

1. _____ Reasonable weather conditions
2. No excess
   - _____ a. wind
   - _____ b. smog or fog
   - _____ c. odors
   - _____ d. soot or dust
3. _____ The area is residential
4. There are no
   - _____ a. factories
   - _____ b. dumps
   - _____ c. highways
   - _____ d. railroads
   - _____ e. airports
   - _____ f. apartments
   - _____ g. commercial buildings
5. _____ City-maintained streets
6. No hazards in the area
   - _____ a. quarries
   - _____ b. storage tanks
   - _____ c. power stations
   - _____ d. unprotected swimming pools

7. Reasonably close to
   - _____ a. work
   - _____ b. schools
   - _____ c. churches
   - _____ d. hospital
   - _____ e. shopping
   - _____ f. recreation
   - _____ g. public transportation
   - _____ h. library
   - _____ i. police protection
   - _____ j. fire protection
   - _____ k. parks
   - _____ l. cultural activities
8. _____ Streets are curved
9. _____ Traffic is slow
10. _____ Intersections are at right angles
11. _____ Street lighting
12. _____ Light traffic
13. _____ Visitor parking
14. _____ Good design in street
15. _____ Paved streets and curbs
16. _____ Area is not deteriorating
17. _____ Desirable expansion
18. _____ Has some open spaces

19. _____ Numerous and healthy trees
20. _____ Pleasant-looking homes
21. _____ Space between homes
22. _____ Water drains off
23. _____ Near sewerage line
24. _____ Storm sewers nearby
25. _____ Mail delivery
26. _____ Garbage pickup
27. _____ Trash pickup
28. _____ No city assessments

The Lot

1. _____ Title is clear
2. _____ No judgments against the seller
3. _____ No restrictions as to the use of the land or the deed
4. _____ No unpaid taxes or assessments
5. _____ Minimum of 70 feet of frontage
6. _____ House does not crowd the lot
7. _____ Possible to build on
8. _____ Few future assessments (sewers, lights, and so forth)
9. _____ Good top soil and soil percolation
10. _____ Good view
11. _____ No low spots to hold water
12. _____ Water drains off land away from the house
13. _____ No fill
14. _____ No water runoff from high ground
15. _____ If cut or graded there is substantial retaining wall
16. _____ Permanent boundary markers
17. _____ Utilities available at property line
18. _____ Utility hookup is reasonable
19. _____ Utility rates are reasonable
20. _____ Taxes are reasonable
21. _____ Water supply is adequate
22. _____ Regular, simply shaped lot
23. _____ Trees
24. _____ Do not have to cut trees
25. _____ Privacy for outside activities
26. _____ Attractive front yard
27. _____ Front and rear yards are adequate
28. _____ Front yard is not divided up by walks and driveway
29. _____ Outdoor walks have stairs grouped

The Floor Plan

1. _____ Designed by licensed architect
2. _____ Purchased from a reputable stock plan company
3. _____ Supervised by skilled contractor
4. Orientation
_____ a. sun
_____ b. view
_____ c. noise
_____ d. breeze
_____ e. contour of land
5. _____ Entry
6. _____ Planned for exterior expansion
7. Planned for interior expansion
_____ a. attic
_____ b. garage
_____ c. basement
8. _____ Simple but functional plan
9. _____ Indoor recreation area
10. _____ Wall space for furniture in each room
11. Well-designed hall
_____ a. leads to all areas
_____ b. no congestions

_____ c. no wasted space
_____ d. 3' minimum widths
12. _____ Easy to clean
13. _____ Easy to keep orderly
14. _____ Plan meets family's needs
15. _____ All rooms have direct emergency escape
16. Doorways functional
_____ a. no unnecessary doors
_____ b. wide enough for moving furniture through
_____ c. can see visitors through locked front door
_____ d. do not swing out into halls
_____ e. swing open against a blank wall
_____ f. do not bump other subjects
_____ g. exterior doors are solid
17. Windows are functional
_____ a. not too small
_____ b. enough but not too many
_____ c. glare-free
_____ d. roof overhang protection where needed
_____ e. large ones have the best view
_____ f. easy to clean
_____ g. no interference with furniture placement
_____ h. over kitchen sink
_____ i. open easily
18. _____ No fancy gadgets
19. _____ Room sizes are adequate
20. _____ Well-designed stairs
_____ a. treads are 9" minimum
_____ b. risers are 8" maximum
_____ c. 36" minimum width
_____ d. 3' minimum landings
_____ e. attractive
_____ f. easily reached
21. _____ Overall plan "fits" family requirements
22. _____ Good traffic patterns
23. _____ Noisy areas separated from quiet areas
24. _____ Rooms have adequate wall space for furniture
25. _____ Halls are 3'6" minimum

The Living Area

1. _____ Minimum space 12' x 16'
2. _____ Front door traffic does not enter
3. _____ Not in a traffic pattern
4. _____ Windows on two sides
5. _____ Has a view
6. _____ Storage for books and music materials
7. _____ Decorative lighting
8. _____ Whole family plus guests can be seated
9. _____ Desk area
10. _____ Fireplace
11. _____ Wood storage
12. _____ No street noises
13. _____ Privacy from street
14. _____ Acoustical ceiling
15. _____ Cannot see or hear bathroom
16. _____ Powder room
17. _____ Comfortable for conversation
18. Dining room
_____ a. used enough to justify
_____ b. minimum of 3' clearance around table
_____ c. can be opened or closed to kitchen and patio
_____ d. can be opened or closed to living room
_____ e. electrical outlets for table appliances

19. Family room
    _____ a. minimum space 10' x 12'
    _____ b. room for family activities
    _____ c. room for noisy activities
    _____ d. room for messy activities
    _____ e. activities will not disturb sleeping area
    _____ f. finish materials are easy to clean and durable
    _____ g. room for expansion
    _____ h. separate from living room
    _____ i. near kitchen
    _____ j. fireplace
    _____ k. adequate storage
20. _____ Dead-end circulation
21. _____ Adequate furniture arrangements

The Entry

1. _____ The entry is a focal point
2. _____ The outside is inviting
3. _____ The landing has a minimum depth of 5'
4. _____ Protected from the weather
5. _____ Has an approach walk
6. _____ Well planted
7. _____ Coat closet
8. _____ Leads to living, sleeping, and service areas
9. _____ Floor material attractive and easy to clean
10. _____ Decorative lighting
11. _____ Space for table
12. _____ Space to hang mirror
13. _____ Does not have direct view into any room

The Bedrooms

1. _____ Adequate number of bedrooms
2. _____ Adequate size—10' x 12' minimum
3. _____ Open into a hall
4. _____ Living space
5. _____ Children's bedroom has study and play area
6. _____ Oriented to north side
7. In quiet area
    _____ a. soundproofing
    _____ b. acoustical ceiling
    _____ c. insulation in walls
    _____ d. thermal glass
    _____ e. double doors
    _____ f. closet walls
8. _____ Privacy
9. _____ 4' minimum wardrobe rod space per person
10. Master bedroom
    _____ a. bath
    _____ b. dressing area
    _____ c. full-length mirror
    _____ d. 12' x 12' minimum
11. Adequate windows
    _____ a. natural light
    _____ b. cross-ventilation
    _____ c. windows on two walls
12. _____ Room for overnight guests
13. _____ Bathroom nearby
14. _____ Wall space for bed, nightstands, and dresser
15. _____ Quiet reading area

The Bathroom

1. _____ Well designed
2. _____ Plumbing lines are grouped
3. _____ Fixtures have space around them for proper use
4. _____ Doors do not interfere with fixtures
5. _____ Noises are insulated from other rooms
6. _____ Convenient to bedrooms
7. _____ Convenient to guests
8. _____ Ventilation
9. _____ Heating
10. _____ Attractive fixtures
11. _____ No windows over tub or shower
12. _____ Wall area around tub and shower
13. _____ Light fixtures are water tight
14. _____ Large medicine cabinet
15. _____ Children cannot open medicine cabinet
16. _____ No bathroom tie-ups
17. _____ Good lighting
18. _____ Accessible electrical outlets
19. _____ No electric appliance or switch near water supply
20. _____ Towel and linen storage
21. _____ Dirty clothes hamper
22. _____ Steamproof mirrors
23. _____ Wall and floor materials are waterproof
24. _____ All finishes are easy to maintain
25. _____ Curtain and towel rods securely fastened
26. _____ Grab bar by tub
27. _____ Mixing faucets
28. _____ Bath in service area
29. _____ No public view into open bathroom door
30. _____ Clean-up area for outdoor jobs and children's play

The Kitchen

1. _____ Centrally located
2. _____ The family can eat informally in the kitchen
3. _____ At least 20' of cabinet space
    _____ a. counter space on each side of major appliances
    _____ b. minimum of 8' counter work area
    _____ c. round storage in corners
    _____ d. no shelf is higher than 72"
    _____ e. floor cabinets 24" deep and 36" high
    _____ f. wall cabinets 15" deep
    _____ g. 15" clearance between wall and floor cabinets
4. _____ Work triangle is formed between appliances
    _____ a. between 12' and 20'
    _____ b. no traffic through the work triangle
    _____ c. refrigerator opens into the work triangle
    _____ d. at least six electric outlets in work triangle
    _____ e. no door between appliances
5. _____ No space between appliances and counters
6. _____ Window over sink
7. _____ No wasted space in kitchen
8. _____ Can close off kitchen from dining area
9. _____ Snack bar in kitchen
10. _____ Kitchen drawers are divided
11. _____ Built-in chopping block
12. _____ Writing and telephone desk
13. _____ Indoor play area visible from kitchen
14. _____ Outdoor play area visible from kitchen
15. _____ Exhaust fan
16. _____ Natural light
17. _____ Good lighting for each work area
18. _____ Convenient access to service area and garage
19. _____ Durable surfaces
20. _____ Dishwasher
21. _____ Disposal
22. _____ Built-in appliances
23. _____ Bathroom nearby

24. _____ Room for freezer
25. _____ Pantry storage

The Utility Room

1. _____ Adequate laundry area
2. _____ Well-lighted work areas
3. _____ 240-volt outlet
4. _____ Gas outlet
5. _____ Sorting area
6. _____ Ironing area
7. _____ Drip-drying area
8. _____ Sewing and mending area
9. _____ On least desirable side of lot
10. _____ Exit to outdoor service area
11. _____ Exit near garage
12. _____ Sufficient cabinet space
13. _____ Bathroom in area
14. _____ Accessible from kitchen
15. _____ Adequate space for washer and dryer
16. _____ Laundry tray
17. _____ Outdoor exit is protected from the weather
18. _____ Window

Working Areas

1. _____ Home repair area
2. _____ Work area for hobbies
3. _____ Storage for paints and tools
4. _____ Garage storage
5. _____ Incinerator area
6. _____ Refuse area
7. _____ Delivery area
8. _____ Near parking
9. _____ 240-volt outlet for power tools

Storage

1. _____ General storage space for each person
2. _____ 4' of rod space for each person
3. _____ Closet doors are sealed to keep out dust
4. _____ Minimum wardrobe closet size is 40" x 22"
5. _____ Cedar closet storage for seasonal clothing
6. _____ Bulk storage area for seasonal paraphernalia
7. _____ Closets are lighted
8. _____ Walk-in closets have adequate turnaround area
9. Storage for:
   _____ a. linen and towels
   _____ b. cleaning materials
   _____ c. foods
   _____ d. bedding
   _____ e. outdoor furniture
   _____ f. sports equipment
   _____ g. toys—indoor
   _____ h. toys—outdoor
   _____ i. bicycles
   _____ j. luggage
   _____ k. out-of-season clothes
   _____ l. storm windows and doors
   _____ m. garden tools
   _____ n. tools and paints
   _____ o. hats
   _____ p. shoes
   _____ q. belts
   _____ r. ties
   _____ s. bridge tables and chairs
   _____ t. camping equipment
   _____ u. china
   _____ v. silver
   _____ w. minor appliances
   _____ x. books

10. _____ Closets are ventilated
11. _____ Closets do not project into room
12. _____ Toothbrush holders in bathrooms
13. _____ Soap holders in bathrooms
14. _____ Adequate built-in storage
15. _____ Drawers cannot pull out of cabinet
16. _____ Drawers slide easily
17. _____ Drawers have divided partitions
18. _____ Adult storage areas easy to reach
19. _____ Children storage areas easy to reach
20. _____ Guest storage near entry
21. _____ Heavy storage areas have reinforced floors
22. _____ Sides of closets easy to reach
23. _____ Tops of closets easy to reach
24. _____ No wasted spaces around stored articles
25. _____ Sloping roof or stairs do not render closet useless
26. _____ Entry closet

The Exterior

1. _____ The design looks "right" for the lot
2. _____ Design varies from other homes nearby
3. _____ Design fits with unity on its site
4. _____ Definite style architecture—not mixed
5. _____ Simple, honest design
6. _____ Garage design goes with the house
7. _____ Attractive on all four sides
8. _____ Colors in good taste
9. _____ Finish materials in good taste
10. _____ Has charm and warmth
11. _____ Materials are consistent on all sides
12. _____ No false building effects
13. _____ Well-designed roof lines—not chopped up
14. _____ Window tops line up
15. _____ Bathroom windows are not obvious
16. _____ Does not look like a box
17. _____ Easy maintenance of finish materials
18. _____ Windows are protected from pedestrian view
19. _____ Attractive roof covering
20. _____ Gutters on roof
21. _____ Downspouts that drain into storm sewer
22. _____ Glass area protected with overhang or trees
23. _____ Dry around the house
24. _____ Several waterproof electric outlets
25. _____ Hose bib on each side
26. _____ Style will look good in the future

Outdoor Service Area

1. _____ Clothes hanging area
2. _____ Garbage storage
3. _____ Can storage
4. _____ On least desirable side of site
5. _____ Next to indoor service area
6. _____ Near garage
7. _____ Delivery area for trucks
8. _____ Fenced off from rest of site

Outdoor Living Area

1. _____ Area for dining
2. _____ Area for games
3. _____ Area for lounging
4. _____ Area for gardening
5. _____ Fenced for privacy
6. _____ Partly shaded
7. _____ Concrete deck at convenient places
8. _____ Garden walks

9. _____ Easy access to house
10. _____ Paved area for bikes and wagons
11. _____ Easy maintenance

Landscaping

1. _____ Planting at foundation ties
2. _____ Garden area
3. _____ Well-located trees
4. _____ Healthy trees
5. _____ Plants of slow-growing variety
6. _____ Landscaping professionally advised
7. _____ Garden walks
8. _____ Easy maintenance
9. _____ Extras as trellis or gazebo

Construction

1. _____ Sound construction
2. _____ All work complies to code
3. _____ Efficient contractor and supervision
4. _____ Honest builders
5. _____ Skilled builders
6. _____ Constructed to plans
7. Floors are well constructed
   _____ a. resilient
   _____ b. subfloor diagonal to joints
   _____ c. flat and even
   _____ d. slab is not cold
   _____ e. floor joists rest on 2" of sill—minimum
   _____ f. girder lengths are joined under points of support
8. Foundation is well constructed
   _____ a. level
   _____ b. sill protected from termites
   _____ c. vapor barrier
   _____ d. no cracks
   _____ e. no water seepage
   _____ f. no dryrot in sills
   _____ g. garage slab drains
   _____ h. waterproofed
   _____ i. walls are 8" thick
   _____ j. basement height 7'6" minimum
   _____ k. sills bolted to foundation
   _____ l. adequate vents
9. Walls are well constructed
   _____ a. plumb
   _____ b. no waves
   _____ c. insulation
   _____ d. flashing at all exterior joints
   _____ e. solid sheathing
   _____ f. siding is neat and tight
   _____ g. drywall joints are invisible
10. Windows are properly installed
    _____ a. move freely
    _____ b. weatherstripped
    _____ c. caulked and sealed
    _____ d. good-quality glass
11. Doors properly hung
    _____ a. move freely
    _____ b. exterior doors weatherstripped
    _____ c. exterior doors are solid-core
    _____ d. interior doors are hollow-core
12. Roof is well constructed
    _____ a. rafters are straight
    _____ b. all corners are flashed
    _____ c. adequate vents in attic
    _____ d. no leaks
    _____ e. building paper under shingles
13. _____ Tile work is tight

14. _____ Hot water lines are insulated
15. _____ Mortar joints are neat
16. _____ Mortar joints do not form shelf to hold water
17. _____ Ceiling is 8'0" minimum
18. _____ No exposed pipes
19. _____ No exposed wires
20. _____ Tight joints at cabinets and appliances
21. _____ Stairs have railings
22. _____ Neat trim application
23. _____ Builder responsible for new home flaws

The Fireplace

1. _____ There is a fireplace
2. _____ Wood storage near the fireplace
3. _____ Draws smoke
4. _____ Hearth in front (minimum 10" on sides; 20" in front)
5. _____ Does not project out into the room
6. _____ Has a clean-out
7. _____ Chimney top 2' higher than roof ridge
8. _____ No leaks around chimney in roof
9. _____ No wood touches the chimney
10. _____ 2" minimum air space between framing members and masonry
11. _____ No loose mortar
12. _____ Has a damper
13. _____ Space for furniture opposite fireplace
14. _____ Doors minimum of 6' from fireplace
15. _____ Windows minimum of 3' from fireplace
16. _____ On a long wall
17. _____ Install "heatilator"
18. _____ Install glass doors to minimize heat loss

Equipment

1. _____ All equipment listed in specifications and plans
2. _____ All new equipment has warranty
3. _____ All equipment is up to code standards
4. _____ All equipment is functional and not a fad
5. _____ Owner's choice of equipment meets builder's allowance
6. _____ Public system for utilities
7. _____ Private well is deep; adequate and healthy water
8. Electrical equipment is adequate
   _____ a. inspected and guaranteed
   _____ b. 240 voltage
   _____ c. 120 voltage
   _____ d. sufficient electric outlets
   _____ e. sufficient electric circuits—minimum of six
   _____ f. circuit breakers
   _____ g. television aerial outlet
   _____ h. telephone outlets
   _____ i. outlets in convenient places
9. Adequate lighting
   _____ a. all rooms have general lighting
   _____ b. all rooms have specific lighting for specific tasks
   _____ c. silent switches
   _____ d. some decorative lighting
   _____ e. light at front door
   _____ f. outdoor lighting
10. _____ Plumbing equipment is adequate
    _____ a. inspected and guaranteed
    _____ b. adequate water pressure
    _____ c. hot water heater—50-gallon minimum
    _____ d. shut-off valves at fixtures

_____ e. satisfactory city sewer or septic tank
_____ f. septic tank disposal field is adequate
_____ g. septic tank is large enough for house (1000 gallons for three-bedroom house, plus 250 gallons for each additional bedroom)
_____ h. water softener for hard water
_____ i. siphon vertex or siphon reverse-trap water closet
_____ j. clean-out plugs at all corners of waste lines
_____ k. water lines will not rust
_____ l. water pipes do not hammer
_____ m. waste lines drain freely
_____ n. cast iron with vitreous enamel bathtub
11. _____ Good ventilation through house and attic
12. Heating and cooling systems are adequate
_____ a. insulation in roof, ceiling, walls
_____ b. air conditioning system
_____ c. heating and cooling outlets under windows
_____ d. air purifier
_____ e. thermostatic control
_____ f. walls are clean over heat outlets
_____ g. comfortable in hot or cold weather
_____ h. automatic humidifier
_____ i. furnace blower is belt-driven
_____ j. quiet-heating plant
_____ k. ducts are tight
13. _____ Windows are of good quality
_____ a. storm windows
_____ b. secure locks
_____ c. screened
_____ d. double glazed in extreme weather (thermal)
_____ e. glass is ripple-free
_____ f. safety or safe thickness of glass
_____ g. moisture-free
_____ h. frost-free
14. Doors are of good quality
_____ a. secure locks on exterior doors
_____ b. attractive hardware
_____ c. hardware is solid brass or bronze
15. All meters easily accessible to meter readers
16. _____ Fire extinguisher in house and garage
17. _____ Acoustical ceiling
18. _____ Facilities to lock mail box
19. _____ Facilities to receive large packages
20. _____ Gas or electric incinerator
21. Adequate small hardware
_____ a. soap dishes
_____ b. toilet-paper holders
_____ c. toothbrush holders
_____ d. towel holders
_____ e. bathtub grab bars
_____ f. door and drawer pulls

The Garage

1. _____ Same style as the house
2. _____ Fits with house
3. _____ Single garage 12' x 22' minimum
4. _____ Double garage 22' x 22' minimum
5. _____ Larger than minimum size if used for storage or workshop
6. _____ Protected passage to house
7. _____ Doors are safe
8. _____ Access to overhead storage

Financial Checklist

1. _____ Do you understand conveyancing fees (closing costs)?
2. _____ Is the house a good investment?
3. _____ Is the total cost approximately three times your annual income?
4. _____ Have you shopped for the best loan?
5. _____ Do you have a constant payment plan (sliding principal and interest)?
6. _____ Is there a prepayment penalty?
7. _____ Will a week's salary cover the total housing expense for one month?
8. _____ Are all the costs itemized in the contract?
9. Do you understand the following closing costs?
_____ a. title search
_____ b. lawyer
_____ c. plot survey
_____ d. insurance, fire, and public liability
_____ e. mortgage tax
_____ f. recording mortgage
_____ g. recording deed
_____ h. bank's commitment fee
_____ i. state and county taxes
_____ j. state and government revenue stamps
_____ k. title insurance (protects lender)
_____ l. homeowner's policy (protects owner)
_____ m. transferring ownership
_____ n. mortgage service charge
_____ o. appraisal
_____ p. notarizing documents
_____ q. attendant fee (paying off previous mortgage)
_____ r. personal credit check
10. _____ Do you have extra cash to cover unforeseen expenses?
11. Can you afford to pay the following?
_____ a. closing costs
_____ b. old assessments or bonds
_____ c. new assessments or bonds
_____ d. downpayment
_____ e. immediate repairs
_____ f. immediate purchases (furniture, appliances, landscape, tools, fences, carpets, drapes, patio)
_____ g. adequate insurance
_____ h. mortgage payments
_____ i. general maintenance
_____ j. utilities (water, heat, electricity, phone, gas, trash pickup)
_____ k. special design features wanted
_____ l. extras not covered in plans and contract
_____ m. prepayment of interest and taxes for first month of transition
_____ n. moving
_____ o. gardener
_____ p. travel to work
_____ q. interest on construction loan
_____ r. advances to contractors
12. _____ Who will pay for the following?
_____ a. supervision costs of architect or contractor
_____ b. inspection fees
_____ c. increased costs during building
_____ d. building permits
_____ e. difficulties in excavation
_____ f. dry wells
_____ g. extra features the building inspector insists upon

The above Checklist is used with permission. It is taken from Home Planners' Guide to Residential Design _by Charles Talcott, Don Hepler, and Paul Wallach; 1986; McGraw-Hill, Inc._

ENGLISH TUDOR VERSIONS ....

have become increasingly popular in recent years. This style has emanated from the more massive two-story with its many gabled roofs, exposed half-timber work, stucco and muntined windows. More correctly identified as Elizabethan style, the Tudor term of reference has become an accepted misnomer. Other distinguishing features include large sculptured chimneys, brick and stone exterior surfaces and panelled doors. Of interest in this section are the houses which feature complete one-story livability, including first floor bedrooms, but deliver bonus sleeping facilities either upstairs or on a lower level. Truly an impressive and distinctive style.

Design V12785
Square Footage: 2,375

● Exceptional Tudor design! Passersby will take a second glance at this fine home wherever it may be located. And the interior is just as pleasing. As one enters the foyer and looks around, the plan will speak for itself in the areas of convenience and efficiency.

Cross room traffic will be avoided. There is a hall leading to each of the three bedrooms and study of the sleeping wing and another leading to the living room, family room, kitchen and laundry with washroom. The formal dining room can be entered from both

the foyer and the kitchen. Efficiency will be the by-word when describing the kitchen. Note the fine features: a built-in desk, pantry, island snack bar with sink and pass-thru to the family room. The fireplace will be enjoyed in the living and family rooms.

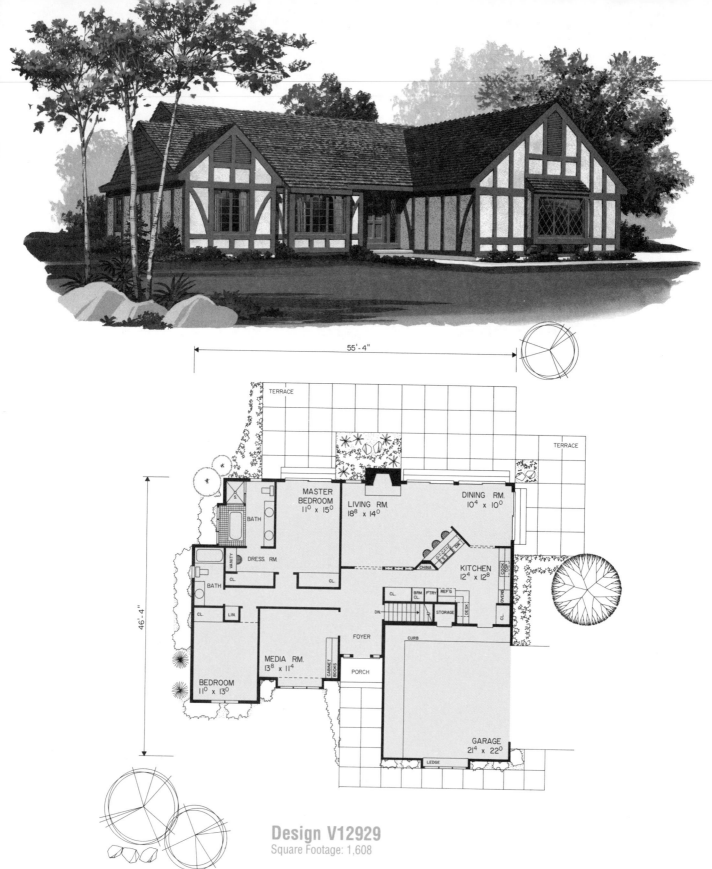

55'- 4"

46'- 4"

TERRACE

TERRACE

MASTER BEDROOM
11⁰ x 15⁰

LIVING RM.
18⁸ x 14⁰

DINING RM.
10⁴ x 10⁰

BATH

DRESS. RM.

VANITY

CL.

CL.

CHINA

KITCHEN
12⁴ x 12⁸

COOK TOP

OVENS

BATH

CL.

CL.

BRM CL.

PTRY

REF'G

CL.

LIN.

DN—

STORAGE

DESK

FOYER

CURB

CABINET BOOKS

MEDIA RM.
13⁸ x 11⁴

BEDROOM
11⁰ x 13⁰

PORCH

GARAGE
21⁴ x 22⁰

LEDGE

Design V12929
Square Footage: 1,608

● Here is a cozy Tudor exterior with a contemporary interior for those who prefer the charm of yesteryear combined with the convenience and practicality of today. This efficient floor plan will cater nicely to the living patterns of the small family; be it a retired couple or newlyweds. The efficient kitch-en is strategically located handy to the garage, dining room, dining terrace and the front door. The spacious living area has a dramatic fireplace that functions with the rear terrace. A favorite spot will be the media room. Just the place for the TV, VCR and stereo systems. The master bedroom is large and has plenty of wardrobe storage along with a master bath featuring twin lavatories and a tub plus stall shower. Don't miss the extra guest room (or nursery). This affordable home has a basement for the development of additional recreational facilities and storage.

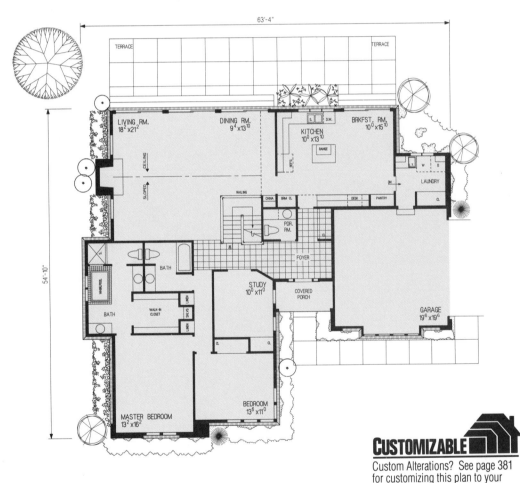

TERRACE

TERRACE

63'-4"

LIVING RM.
18²x21²

DINING RM.
9⁴x13¹⁰

KITCHEN
10⁰x13¹⁰

BRKFST. RM.
10⁰x15¹⁰

RANGE

CEILING

SLOPED

W D

LAUNDRY

RAILING

CHINA

BRM CL.

DESK

PANTRY

CL.

54'-10"

WHIRLPOOL

BATH

PDR. RM.

FOYER

BATH

WALK-IN CLOSET

LINEN

SHLVS

LINEN

STUDY
10⁰x11¹

COVERED PORCH

GARAGE
19⁶x19⁶

CL.

CL.

MASTER BEDROOM
13²x16²

BEDROOM
13⁶x11⁰

CUSTOMIZABLE

Custom Alterations? See page 381
for customizing this plan to your
specifications.

Design V12962
Square Footage: 2,112

● A Tudor exterior with an efficient floor plan favored by many. Each of the three main living zones - the sleeping zone, living zone, and the working zone - are but a couple steps from the foyer. This spells easy, efficient traffic patterns. Open planning, sloping ceil-

ing and plenty of glass create a nice environment for the living-dining area. Its appeal is further enhanced by the open staircase to the lower level recreation/hobby area. The L-shaped kitchen with its island range and work surface is delightfully opened to the

large breakfast room. Again, plenty of glass area adds to the feeling of spaciousness. Nearby is the step-saving first floor laundry. The sleeping zone has the flexibility of functioning as a two or three bedroom area. Notice the economical back-to-back plumbing.

Design V12605
Square Footage: 1,775

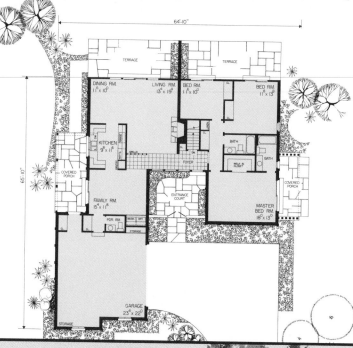

● Here are three modified L-shaped Tudor designs with tremendous exterior appeal and efficient floor plans. While each plan features three bedrooms and 2½ baths, the square footage differences are interesting. Note that each design may be built with or without a basement. This appealing exterior is highlighted by a variety of roof planes, patterned brick, wavy-edged siding and a massive chimney. The garage is oversized and has good storage potential. In addition to the entrance court, there are two covered porches and two terraces for outdoor living. Most definitely a home to be enjoyed by all family members.

Design V12206
Square Footage: 1,769

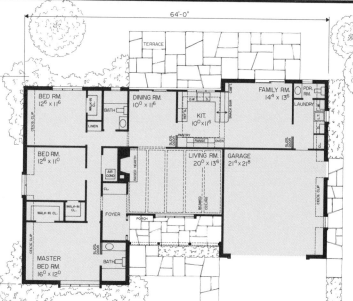

● The charm of Tudor adaptations has become increasingly popular in recent years. And little wonder. Its freshness of character adds a unique touch to any neighborhood. This interesting one-story home will be a standout wherever you choose to have it built. The covered front porch leads to the formal front entry–the foyer. From this point traffic flows freely to the living and sleeping areas. The outstanding plan features a separate dining room, a beamed ceiling living room, an efficient kitchen and an informal family room.

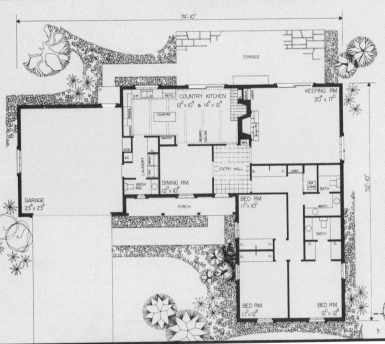

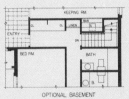

OPTIONAL BASEMENT

Design V12604
Square Footage: 1,956

L D

● A feature that will set the whole wonderful pattern of true living will be the 26 foot wide country kitchen. The spacious, L-shaped kitchen has its efficiency enhanced by the island counter work surface. Beamed ceilings, fireplace and sliding glass doors add to the cozy atmosphere of this area. The laundry, dining room and entry hall are but a step or two away. The big keeping room also has a fireplace and can function with the terrace. Observe the 2½ baths.

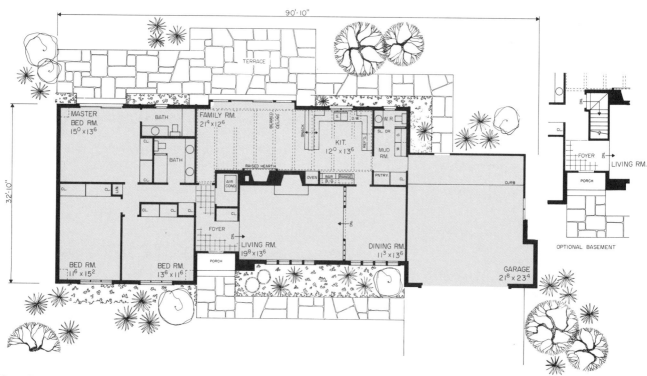

Design V12318
Square Footage: 2,029

● Warmth and charm are characteristics of Tudor adaptations. This modest sized home with its twin front-facing gabled roofs represents a great investment. While it will be an exciting and refreshing addition to any neighborhood, its appeal will never grow old.

The covered, front entrance opens to the center foyer. Traffic patterns flow in an orderly and efficient manner to the three main zones — the formal dining zone, the sleeping zone and the informal living zone. The sunken living room with its fireplace is separated

from the dining room by an attractive trellis divider. A second fireplace, along with beamed ceiling and sliding glass doors, highlights the family room. Note snack bar, mud room, cooking facilities, two full baths and optional basement.

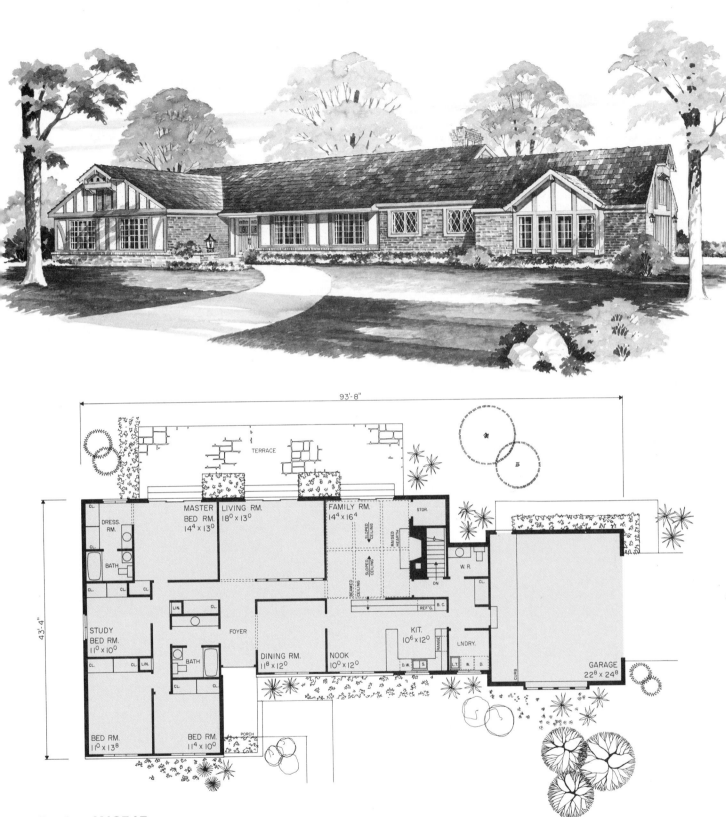

Design V12515
Square Footage: 2,363

D

● Another Tudor adaptation with all the appeal that is inherent in this design style. The brick veneer exterior is effectively complimented by the beam work, the stucco and the window treatment. The carriage lamp, perched on the planter wall, adds a delightful touch as do the dovecotes of the bedroom wing and over the garage door. The livability of the interior is just great. The kitchen, nook and dining room overlook the front yard. The laundry is around the corner from the kitchen. An extra washroom is not far away. Sloping, beamed ceiling and raised hearth fireplace are highlights of the family room. Like the living room and master bedroom, it functions with the rear terrace. Note vanity outside main bath. Wood posts separate the living room and hall.

19

Design V12859
Square Footage: 1,599

● Incorporated into the extremely popular basic one-story floor plan is a super-insulated structure. This means that it has double exterior walls separated by R-33 insulation and a raised roof truss that insures ceiling insulation will extend to the outer wall. More popularity is shown in the always popular Tudor facade. Enter the home through the air-locked vestibule to the foyer. To the left is the sleeping area. To the right of the foyer is the breakfast room, kitchen and stairs to the basement. Viewing the rear yard are the gathering and dining rooms. Study the technical details described in the blueprints of the wall section so you can better understand this super-insulated house.

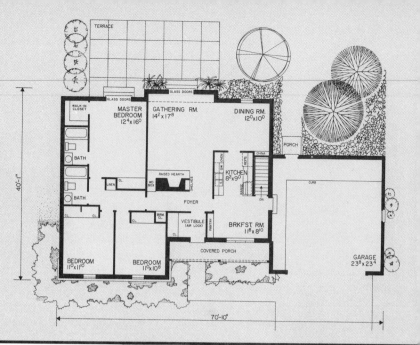

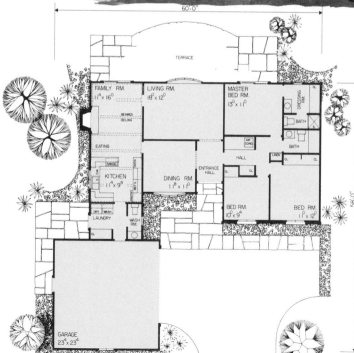

Design V12606
Square Footage: 1,499

L D

CUSTOMIZABLE

Custom Alterations? See page 381 for customizing this plan to your specifications.

● This modest sized house with its 1,499 square feet could hardly offer more in the way of exterior charm and interior livability. Measuring only 60 feet in width means it will not require a huge, expensive piece of property. The orientation of the garage and the front drive court are features which promote an economical use of property. In addition to the formal, separate living and dining rooms, there is the informal kitchen/family room area. Note the beamed ceiling, the fireplace, the sliding glass doors and the eating area of the family room.

OPTIONAL BASEMENT

Design V12737
Square Footage: 1,796

L

● You will be able to build this distinctive, modified U-shaped one-story home on a relatively narrow site. But, then, if you so wished, with the help of your architect and builder you may want to locate the garage to the side of the house. Inside, the living potential is just great. The interior U-shaped kitchen handily services the dining and family rooms and nook. A rear covered porch functions ideally with the family room while the formal living room has its own terrace. Three bedrooms and two baths highlight the sleeping zone (or make it two bedrooms and a study). Notice the strategic location of the washroom, laundry, two storage closets and the basement stairs.

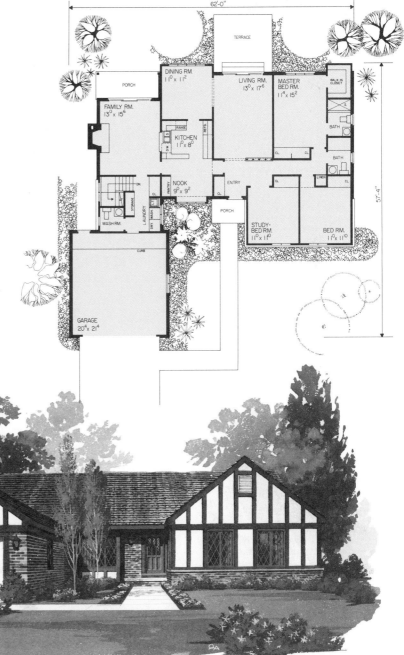

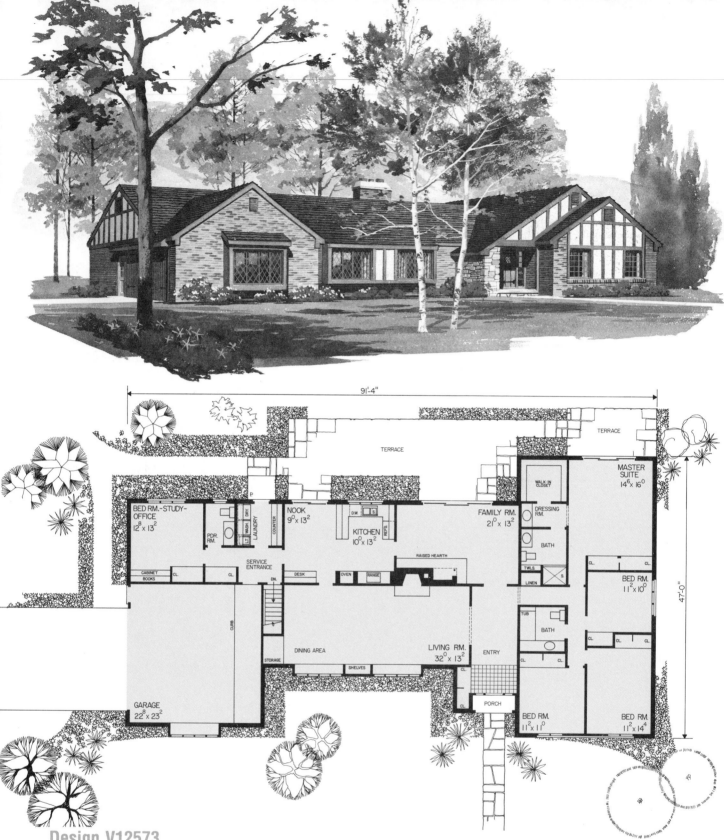

Labels within the floor plan:

TERRACE

91'-4"

TERRACE

BED RM.-STUDY-OFFICE 12⁸ x 13²

PDR. RM.

WASH DRY

LAUNDRY

NOOK 9⁰ x 13²

KITCHEN 10⁰ x 13²

DW S

REFG.

FAMILY RM. 21⁰ x 13²

WALK IN CLOSET

DRESSING RM.

MASTER SUITE 14⁶ x 16⁰

47'-0"

CABINET BOOKS

CL.

CL.

SERVICE ENTRANCE

DN.

DESK

COUNTER

RAISED HEARTH

OVEN RANGE

BATH

TWLS.

LINEN S

BED RM. 11² x 10⁰

CURB

DINING AREA

STORAGE

SHELVES

LIVING RM. 32⁰ x 13²

ENTRY

CL

TUB

BATH

CL. CL.

CL. CL. CL.

GARAGE 22⁸ x 23²

PORCH

BED RM. 11² x 11⁰

BED RM. 11² x 14⁴

Design V12573
Square Footage: 2,747

L D

● A Tudor ranch! Combining brick and wood for an elegant look. It has a living/dining room measuring 32' by 13', large indeed. It is fully appointed with a traditional fireplace and built-in shelves, flanked by diagonally paned windows. There's much more! There is a family room with a raised hearth fireplace and sliding glass doors that open onto the terrace. A U-shaped kitchen has lots of built-ins . . . a range, an oven, a desk. Plus a separate breakfast nook. The sleeping facilities consist of three family bedrooms plus an elegant master bedroom suite. A conveniently located laundry with a folding counter is in the service entrance. Adjacent to the laundry is a washroom. The corner of the plan has a study or make it a fifth bedroom if you prefer.

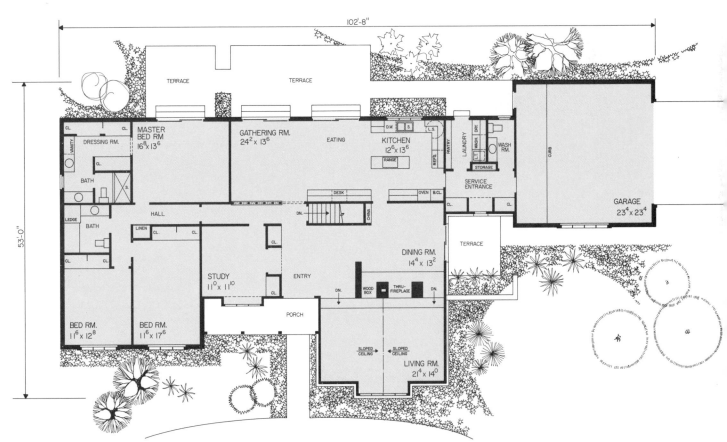

Design V12746
Square Footage: 2,790

D

● This impressive one-story will be the talk-of-the-town. And not surprisingly, either. It embodies all of the elements to assure a sound investment and years of happy family livability. The projecting living room with its stucco, simulated wood beams and effective window treatment adds a dramatic note. Sunken by two steps, this room will enjoy privacy. The massive double front doors are sheltered by the covered porch and lead to the spacious entry hall. The interior is particularly well-zoned. The large, rear gathering room will cater to the family's gregarious instincts. Outdoor enjoyment can be obtained on the three terraces. Also, a study is available for those extra quiet moments. Be sure to observe the plan closely for all of the other fine features.

23

Design V11989
Square Footage: 2,282

L D

● High style with a plan as contemporary as today and tomorrow. There is, indeed, a feeling of coziness that emanates from the ground-hugging qualities of this picturesque home. Inside, there is livability galore. There's the sunken living room and the separate dining room to function as the family's formal living area. Then, over-looking the rear yard, there's the informal living area with its beamed ceiling family room, kitchen and adjacent breakfast room.

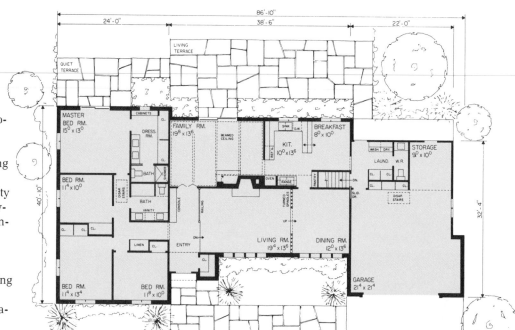

Design V12378
Square Footage: 2,580

● If yours is a preference for an exterior that exudes both warmth and formality, the styling of English Tudor may suit your fancy. A host of architectural features blend together to produce this delightfully appealing exterior. Notice the interesting use of contrasting exterior materials. Don't overlook the two stylish chimneys. The manner in which the interior functions to provide the fine living patterns is outstanding. Each of four main rooms — look out on the rear terrace.

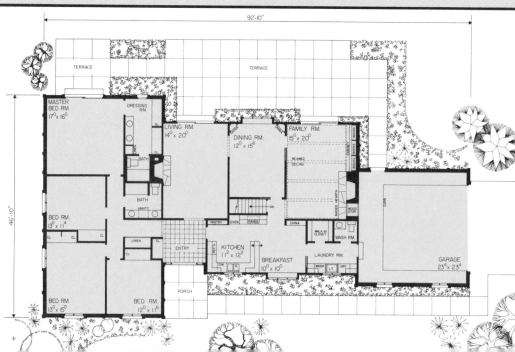

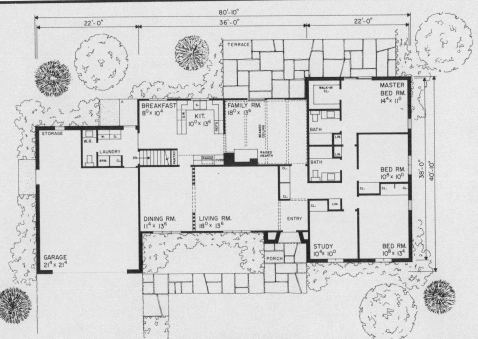

Design V12129
Square Footage: 2,057

● This four bedroom home is zoned for convenient living. The sleeping area, with its two full baths and plenty of closets, will have a lot of privacy. The formal living and dining rooms function together and may be completely by-passed when desired. The informal living areas are grouped together and overlook the rear yard. The family room with its beamed ceiling is but a step from the kitchen. The U-shaped kitchen is handy to both the breakfast and dining rooms.

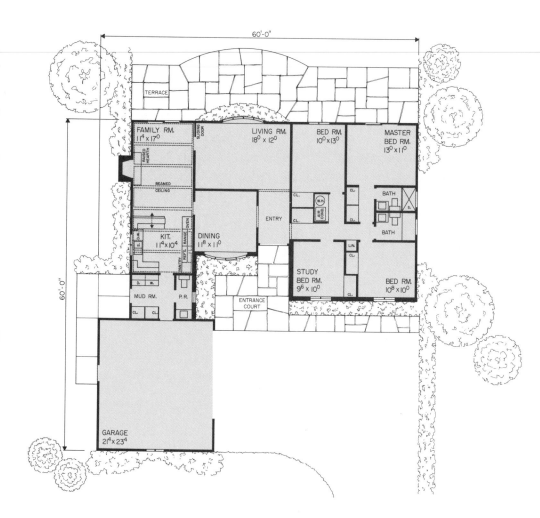

Design V12170
Square Footage: 1,646

● An L-shaped home with an enchanting Olde English styling. The wavy-edged siding, the similated beams, the diamond lite windows, the unusual brick pattern and the interesting roof lines all are elements which set the character of authenticity. The center entry routes traffic directly to the formal living and sleeping zones of the house. Between the kitchen-family room area and the attached two-car garage is the mud room. Here is the washer and dryer with the extra powder room nearby. The family room is highlighted by the beamed ceilings, the raised hearth fireplace and sliding glass doors to the rear terrace. The work center with its abundance of cupboard space will be fun in which to function. Four bedrooms, two full baths and good closet space are features of the sleeping area.

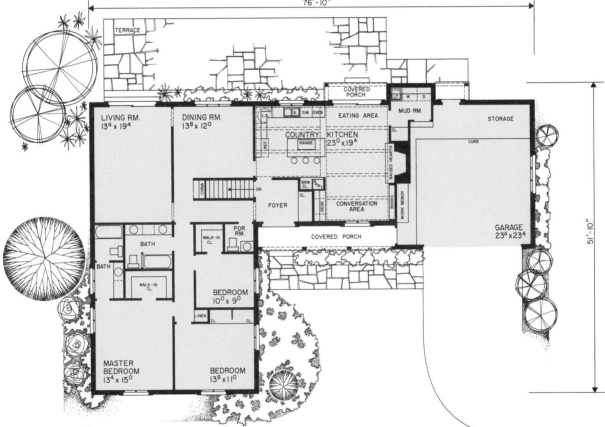

Design V12678
Square Footage: 1,971

L D

● If you've ever desired to have a large country kitchen in your home then this is the design for you. The features of this room are many, indeed. Begin your long list with the island range with snack bar, pantry and broom closets, eating area with sliding glass doors leading to a covered porch, adjacent mud room with laundry facilities and access to the garage, raised hearth fireplace and conversation area with built-in desk on one side and shelves on the other. Now that is some multi-purpose room! There are formal living and dining rooms, too. Two and a half baths, all grouped around the living and sleeping areas. Review the rest of this plan which is surrounded by a delightful Tudor facade. It will surely prove to be a remarkable home to live in for the entire family.

Design V12728
Square Footage: 1,825

L **D**

● Your family's new lifestyle will surely flourish in this charming, L-shaped English adaptation. The curving front driveway produces an impressive approach. A covered front porch shelters the centered entry hall which effectively routes traffic to all areas. The fireplace is the focal point of the spacious, formal living and dining area. The kitchen is strategically placed to service the dining room and any informal eating space developed in the family room. In addition to the two full baths of the sleeping area, there is a handy washroom at the entrance from the garage. A complete, first floor laundry is nearby and has direct access to the yard. Sliding glass doors permit easy movement to the outdoor terrace and side porch. Don't overlook the basement and its potential for the development of additional livability and/or storage.

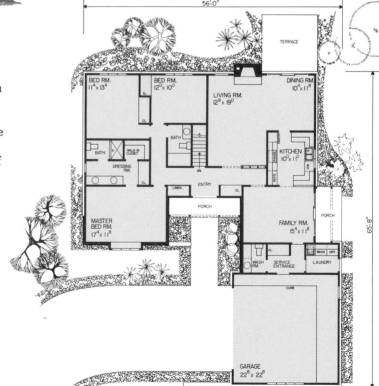

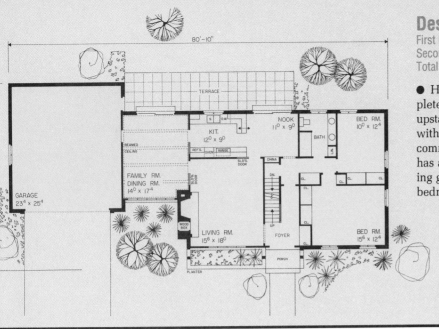

Design V12286
First Floor: 1,496 square feet
Second Floor: 751 square feet
Total: 2,247 square feet

● Here is a subtly styled Tudor design with complete one-floor livability plus two bonus bedrooms upstairs. It retains all the appearance of a one-story with a living room and family/dining room to accommodate all occasions. The convenient kitchen has a pass-through to the nook, which features sliding glass doors to the terrace. The two first-floor bedrooms have an abundance of closet space.

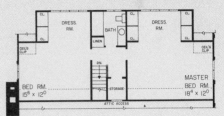

Design V12374
Square Footage: 1,919

● This English adaptation will never grow old. There is, indeed, much here to please the eye for many a year to come. The wavy-edged siding contrasts pleasingly with the diagonal pattern of brick below. The diamond lites of the windows create their own special effect. The projecting brick wall creates a pleasant court outside the covered front porch. The floor plan is well-zoned with the three bedrooms and two baths comprising a distinct sleeping wing. Flanking the entrance hall is the formal living room and the informal, multi-purpose family room. The large dining room is strategically located. The mud room area is adjacent to the extra washroom and the stairs to the basement.

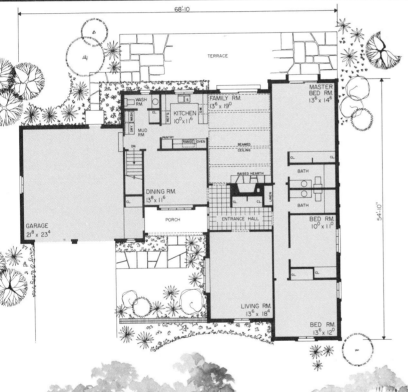

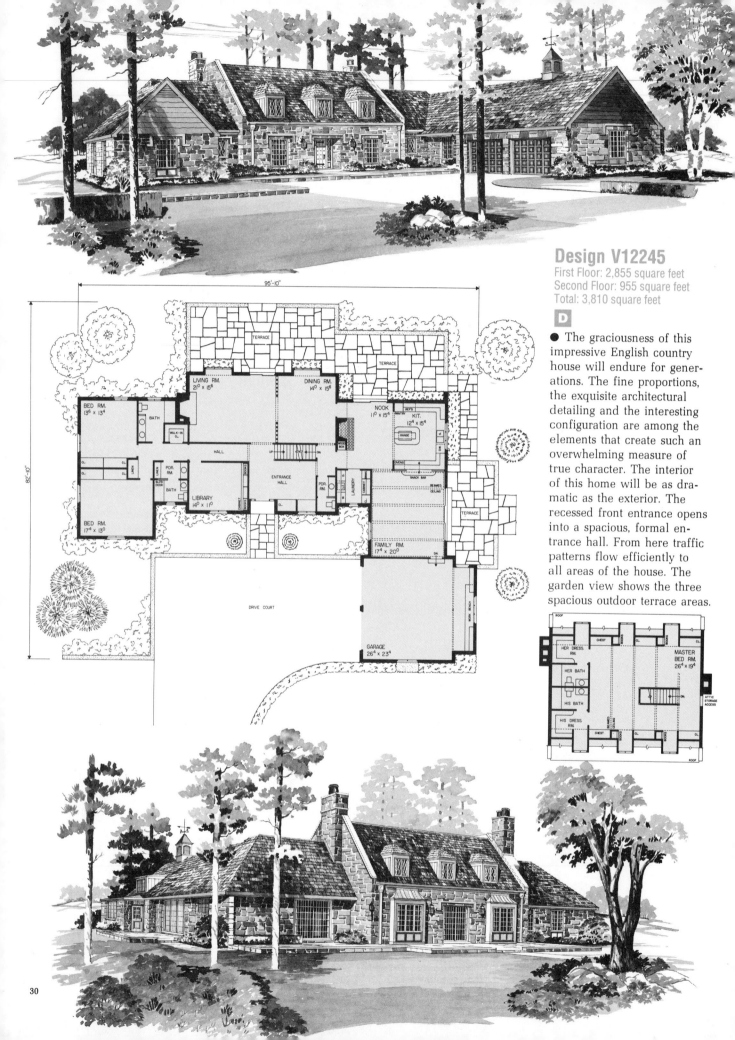

Design V12245

First Floor: 2,855 square feet
Second Floor: 955 square feet
Total: 3,810 square feet

D

● The graciousness of this impressive English country house will endure for generations. The fine proportions, the exquisite architectural detailing and the interesting configuration are among the elements that create such an overwhelming measure of true character. The interior of this home will be as dramatic as the exterior. The recessed front entrance opens into a spacious, formal entrance hall. From here traffic patterns flow efficiently to all areas of the house. The garden view shows the three spacious outdoor terrace areas.

Design V12317
Square Footage: 3,161

● Here's a rambling English manor with its full measure of individuality. Its fine proportions and irregular shape offer even the most casual of passers-by delightful views of fine architecture. The exterior boasts an interesting use of varying materials. In addition to the brick work, there is vertical siding, wavy-edged horizontal siding and stucco. Three massive chimneys provide each of the three major wings with a fireplace. The overhanging roof provides the cover for the long front porch. Note the access to both the foyer as well as the service hall. The formal living room, with its sloping beamed ceiling, and fireplace flanked by bookshelves and cabinets, will be cozy, indeed. Study rest of plan. It's outstanding. Don't miss the three fireplaces and three full baths.

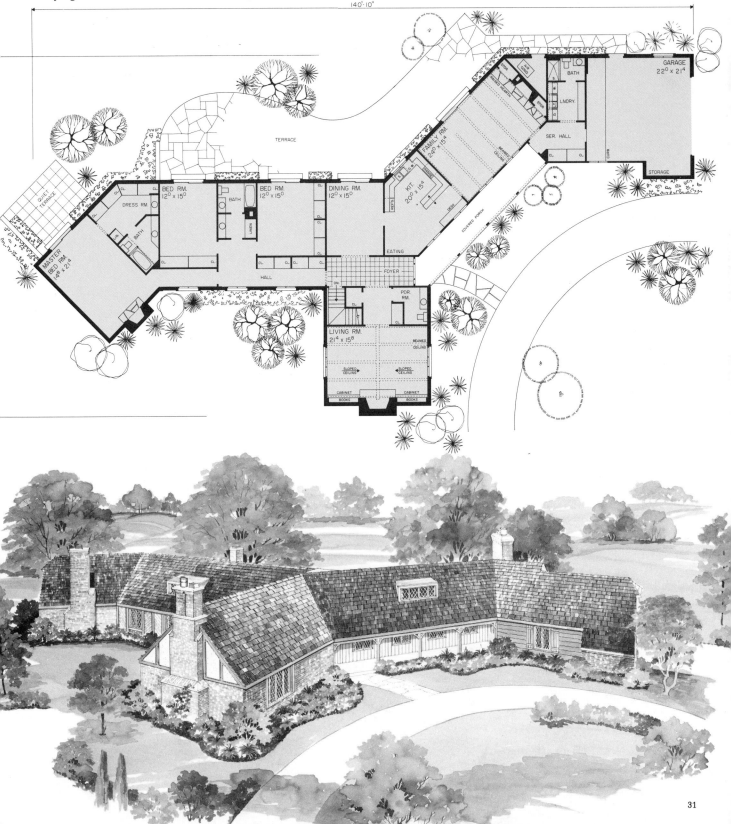

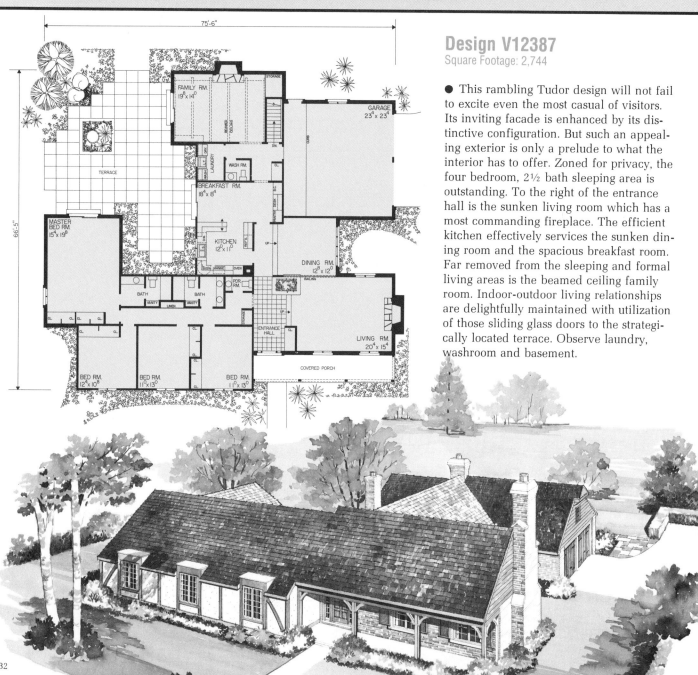

Design V12387
Square Footage: 2,744

● This rambling Tudor design will not fail to excite even the most casual of visitors. Its inviting facade is enhanced by its distinctive configuration. But such an appealing exterior is only a prelude to what the interior has to offer. Zoned for privacy, the four bedroom, 2½ bath sleeping area is outstanding. To the right of the entrance hall is the sunken living room which has a most commanding fireplace. The efficient kitchen effectively services the sunken dining room and the spacious breakfast room. Far removed from the sleeping and formal living areas is the beamed ceiling family room. Indoor-outdoor living relationships are delightfully maintained with utilization of those sliding glass doors to the strategically located terrace. Observe laundry, washroom and basement.

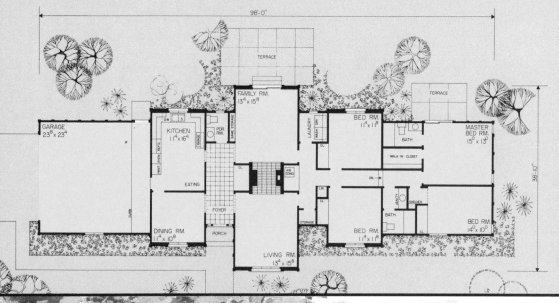

Design V12385
Square Footage: 2,100

● The charm of Tudor styled exterior adaptations is difficult to beat. Here is a hip-roof version which highlights the effective use of stucco, patterned brick and exposed beam work. The varying roof planes and the massive chimney, along with the recessed front entrance enhance the appeal. A study of the floor plan is most revealing. Excellent zoning is readily apparent.

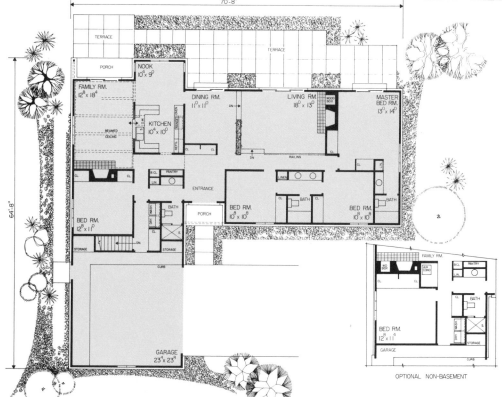

Design V12613
Square Footage: 2,132

● A classic Tudor! With prominent wood and stucco styling. And unique features throughout. Start with the sunken living room where an attractive railing has replaced the anticipated hallway wall. For more good looks, a traditional fireplace with an attached woodbox and sliding glass doors that open onto the terrace. There's a formal dining room, too, also with access onto the terrace. Together these rooms form a gracious center for entertaining! For casual times, a family room with a beamed ceiling, fireplace and summer porch. And a work-efficient kitchen plus a roomy breakfast nook.

OPTIONAL NON-BASEMENT

33

Design V12629

First Floor: 1,555 square feet
Second Floor: 1,080 square feet
Total: 2,635 square feet

● This home will really be fun in which to live. In addition to the sizeable living, dining and family rooms, many extras will be found. There are two fire-places one to serve each of the formal and the informal areas. The back porch is a delightful extra. It will be great to relax in after a long hard day. Note two half baths on the first floor and two full baths on the second floor to serve the three bed-rooms. Count the number of clos-ets in the spacious upstairs. The door from the bedroom leads to storage over garage.

Design V12630

First Floor: 1,491 square feet
Second Floor: 788 square feet
Total: 2,279 square feet

● This distinctive version of Tudor styling will foster many years of prideful ownership and unique, yet practical living patterns. The main portion of the facade is delightfully symmetrical. Inside, the family living will focus on the 29 foot great room with its dramatic fireplace and beam-ed ceiling. The kitchen is outstanding with snack bar and dining nook near-by. Note the three large bedrooms each having its own dressing room. Extra storage space is available above the garage or may be developed into another room. Oversized garage in-cludes a built-in workbench. Study plan carefully. It has much to offer.

Design V12273

First Floor: 1,357 square feet
Second Floor: 1,065 square feet
Total: 2,422 square feet

● Note the traditional charm of this design. Formal/informal dining areas are offered in this plan. The large living room with fireplace will provide a lot of enjoyment. A full bath, storage area and your option of a library/bedroom also are featured on this floor. The second floor has a large master bedroom with a full bath. Two bedrooms and another full bath will serve the rest of the family.

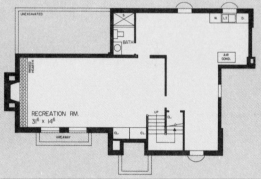

● This is an exquisitely styled Tudor tri-level designed to serve its happy occupants for many years. The contrasting use of material surely makes the exterior eye-catching.

Design V12847
Main Level: 1,874 square feet
Lower Level: 1,131 square feet
Total: 3,005 square feet

L D

DECK

78'- 8"

DINING RM.
11⁰ x 11⁶

LIVING RM.
14⁰ x 19⁴

MASTER BEDROOM
15⁰ x 12⁰

BREAKFAST
11⁰ x 12⁰

THRU FIREPLACE

RAILING

CURB

CHINA

PANTRY   BRM   CL
RANGE

OVEN   DN

BATH

42'- 0"

KITCHEN
16⁸ x 9⁴

DW   S   REF'S   CONSOLE

BATH

GARAGE
23⁶ x 23⁴

LAUNDRY

COVERED PORCH   FOYER   CL   LINEN

CL

CL   CL

BEDROOM
11⁴ x 11⁰

BEDROOM
11⁸ x 13⁰

TERRACE

BEDROOM/STUDY
10⁸ x 11⁶

FAMILY RM.
14⁰ x 22¹⁰

BASEMENT

SAUNA/HOT TUB/DRESSING ROOM
10⁶ x 15⁴

CL

RAISED HEARTH

AIR COND

CL

UP

UNEX

BATH

LINEN   STORAGE   SEAT

SNACK BAR

UNEX

SUMMER KITCHEN
13⁴ x 7⁰

RANGE   REF   STORAGE

SHOP AREA

36

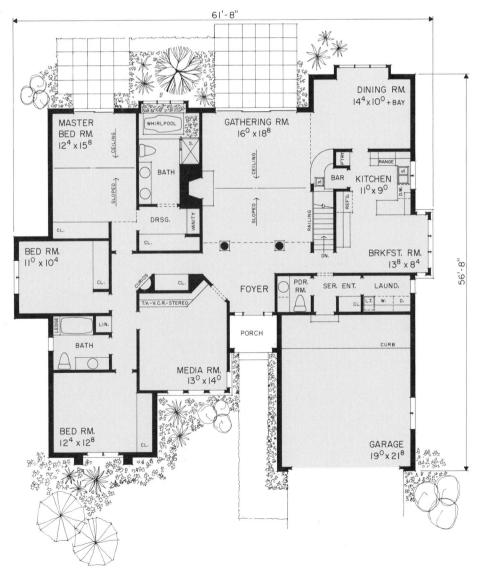

MASTER
BED RM.
12^4 x 15^8

WHIRLPOOL

BATH

GATHERING RM.
16^0 x 18^8

DINING RM.
14^4 x 10^0 + BAY

$\leftarrow$ CEILING

$\leftarrow$ CEILING

SLOPED $\rightarrow$

SLOPED $\rightarrow$

P'TRY

RANGE

BAR

KITCHEN
11^0 x 9^0

DRSG.

VANITY

CL.

RAILING

REF'G.

D.W.

CL.

BED RM.
11^0 x 10^4

CL.

DN.

BRKFST. RM.
13^8 x 8^4

CURIOS

CL.

FOYER

PDR.
RM.

SER. ENT.

LAUND.

T.V.- V.C.R - STEREO

LEDGE

LIN.

BATH

LT.

W.

D.

CL.

PORCH

MEDIA RM.
13^0 x 14^0

CURB

BED RM.
12^4 x 12^8

CL.

GARAGE
19^0 x 21^8

61'-8"

56'-8"

Design V13377
Square Footage: 2,217

● This Tudor design provides a handsome exterior complemented by a spacious and modern floor plan. The sleeping area is positioned to the left side of the home. The master bedroom features an elegant bath with whirlpool, shower, dual lavs and a separate vanity area. Two family bedrooms share a full bath. A media room exhibits the TV, VCR and stereo. The enormous gathering room is set off by columns and contains a fireplace and sliding doors to the rear terrace. The dining room and breakfast room each feature a bay window.

Design V13346
Square Footage: 2,032

● This home boasts a delightful Tudor exterior with a terrific interior floor plan. Though compact, there's plenty of living space: large study with fireplace, gathering room, dining room, and breakfast room. The master bedroom has an attached bath with whirlpool tub. Note the double walk-in closets.

CUSTOMIZABLE
Custom Alterations? See page 381 for customizing this plan to your specifications.

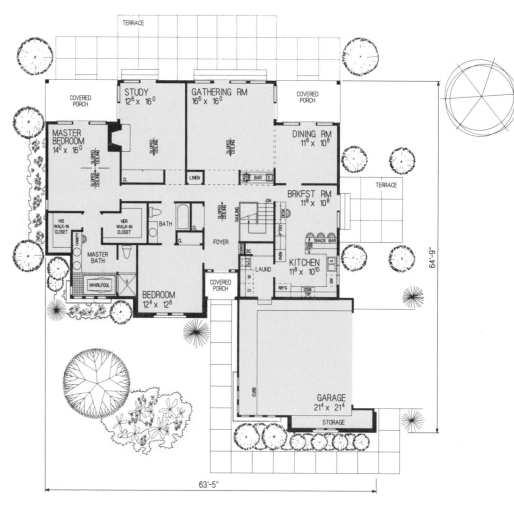

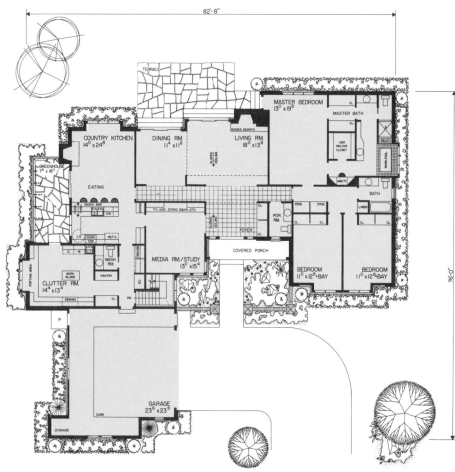

82'-8"

76'-0"

TERRACE

COUNTRY KITCHEN
14⁰ x 24⁸

DINING RM.
11⁴ x 11⁸

LIVING RM.
18⁰ x 13⁸

SLOPED CEILING

RAISED HEARTH

MASTER BEDROOM
13⁰ x 19⁸

MASTER BATH

HER WALK-IN CLOSET

VANITY

BATH

GREENHOUSE
7⁸ x 18⁰

EATING

SNACK BAR

OVEN

TV, VCR, STEREO EQUIP., ETC.

SLOPED CEILING

STOR.

STOR.

LINEN

COOK TOP

REF'S.

D. W.

WASH RM.

PANTRY

PDR. RM.

FOYER

WORK ISLAND

CLUTTER RM.
14⁴ x 13⁴

SEWING

MEDIA RM./STUDY
13⁰ x 15⁴

FREEZER

DN.

COVERED PORCH

BEDROOM
11⁰ x 12⁸+BAY

BEDROOM
11⁰ x 12⁴+BAY

POTTING AREA

GARAGE
23⁶ x 23⁸

CURB

STORAGE

Design V12961
Square Footage: 3,049

● Another interesting and charming L-shaped one-story. This time with Tudor exterior styling. Contributing to the pleasing eye-appeal are the varying roof planes, the cornice detailing, the brick exterior with those accents of stucco and beam-work, the window treatment, and that dramatic front door with its surrounding glass area. The brick wall forming the front courtyard is a nice touch. Inside, the spacious foyer with its slate floor routes traffic most effectively. Highlights include the media room, the clutter room, the country kitchen, the 29 foot formal living-dining room area, and the large master bedroom with its luxurious master bath. Functioning with the country kitchen and clutter room is the glass-walled greenhouse. Its 130 sq. ft. is included in the total above.

Design V12278

First Floor: 1,804 square feet
Second Floor: 939 square feet
Total: 2,743 square feet

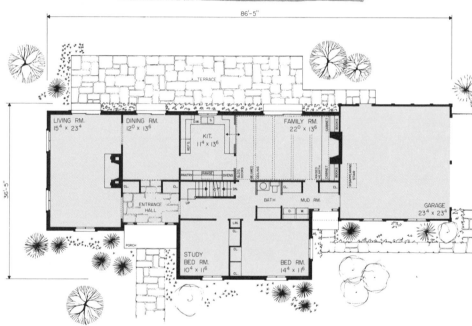

● The Tudor charm is characterized in each of these three one-and-a-half story designs. Study each of them for its own special features.

Design V12674

First Floor: 1,922 square feet
Second Floor: 890 square feet
Total: 2,812 square feet

● This delightful Tudor design's configuration permits a flexible orientation on its site with either the garage doors or the front doors facing the street. One-and-a-half-story designs offer great flexibilty in their livability. Complete livability is offered on the first floor; by utilizing the second floor another three bedrooms and bath are available. First floor features include a sunken family room with fireplace and built-in bookshelves, rear living room with sliding glass doors to the terrace, large formal dining room, first floor laundry and two washrooms.

● This is a most interesting home; both inside and out. Its L-shape with covered front porch and diamond-lite windows is appealing. Its floor plan with extra bedroom, lounge and storage room is exceptional.

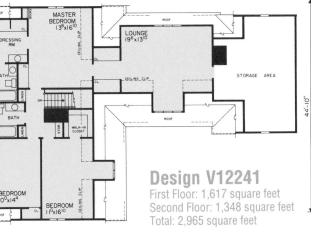

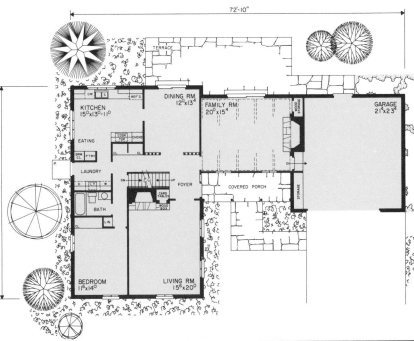

Design V12241

First Floor: 1,617 square feet
Second Floor: 1,348 square feet
Total: 2,965 square feet

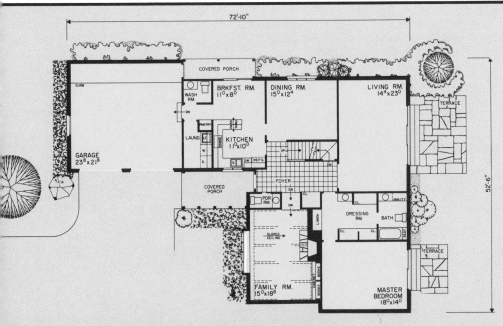

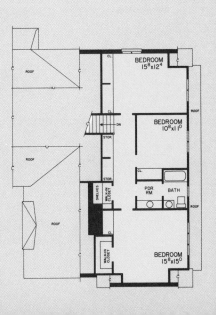

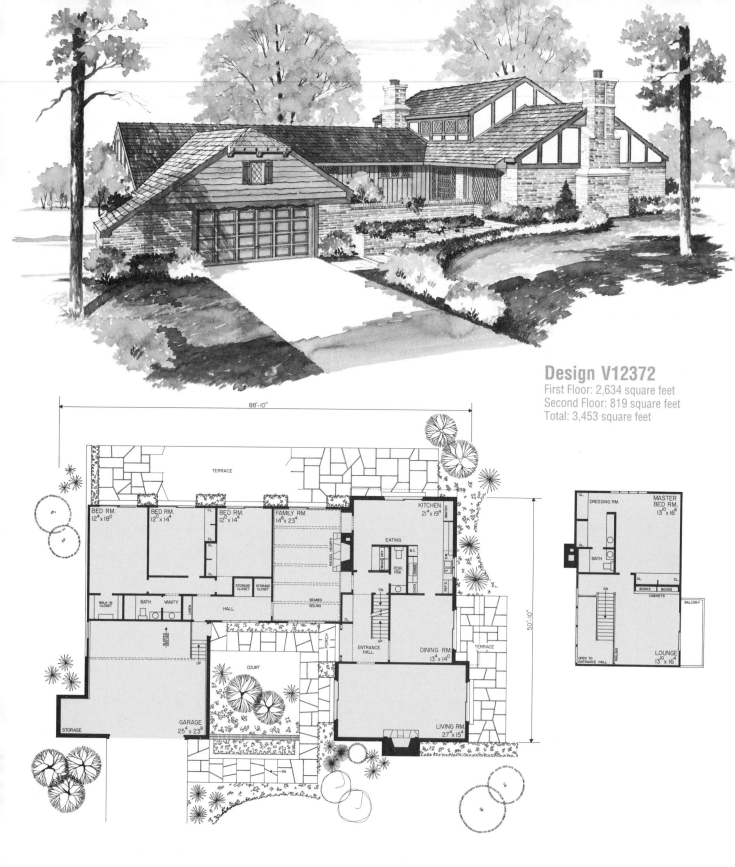

Design V12372

First Floor: 2,634 square feet
Second Floor: 819 square feet
Total: 3,453 square feet

● What a wonderfully unique design — one-story livability with bonus space upstairs. The Tudor styling and the varying roof planes, along with its U-shape, add to the air of distinction. From the driveway, steps lead past a big raised planter up to the enclosed entrance court. A wide overhanging roof shelters the massive patterned double doors flanked by diamond paned sidelites. The living room is outstanding. It is located a distance from other living areas and is quite spacious. The centered fireplace is the dominant feature, while sliding glass doors open from each end onto outdoor terraces. The kitchen, too, is spacious and functions well. Two eating areas are nearby. It is worth noting that each of the major first floor rooms have direct access to the outdoor terraces. Note second floor suite which includes a lounge with built-in book cabinets.

Design V12391

First Floor: 2,496 square feet
Second Floor: 958 square feet
Total: 3,454 square feet

● This impressive English adaptation allows complete one-story convenience with additional sleeping and study space on a second floor. Note the large living areas: family room with raised hearth fireplace and beamed ceiling, L-shaped living/dining room area with bay window — all arranged around the kitchen and breakfast room. Three first floor bedrooms have access to two full baths while an entry hall powder room serves guests nicely. The large three-car garage means no lack of space for the family vehicles and provides a service entrance to the laundry.

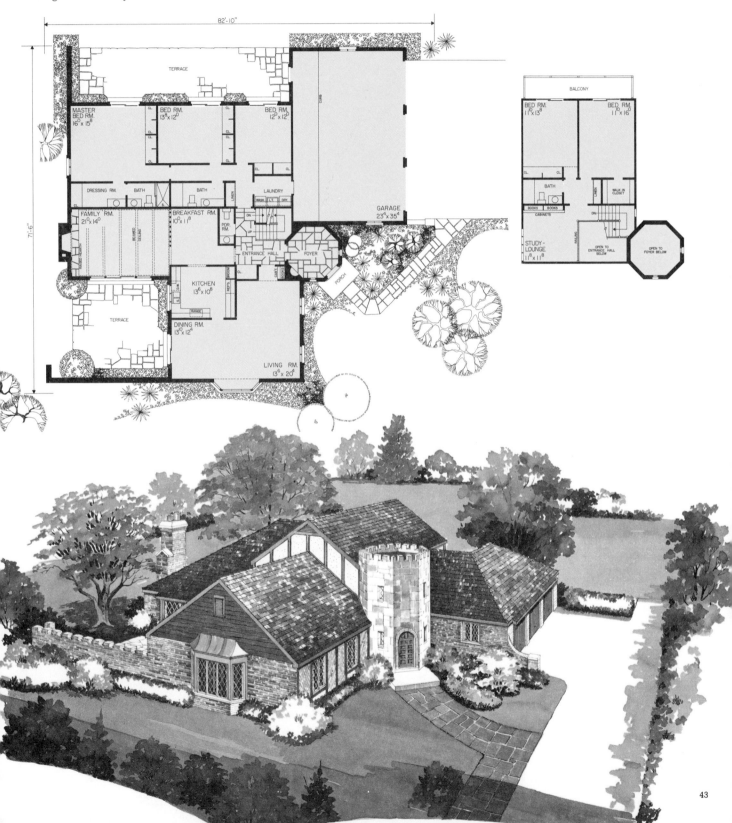

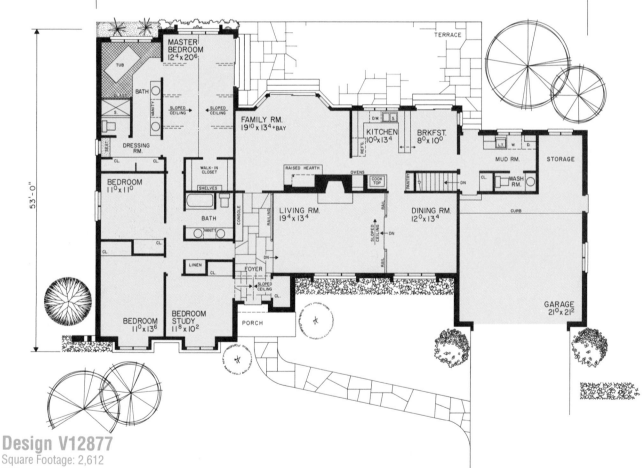

Design V12877
Square Footage: 2,612

D

● Here's a dramatic, Post-Modern exterior with a popular plan featuring an outstanding master bedroom suite. The bedroom itself is spacious, has a sloped ceiling, a large walk-in closet and sliding glass doors to the terrace. Now examine the bath and dressing area. Two large closets, twin vanities, built-in seat and a dramatically presented corner tub are present. The tub will be a great place to spend the evening hours after a long, hard day. Along with this bedroom, there are three more served by a full bath. The living area of this plan has the formal areas in the front and the informal areas in the rear. Both have a fireplace. The spacious work center is efficiently planned.

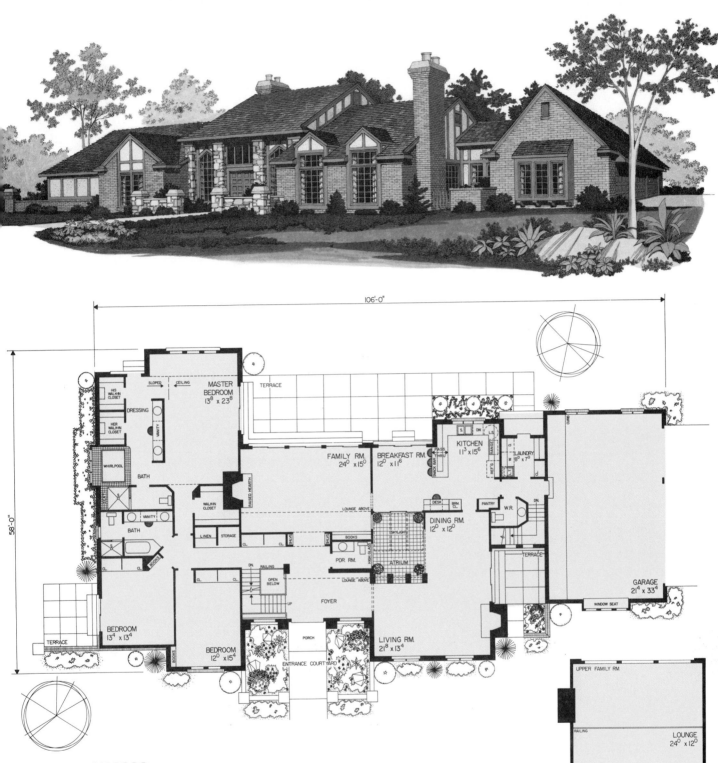

Design V12966
Square Footage: 3,403

● This Tudor adaptation is as dramatic inside as it is outside. As a visitor
approaches the front courtyard there is much that catches the eye. The interesting roof lines, the appealing window treatment, the contrasting exterior
materials and their textures, the inviting panelled front door and the massive
twin chimneys with their protruding clay pots. Inside, the spacious foyer with
its sloping ceiling looks up into the balcony-type lounge. It also looks down
the open stairwell to the lower level area. From the foyer, traffic flows conveniently to other areas. The focal point of the living zone is the delightful
atrium. Both the formal living room and the informal family room feature a
fireplace. Each of the full baths highlights a tub and shower, a vanity and
twin lavatories. Note the secondary access to the basement adjacent to the
door to three car garage. Lounge adds an additional 284 sq. ft.

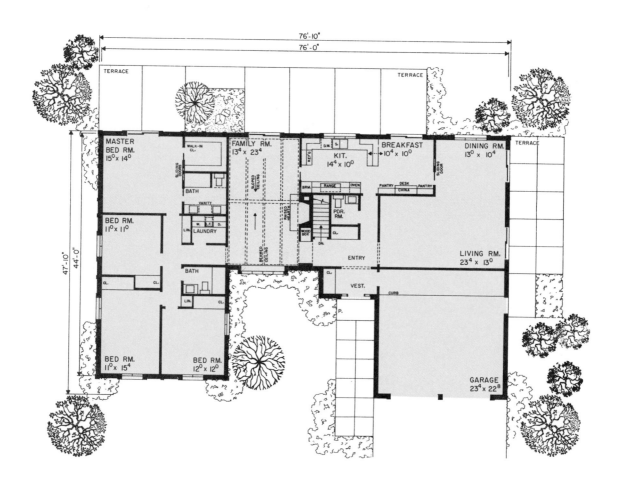

Design V12142
Square Footage: 2,450

● Adaptations of Old England have become increasingly popular in today's building scene. And little wonder; for many of these homes when well-designed have a very distinctive charm. Here is certainly a home which will be like no other in its neighborhood. Its very shape adds an extra measure of uniqueness. And inside, there is all the livability the exterior seems to fortell. The sleeping wing has four bedrooms, two full baths and the laundry room — just where the soiled linen originates. The location of the family room is an excellent one. It is convenient for children because their traffic usually flows between family room and bedrooms. The spacious formal living and dining area will enjoy its privacy and be great fun to furnish.

FRENCH FACADES . . .

have an outstanding charm of their own. Their exterior appeal seems to announce a graciously formal lifestyle. The hip-roof is a distinguishing characteristic of the one-story French house. Shuttered casement windows, brick quoins at the corners of the house, cornice dentils, double front doors with raised panels, massive chimneys and cupolas are among other features that establish the style. In many cases arched window heads and shutters, recessed front entrances, wrought iron grillwork, carriage lamps and entry courts add an extra measure of appeal. In addition to the variety of interior living features, it is worth noting the outdoor living potential.

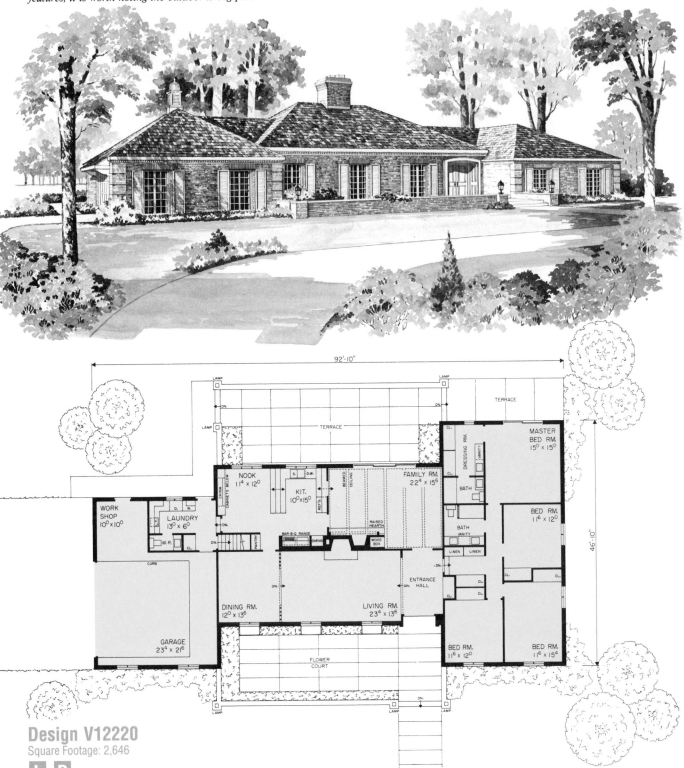

Design V12220
Square Footage: 2,646

L D

● The gracious formality of this home is reminiscent of a popularly accepted French styling. The hip-roof, the brick quoins, the cornice details, the arched window heads, the distinctive shutters, the recessed double front doors, the massive center chimney, and the de-lightful flower court are all features which set the dramatic appeal of this home. This floor plan is a favorite of many. The four bedroom, two bath sleeping wing is a zone by itself. Further, the formal living and dining rooms are ideally located. For enter-taining they function well together and look out upon the pleasant flower court. Overlooking the raised living terrace at the rear are the family and breakfast rooms and work center. Don't miss the laundry, extra wash room and work shop in garage.

● You'll want life's biggest investment — the purchase of a home — to be a source of everlasting enjoyment. To assure such a rewarding dividend, make every effort to match your family's desired living patterns with a workable plan. Of course, you'll want your plan enveloped by a stunning exterior. Consider both the interior and exterior of this design. Each is impressive. The sleeping zone comprises a separate wing and is accessible from both living and kitchen areas. There are four bedrooms, two full baths and plenty of closets. The 32 foot wide living and dining area will be just great fun to decorate. Then, there is the large family room with its raised hearth fireplace and sliding glass doors to the terrace. Note the fine laundry with wash room nearby. The extra curb area in the garage is great for storing small garden equipment.

● This French design is surely impressive. The exterior appearance will brighten any area with its French roof, paned-glass windows, masonry brick privacy wall and double front doors. The inside is just as appealing. Note the unique placement of rooms and features. The entry hall is large and leads to each of the areas in this plan. The formal dining room is outstanding and guests can enter through the entry hall. While serving one can enter by way of the butler's pantry (notice it's size and that it has a sink). To the right of the entry is a sizable parlor. Then there is the gathering room with fireplace, sliding glass doors and adjacent study. The work center is also outstanding. There is the U-shaped kitchen, island range, snack bar, breakfast nook, pantry plus wash room and large laundry near service entrance. Basement stairs are also nearby.

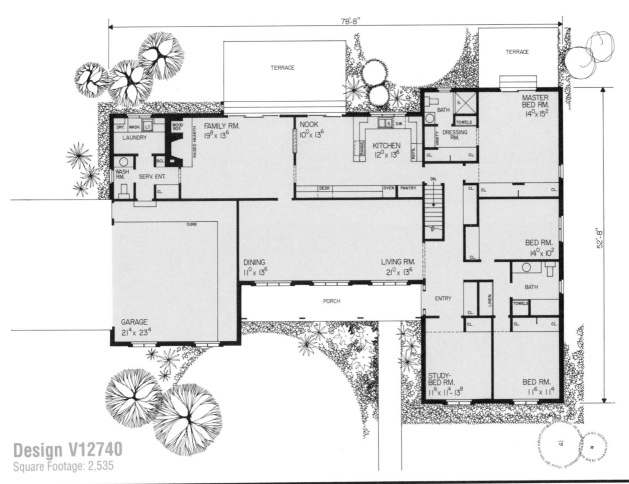

78'-8"

52'-8"

TERRACE

TERRACE

LAUNDRY
DRY. WASH. L.T.
WOOD BOX
RAISED HEARTH

FAMILY RM.
19⁸ x 13⁶

NOOK
10⁰ x 13⁶

BATH
TOWELS

MASTER BED RM.
14⁰ x 15²

WASH RM.
SERV. ENT.
CL.

KITCHEN
12⁰ x 13⁶
RANGE
REFR.
CL.

DRESSING RM.
VANITY
CL.
DN.

DESK
OVEN
PANTRY

CL. CL.
CL.

CURB

DINING
11⁰ x 13⁶

LIVING RM.
21⁰ x 13⁶

ENTRY

BED RM.
14⁰ x 10²

BATH

GARAGE
21⁴ x 23⁴

PORCH

CL.
LINEN
CL.

TOWELS

STUDY-BED RM.
11⁶ x 11-13⁸

BED RM.
11⁶ x 11⁴

Design V12740
Square Footage: 2,535

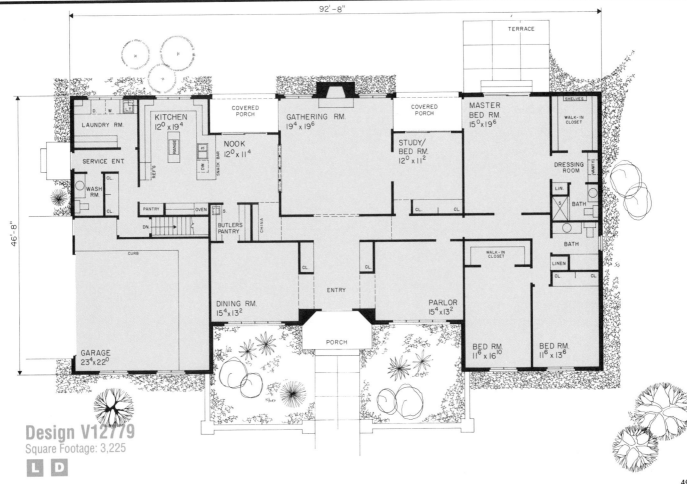

92'-8"

46'-8"

TERRACE

D. W. L.T.

LAUNDRY RM.

KITCHEN
12⁰ x 19⁴
RANGE

COVERED PORCH

GATHERING RM.
19⁴ x 19⁶

COVERED PORCH

MASTER BED RM.
15⁰ x 19⁶

SHELVES
WALK-IN CLOSET

SERVICE ENT.

REF'G

NOOK
12⁰ x 11⁴
SNACK BAR
DW

STUDY/BED RM.
12⁰ x 11²

DRESSING ROOM
VANITY

WASH RM.
CL.

PANTRY
OVEN
DN.
BUTLERS PANTRY
CHINA

CL. CL.

LIN.
BATH

CURB

CL.

WALK-IN CLOSET

BATH

LINEN

CL. CL.

GARAGE
23⁴ x 22⁰

DINING RM.
15⁴ x 13²

ENTRY

PARLOR
15⁴ x 13²

BED RM.
11⁶ x 16¹⁰

BED RM.
11⁶ x 13⁶

PORCH

Design V12779
Square Footage: 3,225

L D

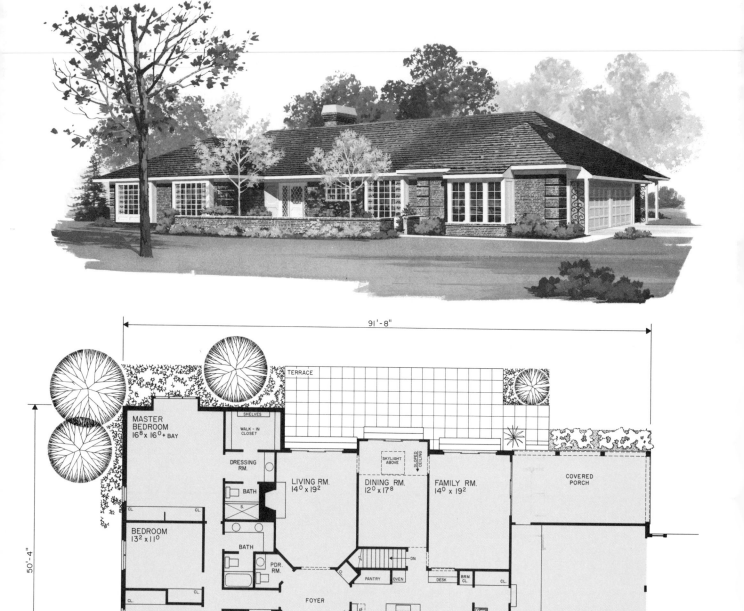

Design V12851
Square Footage: 2,739

L

● This spacious one-story has a classic Country French hip roof. The front entrance creates a charming entry. Beyond the covered porch is an octagonal foyer. A closet, shelves and powder room are contained in the foyer. All of the living areas overlook the rear yard.

Sliding glass doors open each of these areas to the rear terrace. Their features include a fireplace in the living room, skylight in the dining room and a second set of sliding glass doors in the family room leading to a side covered porch. An island range and other built-

ins are featured in the spacious, front kitchen. Adjacent is the breakfast room which will be used for informal dining. The four bedrooms and bath facilities are all clustered in one wing. Note the bay windows in the master bedroom, breakfast room and the three-car garage.

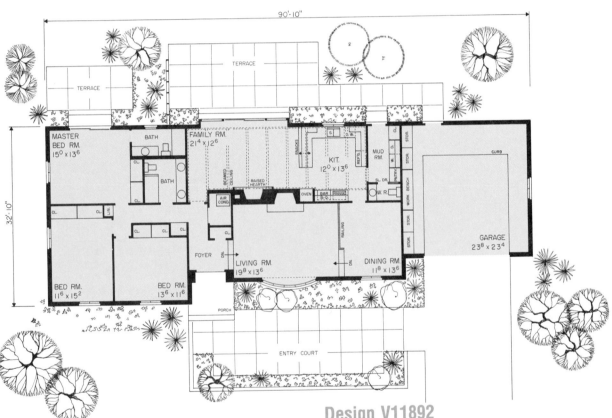

90'-10"

32'-10"

TERRACE

TERRACE

MASTER BED RM.
15⁰ x 13⁶

BATH

BATH

CL.

CL.

CL.

LIN.

FAMILY RM.
21⁴ x 12⁶

BEAMED CEILING

RAISED HEARTH

AIR COND.

SNACKS

KIT.
12⁰ x 13⁶

REFG.

S

D.W.

d

MUD RM.

SL. DR.

PANTRY

W.

W. R.

WORK BENCH

STOR.

STOR.

STOR.

STOR.

STOR.

CURB

OVEN

BAR

RANGE

GARAGE
23⁸ x 23⁴

FOYER

DN.

LIVING RM.
19⁸ x 13⁶

RAILING

DN.

DINING RM.
11⁸ x 13⁶

BED RM.
11⁶ x 15²

BED RM.
13⁶ x 11⁶

CL.

CL.

CL.

CL.

CL.

PORCH

ENTRY COURT

DN.

CL.

DN.

FOYER

LIVING RM.

OPTIONAL BASEMENT

PORCH

Design V11892
Square Footage: 2,036

L D

● The romance of French Provincial is captured here by the hip-roof masses, the charm of the window detailing, the brick quoins at the corners, the delicate dentil work at the cornices, the massive centered chimney, and the recessed double front doors. The slightly raised entry court completes the picture. The basic floor plan is a favorite of many. And little wonder, for all areas work well together, while still maintaining a fine degree of separation of functions. The highlight of the interior, perhaps, will be the sunken living room. The family room, with its beamed ceiling, will not be far behind in its popularity. The separate dining room, mud room, efficient kitchen, complete the livability.

Design V11797
Square Footage: 1,618

● A house to be looked at and lived in —that's what this impressively formal French Provincial adaptation represents. The front court, just inside the brick wall with its attractive iron gate, sets the patterns of formality that are so apparent inside. The formal living and dining rooms separate the sleeping area from the kitchen/family room area. A pass-thru facilitates serving of informal snacks in family room. The three bedrooms will serve the average sized family perfectly. Details for an optional basement are included with this plan.

Design V11272
Square Footage: 1,690

● Designed for the family who wants the refinement of French Provincial, but on a small scale. Keynoting its charm are the long shutters, the delightful entrance porch with its wood posts, the interesting angles of the hip roof and the pair of paneled garage doors. Behind this formal facade is a simple, efficient, up-to-date floor plan. The living patterns for the family occupying this house will be toward the rear where the long living terrace is just a step outside the glass sliding doors of the formal and informal living areas. The two bathrooms in the sleeping area share back-to-back plumbing, which is economical.

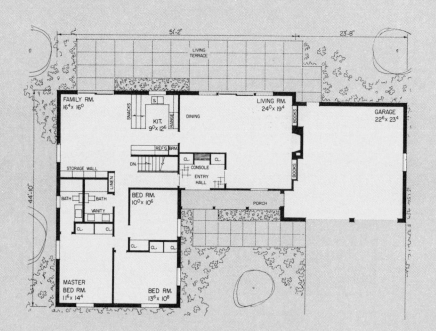

Design V11362
Square Footage: 1,896

● This dramatic L-shaped French adaptation is distinctive indeed. The projecting bedroom wing, consisting of three bedrooms, adds to the exterior appeal. Inside, the traffic patterns are excellent. The blueprints show optional basement details as well as an optional fireplace in the living room. This is most definitely a design to please all family members.

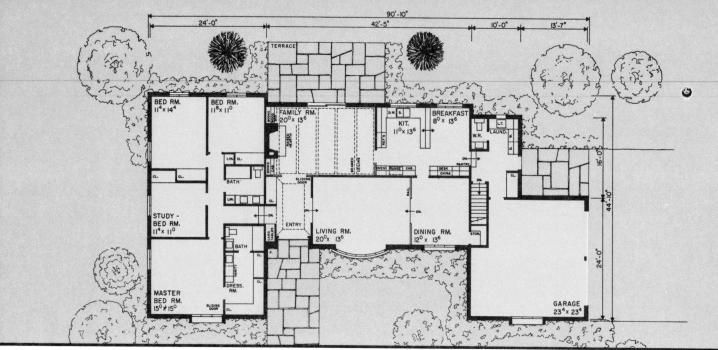

● Here are three delightful French Provincial adaptations, any one of which would surely be an impressive addition to a neighborhood. Each design features a sleeping wing of four bedrooms, two full baths, and plenty of closets. Further, each design has a separate first floor laundry with an adjacent wash room. Observe the sunken living room . . .

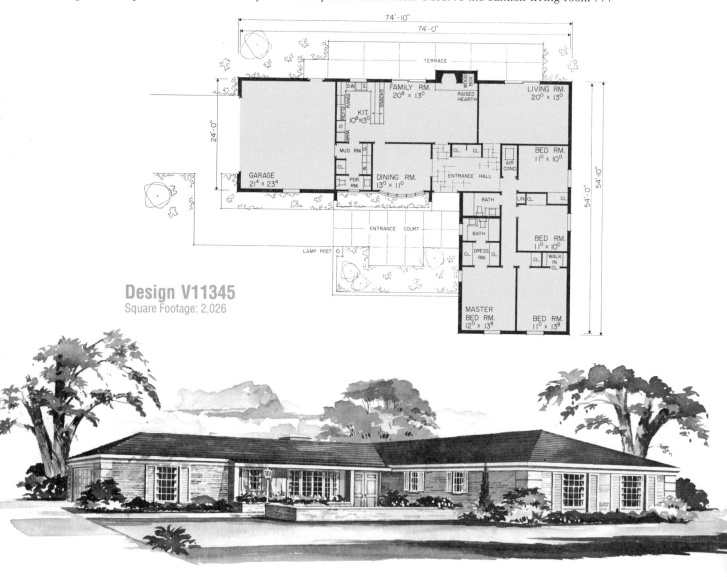

Design V11345
Square Footage: 2,026

Design V12134
Square Footage: 2,530

. . . and the beamed ceiling family room of Design V12134 above. Don't miss its big dressing room or raised hearth fireplace. Design V11345 has both its family and living rooms located to the rear and functioning with the terrace. Design V11054 has an efficient work area and a large formal dining room.

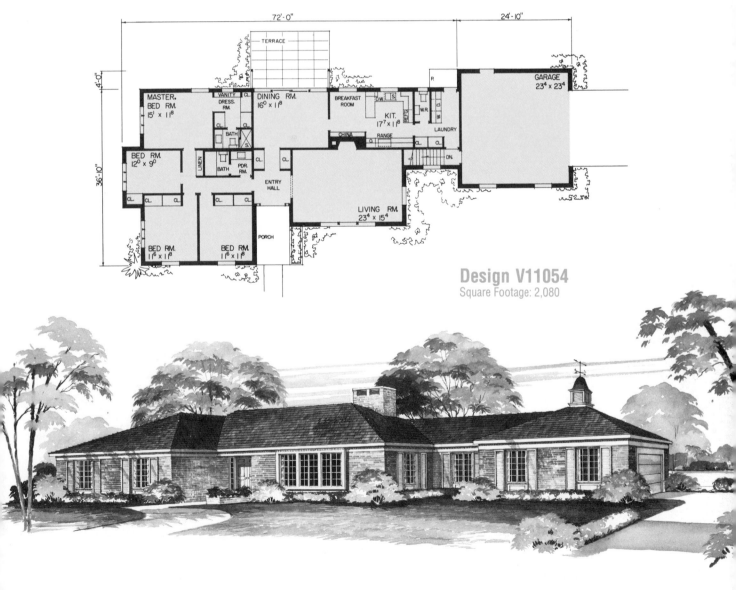

Design V11054
Square Footage: 2,080

Design V11330
Square Footage: 1,820

● A dramatic, formal exterior uses strong horizontal cornice lines to accentuate its low-slung qualities. The brick quoins at the corners, the paneled shutters, the ornamental iron and the hip-roof contribute to a distinctly continental flavor. Inside, the various areas are clearly defined. The bedrooms and living room are away from the noise of the family and service areas. The living room can double as a den-study. The U-shaped kitchen with pass-thru counters serves both the family room and dining area conveniently. The sleeping wing is highlighted by three sizable bedrooms, two baths and an abundance of wardrobe storage facilities. Optional fireplace details are included with the plan.

Design V11326
Square Footage: 2,014

● This pleasing, French Provincial adaptation has an extremely practical basic floor plan which contains many of those "extras" that contribute so much to good living. Among the features that make this such an outstanding home are: two fireplaces—one with raised hearth and wood box, first floor laundry, extra washroom, powder room, snack bar, separate dining room, partial basement, garage storage and workbench. With the four bedrooms and the formal and informal living areas, there is plenty of space in which the large family may move around and enjoy their surroundings.

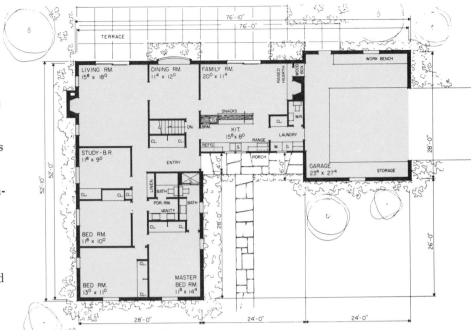

Design V12342
First Floor: 2,824 square feet
Second Floor: 1,013 square feet
Total: 3,837 square feet

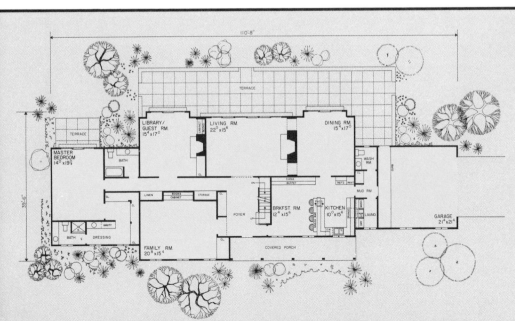

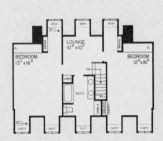

Design V11228

First Floor: 2,583 square feet
Second Floor: 697 square feet
Total: 3,280 square feet

L D

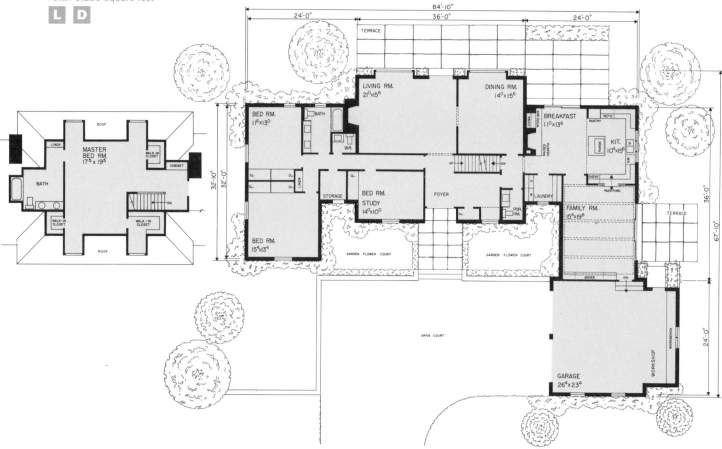

● This beautiful house has a wealth of detail taken from the rich traditions of French Regency design. The roof itself is a study in pleasant dormers and the hips and valleys of a big flowing area. A close examination of the plan shows the careful arrangement of space for privacy as well as good circulation of traffic. The spacious formal entrance hall sets the stage for good zoning. The informal living area is highlighted by the updated version of the old country kitchen. Observe the fireplace, built-in wood box, and china cabinet. While there is a half-story devoted to the master bedroom suite, this home functions more as a one-story country estate design than as a 1½ story.

Design V11784
Square Footage: 2,686

● Truly impressive, and surely a home of which dreams are made. Yet, its basic rectangular shape, its economical use of space, its tremendous livability and its outstanding design make it a worthy lifetime investment. Consider the features which will serve you so well and make you such a proud home-owner for so many years to come. The pleasant formality of the front entrance invites one through the double front doors to a spacious interior. Study the zoning. The formal living and dining rooms will enjoy their deserved privacy and function with their own rear outdoor living facilities. The family room and kitchen function together and have an enclosed court.

● The elegance of pleasing proportion and delightful detailing has seldom been better exemplified than by this classic French country manor adaptation. Approaching the house across the drive court, the majesty of this multi-roofed structure is breathtaking, indeed. An outstanding feature is the maid's suite. It is located above the garage and is easily reached by use of the covered porch connecting the laundry room's service entrance to the garage. If desired, it would make an excellent studio, quiet retreat or even a game room.

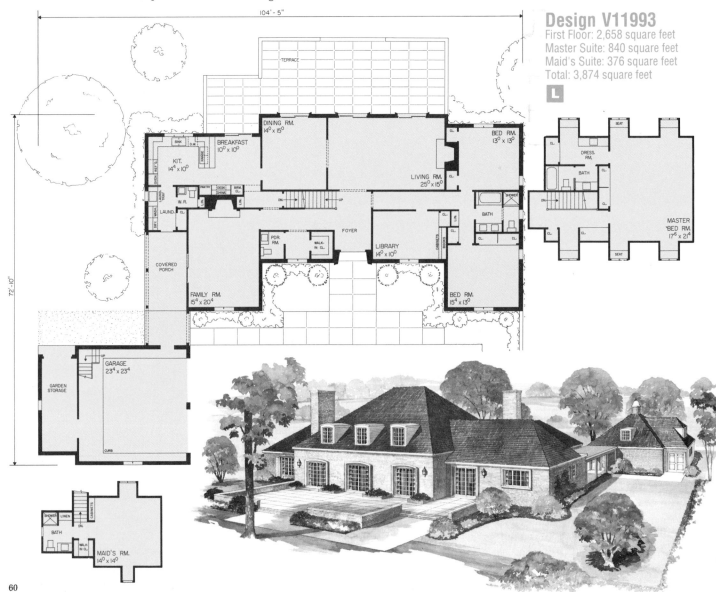

Design V11993
First Floor: 2,658 square feet
Master Suite: 840 square feet
Maid's Suite: 376 square feet
Total: 3,874 square feet

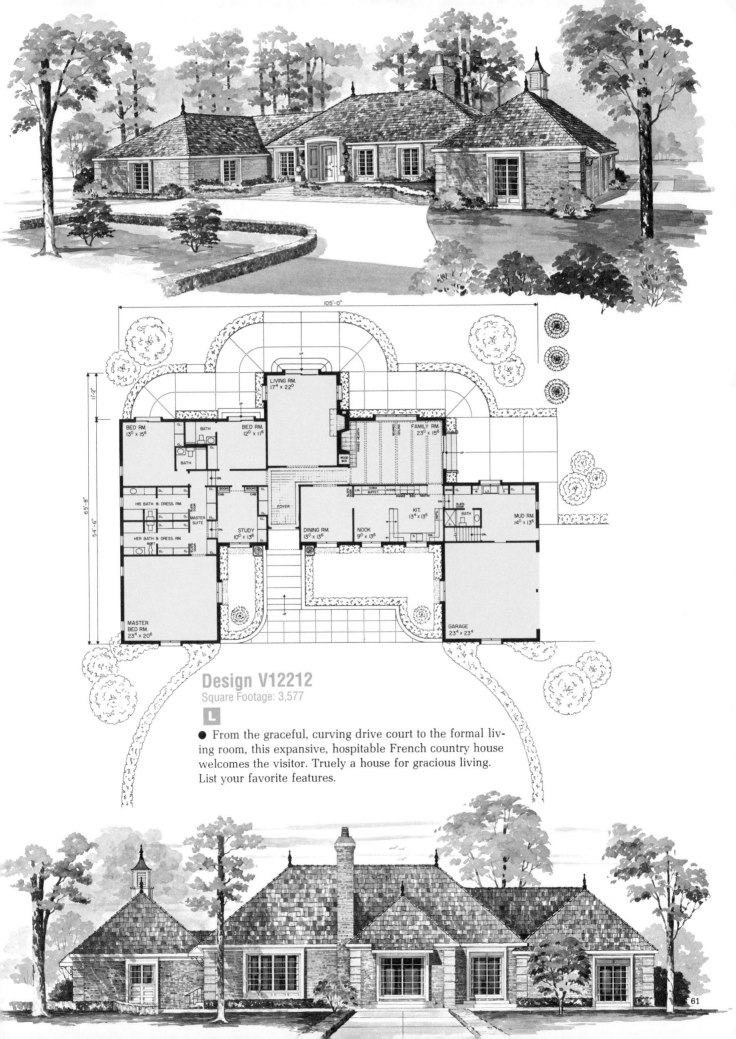

105'-0"

LIVING RM.
17⁴ x 22⁰

BED RM.
13⁰ x 15⁶

BATH

BED RM.
12⁰ x 11⁶

FAMILY RM.
23⁰ x 15⁶

BATH

HIS BATH & DRESS. RM.

MASTER SUITE

BOOKS CAB.

BOOKS CAB.

FOYER

CHINA BUFFET

OVENS

RANGE BBQ PANTRY

KIT.
13⁴ x 13⁶

BATH

MUD RM.
14⁰ x 13⁶

HER BATH & DRESS. RM.

STUDY
10⁰ x 13⁶

DINING RM.
13⁰ x 13⁶

NOOK
9⁰ x 13⁶

MASTER BED RM.
23⁴ x 20⁶

GARAGE
23⁴ x 23⁴

11'-2"

54'-6"

65'-8"

Design V12212
Square Footage: 3,577

L

● From the graceful, curving drive court to the formal living room, this expansive, hospitable French country house welcomes the visitor. Truely a house for gracious living. List your favorite features.

61

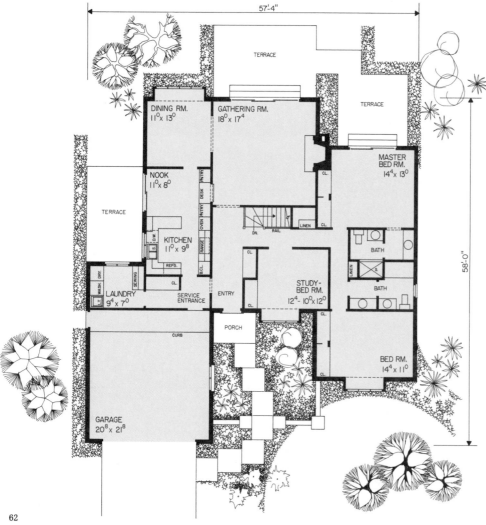

TERRACE

TERRACE

TERRACE

57'-4"

58'-0"

DINING RM.
11⁰ x 13⁰

GATHERING RM.
18⁰ x 17⁴

MASTER
BED RM.
14⁴ x 13⁰

NOOK
11⁰ x 8⁰

CL.

KITCHEN
11⁰ x 9⁸

PANTRY

DESK

OVEN PANTRY

RANGE

REFR.

CL.

DN.   RAIL

LINEN

CL.

BATH

LINEN

LAUNDRY
9⁴ x 7⁰

WASH DRY

SEWING

CL.

SERVICE
ENTRANCE

ENTRY

CL.

STUDY-
BED RM.
12⁴-10⁰ x 12⁰

CL.

BATH

PORCH

CURB

CL.

BED RM.
14⁴ x 11⁰

GARAGE
20⁸ x 21⁸

CL.

Design V12738
Square Footage: 1,898

● Impressive architectural work is indeed apparent in this three bedroom home. The three foot high entrance court wall, the high pitched roof and the paned glass windows all add to this home's exterior appeal. It is also apparent that the floor plan is very efficient with the side, U-shaped kitchen and nook with two pantry closets. Overlooking the backyard, the dining and gathering rooms will serve your every family occasion. Three (or make it two with a study) bedrooms and two baths are in the sleeping wing. Indoor-outdoor living also will be enjoyed in this home with a dining terrace off the nook and a living terrace off the gathering room and master bedroom. Note the fireplace in the gathering room and bay window in dining room. This design will be very livable.

SPANISH & WESTERN VARIATIONS...

can be found to offer a delightful change of pace wherever built. The appealing exterior design highlights include stucco surfaces, arched window heads, porch or courtyard columns, flared chimneys, exposed rafter tails, tiled roofs, window grilles, massive panelled doors, wide overhanging roofs, covered porches and private courtyards. Sloping and beamed ceilings are often among the focal points of these spacious interiors. The rambling nature of the floor plan configurations is consistent with the wide, open spaces from which these designs emanated. This, of course, results in a selection of houses with virtually unlimited livability potential.

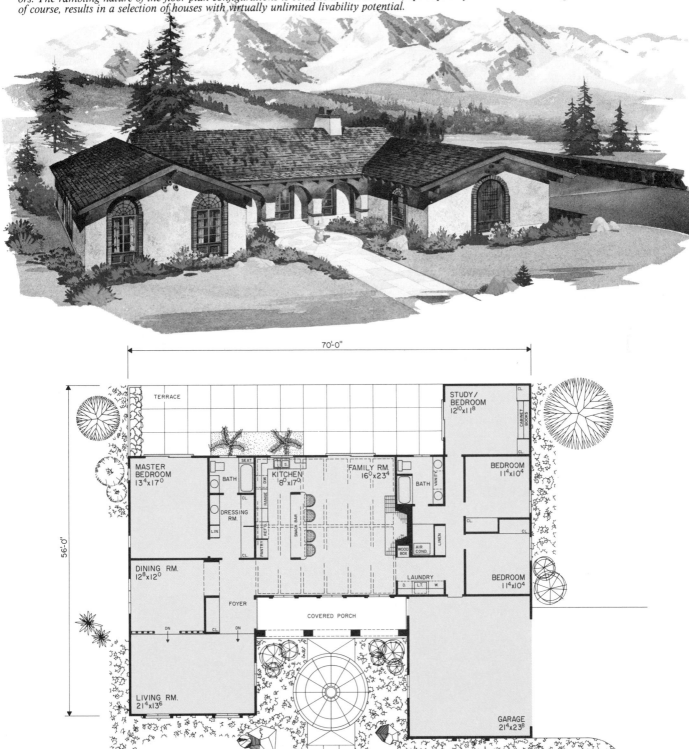

Design V12236
Square Footage: 2,307

● Living in this Spanish adaptation will truly be fun for the whole family. It will matter very little whether the backdrop matches the mountains above, becomes the endless prairie, turns out to be the rolling farmland, or is the backdrop of a suburban area. A family's flair for distinction will be satisfied by this picturesque exterior, while its requirements for everyday living will be gloriously catered to. The hub of the plan will be the kitchen-family room area. The beamed ceiling and raised hearth fireplace will contribute to the cozy, informal atmosphere. The separate dining room and the sunken living room function together formally. The master bedroom will enjoy its privacy from the three children's rooms located at the opposite end of the plan.

Design V12820
Square Footage: 2,261

L D

● A privacy wall around the courtyard with pool and trellised planter area is a gracious area by which to enter this one-story design. The Spanish flavor is accented by the grillework and the tiled roof. Interior livability has a great deal to offer. The front living room has slid-ing glass doors which open to the en-trance court; the adjacent dining room features a bay window. Informal activi-ties will be enjoyed in the rear family room. Its many features include a slop-ed, beamed ceiling, raised hearth fire-place, sliding glass doors to the terrace and a snack bar for those very infor-mal meals. A laundry and powder room are adjacent to the U-shaped kitchen. The sleeping wing can remain quiet away from the plan's activity centers. Notice the three-car garage with an extra storage area.

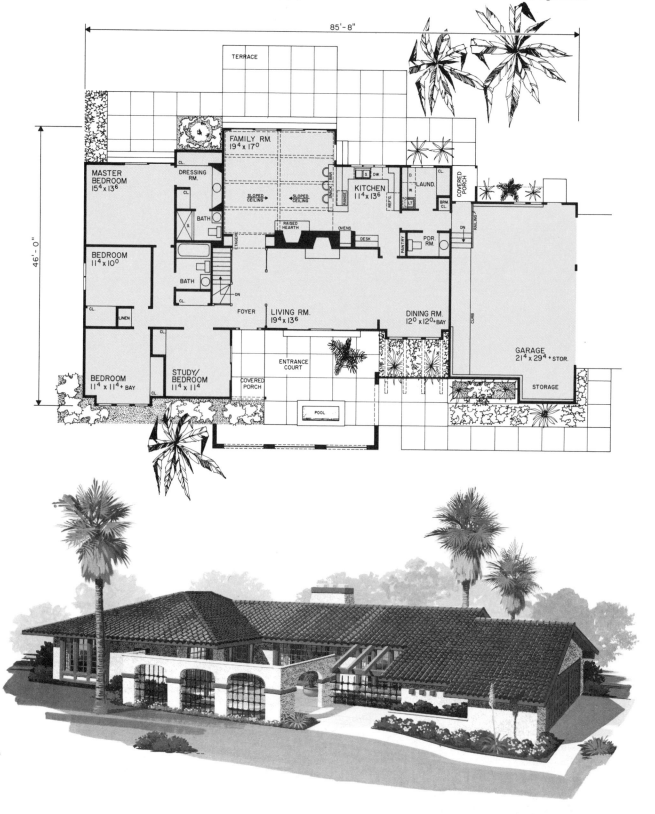

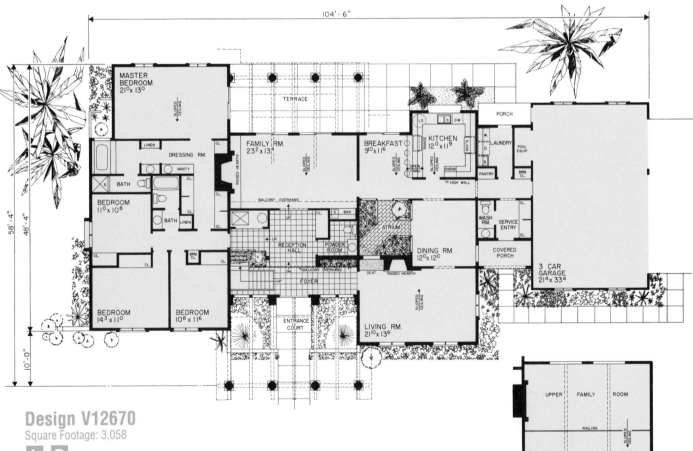

Design V12670
Square Footage: 3,058

L D

● A centrally located interior atrium is one of the most interesting features of this Spanish design. The atrium has a built-in seat and will bring light to its adjacent rooms; living, dining and breakfast. Beyond the foyer, sunken one step, is a tiled reception hall that includes a powder room. This area leads to the sleeping wing and up one step to the family room. Overlooking the family room is a railed lounge, 279 square feet, which can be used for various activities. The work center area will be convenient to work in.

Design V12950
Square Footage: 2,559

● A natural desert dweller, this stucco, tile-roofed beauty is equally comfortable in any clime. Inside, there's a well-planned design. Common living areas — gathering room, formal dining room, and breakfast room — are offset by a quiet study that could be used as a bedroom or guest room. A master suite features two walk-in closets, a double vanity, and whirlpool spa. The two-car garage has a service entrance; close by is an adequate laundry area and a pantry. Notice the warming hearth in the gathering room and the snack bar area for casual dining.

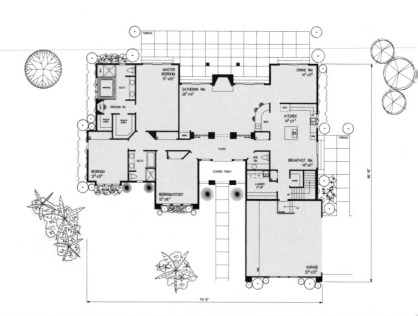

Design V13421
Square Footage: 2,145

● Split-bedroom planning makes the most of a one-story design. In this case the master suite is on the opposite side of the house from two family bedrooms. Gourmets can rejoice at the abundant work space in the U-shaped kitchen and will appreciate the natural light afforded by the large bay window in the breakfast room. A formal living room has a sunken conversation area with a cozy fireplace as its focus. The rear covered porch can be reached through sliding glass doors in the family room.

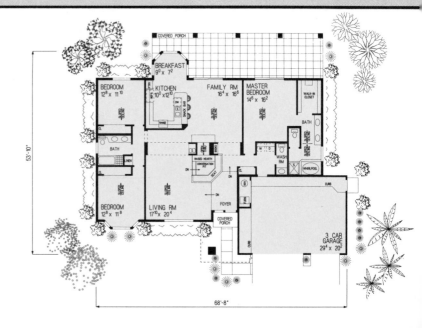

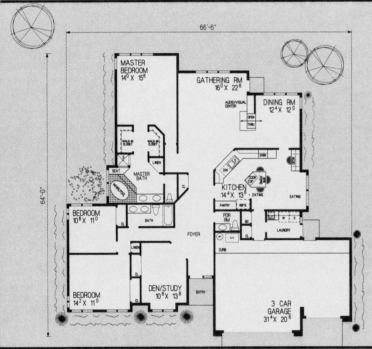

66'-6"

64'-0"

MASTER BEDROOM
14⁰ X 15⁸

GATHERING RM
16⁰ X 22⁶

AUDIO/VISUAL CENTER

OPEN THRU

DINING RM
12⁴ X 12⁰

WALK-IN CLOSET

WALK-IN CLOSET

LINEN

OVEN

SEAT

MASTER BATH

WHIRLPOOL

KITCHEN
14⁴ X 13⁰

COOK TOP

EATING

EATING

BEDROOM
10⁸ X 11⁰

PANTRY

REF'S

BATH

PDR RM

BC

CL

W D

CL

LINEN

FOYER

LAUNDRY

A/C

CURB

BEDROOM
14² X 11⁰

CL

DEN/STUDY
10⁸ X 13⁸

ENTRY

3 CAR GARAGE
31⁴ X 20⁶

Design V13440
Square Footage: 2,300

● Pack 'em in! There's plenty of room for everyone in this three- or optional four-bedroom home. The expansive gathering room welcomes family and guests with a through-fireplace to the dining room, an audio/visual center, and a door to the outside. The kitchen includes a wide pantry, a snack bar, and a separate eating area. Included in the master suite: two walk-in closets, shower, whirlpool tub and seat, dual vanities, and linen storage.

CUSTOMIZABLE

Custom Alterations? See page 381 for customizing this plan to your specifications.

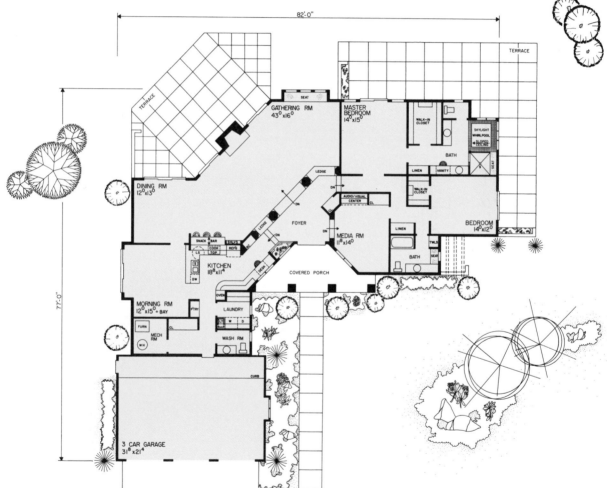

Design V12949
Square Footage: 2,922

● Spanish and western influences take center stage in a long, low stucco design. You'll enjoy the Texas-sized gathering room that opens to a formal dining area and has a snack bar through to the kitchen. More casual dining is accommodated in the nook. A luxurious master suite is graced by plenty of closet space and a soothing whirlpool spa. Besides another bed- room and full bath, there is a media room that could easily double as a third bedroom or guest room.

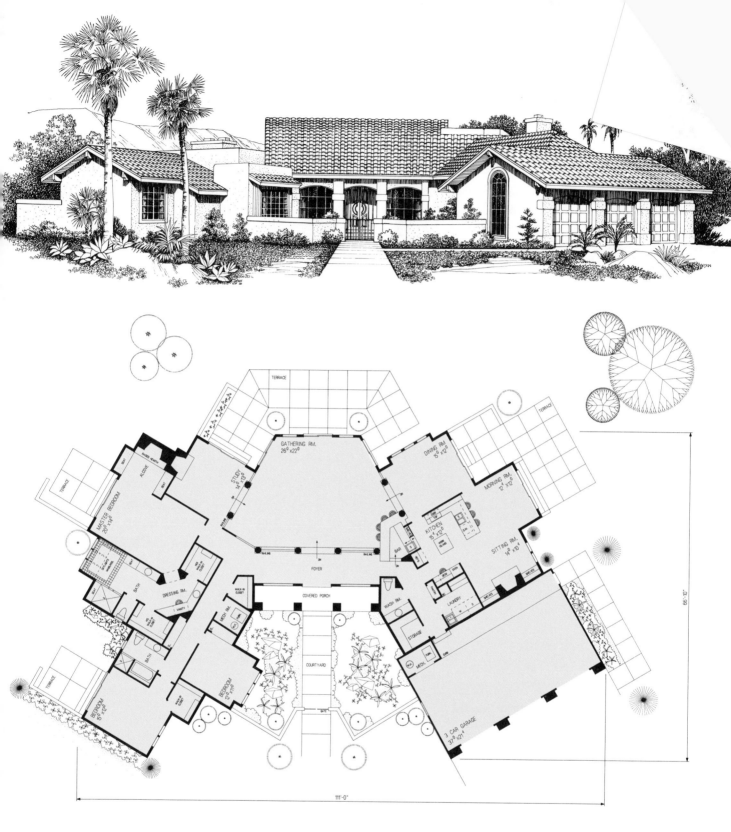

Design V12922
Square Footage: 3,505

● Loaded with custom features, this plan seems to have everything imaginable. There's an enormous sunken gathering room and cozy study. The country-style kitchen contains an efficient work area, as well as space for relaxing in the morning and sitting rooms. Two nice-sized bedrooms and a luxurious master suite round out the plan.

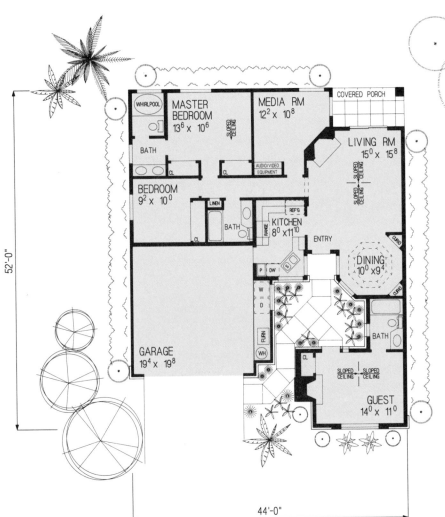

MASTER BEDROOM 13⁶ x 10⁶

WHIRLPOOL

BATH

CL

BEDROOM 9² x 10⁰

LINEN

CL

BATH

MEDIA RM 12² x 10⁸

SLOPED CEILING

AUDIO/VIDEO EQUIPMENT

COVERED PORCH

LIVING RM 15⁰ x 15⁸

SLOPED CEILING   SLOPED CEILING

REF'G

KITCHEN 8⁰ x 11¹⁰

RANGE

ENTRY

P   DW

S

W   D

FURN

WH

GARAGE 19⁴ x 19⁸

DINING 10⁰ x 9⁴

CL'RD

CL'RD

BATH

CL

SLOPED CEILING   SLOPED CEILING

GUEST 14⁰ x 11⁰

52'-0"

44'-0"

CUSTOMIZABLE

Custom Alterations? See page 381 for customizing this plan to your specifications.

Design V13416

Square Footage: 1,375

● Here's a Southwestern design that will be economical to build and a pleasure to occupy. The front door opens into a spacious living room with corner fireplace and dining room with coffered ceiling. The nearby kitchen serves both easily. A few steps away is the cozy media room with built-in space for audio-visual equipment. Down the hall are two bedrooms and two baths; the master features a whirlpool. A guest room is found across the entry court and includes a fireplace and sloped ceiling.

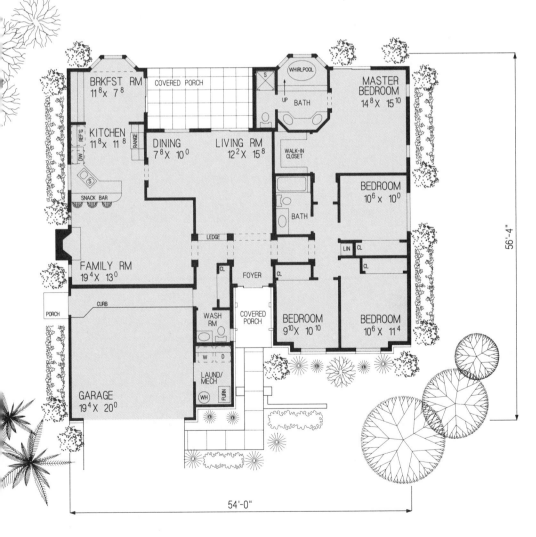

BRKFST RM
11⁸ x 7⁸

COVERED PORCH

KITCHEN
11⁸ x 11⁸

REF'G

DW

RANGE

DINING
7⁸ x 10⁰

LIVING RM
12² x 15⁸

WHIRLPOOL

S

UP

BATH

MASTER BEDROOM
14⁸ x 15¹⁰

WALK-IN CLOSET

SNACK BAR

BEDROOM
10⁶ x 10⁰

BATH

LEDGE

FAMILY RM
19⁴ x 13⁰

LIN

CL

CL

CL

CL

FOYER

CURB

PORCH

WASH RM

COVERED PORCH

BEDROOM
9¹⁰ x 10¹⁰

BEDROOM
10⁶ x 11⁴

W

D

LAUND/ MECH

WH

FURN

GARAGE
19⁴ x 20⁰

56'-4"

54'-0"

Design V13419
Square Footage: 1,965

● This attractive, multi-gabled exterior houses a compact, livable interior. The entry foyer effectively routes traffic to all areas: left to the family room and kitchen, straight back to the dining room and living room, and right to the four-bedroom sleeping area. The spacious family room provides an informal gathering space while the living and dining rooms are perfect for formal occasions. The highlight of the sleeping area is the master bedroom with its whirlpool, walk-in closet and view of the back yard.

CUSTOMIZABLE
Custom Alterations? See page 381 for customizing this plan to your specifications.

71

CUSTOMIZABLE

Custom Alterations? See page 381
for customizing this plan to your
specifications.

Design V13400 Square Footage: 2,784

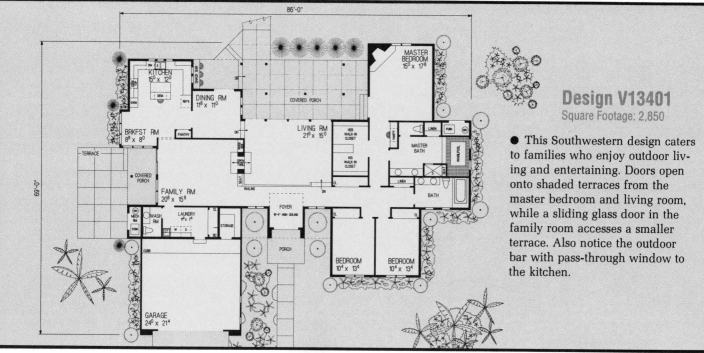

Design V13401
Square Footage: 2,850

● This Southwestern design caters
to families who enjoy outdoor living and entertaining. Doors open
onto shaded terraces from the
master bedroom and living room,
while a sliding glass door in the
family room accesses a smaller
terrace. Also notice the outdoor
bar with pass-through window to
the kitchen.

CUSTOMIZABLE

Custom Alterations? See page 381
for customizing this plan to your
specifications.

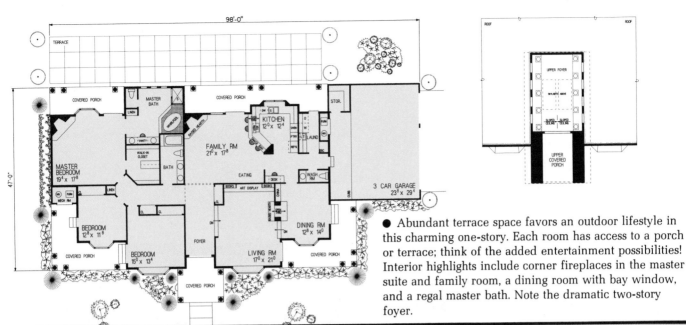

● Abundant terrace space favors an outdoor lifestyle in this charming one-story. Each room has access to a porch or terrace; think of the added entertainment possibilities! Interior highlights include corner fireplaces in the master suite and family room, a dining room with bay window, and a regal master bath. Note the dramatic two-story foyer.

CUSTOMIZABLE

Custom Alterations? See page 381 for customizing this plan to your specifications.

Design V13402
Square Footage: 3,212

● This one-story pairs the customary tile and stucco of Spanish design with a livable floor plan. The sunken living room with its open-hearth fireplace promises to be a cozy gathering place. For more casual occasions, there's a family room with fireplace off the entry foyer. Also noteworthy: a sizable kitchen and a sumptuous master suite.

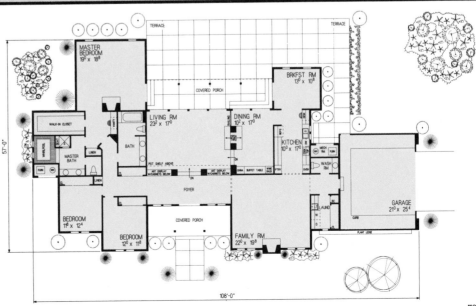

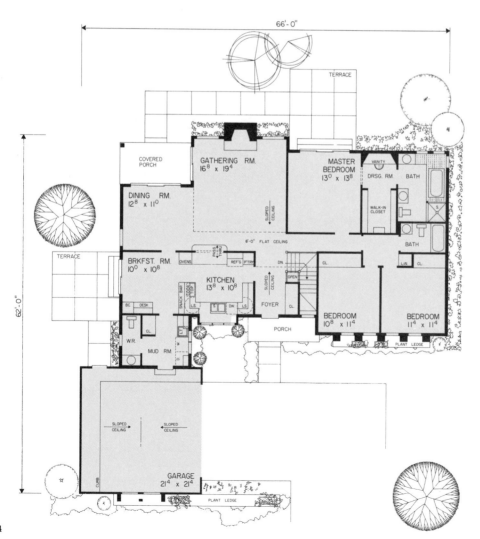

Design V12912
Square Footage: 1,864

● This modern design with smart Spanish styling incorporates careful zoning by room functions with lifestyle comfort. All three bedrooms, including a master bedroom suite, are isolated at one end of the one-story home for privacy and out of traffic patterns. Entry to a breakfast room and kitchen is possible through a mud room off the garage. That's good news for people carrying groceries from car to kitchen or people with muddy shoes during inclement weather. The modern kitchen includes a snack bar and cook top with multiple access to breakfast room, side foyer, and pass-thru to hallway. There's also a nearby formal dining room. A large rear gathering room features sloped ceiling and its own fireplace. Note the two-car garage and built-in plant ledge in front. Gabled end window treatment plus varied roof lines further enhance the striking appearance of this efficient design.

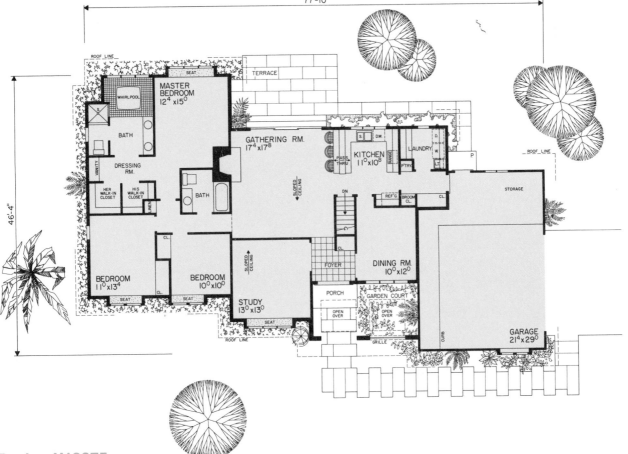

77'-10"

46'-4"

ROOF LINE

SEAT

TERRACE

WHIRLPOOL

MASTER BEDROOM 12⁴x15⁰

BATH

S.

GATHERING RM. 17⁴x17⁸

KITCHEN 11⁰x10⁸

LAUNDRY

D.

ROOF LINE

P

DRESSING RM.

SLOPED CEILING

PASS THRU

S. D.W.

RANGE

P'TRY

VANITY

HER WALK-IN CLOSET

HIS WALK-IN CLOSET

LINEN

BATH

DN

REF'G.

BROOM CL.

CL.

STORAGE

BEDROOM 11⁰x13⁴

CL.

SEAT

BEDROOM 10⁰x10⁰

SEAT

CL.

SLOPED CEILING

FOYER

DINING RM. 10⁰x12⁰

SEAT

STUDY 13⁰x13⁰

PORCH

OPEN OVER

GARDEN COURT

OPEN OVER

GARAGE 21⁴x29⁰

CURB

SEAT

ROOF LINE

GRILLE

Design V12875
Square Footage: 1,913

● This elegant Spanish design incorporates excellent indoor-outdoor living relationships for modern families who enjoy the sun and comforts of a well-planned new home. Note the overhead openings for rain and sun to fall upon a front garden, while a twin arched entry leads to the front porch and foyer. Inside the floor plan features a modern kitchen with pass-thru to a large gathering room with fireplace. Other features include a dining room, laundry room, a study off the foyer, plus three bedrooms including master bedroom with its own whirlpool.

Design V13412
Square Footage: 2,150

CUSTOMIZABLE
Custom Alterations? See page 381 for customizing this plan to your specifications.

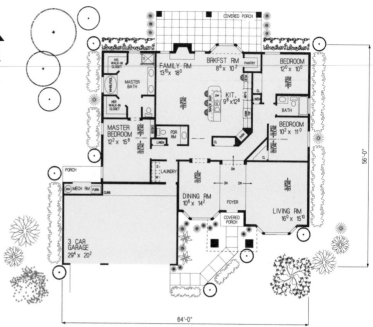

● Although typically Southwestern in design, this home will bring style to any neighborhood. Huge bay windows flood the front living and dining rooms with plenty of natural light. An amenity-filled kitchen with attached family room will be the main gathering area, where the family works and relaxes together. Notice the fireplace, the island snack bar and walk-in pantry. A split sleeping zone separates the master suite with luxurious bath from the two family bedrooms. Also notice the covered porch off the family room.

Design V13430
Square Footage: 2,394

● This dramatic design benefits from open planning. The centerpiece of the living area is a sunken conversation pit which shares a through-fireplace with the family room. The living room and dining room share space beneath a sloped ceiling. The open kitchen features a snack bar and breakfast room and conveniently serves all living areas. Split zoning in the sleeping area places the private master suite to the left of the plan and three more bedrooms, including one with a bay window, to the right.

CUSTOMIZABLE
Custom Alterations? See page 381 for customizing this plan to your specifications.

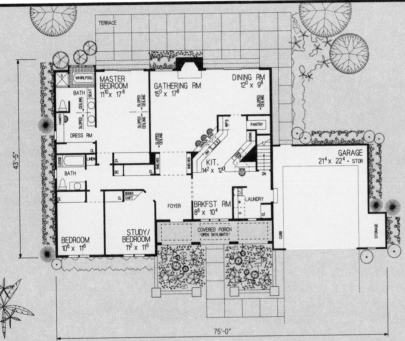

Design V12948
Square Footage: 1,830

● Styled for Southwest living, this home is a good choice in any region. Its highlights include: gathering room/dining room combination with fireplace, a uniquely shaped kitchen, luxurious master suite, and a study or alternate third bedroom. Notice the covered porch with open skylights.

Custom Alterations? See page 381 for customizing this plan to your specifications.

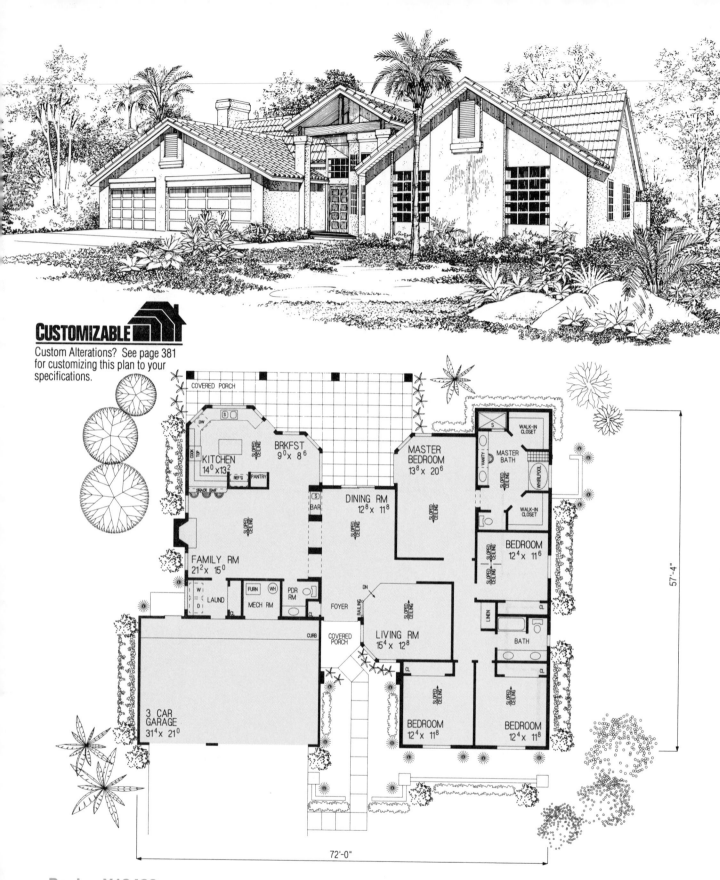

CUSTOMIZABLE
Custom Alterations? See page 381
for customizing this plan to your
specifications.

COVERED PORCH

KITCHEN
14⁰ x 13²

BRKFST
9⁰ x 8⁶

REF'G   PANTRY

SNACK BAR

SLOPED CEILING

FAMILY RM
21² x 15⁰

W   D   LAUND   CL

FURN   WH

MECH RM

PDR RM

CL

DINING RM
12⁸ x 11⁸

BAR

SLOPED CEILING

FOYER

RAILING   DN

COVERED PORCH

CURB

LIVING RM
15⁴ x 12⁸

SLOPED CEILING

3 CAR GARAGE
31⁴ x 21⁰

CL

BEDROOM
12⁴ x 11⁸

SLOPED CEILING

MASTER BEDROOM
13⁸ x 20⁶

SLOPED CEILING

VANITY

MASTER BATH

WHIRLPOOL

WALK-IN CLOSET

WALK-IN CLOSET

SLOPED CEILING

BEDROOM
12⁴ x 11⁶

SLOPED CEILING

LINEN

CL

BATH

CL

BEDROOM
12⁴ x 11⁸

SLOPED CEILING

57'-4"

72'-0"

Design V13423 Square Footage: 2,571

● This spacious Southwestern home will be a pleasure to come home to. Immediately off the foyer are the dining room and step-down living room with bay window. The highlight of the four-bedroom sleeping area is the master suite with porch access and a whirlpool for soaking away the day's worries. The informal living area features an enormous family room with fireplace and bay-windowed kitchen and breakfast room. Notice the snack bar pass-through to the family room.

COVERED PORCH

MASTER BEDROOM
13⁰ x 13⁸

MASTER BATH

WHIRLPOOL

WALK-IN CLOSET

FAMILY RM
12⁸ x 18⁶

BREAKFAST
7⁶ x 9⁴

KIT.
9⁴ x 13⁴

OVENS

SNACK BAR

DW

COOK TOP

REF'G

PANTRY

SLOPED CEILING

BEDROOM
9⁸ x 9¹⁰

CL

BATH

PDR RM

S

BAR

DINING
13⁴ x 9⁶

HALF WALL

CL

BEDROOM
12⁰ x 10⁰

LINEN

LT

LAUND

W

D

STUDY
9⁸ x 9⁶

FOYER

DN

HALF WALL

LIVING RM
13⁴ x 13⁴

SLOPED CEILING

WH

FURN

CL

CURB

COVERED PORCH

GARAGE
21⁴ x 19⁸

60'-0"

50'-0"

Design V13422
Square Footage: 1,932

● An enclosed entry garden greets visitors to this charming Southwestern home. Inside, the foyer is flanked by formal and informal living areas — a living room and dining room to the right and a cozy study to the left. To the rear, a large family room, breakfast room and open kitchen have access to a covered porch and overlook the back yard. Notice the fireplace and bay window. The three-bedroom sleeping area includes a master with a spacious bath with whirlpool.

CUSTOMIZABLE
Custom Alterations? See page 381 for customizing this plan to your specifications.

Design V13411
Square Footage: 2,441

● You'll love the entry to this Southwestern home — it creates a dramatic first impression and leads beautifully to the formal living and dining rooms. Beyond, look for an open family room and dining area in the same proximity as the kitchen. Sliding glass doors here open to a backyard patio. Take your choice of four bedrooms or five, depending on how you wish to use the optional room. The huge master suite is not to be missed.

CUSTOMIZABLE

Custom Alterations? See page 381 for customizing this plan to your specifications.

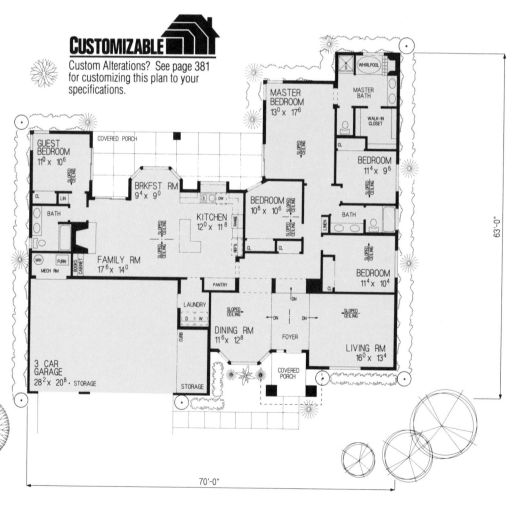

GUEST BEDROOM 11⁰ x 10⁶

COVERED PORCH

BRKFST RM 9⁴ x 9⁰

KITCHEN 12⁰ x 11⁸

BATH

BATH

MASTER BEDROOM 13⁰ x 17⁶

MASTER BATH

WHIRLPOOL

WALK-IN CLOSET

BEDROOM 11⁴ x 9⁶

BEDROOM 10⁸ x 10⁶

FAMILY RM 17⁶ x 14⁰

BOOKS CABINET

WH FURN MECH RM

PANTRY

LAUNDRY

DINING RM 11⁶ x 12⁸

FOYER

BEDROOM 11⁴ x 10⁴

LIVING RM 16⁰ x 13⁴

3 CAR GARAGE 28² x 20⁸ + STORAGE

STORAGE

COVERED PORCH

63'-0"

70'-0"

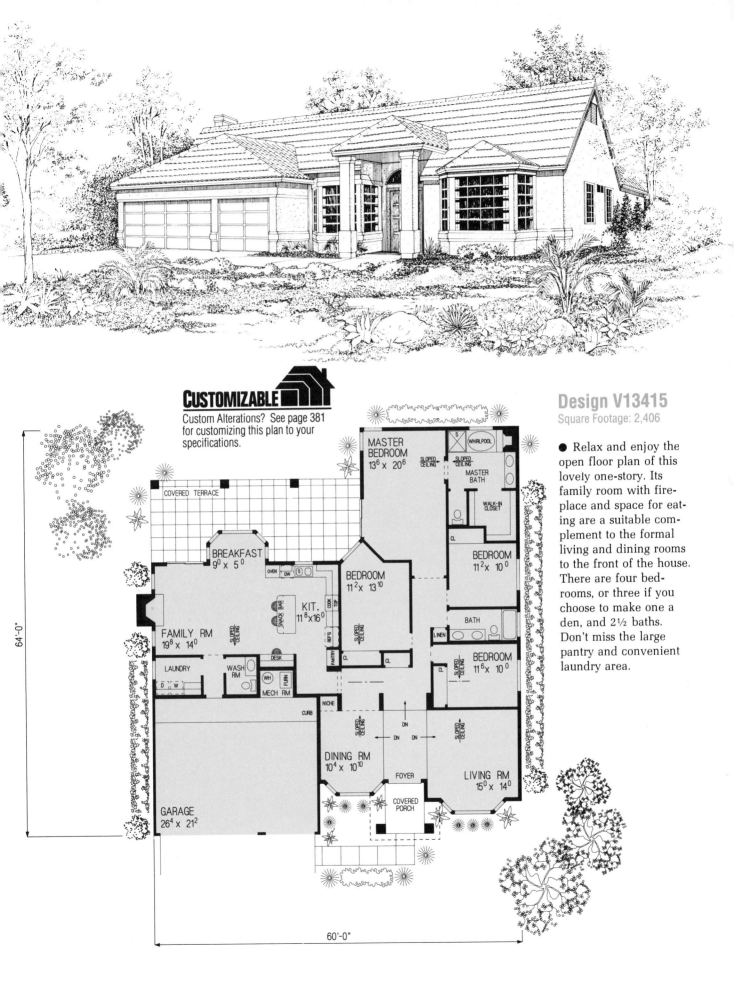

CUSTOMIZABLE

Custom Alterations? See page 381 for customizing this plan to your specifications.

Design V13415
Square Footage: 2,406

● Relax and enjoy the open floor plan of this lovely one-story. Its family room with fireplace and space for eating are a suitable complement to the formal living and dining rooms to the front of the house. There are four bedrooms, or three if you choose to make one a den, and 2½ baths. Don't miss the large pantry and convenient laundry area.

MASTER BEDROOM
13⁶ x 20⁶

SLOPED CEILING

WHIRLPOOL

MASTER BATH

WALK-IN CLOSET

COVERED TERRACE

BREAKFAST
9⁰ x 5⁰

OVEN DW

BEDROOM
11² x 13¹⁰

SLOPED CEILING

BEDROOM
11² x 10⁰

KIT.
11⁸ x 16⁰

SNACK BAR

COOK TOP

REF'S

FAMILY RM
19⁸ x 14⁰

SLOPED CEILING

BATH

LINEN

PANTRY

CL

CL

DESK

LAUNDRY

WASH RM

WH FURN

MECH RM

BEDROOM
11⁶ x 10⁰

CL

SLOPED CEILING

CURB

NICHE

SLOPED CEILING

DN

DN DN

SLOPED CEILING

DINING RM
10⁴ x 10¹⁰

FOYER

LIVING RM
15⁰ x 14⁰

GARAGE
26⁴ x 21²

COVERED PORCH

64'-0"

60'-0"

81

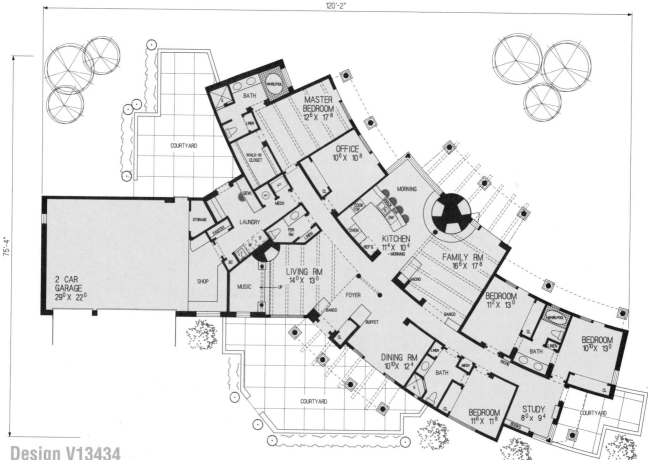

Design V13434
Square Footage: 2,968

● An in-line floor plan follows the tradition of the original Santa Fe-style homes. The slight curve to the overall configuration lends an interesting touch. From the front courtyard, the plan opens to a formal living room and dining room complemented by a family room and kitchen with morning room. The master bedroom is found to one side of the plan while family bedrooms share space at the opposite end. There's also a huge office and a study area for private times. With 3½ baths, a workshop garage, full laundry/sewing area, and three courtyards, this plan adds up to great livability.

CUSTOMIZABLE

Custom Alterations? See page 381 for customizing this plan to your specifications.

Design V13405
Square Footage: 3,144

● In classic Santa Fe style, this home strikes a beautiful combination of historic exterior detailing and open floor planning on the inside. A covered porch running the width of the facade leads to an entry foyer that connects to a huge gathering room with fireplace and formal dining room. The family kitchen allows special space for casual gatherings. The right wing of the home holds two family bedrooms and full bath. The left wing is devoted to the master suite and guest room or study. Built-ins abound throughout the house.

Design V13433
Square Footage: 2,350

● Santa Fe styling creates interesting angles in this one-story home. The master suite features a deluxe bath and a bedroom close at hand, perfect for a nursery, home office or exercise room. Fireplaces in the living room, dining room and covered porch create various shapes. Make note of the island range in the kitchen, extra storage in the garage, and covered porches on two sides.

CUSTOMIZABLE

Custom Alterations? See page 381 for customizing this plan to your specifications.

Design V13436
Square Footage: 2,387

● An expansive gathering room/dining area with sloped ceiling makes a grand impression. The kitchen includes a large pantry and adjoining breakfast area with fireplace. A courtyard in the front can be reached through the dining room or front bedroom, while a covered rear patio is accessible through the gathering room, study, or master bedroom. Each of the three bedrooms includes a walk-in closet and convenient access to a full bath.

CUSTOMIZABLE

Custom Alterations? See page 381 for customizing this plan to your specifications.

Design V12879 Living Area Including Atrium: 3,173 square feet
Upper Lounge/Balcony: 267 square feet
Total: 3,440 square feet

● This plush modern design seems to have it all, including an upper lounge, upper family room, and upper foyer. There's also an atrium with skylight centrally located downstairs. A modern kitchen with snack bar service to a breakfast room also enjoys its own greenhouse window. A deluxe master bedroom includes its own whirlpool and bay window. Three other bedrooms also are isolated at one end of the house downstairs to allow privacy and quiet. A spacious family room in the rear enjoys its own raised-hearth fireplace and view of a rear covered terrace. A front living room with its own fireplace looks out upon a side garden court and the central atrium. There's also a formal dining room situated between the kitchen and living room, plus a three-car garage, covered porches, and sizable laundry with washroom just off the garage.

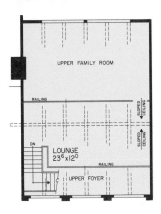

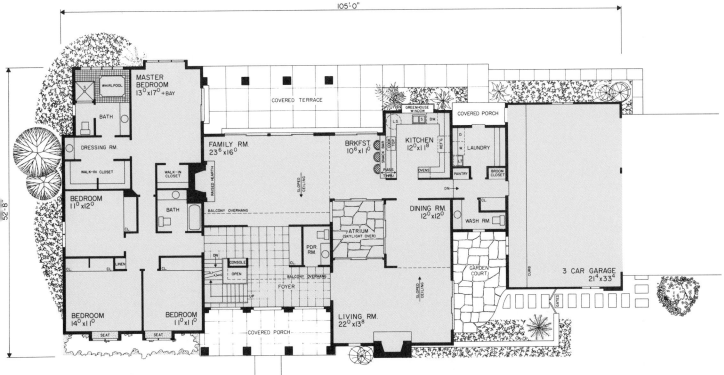

Design V12671
Square Footage: 1,589

L **D**

● A rustic exterior of this one-story home features vertical wood siding. The entry foyer is floored with flagstone and leads to the three areas of the plan: sleeping, living and work center. The sleeping area has three bedrooms, the master bedroom has sliding glass doors to the rear terrace. The living area, consisting of gathering and dining rooms, also has access to the terrace. The work center is efficiently planned. It houses the kitchen with snack bar, breakfast room with built-in china cabinet and stairs to the basement. This is a very livable plan.

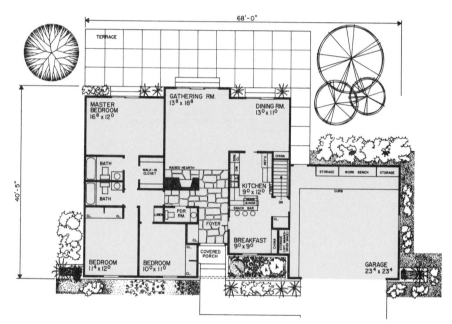

Design V12594 Square Footage: 2,294

D

● A spectacular foyer! Fully 21' long, it offers double entry to the heart of this home . . . a 21' by 21' gathering room, complete with sloped ceiling, raised-hearth fireplace and sliding glass doors onto the terrace. There's a formal dining room, too. Plus a well-located study for solitude or undisturbed work. The kitchen features a snack bar and a breakfast nook with sliding doors onto the terrace. For more convenience, a pantry and first-floor laundry. In the master suite, a dressing room with entry to the bath, four closets and sliding doors onto the terrace! Two more bedrooms if you wish to convert the study, or one easily large enough for two children with a dressing area and private entry to the second bath.

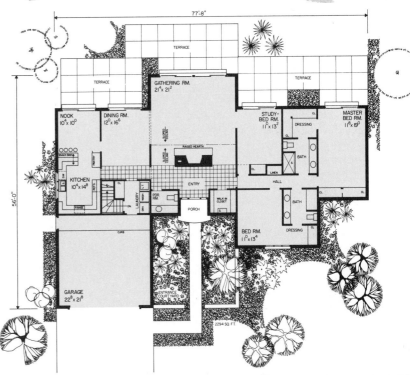

Design V12528
Square Footage: 1,754

D

● This inviting, U-shaped western ranch adaptation offers outstanding living potential behind its double, front doors and flanking glass panels. In but 1,754 square feet there are three bedrooms, 2½ baths, a formal living room and an informal family room, an excellently functioning interior kitchen, an adjacent breakfast nook and good storage facilities. The open stairwell to the lower level basement can be an interesting, interior feature. Note raised-hearth fireplace and sloped ceiling.

Design V12200
Square Footage: 1,695

● The two plans featured here are both housed in this L-shaped ranch home. Its exterior shows a Spanish influence by utilizing a stucco exterior finish, grilled windows and an arched entryway. Beyond the arched entryway is the private front court which leads to the tiled foyer. Interior livability has been well planned in both designs.

OPTIONAL BASEMENT PLAN

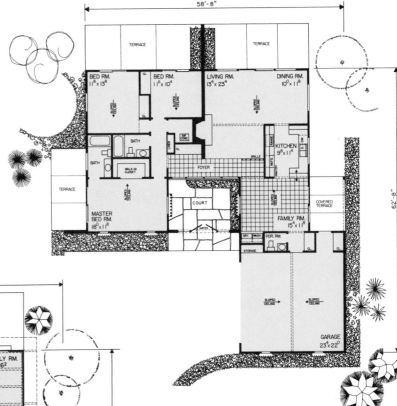

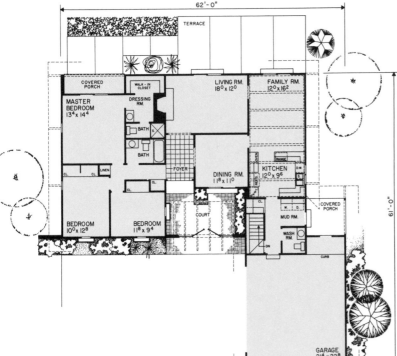

Design V12677
Square Footage: 1,634

● Notice the difference in these plan's livability. Design V12200 has a shared living dining room overlooking the backyard and a front master bedroom with a side terrace where Design V12677 has a separate front dining room, family room with access to the rear terrace and a rear master bedroom with an adjacent covered porch. Both designs have two additional bedrooms besides the master bedroom. Access to the basement varies in each plan.

TRADITIONAL DESIGNS 1,500-2,000 Sq. Ft.

Providing all the livability of much larger plans, the homes in this collection feature the elements that are most in demand: family rooms, breakfast rooms, separate living and dining rooms, and comfortable master bedroom suites. The appealing traditional styling includes amenities like covered porches, wide rear terraces, and lovely classic architectural details. A fine combination in one-story living.

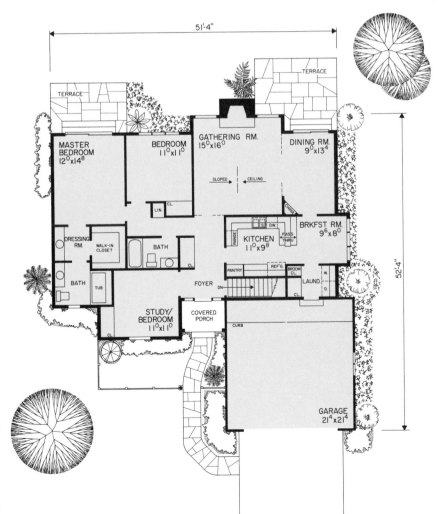

Design V12878
Square Footage: 1,521

L **D**

● This charming one-story Traditional design offers plenty of livability in a compact size. Thoughtful zoning puts all bedroom sleeping areas to one side of the house apart from household activity in the living and service areas. The home includes a spacious gathering room with sloped ceiling, in addition to formal dining room and separate breakfast room. There's also a handy pass-thru between the breakfast room and an efficient, large kitchen. The laundry is strategically located adjacent to garage and breakfast/kitchen areas for handy access. A master bedroom enjoys its own suite with private bath and walk-in closet. A third bedroom can double as a sizable study just off the central foyer. This design offers the elegance of Traditional styling with the comforts of modern lifestyle.

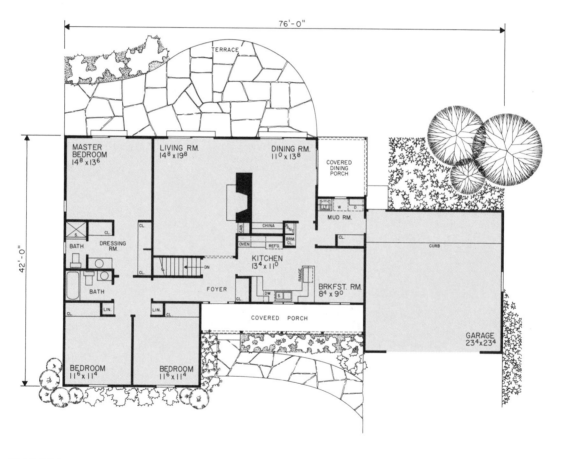

Design V12672

Square Footage: 1,717

● The traditional appearance of this one-story is emphasized by its covered porch, multi-paned windows, narrow clapboard and vertical wood siding. Not only is the exterior eye-appealing but the interior has an efficient plan and is very livable. The front U-shaped kitchen will work with the breakfast room and mud room, which houses the laundry facilities. An access to the garage is here. Outdoor dining can be enjoyed on the covered porch adjacent to the dining room. Both of these areas, the porch and dining room, are convenient to the kitchen. Sleeping facilities consist of three bedrooms and two full baths. Note the three sets of sliding glass doors leading to the terrace.

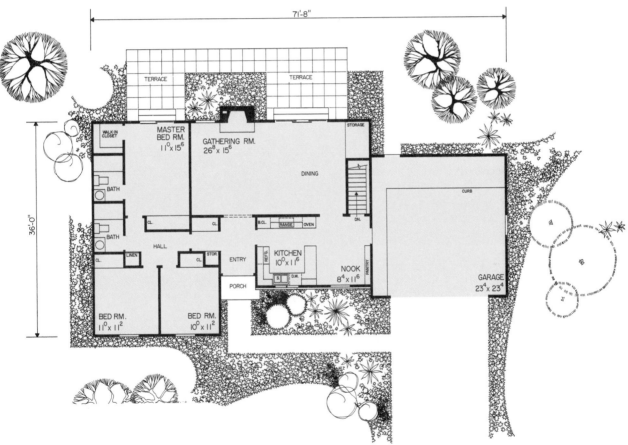

TERRACE

TERRACE

WALK-IN CLOSET

MASTER BED RM.
11⁰ x 15⁶

GATHERING RM.
26⁸ x 15⁶

STORAGE

BATH

DINING

CURB

BATH

CL.

CL.

B.CL.

RANGE

OVEN

DN.

HALL

LINEN

CL.

CL.

STOR.

ENTRY

REF'G.

KITCHEN
10⁰ x 11⁶

NOOK
8⁴ x 11⁶

PANTRY

GARAGE
23⁴ x 23⁴

BED RM.
11⁰ x 11²

BED RM.
10⁰ x 11²

PORCH

S.

D.W.

71'-8"

36'-0"

Design V12597
Square Footage: 1,515

L D

● Whether it be a starter house you are after, or one in which to spend your retirement years, this pleasing frame home will provide a full measure of pride in ownership. The contrast of vertical and horizontal lines, the double front doors and the coach lamp post at the garage create an inviting exterior. The floor plan functions in an orderly and efficient manner. The 26 foot gathering room has a delightful view of the rear yard and will take care of those formal dining occasions. There are two full baths serving the three bedrooms. There are plenty of storage facilities, two sets of glass doors to the terraces, a fireplace in the gathering room, a basement and an attached two-car garage to act as a buffer against the wind. A delightful home, indeed.

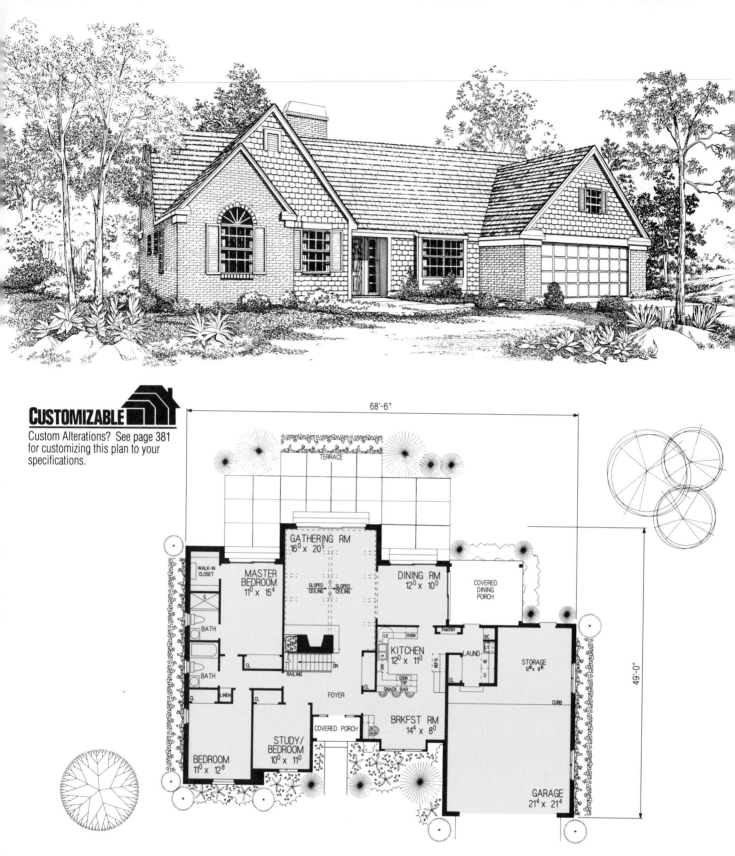

CUSTOMIZABLE

Custom Alterations? See page 381 for customizing this plan to your specifications.

68'-6"

TERRACE

GATHERING RM
16⁰ x 20⁵

DINING RM
12⁰ x 10⁰

COVERED DINING PORCH

WALK-IN CLOSET

MASTER BEDROOM
11⁰ x 15⁴

SLOPED CEILING | SLOPED CEILING

PANTRY

LAUND

BC
LT

STORAGE
12⁰ x 9¹⁰

BATH

KITCHEN
12⁰ x 11⁰

BATH

LINEN

CL

RAILING

DN

FOYER

COOK TOP

SNACK BAR

CL

CURB

49'-0"

BEDROOM
11⁰ x 12⁸

STUDY/
BEDROOM
10⁰ x 11⁰

COVERED PORCH

BRKFST RM
14⁴ x 8⁰

GARAGE
21⁴ x 21⁴

Design V13345 Square Footage: 1,738

● This quaint shingled cottage offers an unexpected amount of living space in just over 1,700 square feet. The large gathering room with fireplace, dining room with covered porch, and kitchen with breakfast room handle formal parties as easily as they do the casual family get-together. Three bedrooms, one that could also serve as a study, are found in a separate wing of the house. Give special attention to the storage space in this home and the extra touches that set it apart from many homes of equal size.

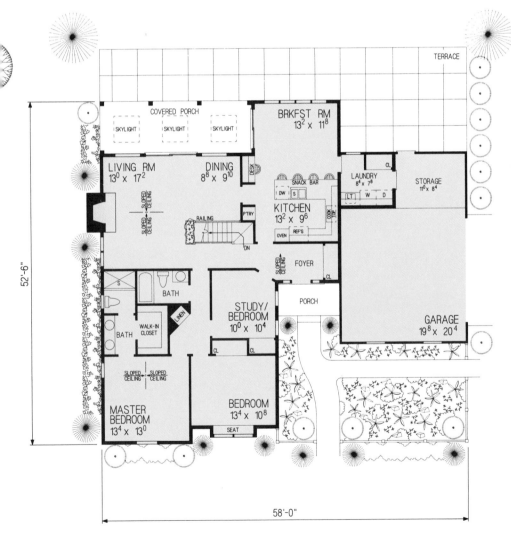

COVERED PORCH

SKYLIGHT   SKYLIGHT   SKYLIGHT

TERRACE

BRKFST RM
13² x 11⁸

LIVING RM
13⁰ x 17²

DINING
8⁸ x 9¹⁰

DESK

SNACK BAR

LAUNDRY
8⁴ x 7⁸

CL

STORAGE
11⁰ x 8⁴

DW   S

SLOPED CEILING

SLOPED CEILING

RAILING

P'TRY

KITCHEN
13² x 9⁶

COOK TOP

LT   W   D

DN

OVEN   REF'G

SLOPED CEILING

FOYER

S

BATH

CL

PORCH

BATH

WALK-IN CLOSET

LINEN

STUDY/ BEDROOM
10⁰ x 10⁴

CL

CL

GARAGE
19⁸ x 20⁴

SLOPED CEILING   SLOPED CEILING

MASTER BEDROOM
13⁴ x 13⁰

BEDROOM
13⁴ x 10⁸

SEAT

52'-6"

58'-0"

Design V13340
Square Footage: 1,611

● You may not decide to build this design simply because of its delightful covered porch. But it certainly will provide its share of enjoyment if this plan is your choice. Notice also how effectively the bedrooms are arranged out of the traffic flow of the house. One bedroom could double nicely as a TV room or study. The living room/dining area is highlighted by a fireplace, sliding glass doors to the porch, and an open staircase with built-in planter to the basement.

Design V11337
Square Footage: 1,606

● A pleasantly traditional facade which captures a full measure of warmth. Its exterior appeal results from a symphony of such features as: the attractive window detailing; the raised planter; the paneled door, carriage light and cupola of the garage; the use of both horizontal siding and brick. The floor plan has much to recommend this design to the family whose requirements include formal and informal living areas. There is an exceptional amount of livability in this modest-sized design.

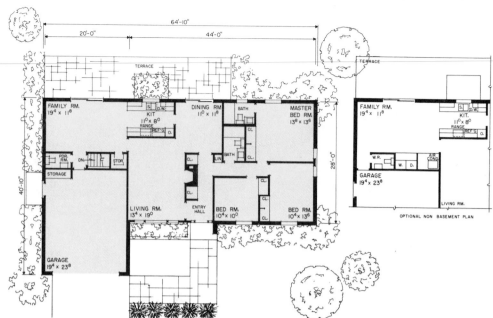

Design V11890
Square Footage: 1,628

● The pediment gable and columns help set the charm of this modestly sized home. Here is graciousness normally associated with homes twice its size. The pleasant symmetry of the windows and the double front doors complete the picture. Inside, each square foot is wisely planned to assure years of convenient living. There are three bedrooms, each with twin wardrobe closets. There are two full baths economically grouped with the laundry and heating equipment. A fine feature.

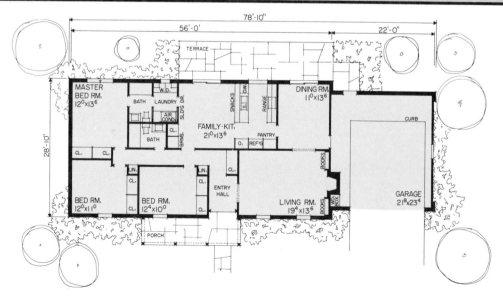

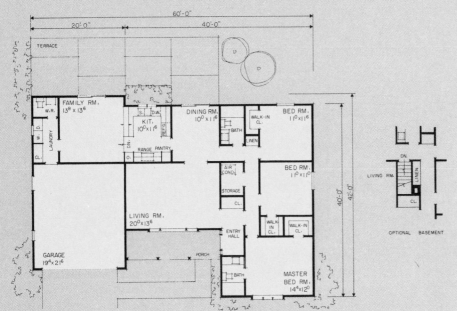

Design V11920
Square Footage: 1,600

L **D**

● A charming exterior with a truly great floor plan. The front entrance with its covered porch seems to herald all the outstanding features to be found inside. Study the sleeping zone with its three bedrooms and two full baths. Each of the bedrooms has its own walk-in closet. Note the efficient U-shaped kitchen with the family and dining rooms to each side. Observe the laundry and the extra wash room. Blueprints for this design include details for both basement and non-basement construction.

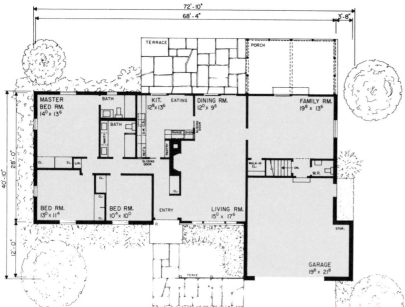

Design V11100
Square Footage: 1,752

● This modest sized, brick veneer home has a long list of things in its favor—from its appealing exterior to its feature-packed interior. All of the elements of its exterior complement each other to result in a symphony of attractive design features. The floor plan features three bedrooms, two full baths, an extra wash room, a family room, kitchen eating space, a formal dining area, two sets of sliding glass doors to the terrace and one set to the covered porch, built-in cooking equipment, a pantry and vanity with twin lavatories. Further, there is the living room fireplace, attached two-car garage with a bulk storage unit and a basement for extra storage and miscellaneous recreational activities. A fine investment.

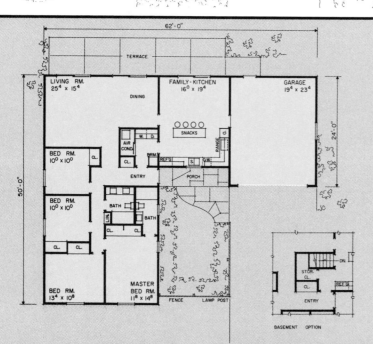

Design V11343
Square Footage: 1,620

L

● This is truly a prize-winner! The traditional, L-shaped exterior with its flower court and covered front porch is picturesque, indeed. The formal front entry routes traffic directly to the three distinctly zoned areas—the quiet sleeping area; the spacious; formal living and dining area; the efficient, informal family-kitchen. A closer look at the floor plan reveals four bedrooms, two full baths, good storage facilities, a fine snack bar and sliding glass doors to the rear terrace. The family-kitchen is ideally located. In addition to being but a few steps from both front and rear entrances, one will enjoy the view of both yards. Blueprints include basement and non-basement details.

Design V11896
Square Footage: 1,690

● Complete family livability is provided by this exceptional floor plan. Further, this design has a truly delightful traditional exterior. The fine layout features a center entrance hall with storage closet in addition to the wardrobe closet. Then, there is the formal, front living room and the adjacent, separate dining room. The U-shaped kitchen has plenty of counter and cupboard space. There is even a pantry. The family room functions with the kitchen and is but a step from the outdoor terrace. The mud room has space for storage and laundry equipment. The extra wash room is nearby. The large family will find those four bedrooms and two full baths just the answer to sleeping and bath accommodations.

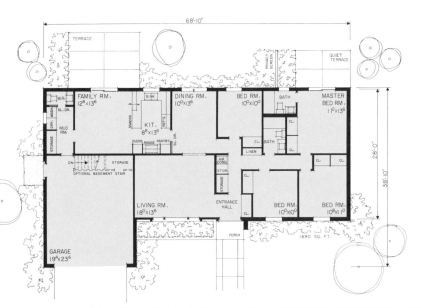

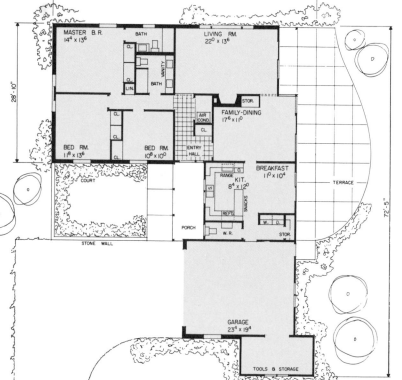

Design V13144
Square Footage: 1,760

● If you are short on space and searching for a home that is long on both good looks and livability, search no more! This impressive L-shaped home measures merely 56'-5'' in width. It, therefore, qualifies for placement on a relatively narrow building site. Of course with land costs so high, the purchase of a smaller and less expensive building site can significantly reduce the building budget. Whether you build with, or without, a basement (blueprints include details for both types of construction) the outstanding livability remains. There are three bedrooms, two baths, a formal rear living room, a big breakfast room, an excellent kitchen, a wash room and laundry and a huge bulk storage area projecting from the front of the garage. Note window treatment.

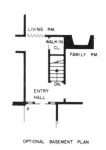

OPTIONAL BASEMENT PLAN

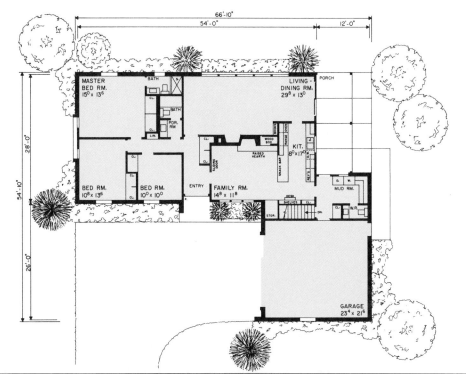

Design V11280
Square Footage: 1,730

● This medium-sized, L-shaped ranch home with its touch of traditional styling is, indeed, pleasing to the eye. Hub of this plan is the centrally located foyer which controls traffic to the bedrooms, living/dining room and family room. Economically planned circulation spends very little floor space on hallways. Back-to-back fireplaces in the family room and the living room are an effective sound barrier between the informal and formal areas. Strategically placed kitchen allows for a convenient observation post overlooking family room. The kitchen features a snack bar, built-in desk with shelves and adjacent mud room with washroom. This design includes a basement for future development or storage space.

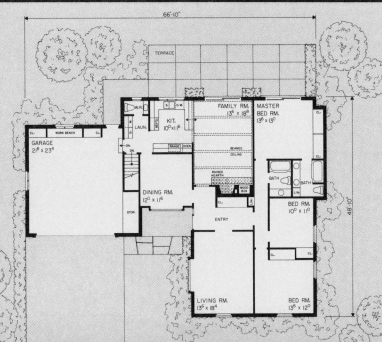

Design V12261
Square Footage: 1,825

● This distinctive L-shaped home virtually exudes traditional warmth and charm. And little wonder, for the architectural detailing is, indeed, exquisite. Notice the fine window detailing, the appealing cornice work, the attractiveness of the garage door and the massive chimney. The dovecote and the weather vane add to the design impact. The covered front porch shelters the entry which is strategically located to provide excellent traffic patterns. A service entry from the garage is conveniently located handy to the laundry, washroom, kitchen and stairs to the basement. The beamed-ceilinged family room will naturally be everyone's favorite spot for family living.

Design V11758
Square Footage: 1,872

● Setting the delightful character of this L-shaped traditional one-story home are such design features as: the wood columns of the covered front porch; the pediment, gabled ends; the attractive window treatment and the front entrance detail. The floor plan is an exceptional one. The nicely sized formal entry hall routes traffic ideally to the major areas of the house. The two large living areas - the informal family-kitchen and the quiet, formal living room - look out upon the rear terrace through sliding glass doors. The work center is efficient.

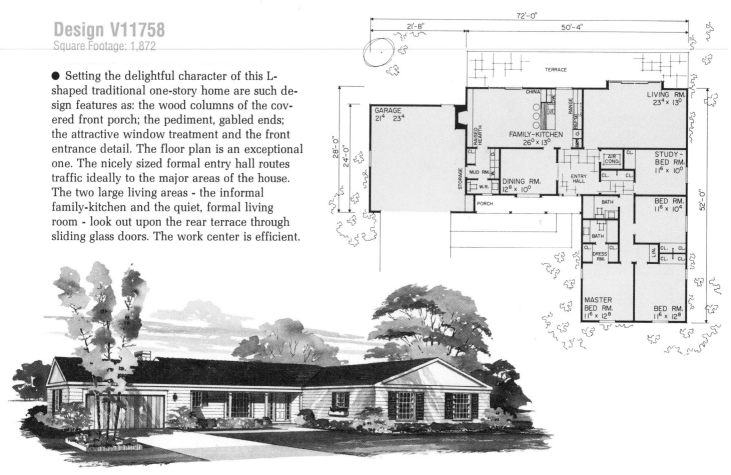

Design V11346
Square Footage: 1,644

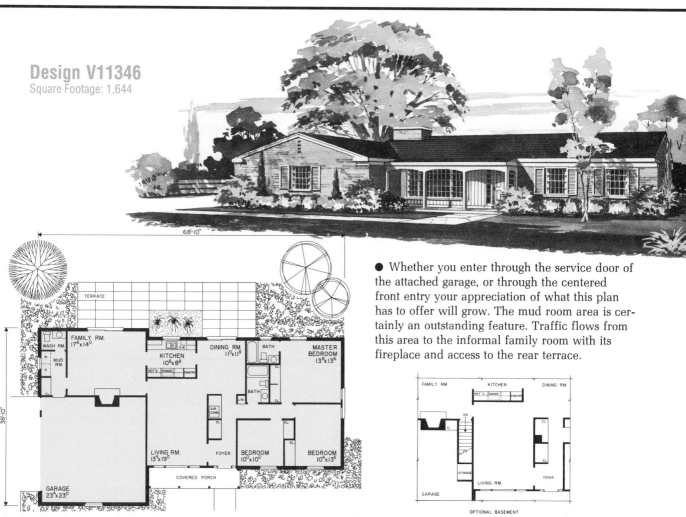

● Whether you enter through the service door of the attached garage, or through the centered front entry your appreciation of what this plan has to offer will grow. The mud room area is certainly an outstanding feature. Traffic flows from this area to the informal family room with its fireplace and access to the rear terrace.

Design V11091
Square Footage: 1,666

D

● What could be finer than to live in a delightfully designed home with all the charm of the exterior carried right inside. The interior points of interest are many. However, the focal point will surely be the family-kitchen. The work center is U-shaped and most efficient. The family activity portion of the kitchen features an attractive fireplace which will contribute to a feeling of warmth and fellowship. Nearby is the wash room and stairs to the basement.

● The paneled, front door, flanked by attractive vertical glass panels, will welcome callers to this traditional exterior with a refreshingly different floor plan. The highlight of the interior is the unique location of the family room. While it functions conveniently with the kitchen, it is also easily accessible from the front entry hall, the attached two-car garage and the covered, rear porch. A raised hearth fireplace, snack bar and sliding glass doors are plus features of this multi-purpose area. The strategic location of the extra washroom will reduce thru-the-house traffic from the outdoors. Spaciousness, resulting from the open planning of the formal living and dining rooms, permits the creation of a most gracious atmosphere.

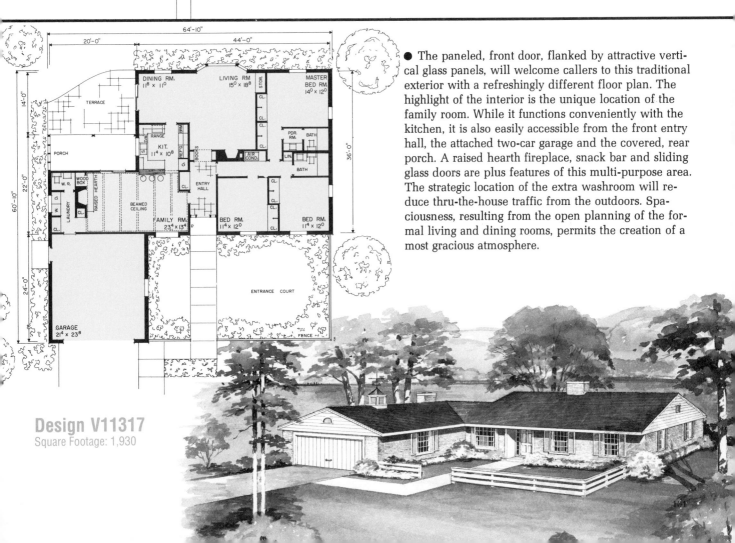

Design V11317
Square Footage: 1,930

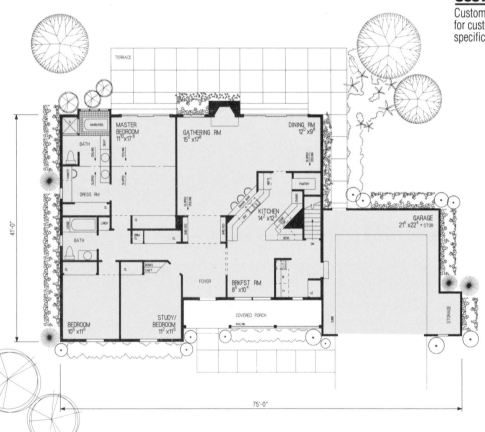

CUSTOMIZABLE

Custom Alterations? See page 381 for customizing this plan to your specifications.

Design V12947
Square Footage: 1,830

● This charming one-story Traditional home greets visitors with a covered porch. A galley-style kitchen shares a snack bar with the spacious gathering room where a fireplace is the focal point. An ample master suite includes a luxury bath with whirlpool tub and separate dressing room. Two additional bedrooms, one that could double as a study, are located at the front of the home.

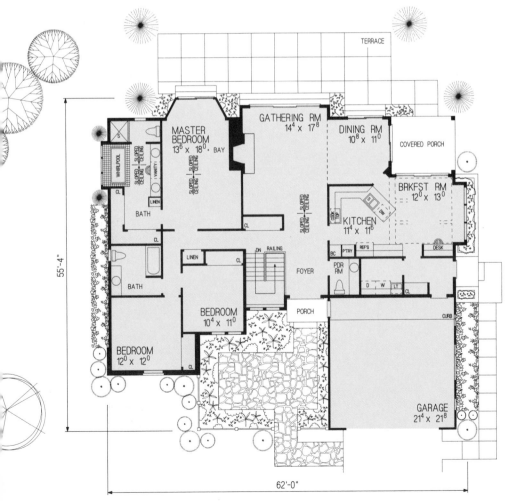

TERRACE

MASTER BEDROOM
13⁶ x 18⁰. BAY

GATHERING RM
14⁴ x 17⁸

DINING RM
10⁸ x 11⁰

COVERED PORCH

WHIRLPOOL

SLOPED · SLOPED
CEILING · CEILING

VANITY

SLOPED · SLOPED
CEILING · CEILING

BRKFST RM
12⁰ x 13⁰

LINEN

CL

BATH

SLOPED · SLOPED
CEILING · CEILING

COOK
TOP

KITCHEN
11⁴ x 11⁶

DN

CL

DESK

CL

LINEN

DN   RAILING

REF'G

BC   P'TRY

BATH

CL

FOYER

PDR
RM

D W LT
CL

BEDROOM
10⁴ x 11⁰

PORCH

CURB

BEDROOM
12⁰ x 12⁰

GARAGE
21⁴ x 21⁸

CL

55'-4"

62'-0"

Design V13336
Square Footage: 2,022

● Compact and comfortable! This three-bedrooom home is a good consideration for a small family or empty-nester retirees. Of special note are the covered eating porch and sloped ceilings in the gathering room and master bedroom. A well-placed powder room is found at the front entry.

Design V11252
Square Footage: 1,985

● Here is a traditional adaptation which embodies all the warmth and appeal to make its occupants swell with pride. The projection of the bedroom wing, the recessed front entrance, the boxed bay windows and the set-back attached two-car garage all contribute to the interesting lines of the front exterior. The floor plan is one which contains all the features an active family would require to assure years of exceptional livability. There are two full baths in the three bedroom sleeping area, a sunken formal living room, a separate dining room and a spacious rear family room.

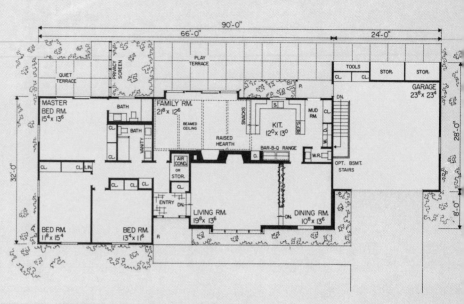

Design V12550
Square Footage: 1,892

D

● An enchanting low-slung traditional ranch with exceptional appeal. The low-pitched roof has a wide overhang and exposed beams. Stone and vertical siding offer a pleasing contrast. However, you may wish to substitute other materials of your choice. The diamond lite windows, the fence with its lamp post, the double front doors and the dovecote above the carriage lamp of the garage are among the interesting exterior features. Inside, there are four bedrooms and two full baths in the sleeping wing. The L-shaped living area is spacious and features a sloping ceiling for the gathering and dining rooms. The open stairwell to the basement recreation area is attractive. The pleasant kitchen is flanked by the nook and laundry.

Design V11186
Square Footage: 1,872

● This appealing home has an interesting and practical floor plan. It is cleverly zoned to cater to the living patterns of both the children and the parents. The children's bedroom wing projects to the rear and functions with their informal family room. The master bedroom is ideally isolated and is located in a part of the plan's quietly formal wing. The efficient kitchen looks out upon the rear terrace and functions conveniently with the dining area and family room. A full bath serves each of the two main living areas. A built-in vanity highlights each bath. The mud room features laundry equipment, storage unit and stairs to the basement. The blueprints show details for basement and non-basement construction.

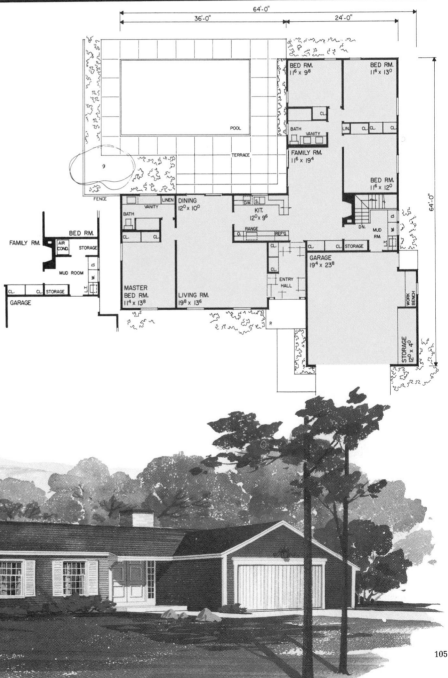

Design V12603
Square Footage: 1,949

L **D**

● Surely it would be difficult to beat the appeal of this traditional one-story home. Its slightly modified U-shape with the two front facing gables, the bay window, the covered front porch and the interesting use of exterior materials all add to the exterior charm. Besides, there are three large bedrooms serviced by two full baths and three walk-in closets. The excellent kitchen is flanked by the formal dining room and the informal family room. Don't miss the pantry, the built-in oven and the pass-thru to the snack bar. The handy first floor laundry is strategically located to act as a mud room. The extra wash room is but a few steps away. The sizable living room highlights a fireplace and a picture window. Note the location of the basement stairs.

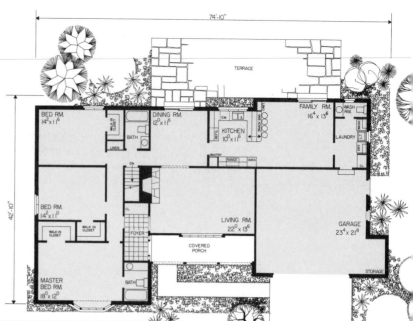

Design V13177
Square Footage: 1,888

● It would certainly be difficult to pack more living potential into such a modestly sized home than this. The family's living patterns will be just great with "convenience" as the byword. Consider: three bedrooms serviced by two full baths; a formal living room and a formal dining room overlooking the rear terrace and free from unnecessary cross-room traffic; an interior kitchen functioning ideally with the dining room, the family room and the laundry; a powder room handy to living and family rooms and kitchen. Observe: stall shower, fireplace, abundant wardrobe closets, built-in planter, snack bar, family room storage wall and sliding glass doors. The exterior is charming.

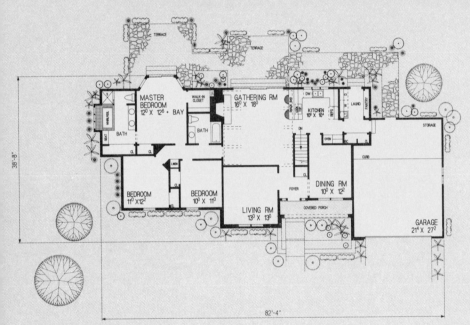

Design V13350
Square Footage: 1,744

● Though smaller in size, this traditional one-story provides a family-oriented floor plan that leaves nothing out. Besides the formal living room (or study if you prefer) and dining room, there's a gathering room with fireplace, snack bar, and sliding glass doors to the rear terrace. The U-shaped kitchen is in close proximity to the handy utility area. Of particular note is the grand master bedroom with garden whirlpool tub, walk-in closet, and private terrace. The sleeping area is completed with two family bedrooms to the front.

Design V13376
Square Footage: 1,999

● Small families or empty nesters will appreciate the layout of this traditional ranch. The foyer opens to the gathering room with fireplace and sloped ceiling. The dining room is open to the gathering room for entertaining ease and contains sliding doors to a rear terrace. The breakfast room also provides access to a covered porch for dining outdoors. The media room to the left of the home offers a bay window and a wet bar, or it can double as a third bedroom.

Design V11222
Square Footage: 1,657

● How will you call upon this home to function? As a three or four bedroom home? The study permits all kinds of flexibility in your living patterns. If you wish, the extra room could serve the family as a TV area or an area for sewing, hobbies or guests. The 27 foot living room features a formal dining area which is but a step from the secluded, covered dining porch and efficient kitchen. There is a strategically located mud room which houses the washer and dryer and adjacent washroom. The stairs leading to the basement are also in this area.

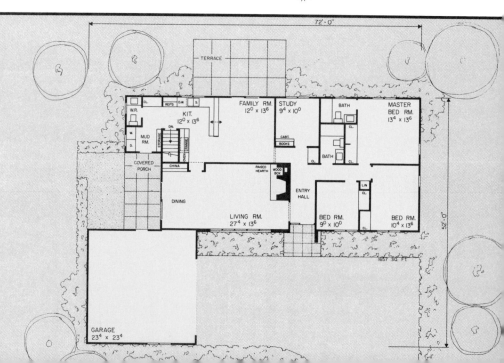

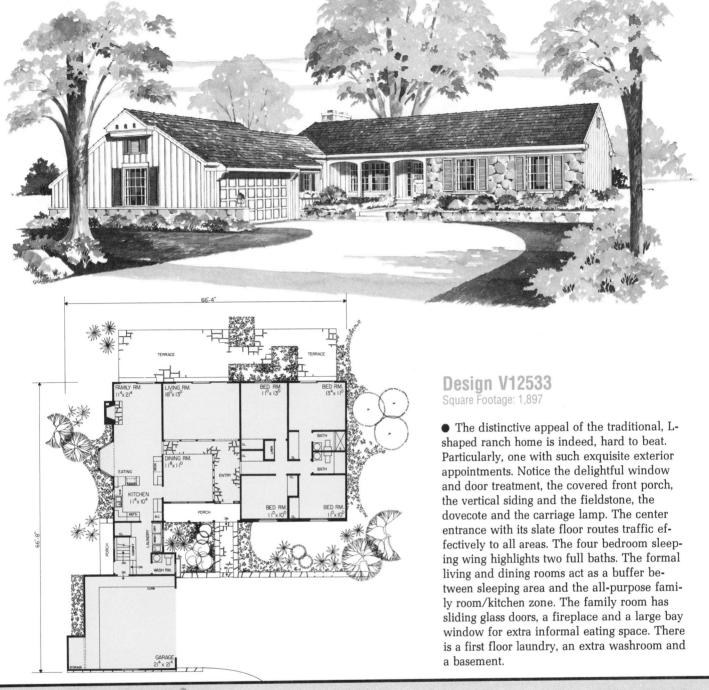

Design V12533
Square Footage: 1,897

● The distinctive appeal of the traditional, L-shaped ranch home is indeed, hard to beat. Particularly, one with such exquisite exterior appointments. Notice the delightful window and door treatment, the covered front porch, the vertical siding and the fieldstone, the dovecote and the carriage lamp. The center entrance with its slate floor routes traffic effectively to all areas. The four bedroom sleeping wing highlights two full baths. The formal living and dining rooms act as a buffer between sleeping area and the all-purpose family room/kitchen zone. The family room has sliding glass doors, a fireplace and a large bay window for extra informal eating space. There is a first floor laundry, an extra washroom and a basement.

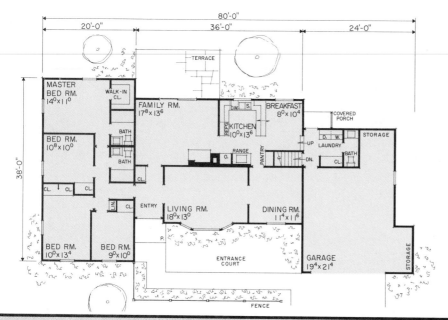

Design V11829
Square Footage: 1,800

L D

● All the charm of a traditional heritage is wrapped up in this U-shaped home with its narrow, horizontal siding, delightful window treatment and high-pitched roof. The massive center chimney, the bay window and the double front doors are plus features. Inside, the living potential is outstanding. The sleeping wing is self-contained and has four bedrooms and two baths. The large family and living rooms cater to the divergent age groups.

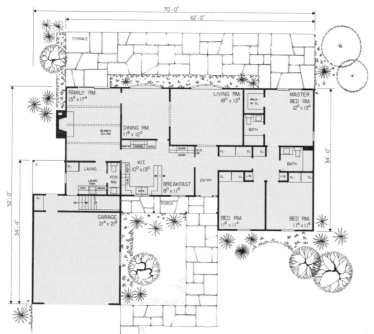

Design V11980
Square Footage: 1,901

● Planned for easy living, the daily living patterns of the active family will be pleasant ones, indeed. All the elements are present to assure a wonderful family life. The impressive exterior is enhanced by the recessed front entrance area with its covered porch. The center entry results in a convenient and efficient flow of traffic. A secondary entrance leads from the covered side porch, or the garage, into the first floor laundry. Note the powder room nearby.

Design V12360
Square Footage: 1,936

● There is no such thing as taking a fleeting glance at this charming home. Fine proportion and pleasing lines assure a long and rewarding study. Inside, the family's everyday routine will enjoy all the facilities which will surely guarantee pleasurable living. Note the sunken living room with its fireplace flanked by storage cabinets and book shelves. Observe the excellent kitchen just a step from the dining room and the nook.

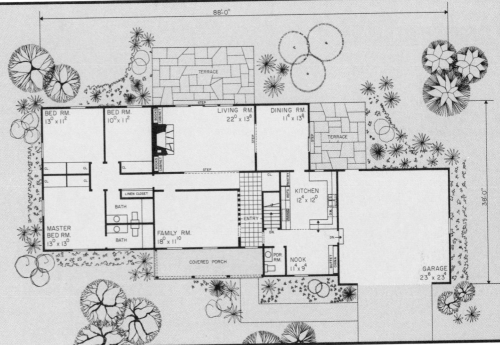

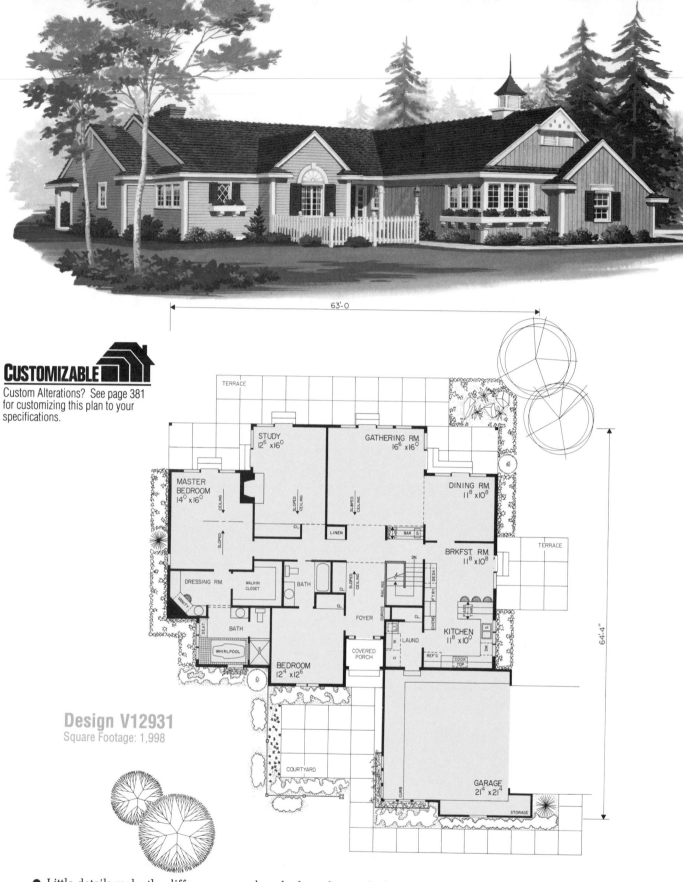

CUSTOMIZABLE

Custom Alterations? See page 381 for customizing this plan to your specifications.

63'-0

TERRACE

STUDY
12⁶ x 16⁰

GATHERING RM.
16⁶ x 16⁰

MASTER BEDROOM
14⁰ x 16⁰

SLOPED CEILING

SLOPED CEILING

DINING RM.
11⁸ x 10⁸

CL.

LINEN

BAR   S.

TERRACE

DRESSING RM.

WALK-IN CLOSET

BATH

SLOPED CEILING

CL.

BRKFST. RM.
11⁸ x 10⁸

DN.

PT'RY   DESK

VANITY

BATH

SEAT

CL.

FOYER

CURIOS   RAILING

CL.

OVENS

PASS THRU

KITCHEN
11⁸ x 10⁰

WHIRLPOOL

S

LAUND.

REF'G

COOK TOP

DW

64'-4"

BEDROOM
12⁴ x 12⁶

COVERED PORCH

CURB

Design V12931
Square Footage: 1,998

COURTYARD

CURB

GARAGE
21⁴ x 21⁴

STORAGE

● Little details make the difference. Consider these that make this such a charming showplace: Picket fenced courtyard, carriage lamp, window boxes, shutters, muntined windows, multi-gabled roof, cornice returns, vertical and horizontal siding with corner

boards, front door with glass side lites, etc. Inside this appealing exterior there is a truly outstanding floor plan for the small family or empty-nesters. The master bedroom suite is long on luxury, with a separate dressing room, private vanities, and whirlpool bath. An

adjacent study is just the right retreat. There's room to move and - what a warm touch! - it has its own fireplace. Other attractions: roomy kitchen and breakfast area, spacious gathering room, rear and side terraces, and an attached two-car garage with storage.

Design V13314
Square Footage: 1,951

● Formal living areas in this plan are joined by a sleeping wing that holds three bedrooms. Two verandas and a screened porch enlarge the plan and enhance indoor/outdoor livability. Notice the abundant storage space.

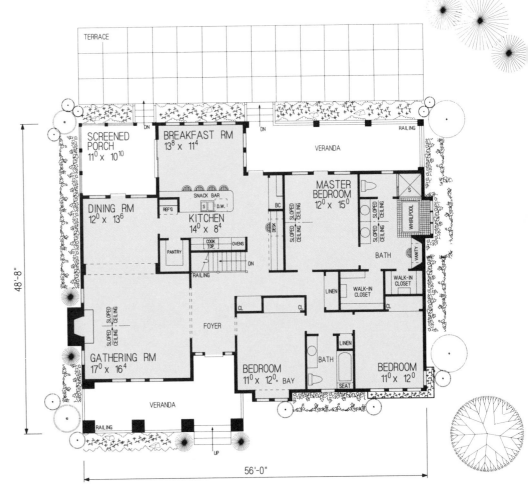

TERRACE

SCREENED PORCH
11⁰ x 10¹⁰

BREAKFAST RM
13⁸ x 11⁴

VERANDA

RAILING

DINING RM
12⁰ x 13⁶

REF'G

SNACK BAR

S   D.W.

KITCHEN
14⁰ x 8⁴

MASTER BEDROOM
12⁰ x 15⁰

SLOPED CEILING

SLOPED CEILING

WHIRLPOOL

S

BATH

PANTRY

COOK TOP

OVENS

DESK

RAILING

DN

VANITY

WALK-IN CLOSET

LINEN

WALK-IN CLOSET

SLOPED CEILING

SLOPED CEILING

FOYER

CL

CL

CL

GATHERING RM
17⁰ x 16⁴

BEDROOM
11⁰ x 12⁰ BAY

BATH

LINEN

SEAT

BEDROOM
11⁰ x 12⁰

VERANDA

RAILING

UP

48'-8"

56'-0"

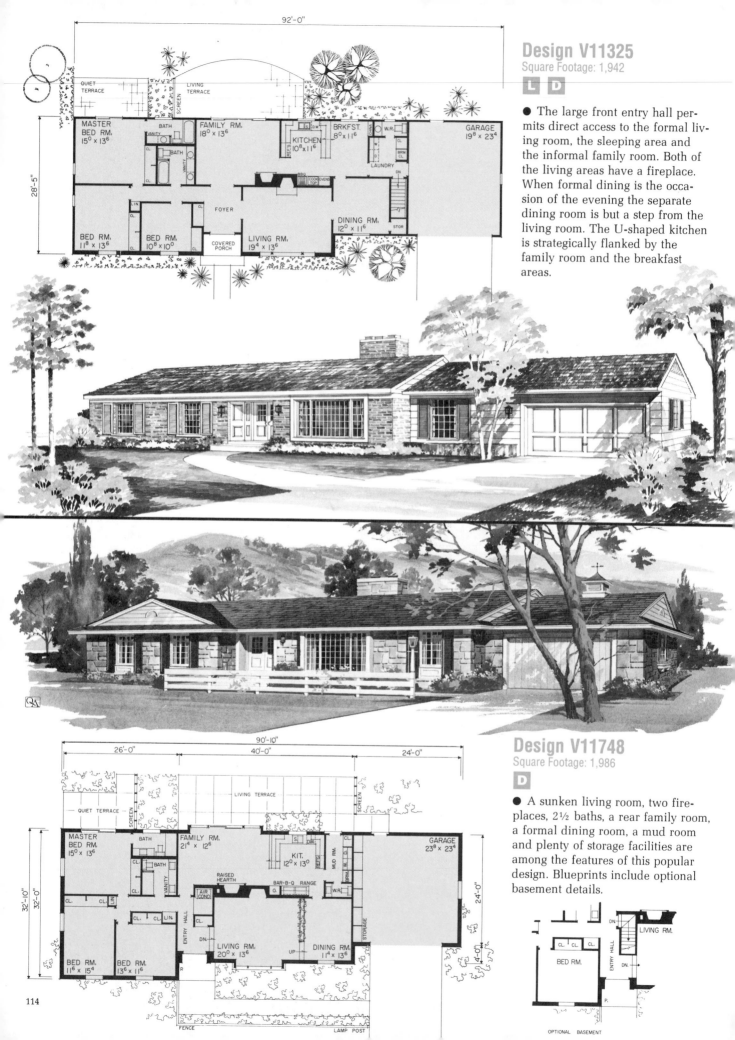

92'-0"

28'-5"

QUIET TERRACE

LIVING TERRACE

SCREEN

MASTER BED RM. 15⁰ x 13⁶

BATH

VANITY

BATH

CL.

CL.

FAMILY RM. 18⁰ x 13⁶

KITCHEN 10⁸ x 11⁶

BRKFST. 8⁰ x 11⁶

W.R.

GARAGE 19⁸ x 23⁴

LAUNDRY

BBQ

COOK TOP

OVENS

DN.

LIN.

CL.

FOYER

STOR.

BED RM. 11⁸ x 13⁶

BED RM. 10⁸ x 10⁰

CL.

COVERED PORCH

LIVING RM. 19⁴ x 13⁶

DINING RM. 12⁰ x 11⁶

Design V11325
Square Footage: 1,942

L D

● The large front entry hall permits direct access to the formal living room, the sleeping area and the informal family room. Both of the living areas have a fireplace. When formal dining is the occasion of the evening the separate dining room is but a step from the living room. The U-shaped kitchen is strategically flanked by the family room and the breakfast areas.

Design V11748
Square Footage: 1,986

D

● A sunken living room, two fireplaces, 2½ baths, a rear family room, a formal dining room, a mud room and plenty of storage facilities are among the features of this popular design. Blueprints include optional basement details.

90'-10"

26'-0" **40'-0"** **24'-0"**

32'-10"

32'-0"

24'-0"

4'-0"

QUIET TERRACE

SCREEN

LIVING TERRACE

SCREEN

MASTER BED RM. 15⁰ x 13⁶

BATH

CL.

BATH

VANITY

CL.

FAMILY RM. 21⁴ x 12⁶

KIT. 12⁰ x 13⁰

MUD RM.

BRM.

W.

D.

CL.

GARAGE 23⁸ x 23⁴

CL.

CL.

LIN.

RAISED HEARTH

AIR COND.

BAR-B-Q RANGE

O.

W.R.

STORAGE

CL.

CL.

LIN.

ENTRY HALL

DN.

LIVING RM. 20⁴ x 13⁶

UP

DINING RM. 11⁴ x 13⁶

BED RM. 11⁶ x 15⁴

BED RM. 13⁶ x 11⁶

FENCE

LAMP POST

DN.

CL. CL.

BED RM.

ENTRY HALL

DN.

LIVING RM.

P.

OPTIONAL BASEMENT

114

Shared Expense – Shared Livability

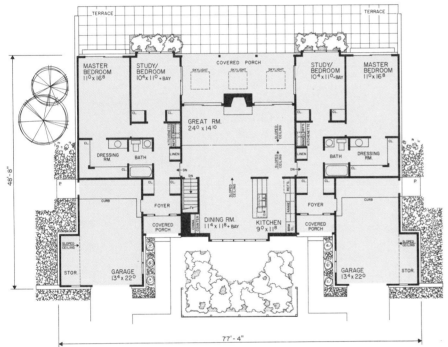

Design V12869
Square Footage: 1,986

● This traditional one-story design offers the economical benefits of shared living space without sacrificing privacy. The common area of this design is centrally located between the two private, sleeping wings. The common area, 680 square feet, is made up of the great room, dining room and kitchen. Sloping the ceiling in this area creates an open feeling as will the sliding glass doors on each side of the fireplace. These doors lead to a large covered porch with skylights above. Separate outdoor entrances lead to each of the sleeping wings. Two bedrooms, dressing area, full bath and space for an optional kitchenette occupy 653 square feet in each wing. Additional space will be found in the basement which is the full size of the common area. Don't miss the covered porch and garage with additional storage space.

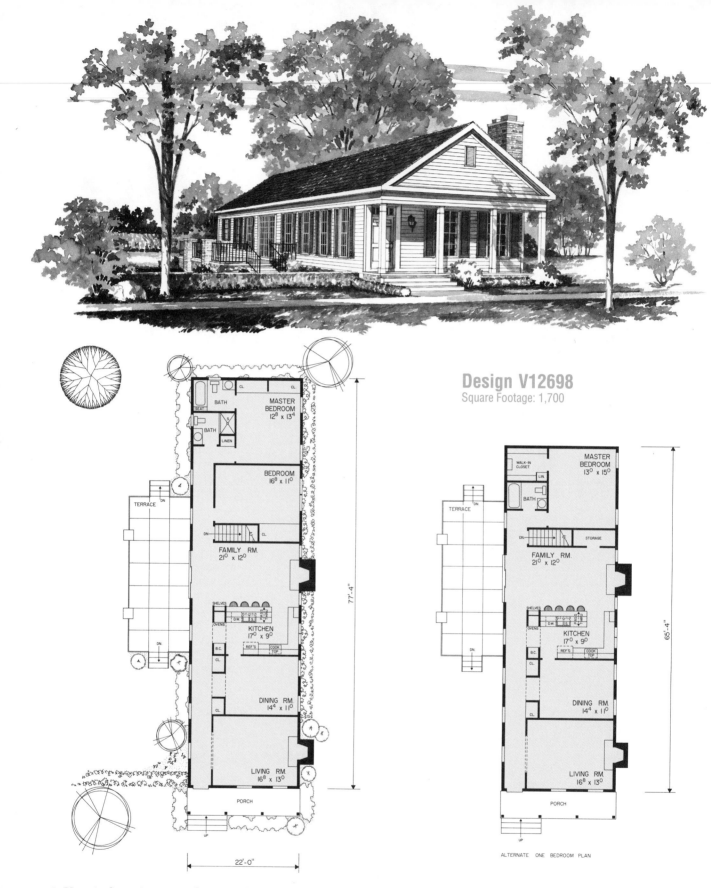

Design V12698
Square Footage: 1,700

ALTERNATE ONE BEDROOM PLAN

● Here is the quintessential narrow lot house. It was found in 19th Century New Orleans and many other southern towns. Its origins go back to the West Indies and Africa and has been called, the "shotgun house". A name derived from the fact that a bullet could travel through the front door and exit the rear without striking a partition. For the sake of contemporary floor planning this version forsakes the rear door in favor of two full baths. Despite its small size, the facade with its projecting gable and columned front porch is charming, indeed. As a starter home, or even as a retirement home, this unique house will serve its occupants well. An alternate one bedroom version contains 1,436 sq. ft. Notice that all of the amenities to be found in the other rooms remain the same.

TRADITIONAL DESIGNS 2,000-3,000 Sq. Ft.

The larger one-story home offers a full measure of living potential. With all the plusses of the traditional two-story, it has the added advantage of complete livability on one level. Generally, a large home offers larger rooms and practical, efficient traffic patterns that accommodate not only the family's favorite pursuits but the demands of social gatherings as well.

Design V12777
Square Footage: 2,006

L D

● Many years of delightful living will be enjoyed in this one-story traditional home. The covered, front porch adds a charm to the exterior as do the paned windows and winding drive. Inside, there is livability galore. An efficient kitchen with island range and adjacent laundry make this work area very pleasing. A breakfast nook with bay window and built-in desk will serve the family when informal dining is called upon. A formal dining room with sliding glass doors leads to the rear terrace. The large gathering room with raised hearth fireplace can serve the family on any occasion gracefully. The sleeping wing consists of two bedrooms and a study (or make it three bedrooms). The master bedroom includes all of the fine features one would expect: a huge walk-in closet, a vanity, a bath and sliding glass doors to a private terrace.

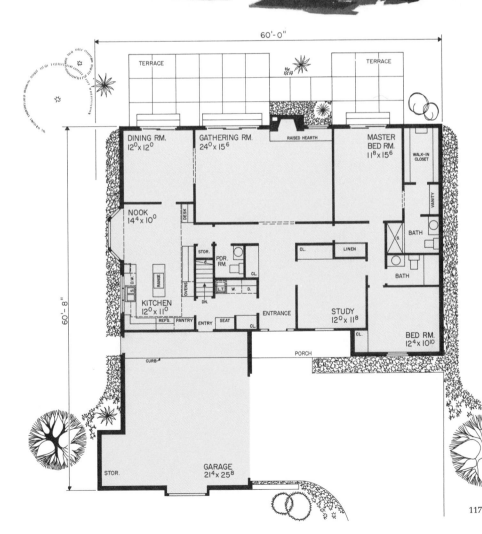

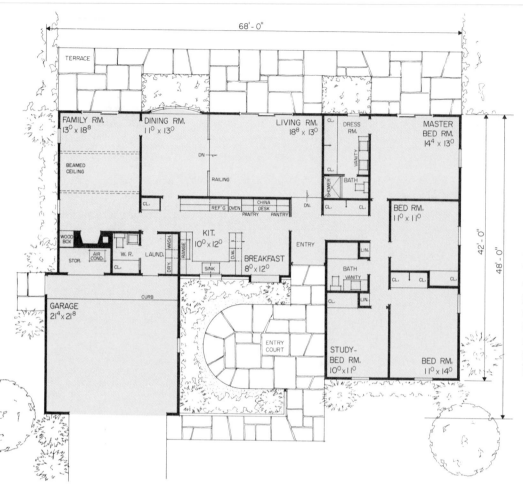

● If you were to count the various reasons that will cause excitement over the prospect of moving into this home, you would certainly be able to compile a long list. You might head your list with the grace and charm of the front exterior. You'd certainly have to comment on the delightful entry court, the picket fence and lamp post and the recessed front entrance. Comments about the interior obviously would begin with the listing of such features as: spaciousness galore; sunken living room; separate dining room; family room with beamed ceiling; excellent kitchen with pass-thru to breakfast room; two full baths, plus washroom, etc.

Design V11102
Square Footage: 2,348

● This quietly impressive home
with curving front drive, covered
front porch, delightful muntined
windows, and panelled door
flanked by patterned side-lites,
houses a fine floor plan. The
center entry hall joins another
hall which runs the width of the
home and routes traffic directly
to each room. There are four
bedrooms, two full baths, and
plenty of storage potential in
sleeping area. A covered rear
porch off the master bedroom
will be nice on hot, summer
evenings. The living and dining
rooms are sure to enjoy their
privacy. The focal point of the
plan, is perhaps the 27 foot
family-kitchen. Don't miss the
strategic location of the mud
room. A snack bar provides a
handy spot for the enjoyment of
quick and easy meals.

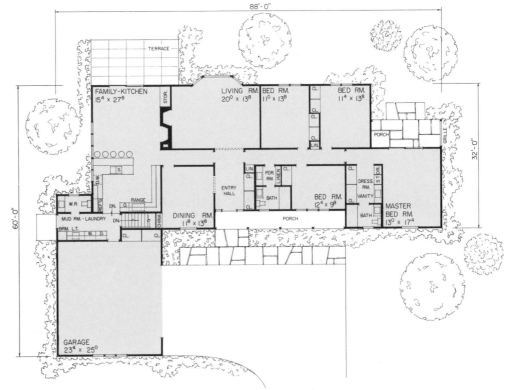

Design V11149
Square Footage: 2,040

● The very shape of this traditional adaptation seems to spell, "welcome". A study of the floor plan reflects excellent zoning. The sleeping area consists of four bedrooms and two full baths. The formal area, located to the front of the house, consists of a separate dining room with built-in china cabinet and living room with fireplace and accompanying woodbox. Study the work center of the kitchen, laundry and wash room. An informal family room. It is only a couple of steps from the kitchen and functions with the outdoor terrace.

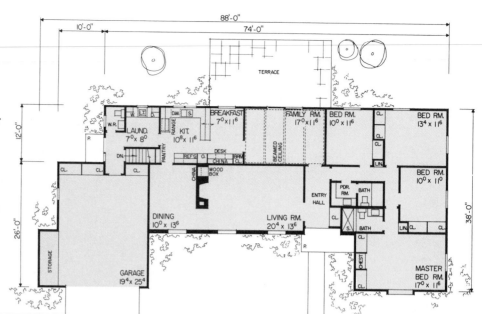

Design V12316
Square Footage: 2,000

L D

● Here is a basic floor plan which is the favorite of many. It provides for the location, to the front of the plan, of the more formal areas (living and dining rooms); while the informal areas (family room and kitchen) are situated to the rear of the plan and function with the terrace. To the left of the center entrance is the four bedroom, two bath sleeping zone. Adjacent to the kitchen is the utility room with a wash room nearby. The garage features a storage room and work shop area with more storage.

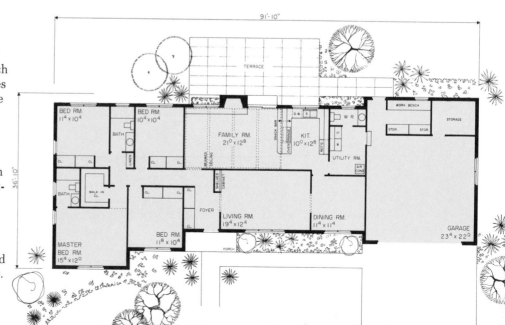

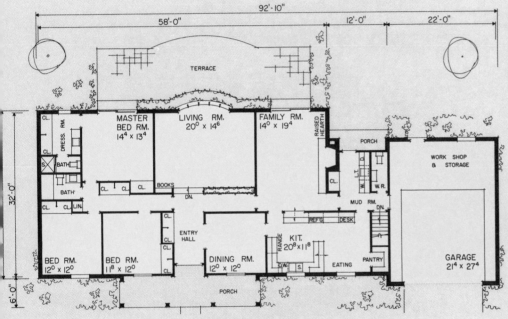

Design V11788
Square Footage: 2,218

L **D**

● "Charm" is one of the many words which may be used to correctly describe this fine design. In addition to its eye-appeal, it has a practical and smoothly functioning floor plan. The detail of the front entrance, highlighted by columns supporting the projecting pediment gable, is outstanding. Observe the window treatment and the double, front doors. Perhaps the focal point of the interior will be the formal living room. It is, indeed, dramatic with its bay window overlooking the backyard. Three bedrooms and two baths are in the private area.

Floor plan labels: 92'-10", 58'-0", 12'-0", 22'-0", 32'-0", 6'-0", TERRACE, MASTER BED RM. 14⁴ x 13⁴, LIVING RM. 20⁰ x 14⁶, FAMILY RM. 14⁰ x 19⁴, RAISED HEARTH, PORCH, WORK SHOP & STORAGE, DRESS. RM., BATH, BATH, CL., CL., CL., CL., CL., LIN., BOOKS, DN., W.T., D., W.R., MUD RM., DN., REF'G, DESK, BED RM. 12⁰ x 12⁰, BED RM. 11⁸ x 12⁰, ENTRY HALL, DINING RM. 12⁰ x 12⁰, RANGE, KIT. 20⁸ x 11⁸, DW., S., EATING, PANTRY, GARAGE 21⁴ x 27⁴, PORCH

Design V12204
Square Footage: 2,016

● Your life's investment hardly could be more wisely made than for the choice of this delightful design as your family's next home. Over the years its charm will not diminish. This is a favorite plan of many. It establishes a quiet sleeping zone, a formal living-dining zone and an informal family-kitchen zone. Sliding glass doors permit the master bedroom, family room and breakfast nook to have easy access to the rear terrace. Entering the house from the garage, all will appreciate the proximity of the closets, the washroom and the basement stairs.

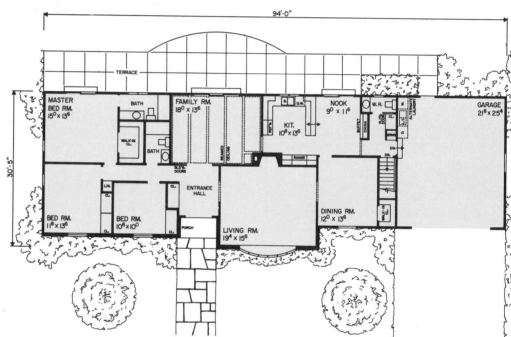

Design V12260
Square Footage: 2,041

● Upon entering this hip-roof traditional, you will view the built-in planter atop a practical storage cabinet. A look into the living room reveals an attractive fireplace flanked by bookshelves, cabinet and wood box. A step into the master bedroom brings into view the twin walk-in closets and sliding glass doors to the rear terrace. Moving into the kitchen, the fine counter and cupboard space will be appreciated. This efficient work area is but a step from the informal nook and the formal dining room. Behind the garage is a large, covered screened porch.

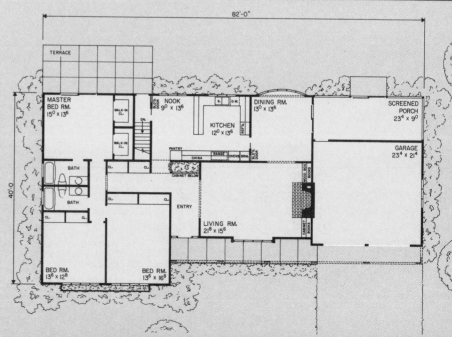

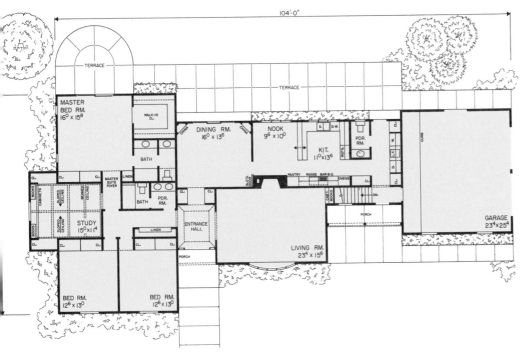

Design V12208
Square Footage: 2,522

● You really won't need a half acre to build this home. Its very breadth will guarantee plenty of space to the front, thus providing a fine setting. The pedimented gables, horizontal siding, corner boards, window and door treatment, two covered porches and the cupola set the note of distinction. An excellent feature is the service entrance, adjacent to the garage. The bedroom wing is positively outstanding. In addition to the three bedrooms and two baths, there is the private study. It has a sloping, beamed ceiling, bookshelves, cabinets and two closets.

Design V12916
Square Footage: 2,129

● Pride of ownership will be forever yours as the occupant of this Early American styled one-story house. The covered front porch provides a shelter for the inviting panelled front door with its flanking side lites. Designed for fine family living, this three bedroom, 2½ bath home offers wonderful formal and informal living patterns. The 27 foot country kitchen has a beamed ceiling and a fireplace. The U-shaped work center is efficient. It is but a step from the mud room area with its laundry equipment, closets, cupboards, counter space and washroom. There are two dining areas - an informal eating space and a formal separate dining room. The more formal gathering room is spacious with a sloping ceiling and two sets of sliding glass doors to the rear terrace.

Design V13332
Square Footage: 2,168

● Nothing completes a traditional-style home quite as well as a country kitchen with fireplace. Notice also the sloped-ceiling living room and well-appointed master suite. A handy washroom is near the laundry, just off the garage.

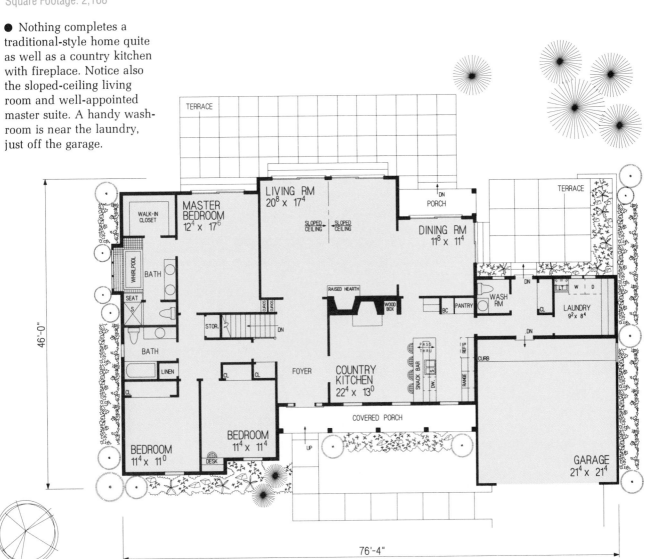

125

Design V12353
Square Footage: 2,302

● Here is an inviting Colonial Ranch home with matching pediment gables projecting toward the street. Deep double-hung windows flanked by shutters enhance the exterior charm. The massive chimney, the raised planter, the panelled front door, and the patterned garage door add their extra measure of appeal. The interior offers loads of livability. Note the sunken living room, the beamed-ceilinged family room, and the efficient kitchen strategically located between the breakfast nook and the formal dining room.

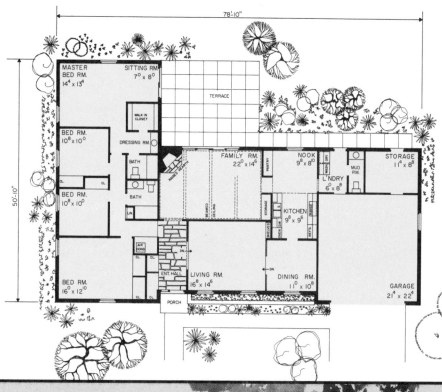

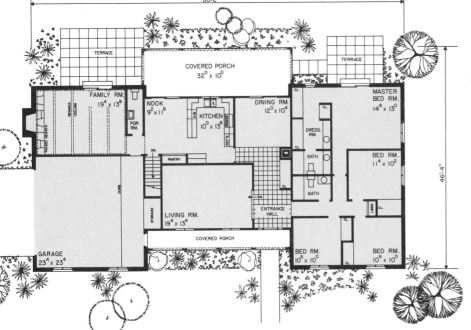

Design V12362
Square Footage: 2,166

● Here is a ground-hugging, traditional adaptation with plenty of exterior appeal and a fine functioning floor plan. Observe the interior zoning. The sunken living room will have plenty of privacy. The four bedroom sleeping area is a wing by itself. The U-shaped kitchen is strategically flanked by the two eating areas. Study the exceptional family room. Note powder room. The indoor-outdoor living relationships are excellent. The covered rear porch will be a popular spot for summer outdoor eating and relaxation.

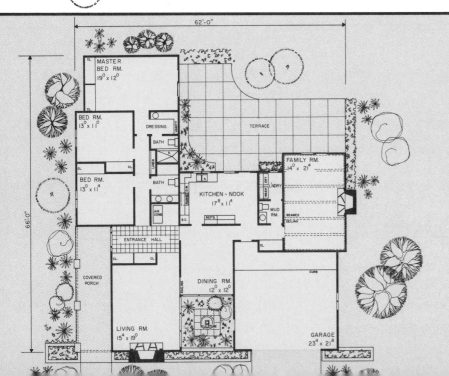

Design V12352
Square Footage: 2,179

● This enchanting hip-roof traditional has a distinctive air of its own. From the recessed gardening area between the living room and garage to the master bedroom vanity, this plan is replete with features. Notice the covered front porch, the spacious kitchen, the quiet living room, the beamed ceilinged family room, the laundry/mud room, the sliding glass doors to terrace, etc. The planting court, so completely visible from the formal living and dining rooms, will be great fun for the amateur horticulturist during the warm months.

127

Design V11835
Square Footage: 2,144

L D

● Cedar shakes and quarried natural
stone are the exterior materials which
adorn this irregularly shaped traditional ranch home. Adding to the appeal of
the exterior are the cut-up windows,
the shutters, the pediment gable, the
cupola and the double front doors. The
detail of the garage door opening adds
further interest. Inside, this favorite
among floor plans, reflects all the features necessary to provide complete
livability for the large family. The
sleeping zone is a 24' x 40' rectangle
which contains four bedrooms and two
full baths. A dressing room with a vanity and a wall of wardrobe storage
highlights the master bedroom. Both
the informal family room and the formal living room have a fireplace.

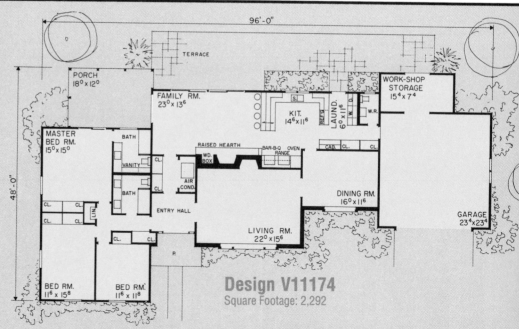

● Whatever the setting, here
is a traditional, one story
home that is truly impressive. Zoned in a most practical manner, the floor plan
features an isolated bedroom
wing, formal living and dining rooms and, across the
rear of the house, the informal living areas.

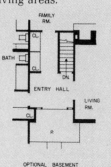

Design V11174
Square Footage: 2,292

TERRACE

| LIVING RM. 23⁴ x 13⁶ | DINING RM. 12⁰ x 13⁶ | EATING | W. R. |
| KITCHEN 19⁴ x 13⁶ | | | CL. |

RANGE · S · D.W.

BED RM. 13⁶ x 11⁰

STOR.

DN.

FOYER

PANTRY

REF'G O.

DN.

MUD. RM.

W. D.

DN.

STOR.

LIN.

CL. CL.

ENTRY

FAMILY RM. 20⁸ x 13⁶

STOR.

CL. CL. CL. CL.

PDR. RM.

BATH

CL.

PORCH

GARAGE 21⁸ x 21⁴

BED RM. 13⁶ x 12⁰

BATH

DRESS. RM.

WALK-IN CL.

S.

VANITY

MASTER BED RM. 13⁶ x 17⁸

78'-10"

64'-0"

14'-0"

50'-10"

Design V11786
Square Footage: 2,370

● Like this? If the answer is, yes, it is easy to understand. This is an extremely appealing design, highlighted by its brick masses, its window detailing, its interesting shape, and its inviting covered front entrance. The foyer is centrally located and but a step or two from all areas. The house, while it features all the facilities for family living, assures a full measure of privacy for all. The bedroom wing is distinctly defined. The quiet, sunken living room is off by itself. There is a separate, formal dining room. The family room is one which will function alone and cater to numerous activities. The kitchen, with its eating space, is of good size. The mud-room area is a true convenient living feature.

Design V12867
Square Footage: 2,388

● A live-in relative would be very comfortable in this home. This design features a self-contained suite (473 sq. ft.) consisting of a bedroom, bath, living room and kitchenette with dining area. This suite is nestled behind the garage away from the main areas of the house. The rest of this traditional, one-story house, faced with fieldstone and vertical wood siding, is also very livable. One whole wing houses the four family bedrooms and bath facilities. The center of the plan has a front, U-shaped kitchen and breakfast room. The formal dining room and large gathering room will enjoy the view, and access to, the backyard. The large, covered porch will receive much use.

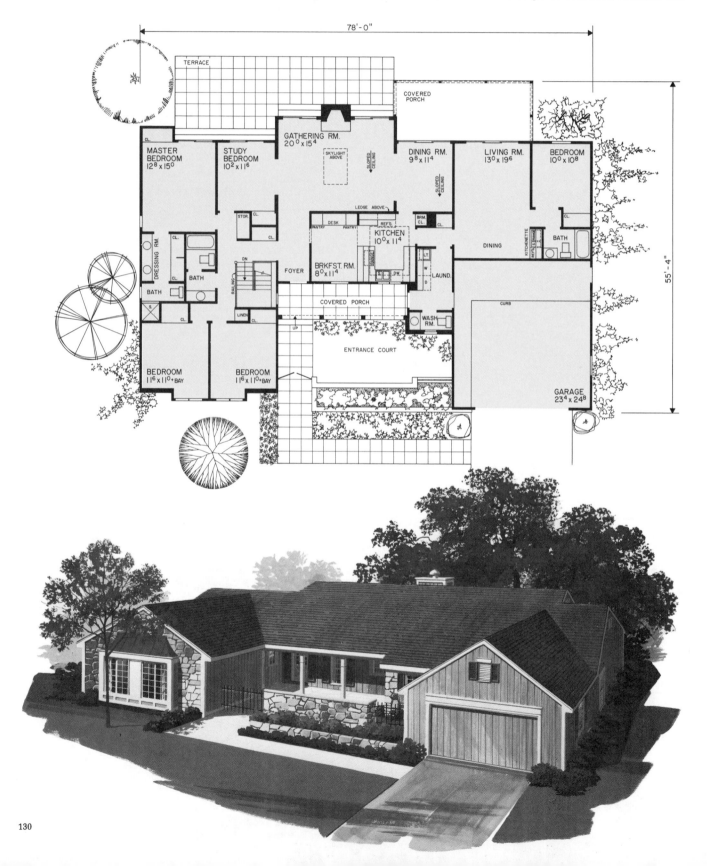

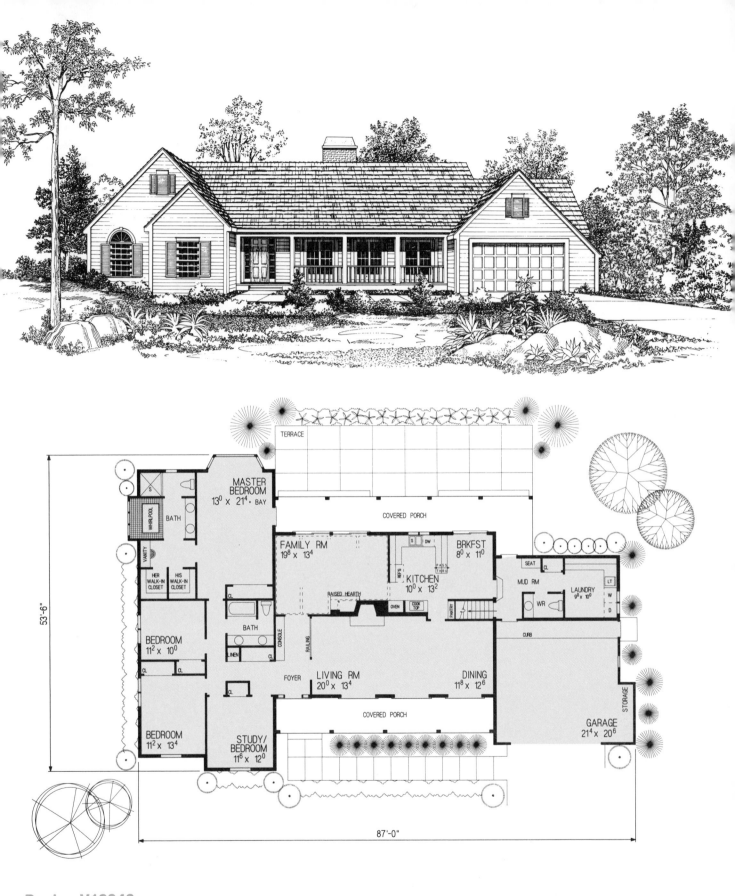

Design V13348 Square Footage: 2,549

● Covered porches front and rear will be the envy of the neighborhood when this house is built. The interior plan meets family needs perfectly in well-zoned areas: a sleeping wing with four bedrooms and two baths, a living zone with formal and informal gathering space, and a work zone with U-shaped kitchen and laundry with washroom. The two-car garage has a huge storage area.

Design V11929
Square Footage: 2,312

D

● There's more to this U-shaped, traditional adaptation than meets the eye. Much more! And, yet, what does meet the eye is positively captivating. The symmetry of the pediment gables, the window styling, the projecting garden wall, the iron gates, and the double front doors, are extremely pleasing. Once inside, a quick tour reveals plenty of space and a super-abundance of features. Each of the rooms is extra large and allows for fine furniture placement. In addition to the raised hearth fireplace, the family room highlights built-in book shelves, sliding glass doors and beamed ceilings.

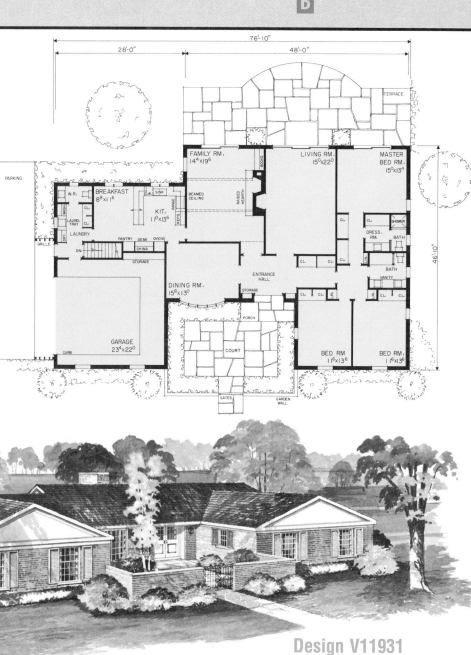

Design V11931
Square Footage: 2,424

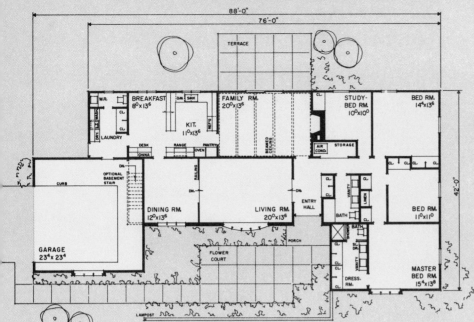

Labels in top floor plan:
88'-0"
76'-0"
TERRACE
W.R. | BREAKFAST 8⁰x13⁶ | DR. SINK | FAMILY RM. 20⁰x13⁶ | CL. | STUDY-BED RM. 10⁰x10⁰ | BED RM. 14⁰x13⁶
CL. | LAUNDRY | KIT. 11⁰x13⁶ | NEF'G | STORAGE
DESK | RANGE | OVEN | PANTRY | AIR COND.
CHINA
42'-0"
DN. | OPTIONAL BASEMENT STAIR | BEAMED CEILING
CURB | DN. | RAILING | DN. | CL. | CL. | CL.
VANITY | LINEN | BED RM. 11⁰x11⁰
DINING RM. 12⁰x13⁶ | LIVING RM. 20⁰x13⁶ | ENTRY HALL | BATH | SL. DR.
BATH | VANITY
GARAGE 23⁴x23⁴ | PORCH | DRESS. RM. | MASTER BED RM. 15⁴x13⁸
FLOWER COURT
LAMPOST | FENCE

● This home will lead the hit parade in your new subdivision. Its sparkling, traditionally styled exterior will be the favorite of all that pass. And, once inside, friends will marvel at how the plan just seems to cater to your family's every activity. When it comes to eating, you can eat in the informal breakfast room or the formal dining room. As you come in the front door you may sit down and relax in the sunken living room or the beamed ceiling family room. Two full baths with built-in vanities, plus the extra wash room will more than adequately serve the family.

Design V11872
Square Footage: 2,212

● If exceptional exterior appeal means anything to interior living potential then this traditional home should have unlimited livability. And, indeed, it has! There are five bedrooms (and a study if you so wish), two full baths and loads of storage in the sleeping wing. The formal living zone highlights a quiet living room and separate dining room. Each completely free of cross-room traffic. For informal living there is the family-kitchen with a snack bar, fireplace and sliding glass doors to the terrace. The work center is outstanding with laundry and washroom nearby. There are plenty of cupboards and lots of counter space. The laundry, with more cupboards and twin closets, is nearby. Note washroom and covered side porch.

Labels in bottom floor plan:
80'-0"
70'-0"
TERRACE
FAMILY-KITCHEN 15⁴x29⁴ | LIVING RM. 18⁰x13⁴ | BED RM. 10⁰x13⁴ | BED RM. 10⁰x13⁴ | BED RM. 12⁰x12⁰
CL. | CL. | CL.
SNACK BAR
STOR | LINEN | STOR | CL. | CL.
30'-0"
60'-5"
COVERED PORCH | REFG | DW. | RANGE | PANTRY | O. | ENTRY HALL | BATH
DN. | CHINA | BATH
DN. | CL. | DINING RM. 12⁰x12⁰ | STUDY-BED RM. 10⁰x10⁴ | MASTER BED RM. 14⁰x12⁰
LAUNDRY | W.R. | CL.
L.T. | D. | W. | P.
GARAGE 23⁴x21⁴ | DRIVE COURT

Design V11924 Square Footage: 2,504

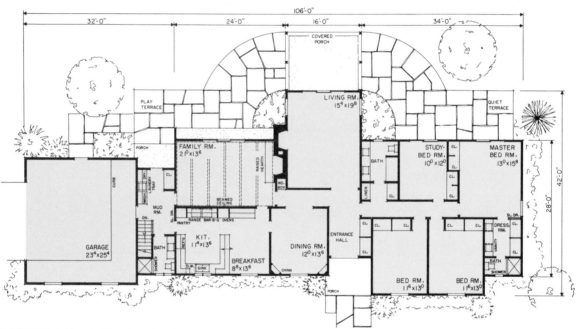

Design V11851 Square Footage: 2,450

134

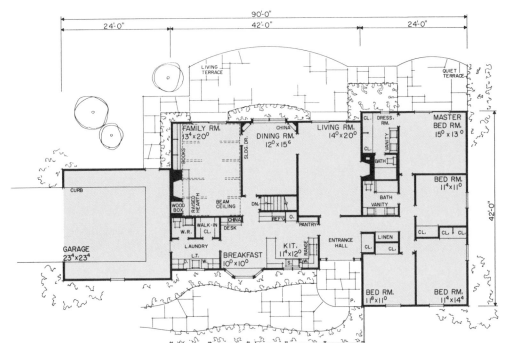

Design V11886
Square Footage: 2,352

Top floor plan labels:
90'-0" / 24'-0" / 42'-0" / 24'-0"
42'-0"

LIVING TERRACE
QUIET TERRACE
FAMILY RM. 13⁴x20⁰
DINING RM. 12⁰x15⁶
LIVING RM. 14⁰x20⁰
MASTER BED RM. 15⁰x13⁰
CL.
DRESS. RM.
VANITY
BATH
BED RM. 11⁴x11⁰
BOOKS
CHINA
CL.
BATH
VANITY
BEAM CEILING
RAISED HEARTH
WOOD BOX
SLDG. DR.
DN.
CURB
GARAGE 23⁴x23⁴
WALK-IN CL.
W.R.
CHINA
DESK
REF'G
O.
PANTRY
LINEN
ENTRANCE HALL
CL.
CL.
LAUNDRY
L.T.
D.
W.
BREAKFAST 10⁰x10⁰
KIT. 11⁴x12⁰
RANGE
S.
CL.
CL.
CL.
BED RM. 11⁸x11⁰
BED RM. 11⁴x14⁴
P.

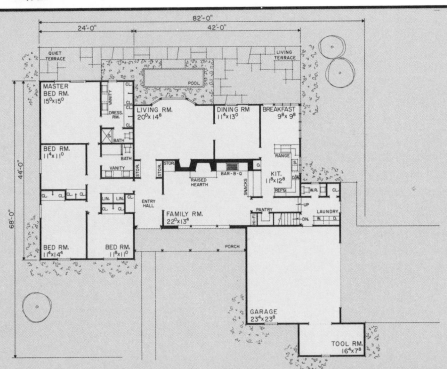

Bottom floor plan labels:
82'-0" / 24'-0" / 42'-0"
44'-0"
68'-0"

QUIET TERRACE
LIVING TERRACE
POOL
MASTER BED RM. 15⁰x15⁰
VANITY
DRESS. RM.
LIVING RM. 20⁰x14⁸
DINING RM. 11⁴x13⁰
BREAKFAST 9⁸x9⁸
BATH
BATH
RANGE
BED RM. 11⁴x11⁰
VANITY
STOR.
STOR.
RAISED HEARTH
BAR-B-Q
O.
KIT. 11⁸x12⁸
D.W.
REF'G
W.R.
S.
CL.
CL.
CL.
LIN.
LIN.
CL.
ENTRY HALL
SNACKS
HI-FI
UP
PANTRY
DN.
LAUNDRY
W.
D.
BED RM. 11⁴x14⁴
BED RM. 11⁸x11⁰
FAMILY RM. 22⁰x13⁴
PORCH
GARAGE 23⁴x23⁸
TOOL RM. 16⁴x7⁸

● Here are three designs each featuring four bedrooms and two plus baths. While each home has a basement, it also highlights a first floor laundry. The differing arrangements of the living, dining, and family rooms are most interesting. The kitchen functions directly with the breakfast rooms, yet again, their locations vary. Raised hearth fireplaces are a focal point of the family rooms, while a second fireplace can be found in the living rooms. Note the side opening garages. Design V11851 has a handy tool room for heavy equipment.

135

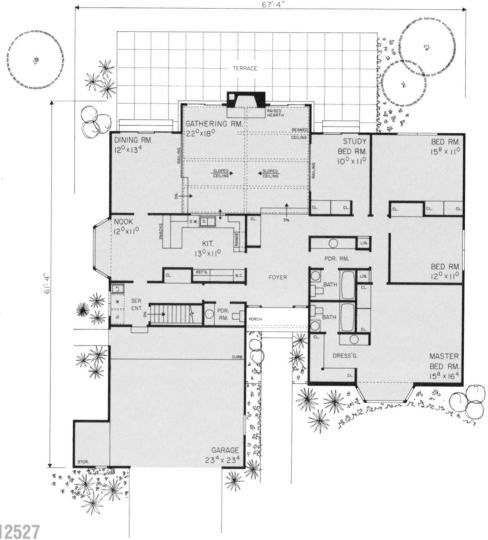

Design V12527
Square Footage: 2,392

D

● Vertical boards and battens, fieldstone, bay window, a dovecote, a gas lamp and a recessed front entrance are among the appealing exterior features of this U-shaped design. Through the double front doors, flanked by glass side lites, one enters the spacious foyer. Straight ahead is the cozy sunken gathering room with its sloping, beamed ceiling, raised hearth fireplace and two sets of sliding glass doors to the rear terrace. To the right of the foyer is the sleeping wing with its three bedrooms, study (make it the fourth bedroom if you wish) and two baths. To the left is the strategically located powder room and large kitchen with its delightful nook and bay window.

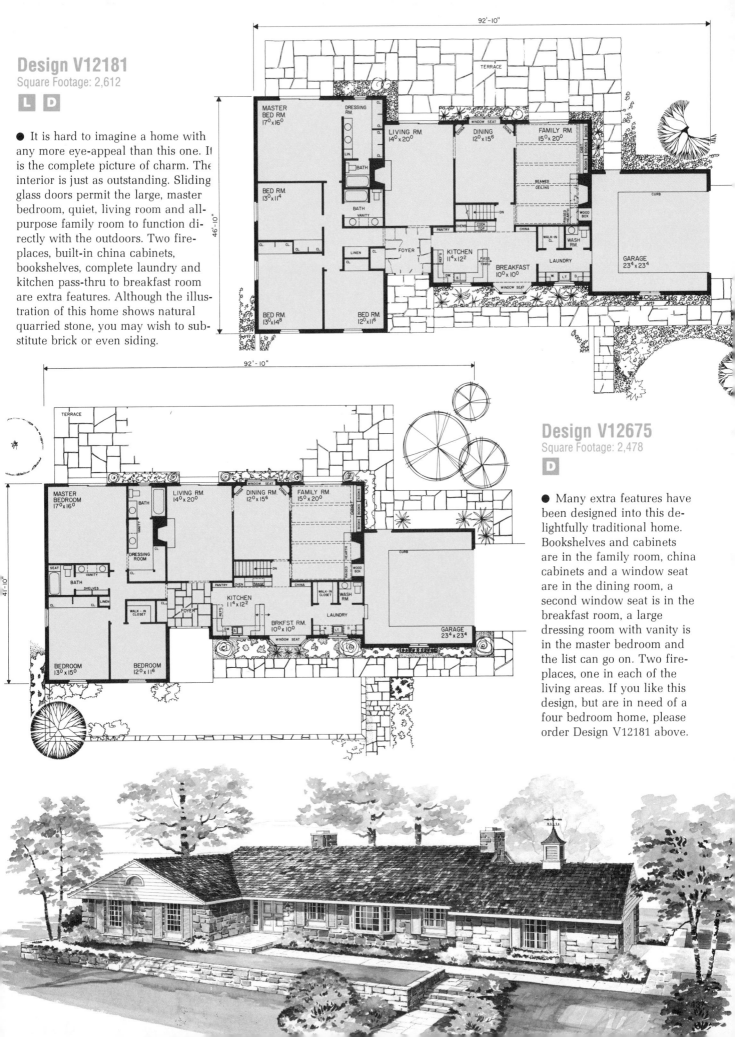

Design V12181
Square Footage: 2,612

L **D**

● It is hard to imagine a home with any more eye-appeal than this one. It is the complete picture of charm. The interior is just as outstanding. Sliding glass doors permit the large, master bedroom, quiet, living room and all-purpose family room to function directly with the outdoors. Two fireplaces, built-in china cabinets, bookshelves, complete laundry and kitchen pass-thru to breakfast room are extra features. Although the illustration of this home shows natural quarried stone, you may wish to substitute brick or even siding.

Design V12675
Square Footage: 2,478

D

● Many extra features have been designed into this delightfully traditional home. Bookshelves and cabinets are in the family room, china cabinets and a window seat are in the dining room, a second window seat is in the breakfast room, a large dressing room with vanity is in the master bedroom and the list can go on. Two fireplaces, one in each of the living areas. If you like this design, but are in need of a four bedroom home, please order Design V12181 above.

Design V12209
Square Footage: 2,659

● Such an impressive home would, indeed, be difficult to top. And little wonder when you consider the myriad of features this one-story Colonial possesses. Consider the exquisite detailing, the fine proportions, and the symmetry of the projecting wings. The gracious and inviting double front doors are a prelude to the exceptional interior. Consider the four bedroom, two-bath sleeping wing. Formal entertaining can be enjoyed in the front living and dining rooms. For informal living there is the rear family room.

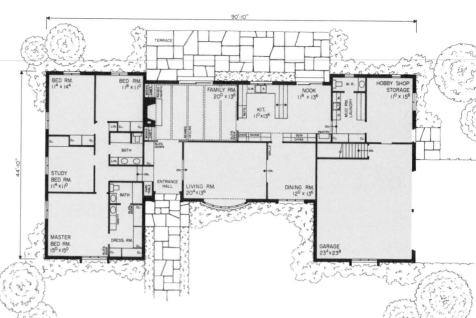

Design V12264
Square Footage: 2,352

● This U-shaped traditional will be a welcomed addition on any site. It has living facilities which will provide your family with years of delightful livability. The two living areas are located to the rear and function with the outdoor terrace. The outstanding kitchen is strategically located handy to the family room and the eating areas. A separate laundry area with fine storage and nearby powder room is a favorite feature. Note garage size and storage potential. Also notice stairway to attic.

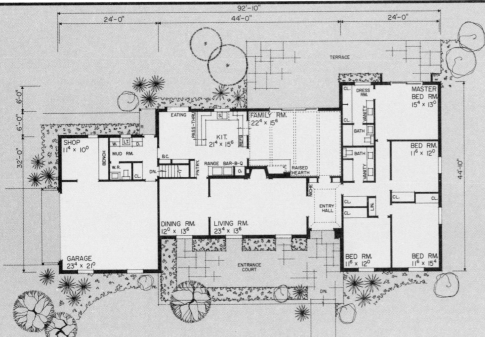

Design V11761
Square Footage: 2,548

L D

● Low, strong roof lines and solid, enduring qualities of brick give this house a permanent, here-to-stay appearance. Bedroom wing is isolated, and the baths and closets deaden noise from the rest of the house. Center fireplaces in family and living rooms make furniture arrangement easy. There are a number of extras – a workshop, an unusually large garage, and an indoor barbecue. Garage has easy access to both basement and kitchen area. There are two eating areas – a formal dining room and a breakfast nook next to the delightful kitchen.

Design V12270
Square Footage: 2,505

● Four bedrooms and two baths make up the sleeping area of this delightful design. There are spacious living areas, too. The family room will serve the informal, family needs; while the living room is available for those more formal times. Both formal and informal dining areas are available to serve every family occasion. They both have easy access to the U-shaped kitchen. Complimenting the work center, an adjacent laundry and washroom will be appreciated. Outstanding storage facilities will be found throughout the plan. These are but some of the highlights of this family-oriented design.

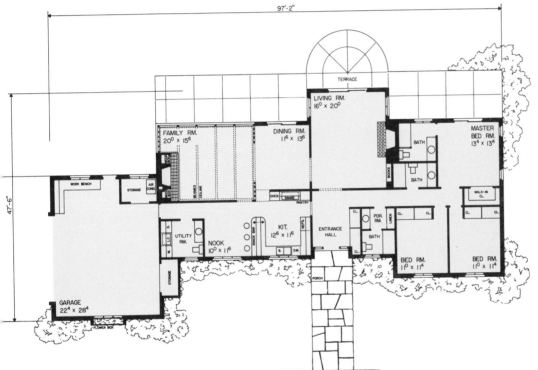

Design V12271
Square Footage: 2,317

● Here's a plan with both formal and informal living areas functioning with the rear terrace. Why let the beauty of your backyard be wasted on the laundry room? This puts the kitchen in the front of the plan. Working in the kitchen, you will be able to see approaching visitors. Among the other features, there are two fireplaces, three full baths, three bedrooms, nook and snack bar and extra garage storage. List the other features that will serve your family.

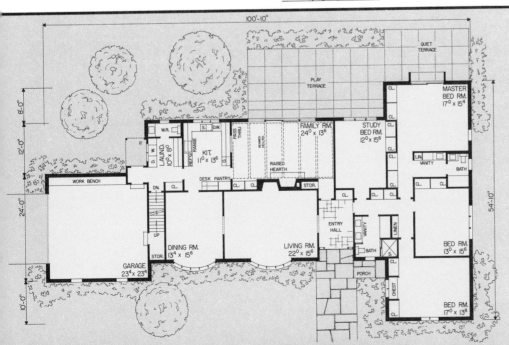

Design V11201
Square Footage: 2,960

● If it's formal living you are after, then the elegance and spaciousness of this richly detailed design should meet your specifications. The large bow windows, the overhanging roof, the massive chimney and the ornamental cupola give this house a stately facade. As you study the plan, note the generous size of the various rooms. Observe the excellence of the zoning and how the elements of each zone - sleeping, formal and informal living and work area - function together smoothly.

141

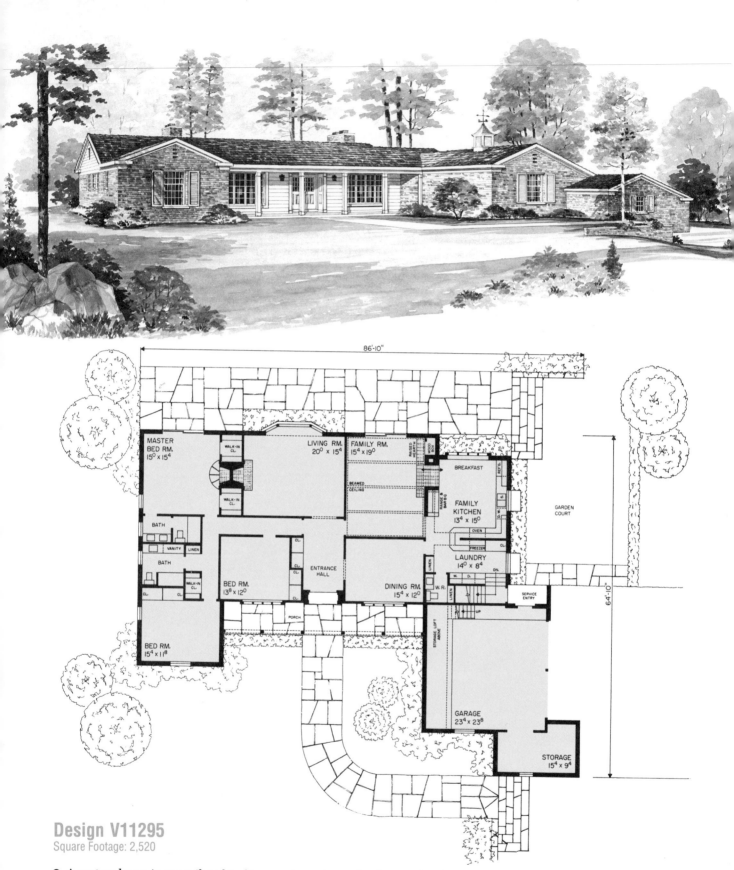

MASTER BED RM. 15⁰ x 15⁴

WALK-IN CL.

WALK-IN CL.

LIVING RM. 20⁰ x 15⁴

FAMILY RM. 15⁴ x 19⁰

RAISED HEARTH

WOOD

BREAKFAST

REFR.

BEAMED CEILING

RANGE & BAR'B'Q

FAMILY KITCHEN 13⁴ x 15⁰

D.W.

BATH

VANITY

LINEN

OVEN

GARDEN COURT

BATH

WALK-IN CL.

CL.

CL.

CL.

CL.

ENTRANCE HALL

FREEZER

CL.

LAUNDRY 14⁰ x 8⁴

DN.

LINEN

BED RM. 13⁸ x 12⁰

CL.

DINING RM. 15⁴ x 12⁰

W.R.

W. D.

LINEN

SERVICE ENTRY

PORCH

STORAGE LOFT ABOVE

UP

BED RM. 15⁴ x 11⁸

GARAGE 23⁴ x 23⁸

STORAGE 15⁴ x 9⁴

86'-10"

64'-10"

Design V11295
Square Footage: 2,520

● A custom home is one tailored to fit the needs and satisfy the living patterns of a particular family. Here is a traditional home which stands ready to serve its occupants ideally. The overhanging roof creates the covered porch with its attractive wood columns. The center entrance leads to an interior which will cater to the formal as well as the informal activities of the family. Two fireplaces, back-to-back, serve the master bedroom and the quiet, formal living room. Another two-way fireplace can be enjoyed from the large, family room and the gaily, informal family kitchen. Adjacent to the kitchen is the formal dining room, the spacious laundry and the powder room. No storage problems here. Of particular interest is the storage room and the storage balcony in the garage.

142

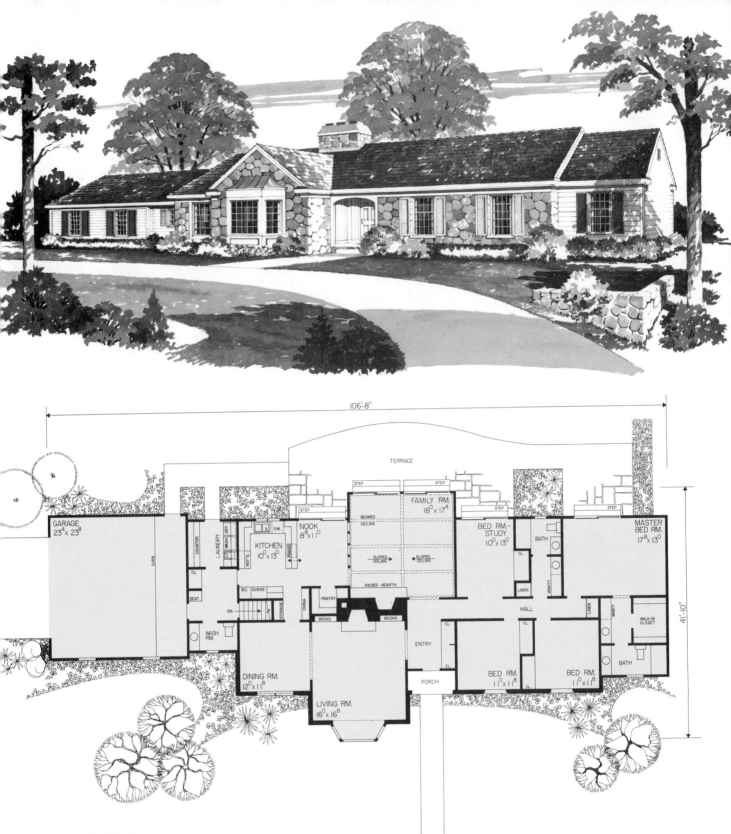

Design V12544
Square Footage: 2,527

D

● A blend of exterior materials enhance the beauty of this fine home. Here, the masonry material used is fieldstone to contrast effectively with the horizontal siding. You may substitute brick or quarried stone if you wish. Adding to the appeal are the various projections and their roof planes, the window treatment and the recessed front entrance. Two large living areas highlight the interior. Each has a fireplace. The homemaking effort will be easily and enjoyably dispatched with such features as the efficient kitchen, the walk-in pantry, the handy storage areas, the first floor laundry and extra washroom. The sleeping zone has four bedrooms, two baths with vanities and good closet accommodations. There's a basement for additional storage and recreation activities.

143

Clutter Room, Media Room To The Fore

Design V12880
Living Area: 2,758 square feet
Greenhouse: 149 square feet
Total: 2,907 square feet

L **D**

● This comfortable traditional home offers plenty of modern livability. A clutter room off the two-car garage is the perfect space for workbench, sewing, and hobbies. It includes a work island and bench space. Across the hall one finds a modern media room, the perfect place for stereo speakers, videos, and more. A spacious country kitchen off the greenhouse is a cozy gathering place for family and friends, as well as convenient work area. The 149-foot greenhouse itself easily could be the focal point of this home filled with modern amenities. The house also features a formal dining room, living room with fireplace, covered porch, and three bedrooms including a master bedroom suite.

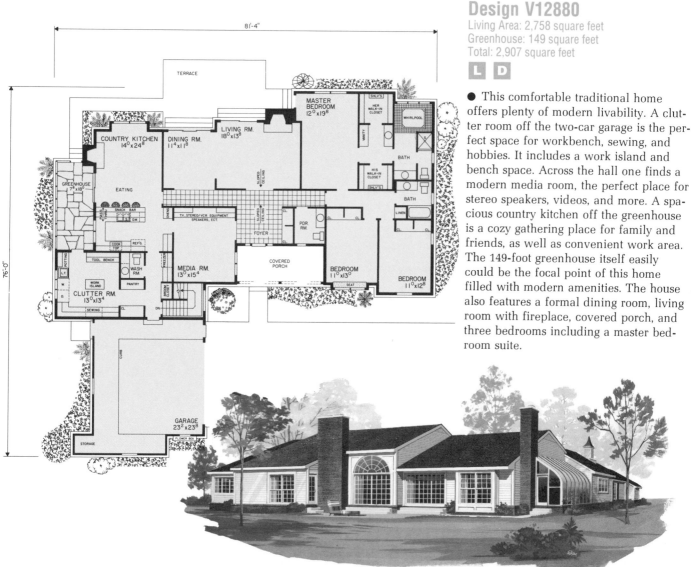

Design V11952
Square Footage: 2,705

● This delightful home has been designed for country-estate living. L-shaped, this traditional will be a worthy addition to any building site. Its pleasing proportions are almost breathtaking. They seem to foretell the tremendous amount of livability its inhabitants are to enjoy. The interior zoning hardly could be improved upon. The children's bedrooms function together in a wing with their own bath. There is a large master bedroom suite. It features Mr. and Mrs. dressing rooms, each with a vanity, with a full bath in the middle. The dining room is nestled between the living and family rooms. Both of these living areas have a beamed ceiling and a fireplace. All of the work area, kitchen, breakfast room, laundry and washroom, is in the front of the plan.

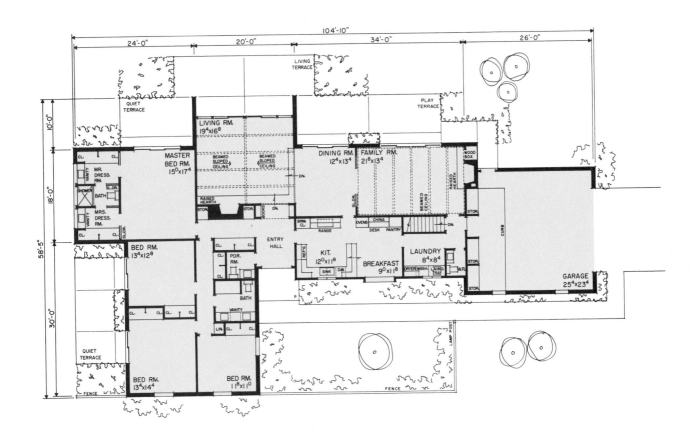

Design V12766
Square Footage: 2,711

D

● A sizable master bedroom has a dressing area featuring two walk-in closets, a twin lavatory and compartmented bath. The two-bedroom children's area has a full bath and supporting study. Formal living and dining zone is separated by a thru-fireplace. A spacious kitchen-nook is cheerfully informal with a sun room just a step away through sliding glass doors. The service area has a laundry, storage, washroom and stairs to basement. An array of sliding glass doors lead to outdoor living on the various terraces. These are but some of the highlights of this appealing, L-shaped traditional home. Be sure to note the large number of sizable closets for a variety of uses.

Design V12778
Square Footage: 2,761

D

● No matter what the occasion, family and friends alike will enjoy this sizable gathering room. A spacious 20' x 23', this room has a thru fireplace to the study and two sets of sliding glass doors to the large, rear terrace. Indoor-outdoor living also can be enjoyed from the dining room, study and master bedroom. There is also a covered porch accessible through sliding glass doors in the dining room and breakfast nook.

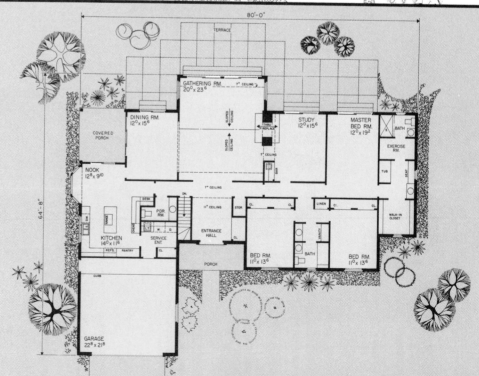

TERRACE

TERRACE

BED RM.
16⁸ x 13⁸

LIVING RM.
21⁴ x 14⁰

NOOK
11⁶ x 9⁸

FAMILY RM.
15¹⁰ x 21⁸

BATH

BED RM
13⁰ x 12⁰

KITCHEN
11⁶ x 12⁰

RAISED HEARTH

AIR COND.

DINING RM.
14⁰ x 13⁰

PANTRY

REF'G

LAUNDRY

LINEN

CL

CL

GALLERY

STUDY
10⁸ x 10⁴

BATH

DRESSING RM.

VANITY

TUB

PORCH

WALK-IN CLOSET

MASTER BED RM.
13⁰ x 18⁴

GARAGE
21¹⁰ x 23⁸

76'-0"

66'-8"

Design V12784
Square Footage: 2,980

● The projection of the master bedroom and garage create an inviting U-shaped area leading to the covered porch of this delightful traditionally styled design. After entering through the double front doors, the gallery will lead to each of the three living areas: the sleeping wing of two bedrooms, full bath and study; the informal area of the family room with raised hearth fireplace and sliding glass doors to the terrace and the kitchen/nook area (the kitchen has a pass--thru snack bar to the family room); and the formal area consisting of a separate dining room with built-in china cabinets and the living room. Note the privacy of the master bedroom.

● What a pleasing, traditional exterior. And what a fine, convenient living interior! The configuration of this home leads to interesting roof planes and even functional outdoor terrace areas. The front court and the covered porch with its stolid pillars strike an enchanting note. The gathering room will be just that. It will be the family's multipurpose living area. Sunken to a level of two steps, its already spacious feeling is enhanced by its open planning with the dining room and study. This latter room may be closed off for more privacy if desired. Just adjacent to the foyer is the open stairwell to the basement level. Here will be the possibility of developing recreation space.

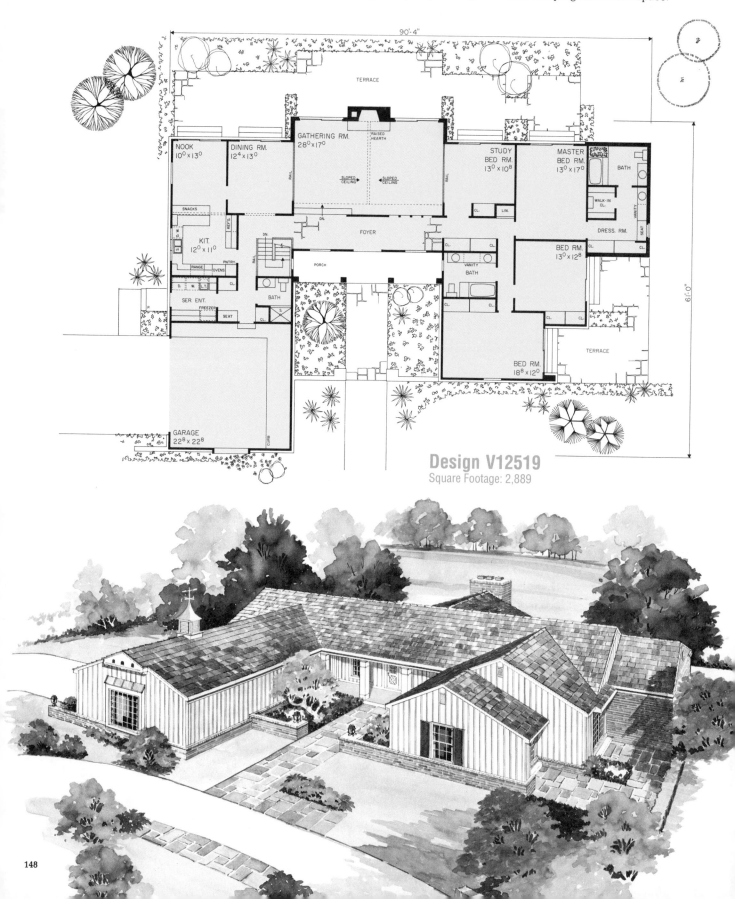

Design V12519
Square Footage: 2,889

TRADITIONAL and CONTEMPORARY . .

as highlighted in this interesting section have both traditional and contemporary exteriors. Each design offers square footage over 3000 sq. ft. In a couple of designs, bonus square footage and livability are picked-up by the addition of the upstairs sleeping quarters. These houses deliver all the livability potential and amenities one would want in a house designed for the unrestricted budget. Provisions are made for both formal and informal living patterns. Flexible and varied indoor-outdoor living relationships have been provided. The configurations of these floor plans are important for they represent, with thoughtful siting, the opportunity to enjoy solar orientation.

Design V12888
Square Footage: 3,018

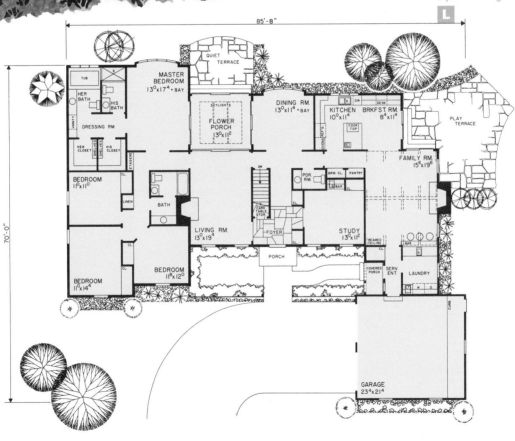

● This is an outstanding Early American design for the 20th-Century. The exterior detailing with narrow clap boards, multi-paned windows and cupola are the features of yesteryear. Interior planning, though, is for today's active family. Formal living room, informal family room plus a study are present. Every activity will have its place in this home. Picture yourself working in the kitchen. There's enough counter space for two or three helpers. Four bedrooms are in the private area. Stop and imagine your daily routine if you occupied the master bedroom. Both you and your spouse would have plenty of space and privacy. The flower porch, accessible from the master bedroom, living and dining rooms, is a very delightful "plus" feature. Study this design's every detail.

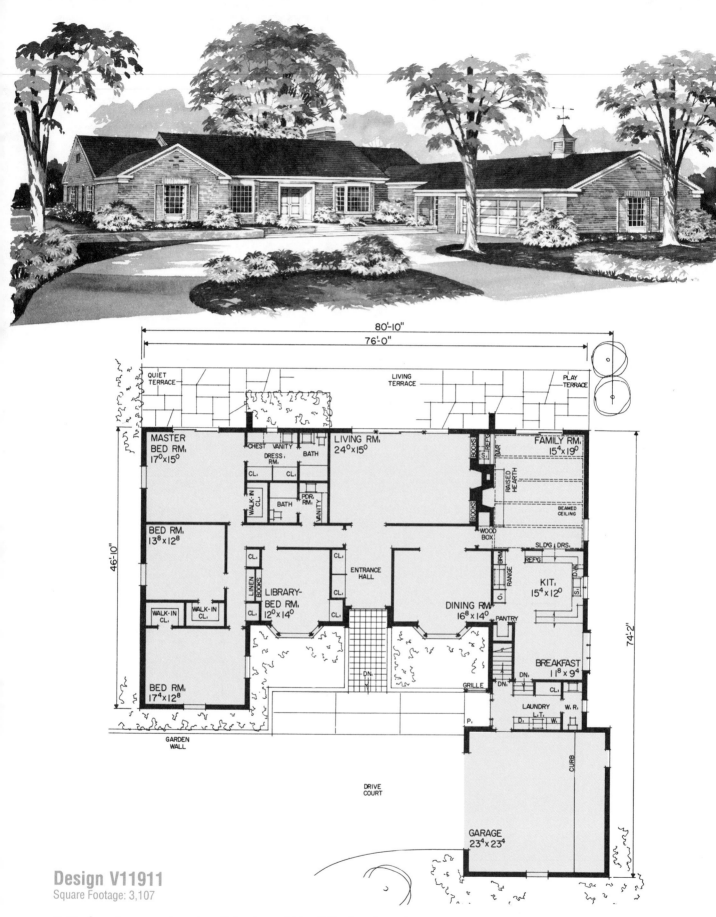

Design V11911
Square Footage: 3,107

● For luxurious, country-estate living it would be difficult to beat the livability offered by these two impressive traditional designs. To begin with, their exterior appeal is, indeed, gracious. Their floor plans highlight plenty of space, excellent room arrangements, fine traffic circulation, and an abundance of convenient living features. It is interesting to note that each design features similar livability facilities. Both may function as four bedroom homes . . .

150

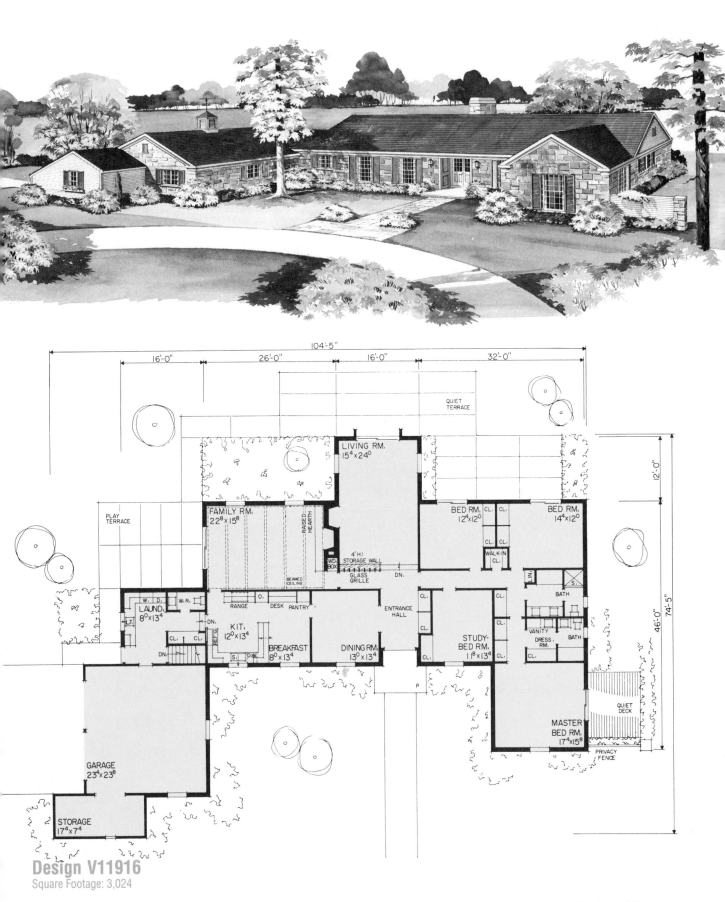

Design V11916
Square Footage: 3,024

● . . . or three bedroom with a study or library. There are first floor laundries, two fireplaces, formal and informal living and dining areas, fine storage potential, and delightful indoor-outdoor living relationships. You'll have fun listing the built-in features. The two family rooms have beamed ceilings and sliding glass doors to the play terraces. The two living rooms are spacious and enjoy a full measure of privacy. They are but a step from outdoor living.

151

Design V12783
Square Footage: 3,210

● The configuration of this traditional design is outstanding indeed. The garage-bedroom wing on one side and the master bedroom on the other create an inviting U-shaped entry court. This area is raised two steps from the driveway and has a 6 foot high masonry wall with coach lamps for an added attraction. Upon entrance through the double front doors one will begin to enjoy the livability that this design has to offer. Each room is well planned and deserves praise. The sizeable master bedroom has a fireplace and sliding glass doors to the entry court. Another sizeable room, the gathering room, has access to the rear terrace along with the dining room, family room and rear bedroom. Note interior kitchen which is adjacent to each of the major rooms.

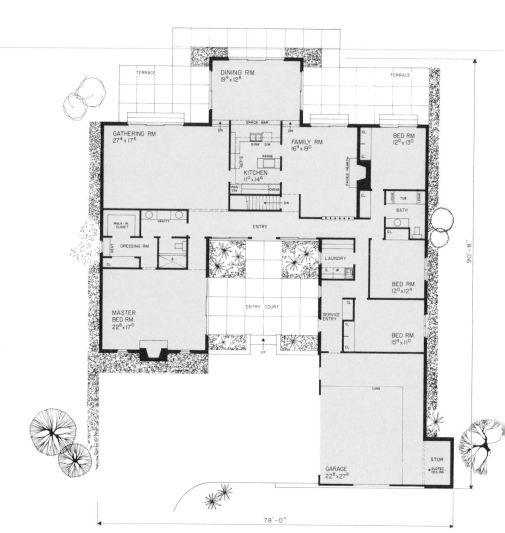

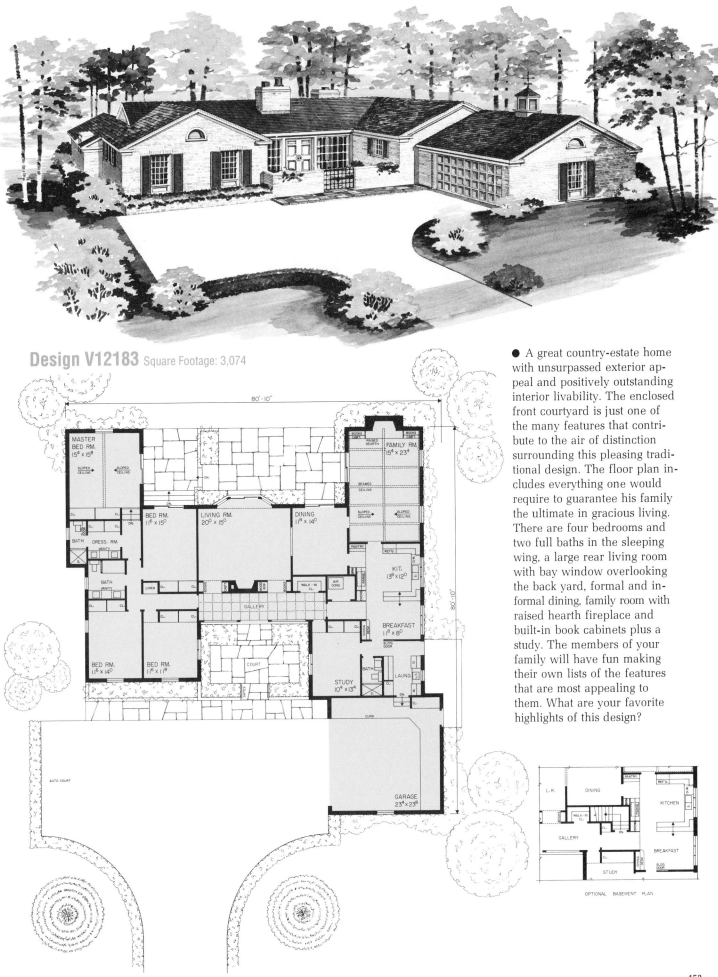

Design V12183 Square Footage: 3,074

MASTER BED RM. 15⁴ x 15⁸

SLOPED CEILING

SLOPED CEILING

BATH

DRESS. RM.

VANITY

BATH

VANITY

LINEN

BED RM. 11⁶ x 15⁰

LIVING RM. 20⁰ x 15⁰

DINING 11⁸ x 14⁰

BOOKS

RAISED HEARTH

FAMILY RM. 15⁴ x 23⁴

BEAMED CEILING

SLOPED CEILING

SLOPED CEILING

PANTRY

REF'G.

KIT. 13⁸ x 12⁰

RANGE

WALK-IN CL.

AIR COND.

GALLERY

BREAKFAST 11⁸ x 8⁰

SLDG. DOOR

BED RM. 11⁶ x 14⁰

BED RM. 11⁶ x 11⁸

COURT

BATH

LAUND.

STUDY 10⁴ x 13⁴

80'-10"

80'-10"

CURB

AUTO COURT

GARAGE 23⁴ x 23⁸

● A great country-estate home with unsurpassed exterior appeal and positively outstanding interior livability. The enclosed front courtyard is just one of the many features that contribute to the air of distinction surrounding this pleasing traditional design. The floor plan includes everything one would require to guarantee his family the ultimate in gracious living. There are four bedrooms and two full baths in the sleeping wing, a large rear living room with bay window overlooking the back yard, formal and informal dining, family room with raised hearth fireplace and built-in book cabinets plus a study. The members of your family will have fun making their own lists of the features that are most appealing to them. What are your favorite highlights of this design?

L.R.

DINING

PANTRY

REF'G.

KITCHEN

BOOKS

WALK-IN CL.

GALLERY

CL.

STUDY

BREAKFAST

SLDG. DOOR

OPTIONAL BASEMENT PLAN

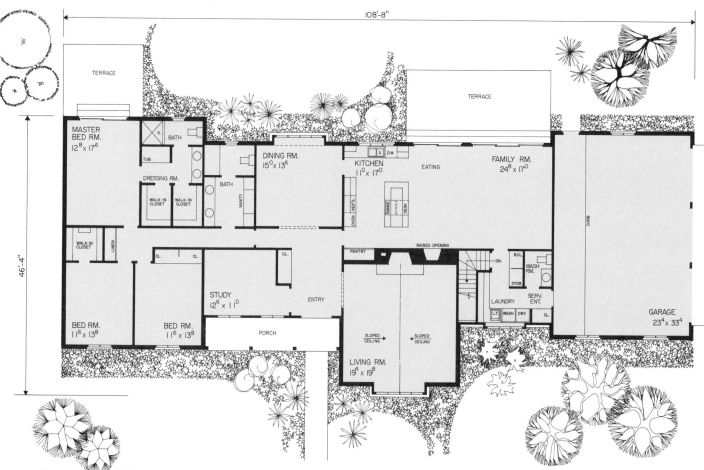

108'-8"

TERRACE

TERRACE

MASTER BED RM.
12⁸ x 17⁶

BATH

TUB

DRESSING RM.

WALK-IN CLOSET

WALK-IN CLOSET

BATH

VANITY

DINING RM.
15⁰ x 13⁶

KITCHEN
11⁰ x 17⁰

OVEN REF'G.

RANGE

DESK

EATING

FAMILY RM.
24⁸ x 17⁰

CURB

WALK-IN CLOSET

LINEN

CL.

CL.

CL.

PANTRY

RAISED OPENING

DN.

B.CL.

WASH RM.

STOR.

STUDY
12⁶ x 11⁰

ENTRY

LAUNDRY

L.T.

WASH.

DRY.

CL.

SERV. ENT.

BED RM.
11⁶ x 13⁸

BED RM.
11⁶ x 13⁸

PORCH

SLOPED CEILING

SLOPED CEILING

LIVING RM.
19⁴ x 19⁸

GARAGE
23⁴ x 33⁴

46'-4"

Design V12767
Square Footage: 3,000

D

● What a sound investment this impressive home will be. And while its value withstands the inflationary pressures of ensuing years, it will serve your family well. It has all the amenities to assure truly pleasurable living. The charming exterior will lend itself

to treatment other than the appealing fieldstone, brick and frame shown. Inside, the plan will impress you with large, spacious living areas, formal and informal dining areas, three large bedrooms, two full baths with twin lavatories, walk-in closets and a fine study.

The kitchen features an island work center with range and desk. The two fireplaces will warm their surroundings in both areas. Two separate terraces for a variety of uses. Note laundry, wash room and three-car garage with extra curb area.

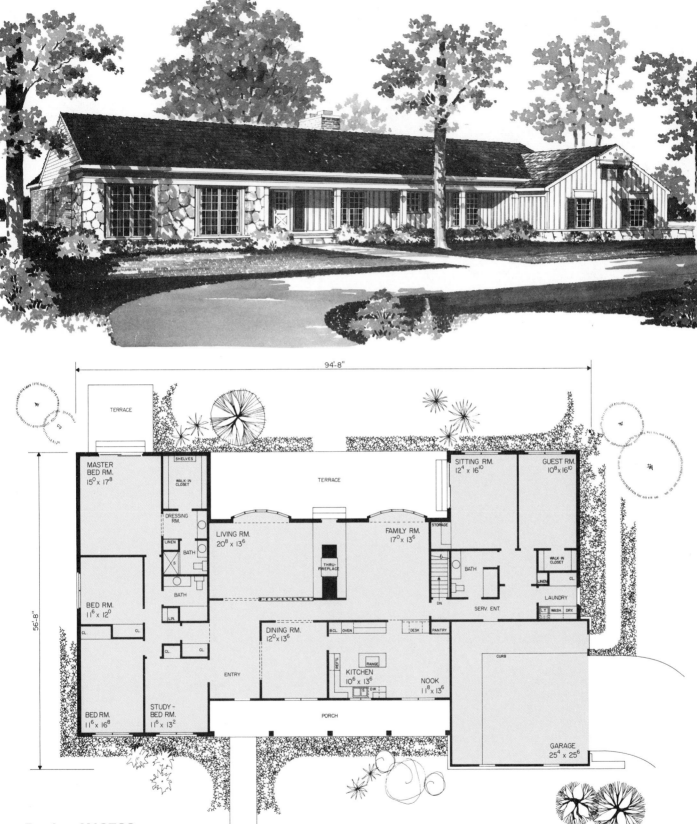

Design V12768
Square Footage: 3,436

TERRACE

MASTER BED RM. 15⁰ x 17⁸

SHELVES

WALK-IN CLOSET

DRESSING RM.

LINEN

BATH

BATH

BED RM. 11⁶ x 12⁰

CL.

CL.

LIN.

CL.

CL.

BED RM. 11⁶ x 16⁸

STUDY - BED RM. 11⁶ x 13²

ENTRY

LIVING RM. 20⁸ x 13⁶

THRU-FIREPLACE

TERRACE

FAMILY RM. 17⁰ x 13⁶

SITTING RM. 12⁴ x 16¹⁰

GUEST RM. 10⁸ x 16¹⁰

STORAGE

BATH

WALK-IN CLOSET

LINEN

CL.

LAUNDRY

L.T WASH DRY

SERV. ENT.

DN

DINING RM. 12⁰ x 13⁶

B.CL. OVEN

DESK

PANTRY

REF'G.

RANGE

KITCHEN 10⁶ x 13⁶

S DW

NOOK 11⁸ x 13⁶

PORCH

CURB

GARAGE 25⁴ x 25⁶

94'-8"

56'-8"

● Besides its elegant traditionally styled exterior with its delightfully long covered front porch, this home has an exceptionally livable interior. There is the outstanding four bedroom and two-bath sleeping wing. Then, the efficient front kitchen with island range flanked by the formal dining room and the informal breakfast nook. Separated by the two-way, thru fireplace are the living and family rooms which look out on the rear yard. Worthy of particular note is the development of a potential live-in relative facility. These two rooms would also serve the large family well as a hobby room and library or additional bedrooms. A full bath is adjacent as well as the laundry. Note curb area in the garage for the storage of outdoor equipment.

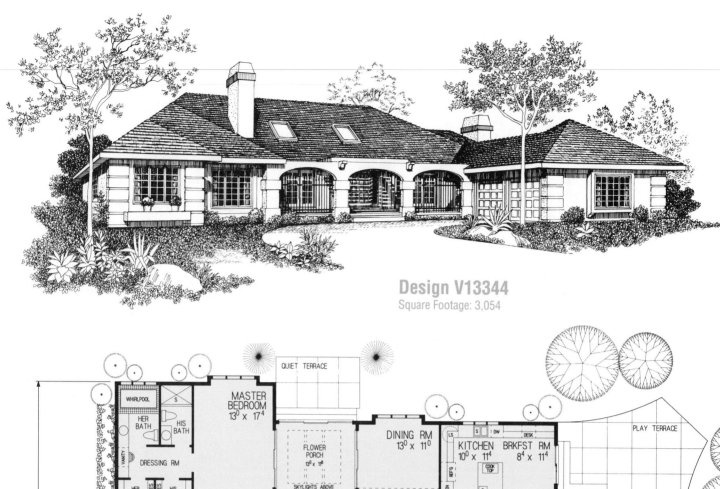

Design V13344
Square Footage: 3,054

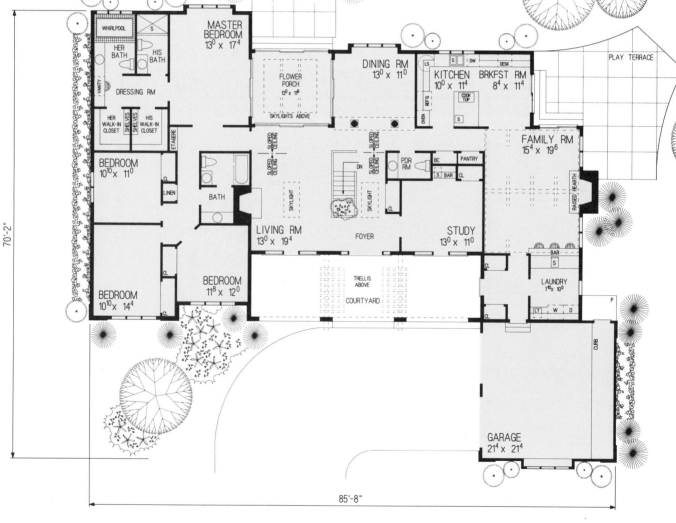

QUIET TERRACE

WHIRLPOOL S

HER BATH · HIS BATH

MASTER BEDROOM
13⁰ x 17⁴

DINING RM
13⁰ x 11⁰

LS · S · DW DESK

PLAY TERRACE

DRESSING RM

FLOWER PORCH
13⁰ x 11⁸

KITCHEN
10⁰ x 11⁴

BRKFST RM
8⁴ x 11⁴

COOK TOP

OVEN · S

HER WALK-IN CLOSET · SHELVES SHELVES · HIS WALK-IN CLOSET

SKYLIGHTS ABOVE

REFG

FAMILY RM
15⁴ x 19⁶

BEDROOM
10¹⁰ x 11⁰

ETAGERE

SLOPED CEILING · SLOPED CEILING

DN

SLOPED CEILING

PDR RM

BC · PANTRY

CL

RAISED HEARTH

CL

LINEN

BATH

SKYLIGHT

SKYLIGHT

LIVING RM
13⁰ x 19⁴

FOYER

STUDY
13⁰ x 11⁰

BAR · S

BAR · S · CL

CL

LAUNDRY
7⁴ x 10⁰

BEDROOM
11⁸ x 12⁰

TRELLIS ABOVE

COURTYARD

CL

LT · W · D

BEDROOM
10¹⁰ x 14⁴

P

GARAGE
21⁴ x 21⁴

70'-2"

85'-8"

● This home features interior planning for today's active family. Living areas include a living room with fireplace, a cozy study and family room with wet bar. Convenient to the kitchen is the formal dining room with attractive bay window overlooking the back yard. The four-bedroom sleeping area contains a sumptuous master suite. Also notice the cheerful flower porch with access from the master suite, living room and dining room.

Design V13315
Square Footage: 3,248

● Besides the covered front veranda, look for another full-width veranda to the rear of this charming home. The master bedroom, breakfast room, and gathering room all have French doors to this outdoor space. A handy wet bar/tavern enhances entertainment options. The upper lounge could be a welcome haven.

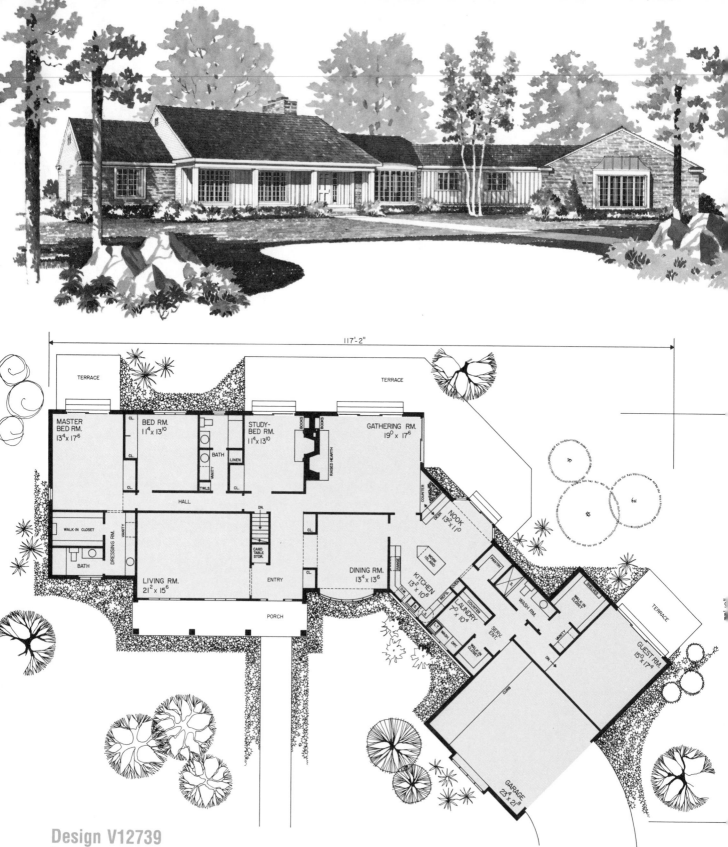

Measurements on floor plan:
117'-2"

TERRACE   TERRACE   TERRACE

MASTER BED RM. 13⁴ x 17⁶
BED RM. 11⁴ x 13¹⁰
STUDY-BED RM. 11⁴ x 13¹⁰
GATHERING RM. 19⁰ x 17⁶
NOOK 13 x 11⁰
GUEST RM. 15⁰ x 17⁴

CL. BATH VANITY LINEN TWLS.
HALL
BOOKS BOOKS RAISED HEARTH
COUNTER
REF. PANTRY WASH RM. WALK-IN CLOSET

WALK-IN CLOSET
VANITY DRESSING RM.
BATH
DN.
CARD TABLE STOR.
ENTRY
CL.
CL.
DINING RM. 13⁴ x 13⁶
WORK ISLAND
KITCHEN 13 x 10⁶
RANGE
COUNTER
LAUNDRY 7⁰ x 10⁴
WASH DRY
WALK-IN CLOSET
SERV. ENT.
VANITY
DN.

LIVING RM. 21² x 15⁶

PORCH

CURB

GARAGE 23⁴ x 21⁸

Design V12739
Square Footage: 3,313

● If you and your family are looking for new living patterns, try to envision your days spent in this traditionally styled home. Its Early American flavor is captured by effective window and door treatment, cornice work and porch pillars. Its zoning is interesting.

The spacious interior leaves nothing to be desired. There are three bedrooms and two full baths in the sleeping area. A quiet, formal living room is separated from the other living areas. The gathering and dining rooms are adjacent to each other and function with

the excellent kitchen and its breakfast eating area. Note work island, pantry and pass-thru. Then, there is an extra guest room sunken one step. A live-in relative would enjoy the privacy of this room. Full bath is nearby. This is definitely a home for all to enjoy.

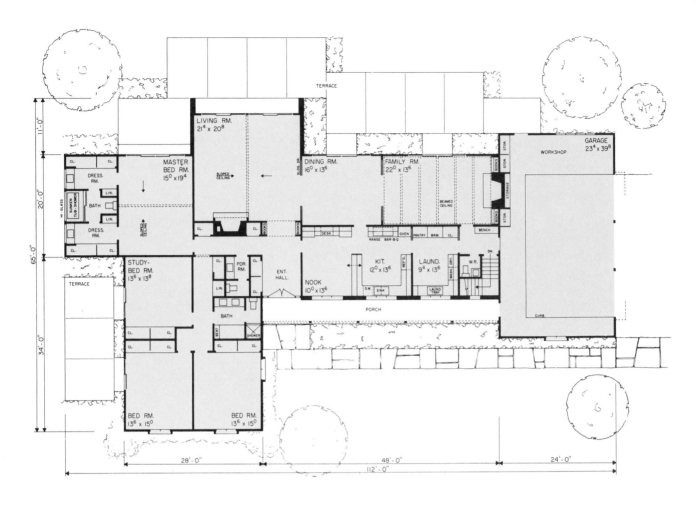

Design V11936
Square Footage: 3,280

● Country-estate living will be experienced in this 3,280 square foot home. The arrangement of the numerous rooms places the major living areas to the rear. They will enjoy their privacy and function with the outdoors. Count the sliding glass door units. Visualize the gracious indoor/outdoor living to be enjoyed by all the members of the family. Even the children's rooms have a terrace. The homemaker's work center overlooks the front yard and is efficient, indeed. There is a breakfast nook, a U-shaped kitchen, a separate laundry room, an extra washroom, and a whole wall of storage facilities. Be sure you notice the powder room near the entrance hall.

159

Created Especially For *Colonial Homes*

Design V12977
First Floor: 4,104 square feet
Second Floor: 979 square feet
Total: 5,083 square feet

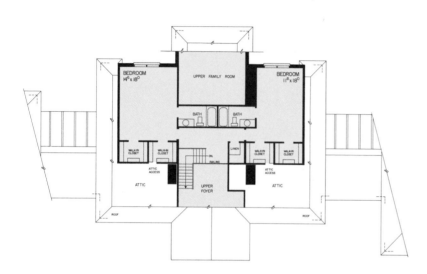

● Beautifully balanced, both front and rear facades of this elegant brick manor depict classic Georgian symmetry. A columned, Greek entry opens to an impressive two-story foyer. Fireplaces, built-in shelves, and cabinets highlight each of the four main gathering areas: living room, dining room, family room, and library. The kitchen features a handy work island, pass-through to the dining room and snack bar that opens to the two-story family room. The master suite is located in its own wing and has a private atrium entrance and lounge/exercise room. A fifth fireplace graces the master bedroom and additional features include His and Hers walk-in closets, built-in vanity, and whirlpool bath. Two bedrooms, each with private bath and double walk-in closets, are located on the second floor. A bonus guest or hobby room is located on the first floor. The lovely rear terrace features double sets of stairs to the rear yard and each of the main wings has a grand fan-shaped window with multi-panes that overlooks the view.

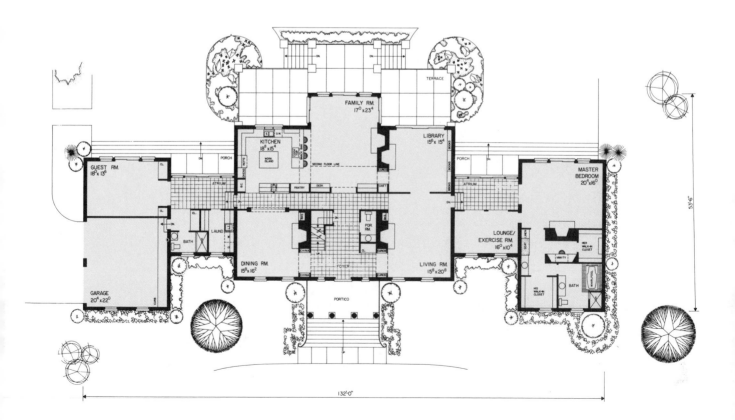

Popular History House Series

Design V12997
Square Footage: 3,442

● The fine features of this home include five fireplaces. One fireplace warms the master bedroom with expansive bath and dressing area, plus access to a private rear terrace. Two additional bedrooms each adjoin a full bath. Large living areas include the living room, dining room and family room with snack bar. A library with fireplace, sloped ceiling and built-in shelves is tucked away in the rear of the home. The exterior of this Georgian manor is just as impressive as the interior.

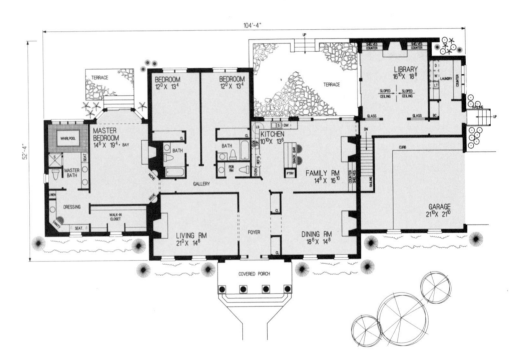

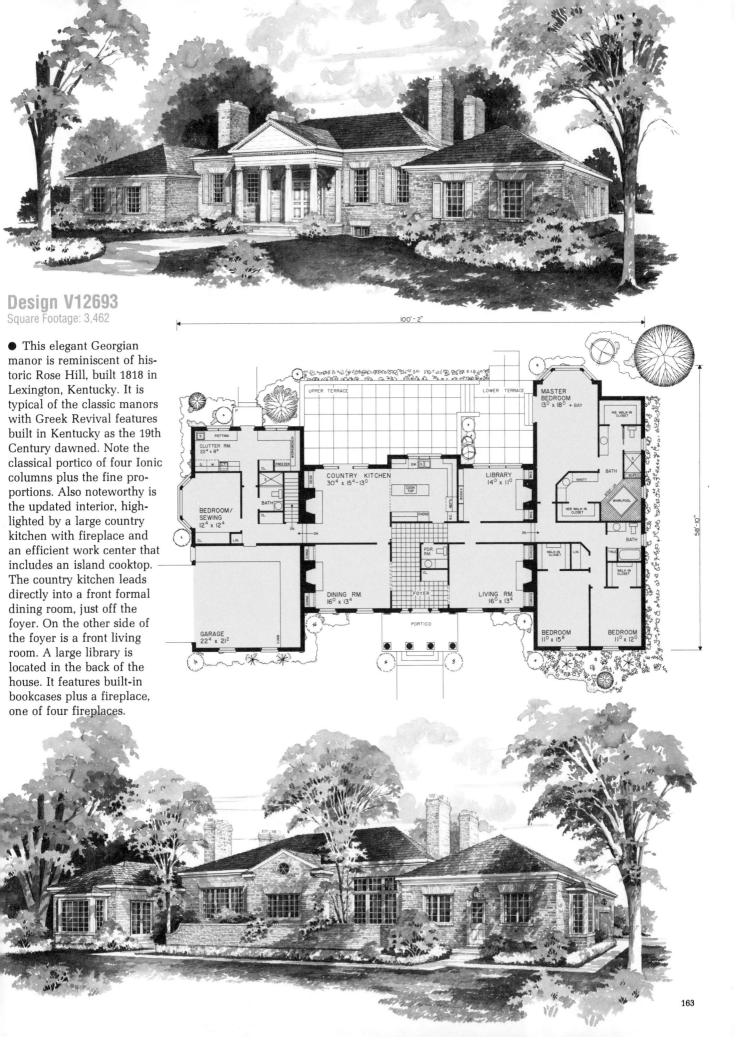

Design V12693
Square Footage: 3,462

● This elegant Georgian manor is reminiscent of historic Rose Hill, built 1818 in Lexington, Kentucky. It is typical of the classic manors with Greek Revival features built in Kentucky as the 19th Century dawned. Note the classical portico of four Ionic columns plus the fine proportions. Also noteworthy is the updated interior, highlighted by a large country kitchen with fireplace and an efficient work center that includes an island cooktop. The country kitchen leads directly into a front formal dining room, just off the foyer. On the other side of the foyer is a front living room. A large library is located in the back of the house. It features built-in bookcases plus a fireplace, one of four fireplaces.

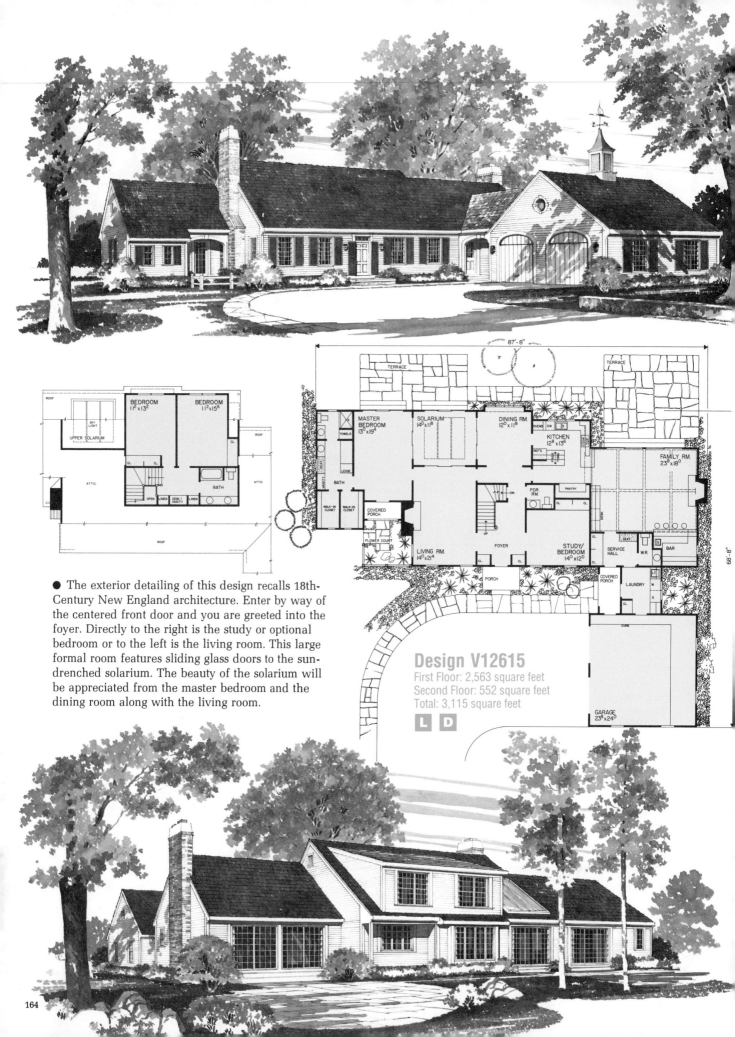

Second Floor Plan labels:
- BEDROOM 11² x 13²
- BEDROOM 11² x 15⁶
- ROOF
- SKY LIGHT
- UPPER SOLARIUM
- ROOF
- CL
- CL
- CL
- BATH
- ATTIC
- ATTIC
- OPEN
- LINEN
- DESK / VANITY
- LINEN
- ROOF

First Floor Plan labels:
- 87'-8"
- TERRACE
- TERRACE
- TOWELS
- MASTER BEDROOM 13⁰ x 19⁴
- SOLARIUM 14⁰ x 11⁸
- DINING RM. 12⁰ x 11⁸
- OVENS
- DW
- KITCHEN 12⁸ x 13⁶
- REF'S
- FAMILY RM. 23⁸ x 18⁰
- BATH
- LEDGE
- VANITY
- SEAT
- WALK-IN CLOSET
- WALK-IN CLOSET
- COVERED PORCH
- PDR. RM.
- PANTRY
- CL
- UP
- DN
- DESK
- FLOWER COURT
- LIVING RM. 14⁰ x 21⁴
- CL
- FOYER
- STUDY/ BEDROOM 14⁰ x 12⁰
- CL
- CL
- SERVICE HALL
- W.R.
- SEAT
- BAR
- 68'-8"
- PORCH
- COVERED PORCH
- LAUNDRY
- W.
- D.
- CL
- CURB
- GARAGE 23⁸ x 24⁰

● The exterior detailing of this design recalls 18th-Century New England architecture. Enter by way of the centered front door and you are greeted into the foyer. Directly to the right is the study or optional bedroom or to the left is the living room. This large formal room features sliding glass doors to the sun-drenched solarium. The beauty of the solarium will be appreciated from the master bedroom and the dining room along with the living room.

Design V12615
First Floor: 2,563 square feet
Second Floor: 552 square feet
Total: 3,115 square feet

L D

Design V11787

First Floor: 2,656 square feet
Second Floor: 744 square feet
Total: 3,400 square feet

D

● Can't you picture this dramatic home sitting on your property? The curving front drive is impressive as it passes the walks to the front door and the service entrance. The roof masses, the centered masonry chimney, the window symmetry and the 108 foot expanse across the front are among the features that make this a distinctive home. Of interest are the living and family rooms — both similar in size and each having its own fireplace.

● Organized zoning by room functions makes this Traditional design a comfortable home for living, as well as classic in its styling. A central foyer facilitates flexible traffic patterns. Quiet areas of the house include a media room and luxurious master bedroom suite with fitness area, spacious closet space and bath, as well as a lounge or writing area. Informal living areas of the house include a sun room, large country kitchen, and efficient kitchen with an island. Service areas include a room just off the garage for laundry, sewing, or hobbies. The second floor garage can double as a practical shop. Formal living areas include a living area and formal dining room. The second floor holds two bedrooms that would make a wonderful children's suite, with a study or TV area also upstairs.

Design V12921

First Floor: 3,215 square feet
Sun Room: 296 square feet
Second Floor: 711 square feet
Total: 4,222 square feet

L D

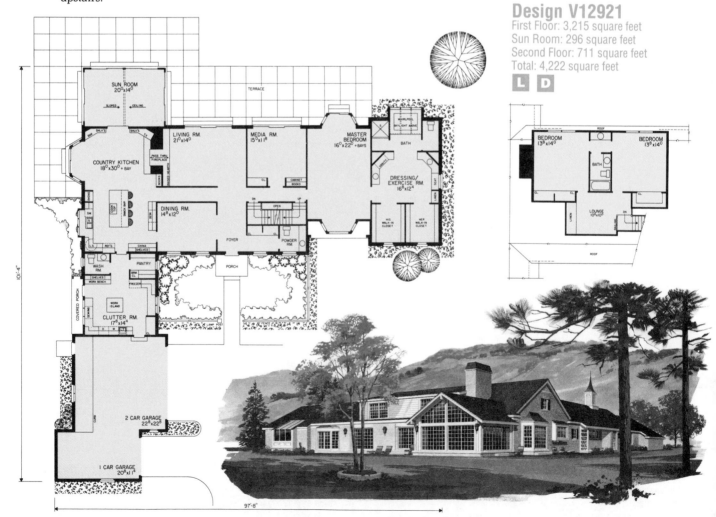

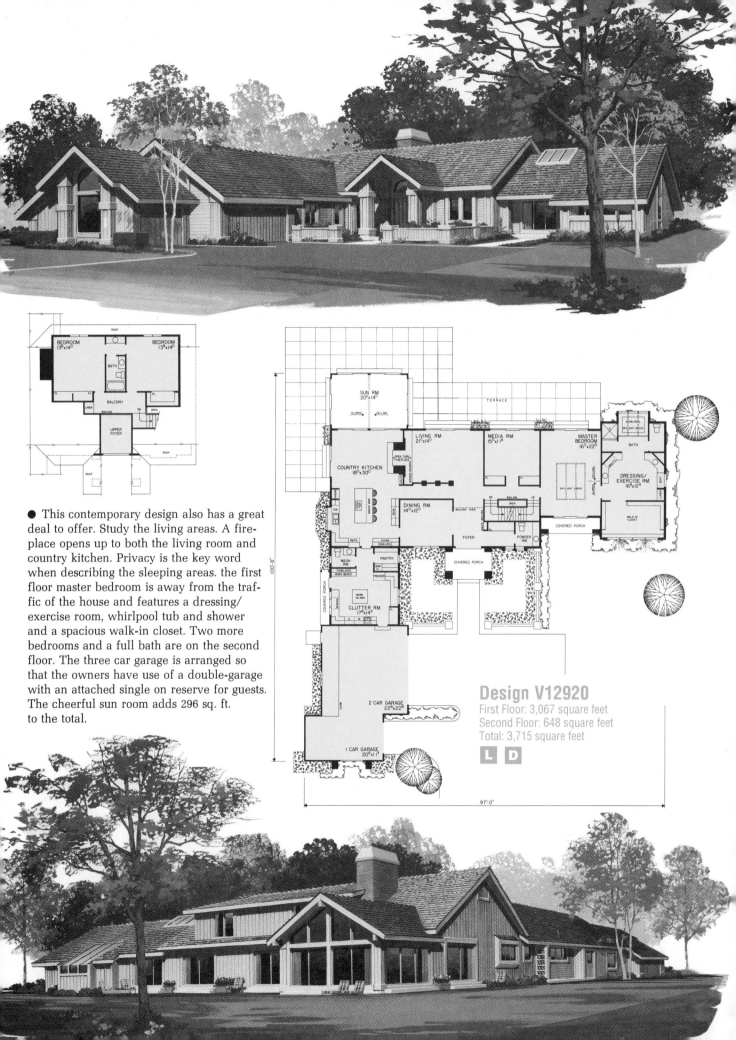

BEDROOM 13⁸x14⁰

BEDROOM 13⁸x14⁰

BATH

BALCONY

RAILING

UPPER FOYER

ROOF

● This contemporary design also has a great deal to offer. Study the living areas. A fireplace opens up to both the living room and country kitchen. Privacy is the key word when describing the sleeping areas. the first floor master bedroom is away from the traffic of the house and features a dressing/exercise room, whirlpool tub and shower and a spacious walk-in closet. Two more bedrooms and a full bath are on the second floor. The three car garage is arranged so that the owners have use of a double-garage with an attached single on reserve for guests. The cheerful sun room adds 296 sq. ft. to the total.

SUN RM. 20⁰x14⁰

SLOPED   CEILING

TERRACE

LIVING RM. 21⁰x14⁰

MEDIA RM. 15⁰x11⁸

MASTER BEDROOM 16⁸x22⁰

BATH

COUNTRY KITCHEN 18⁰x30⁰

OPEN THRU FIREPLACE

RAISED HEARTH

SNACK BAR

DINING RM. 14⁰x12⁰

BALCONY OVER

OPEN   UP

SKYLIGHT ABOVE

DRESSING/ EXERCISE RM. 16⁸x12⁴

WALK-IN CLOSET

REF.

CHINA SHELVES

FOYER

POWDER RM.

COVERED PORCH

COVERED PORCH

WASH RM.

SHELVES

WORK BENCH

PANTRY

FREEZER

COVERED PORCH

CLUTTER RM. 17⁰x14⁴

WORK ISLAND

Design V12920
First Floor: 3,067 square feet
Second Floor: 648 square feet
Total: 3,715 square feet

L   D

2 CAR GARAGE 22⁸x22⁸

1 CAR GARAGE 20⁸x11⁸

97'-0"

Design V11928
Square Footage: 3,272

● You'll find this contemporary home is worthy of your consideration if you're looking for a house of distinction. The dramatic exterior is a sure-fire stopper. Even the most casual passer-by will take a second look. In-teresting roof surfaces, massive brick chimney wall, recessed entrance, rais-ed planters and garden wall are among the features that spell design distinc-tion. And yet, the exterior is only part of the story this home has to tell. Its in-terior is no less unique. Consider the sunken living room, sloping, beamed ceiling of the family room, wonderful kitchen/laundry area, four-bedroom sleeping area with all those closets, bath facilities and sliding doors.

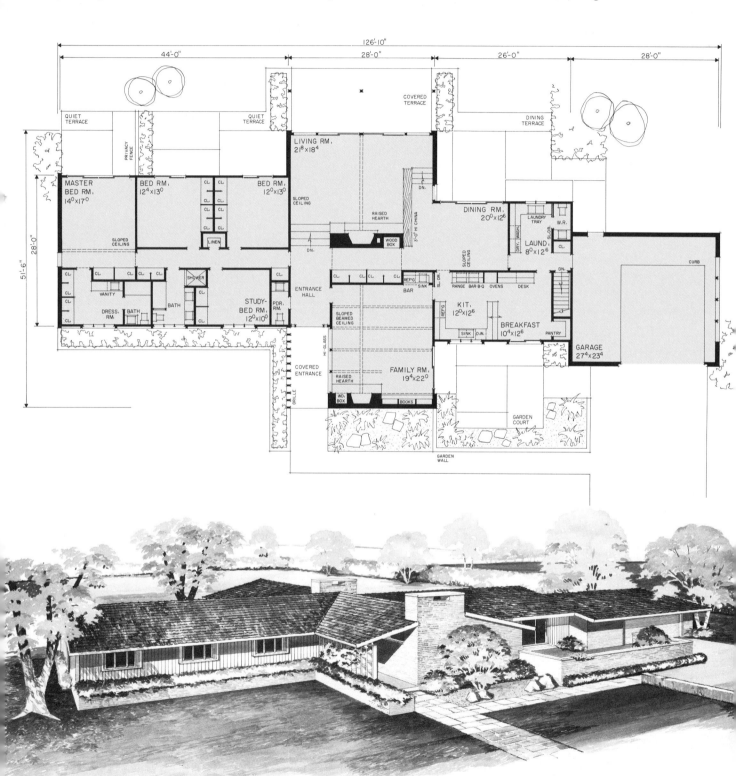

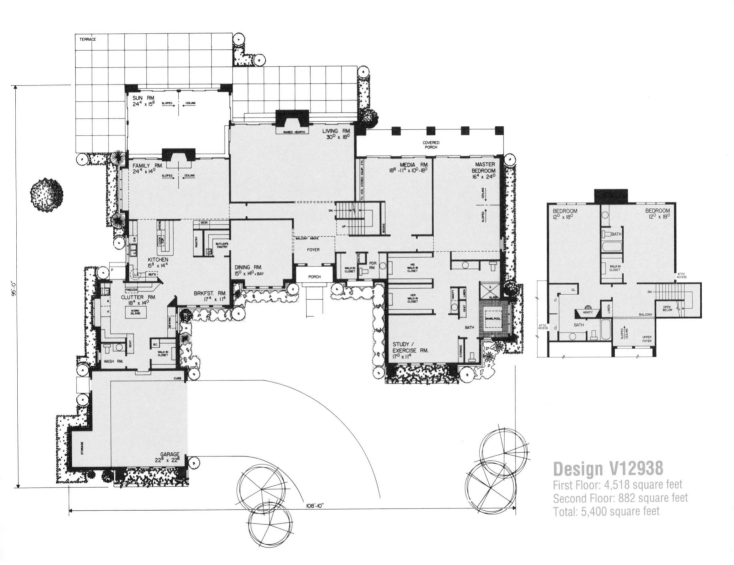

Design V12938
First Floor: 4,518 square feet
Second Floor: 882 square feet
Total: 5,400 square feet

● A semi-circular fanlight and sidelights grace the entrance of this striking contemporary. The lofty foyer, with balcony above, leads to an elegant, two-story living room with fireplace. The family room, housing a second fireplace, leads to a glorious sunroom; both have dramatic sloped ceilings.

The kitchen and breakfast room are conveniently located for access to the informal family room or to the formal dining room via the butler's pantry. The large adjoining clutter room with work island offers limitless possibilities for the seamstress, hobbyist, or indoor gardener. An executive-sized, first-

floor master suite offers privacy and relaxation; the bath with whirlpool tub and dressing area with twin walk-in closets open to a study that could double as an exercise room. Two second-floor bedrooms with private baths and walk-in closets round out the livability in this gracious home.

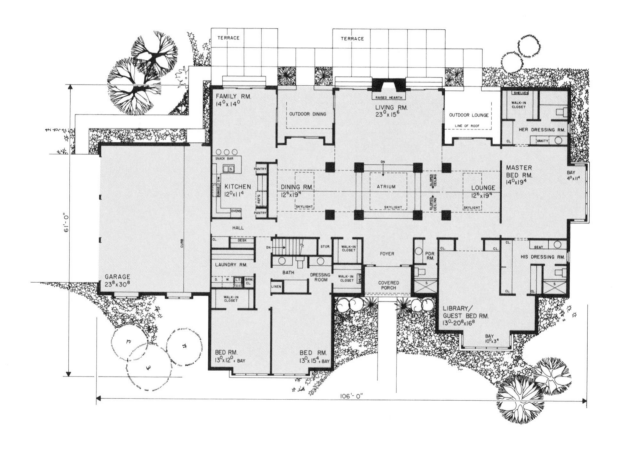

Design V12791
Square Footage: 3,809

● The use of vertical paned windows and the hipped roof highlight the exterior of this unique design. Upon entrance one will view a charming sunken atrium with skylight above plus a skylight in the dining room and one in the lounge. Formal living will be graciously accommodated in the living room. It features a raised hearth fireplace, two sets of sliding glass doors to the rear terrace plus two more sliding doors, one to an outdoor dining terrace and the other to an outdoor lounge. Informal living will be enjoyed in the family room with snack bar and in the large library. All will praise the fine planning of the master suite. It features a bay window, "his" and "her" dressing room with private baths and an abundance of closet space.

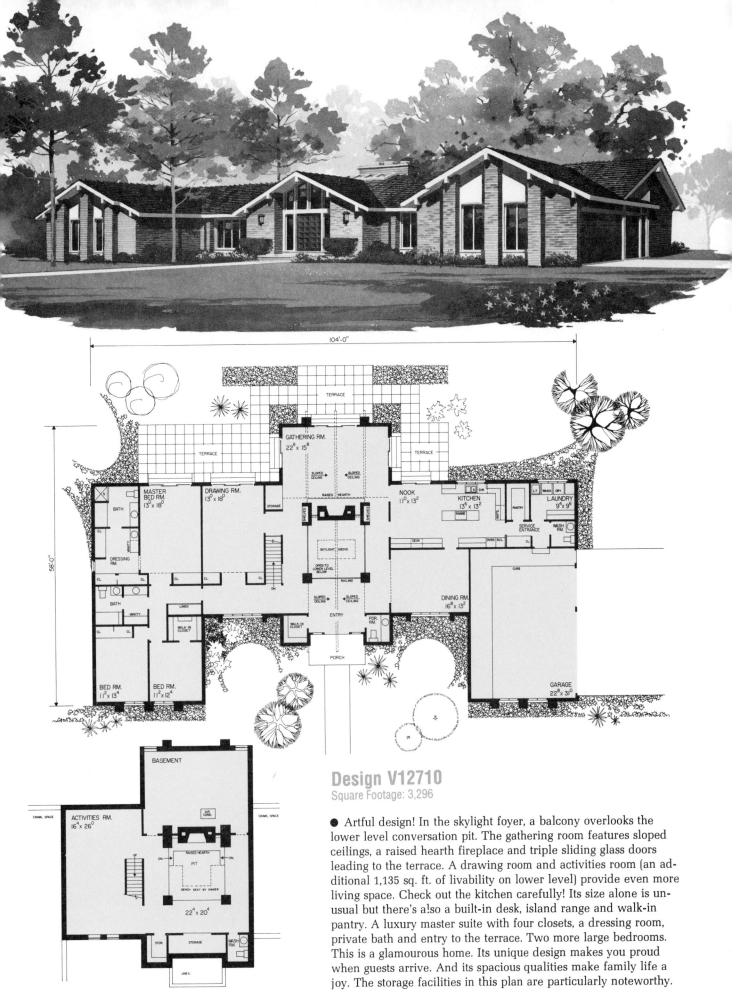

104'-0"

58'-0"

TERRACE

GATHERING RM.
22⁸ x 15⁸

TERRACE

TERRACE

SLOPED CEILING   SLOPED CEILING
RAISED HEARTH

MASTER BED RM.
13⁰ x 18⁰

DRAWING RM.
13⁰ x 18⁰

STORAGE

NOOK
11⁰ x 13²

KITCHEN
13⁶ x 13²

LAUNDRY
9⁸ x 9⁶

BATH

VANITY

SHELVES   SHELVES

RANGE

PANTRY

SERVICE ENTRANCE

WASH RM.

DRESSING RM.

CL   CL   CL   CL   CL   CL

SKYLIGHT ABOVE

DESK

OVEN B.CL

CL

OPEN TO LOWER LEVEL BELOW

DN

CURB

BATH

VANITY

LINEN

SLOPED CEILING   SLOPED CEILING

RAILING

DINING RM.
16⁸ x 13²

CL   CL

WALK-IN CLOSET

WALK-IN CLOSET

ENTRY

PDR RM.

BED RM.
11² x 13⁴

BED RM.
11² x 12⁴

PORCH

GARAGE
22⁸ x 31⁰

BASEMENT

CRAWL SPACE

ACTIVITIES RM.
16⁴ x 26⁰

CRAWL SPACE

AIR COND.

UP

DN   RAISED HEARTH   DN

PIT

BENCH SEAT BY OWNER

22⁴ x 20⁴

STOR.

STORAGE

WASH RM.

UNEX.

Design V12710
Square Footage: 3,296

● Artful design! In the skylight foyer, a balcony overlooks the lower level conversation pit. The gathering room features sloped ceilings, a raised hearth fireplace and triple sliding glass doors leading to the terrace. A drawing room and activities room (an additional 1,135 sq. ft. of livability on lower level) provide even more living space. Check out the kitchen carefully! Its size alone is unusual but there's also a built-in desk, island range and walk-in pantry. A luxury master suite with four closets, a dressing room, private bath and entry to the terrace. Two more large bedrooms. This is a glamourous home. Its unique design makes you proud when guests arrive. And its spacious qualities make family life a joy. The storage facilities in this plan are particularly noteworthy.

171

Design V12765
Square Footage: 3,365

D

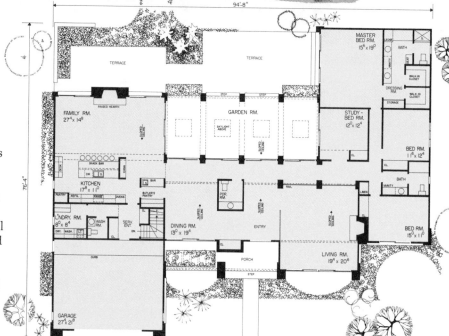

● This three (optional four) bedroom contemporary is a most appealing design. It offers living patterns that will add new dimensions to your everyday routine. The sloped ceilings in the family room, dining room and living room add much spaciousness to this home. The efficient kitchen has many fine features including the island snack bar and work center, built-in desk, china cabinet and wet bar. Adjacent to the kitchen is a laundry room, washroom and stairs to the basement. Formal and informal living will each have its own area. A raised hearth fireplace and sliding glass doors to the rear terrace in the informal family room. Another fireplace in the front formal living room. You will enjoy all that natural light in the garden room from the skylights in the sloped ceiling.

Design V12747
Square Footage: 3,211

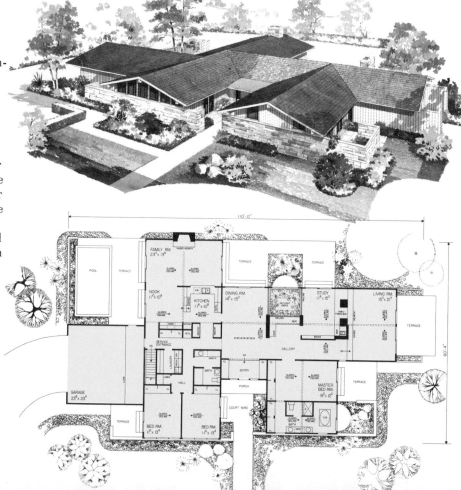

● This home will provide its occupants with a glorious adventure in contemporary living. Its impressive exterior seems to foretell that great things are in store for even the most casual visitor. A study of the plan reveals a careful zoning for both the younger and older family members. The quiet area consists of the exceptional master bedroom suite with private terrace, the study and the isolated living room. For the younger generation, there is a zone with two bedrooms, family room and nearby pool. The kitchen is handy and serves the nook and family rooms with ease. Be sure not to miss the sloping ceilings, the dramatic planter and the functional terrace.

Design V12343
Square Footage: 3,110

● If yours is a growing active family the chances are good that they will want their new home to relate to the outdoors. This distinctive design puts a premium on private outdoor living. And you don't have to install a swim- ming pool to get the most enjoyment from this home. Developing this area as a garden court will provide the in- door living areas with a breathtaking awareness of nature's beauty. Notice the fine zoning of the plan and how each area has its sliding glass doors to provide an unrestricted view. Three bedrooms plus study are serviced by three baths. The family and gathering rooms provide two great living areas. The kitchen is most efficient.

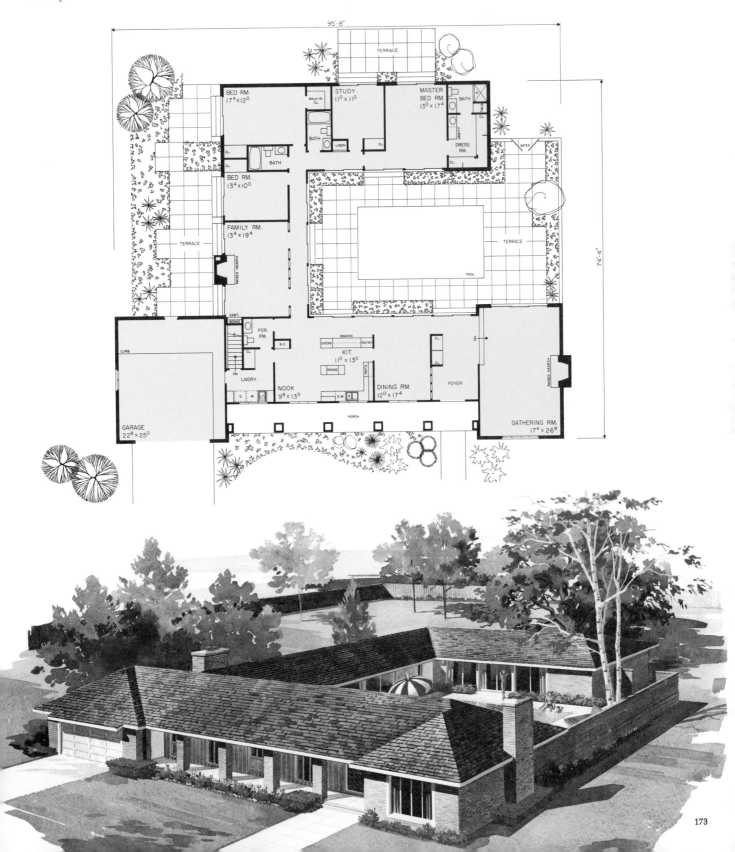

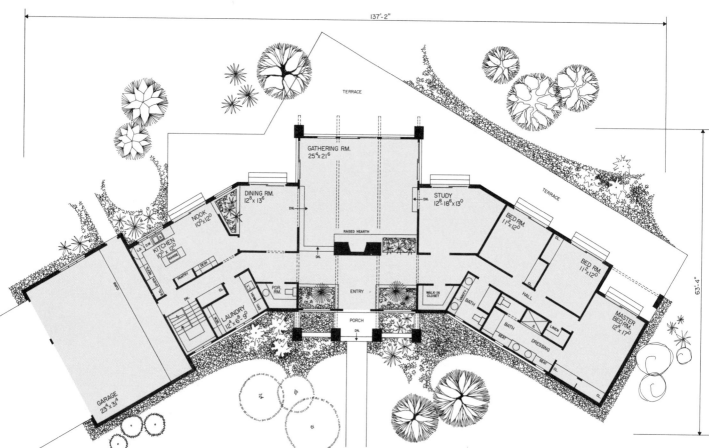

Design V12720
Square Footage: 3,130

● A raised hearth fireplace lights up the sunken gathering room which is exceptionally large and located at the very center of this home! For more living space, a well-located study and formal dining room each having a direct entrance to the gathering room. Plus a kitchen with all the right fea-

tures . . . an island range, pantry, built-in desk and separate breakfast nook. There's an extended terrace, too . . . accessible from every room! And a master suite with double closets, dressing room and private bath. Plus two family bedrooms, a first-floor laundry and lots of storage

space. A basement too, for additional space. This is a liveable home! You can entertain easily or you can hide-out with a good book. Study this plan with your family and pick out your favorite features. Don't miss the dramatic front entry planting areas, or the extra curb area in the garage.

Design V12534
Square Footage: 3,262

L

● The angular wings of this ranch home surely contribute to the unique character of the exterior. These wings effectively balance what is truly a dramatic and inviting front entrance. Massive masonry walls support the wide overhanging roof with its exposed wood beams. The patterned double front doors are surrounded by delightful expanses of glass. The raised planters and the masses of quarried stone (make it brick if you prefer) enhance the exterior appeal. Inside, a distinctive and practical floor plan stands ready to shape and serve the living patterns of the active family. The spacious entrance hall highlights sloped ceiling and an attractive open stairway to the lower level recreation area. An impressive fireplace and an abundance of glass are features of the big gathering room. Interestingly shaped dining room and study flank this main living area. The large kitchen offers many of the charming aspects of the family-kitchen of yesteryear. The bedroom wing has a sunken master suite.

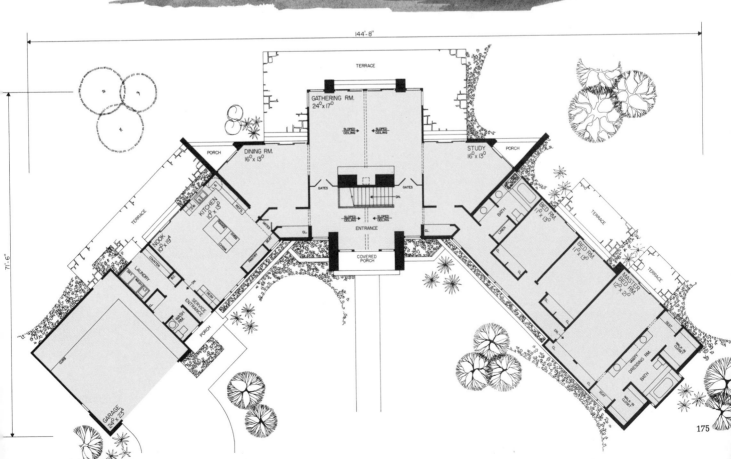

175

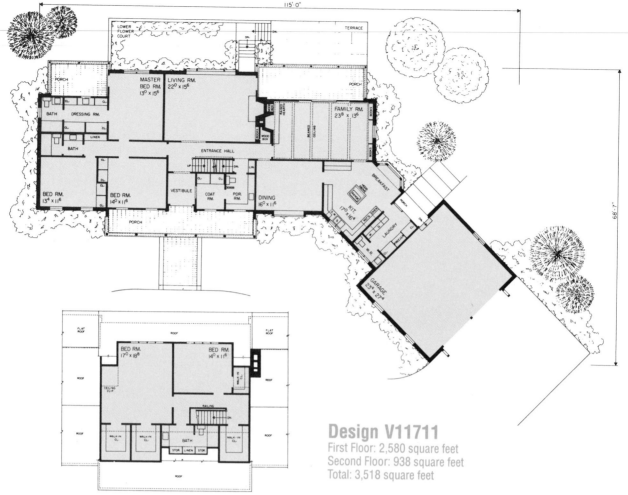

Design V11711
First Floor: 2,580 square feet
Second Floor: 938 square feet
Total: 3,518 square feet

● If the gracious charm of the Colonial South appeals to you, this may be just the house you've been waiting for. There is something solid and dependable in its well-balanced facade and wide, pillared front porch. Much of the interest generated by this design comes from its interesting expanses of roof and angular projection of its kitchen and garage. The feeling of elegance is further experienced upon stepping inside, through double doors, to the spacious entrance hall where there is the separate coat room. Adjacent to this is the powder room, also convenient to the living areas. The work area of the kitchen and laundry room is truly outstanding. Designed as a five bedroom house, each is large. Storage and bath facilities are excellent.

TRADITIONAL DESIGNS UNDER 1500 Sq. Ft. . . .

as featured in the following pages, capture the warmth and charm of an early period in our history. Here we see appealing examples of the one-story house reflecting the beauty that results from effective and prudent use of early American design features. These include, double-hung, muntined windows, panelled doors with sidelights, shutters, cupolas, flower boxes, carriage lamps, wood siding with corner boards, covered front entrances, etc. And above all, pleasing proportion is a prime requisite for achieving that delightful exterior appeal that assures a lasting value for, perhaps, life's biggest single investment. Here are houses for the modest budget.

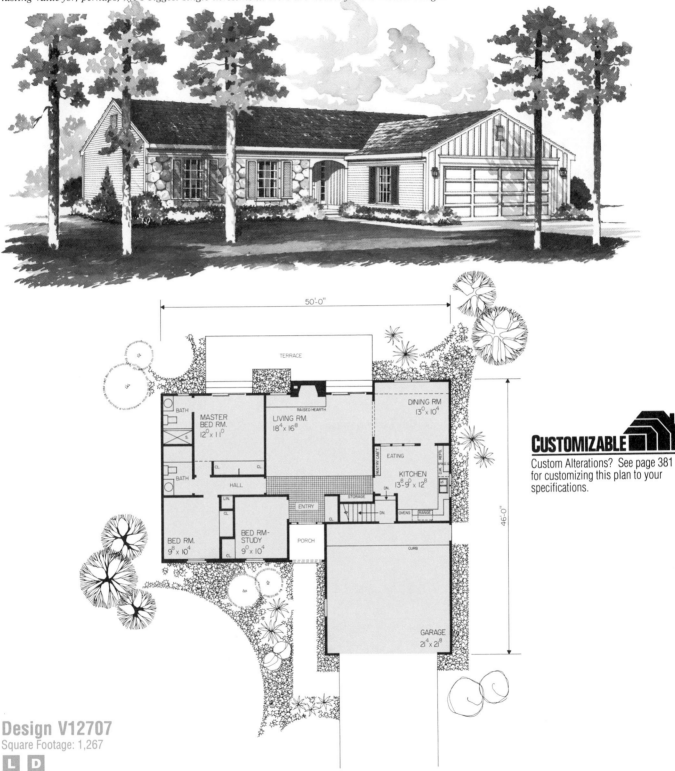

CUSTOMIZABLE
Custom Alterations? See page 381 for customizing this plan to your specifications.

Design V12707
Square Footage: 1,267

L **D**

● Here is a charming Early American adaptation that will serve as a picturesque and practical retirement home. Also, it will serve admirably those with a small family in search of an efficient, economically built home. The living area, highlighted by the raised hearth fireplace, is spacious. The kitchen features eating space and easy access to the garage and basement. The dining room is adjacent to the kitchen and views the rear yard. Then, there is the basement for recreation and hobby pursuits. The bedroom wing offers three bedrooms and two full baths. Don't miss the sliding doors to the terrace from the living room and the master bedroom. Storage units are plentiful including a pantry cabinet in the eating area of the kitchen. This plan will be efficient and livable.

Design V13355
Square Footage: 1,387

● Though it's only just under 1,400 total square feet, this plan offers three bedrooms (or two with study) and a sizable gathering room with fireplace and sloped ceiling. The galley kitchen provides a pass-through snack bar and has a planning desk and attached breakfast room. Besides two smaller bedrooms with a full bath, there's an extravagant master suite with large dressing area, double vanity and raised whirlpool tub.

CUSTOMIZABLE
Custom Alterations? See page 381 for customizing this plan to your specifications.

Design V11193
Square Footage: 1,396

● This L-shaped, one-story with its attached two-car garage incorporates many of the time-tested features of older New England. The attractive cut-up windows, the shutters, the panelled door, the fence and the wood siding contribute to the charm of the exterior. The floor plan is outstanding by virtue of such proven features as the separate dining room, the family-kitchen, the quiet living room with its bay window and the privacy of the bedroom area. The U-shaped work center will be easy to work in.

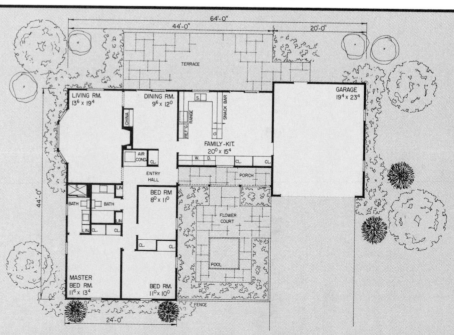

Design V11327
Square Footage: 1,392

OPTIONAL BASEMENT PLAN

● A design to overcome the restrictions of a relatively narrow building site. This home has one of the best one-story plans you'll ever see. Its four bedrooms and two baths form what amounts to a separate wing. The fourth bedroom is located next to the living room so it may serve as a study, if needed. The traffic plan pivoting in the front entry, is excellent. And the kitchen is in just the right place - next to the dining and family rooms, close to the front and side doors and near the laundry. Another fine quality of the kitchen is its snack bar pass-thru to the family room. Formal living will take place in the rear living/dining room. This area can open up to the rear terrace by two sets of sliding glass doors (another set is in the family room). An optional basement plan is included with the purchase of this design.

Design V11316
Square Footage: 1,488

● As picturesque as they come. Within 1,488 square feet, there are the fine sleeping facilities, two full baths, family room, a formal dining area, a big living room, an excellent kitchen and plenty of closets. Other noteworthy features include the fire-place, sliding glass doors to the rear terrace, a fine basement, a pass-thru to family room from kitchen, an attached garage and an appealing front porch.

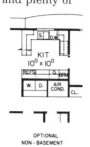

OPTIONAL
NON - BASEMENT

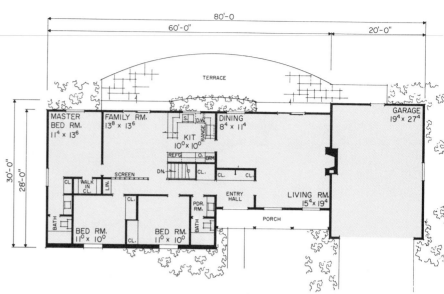

Design V11939
Square Footage: 1,387

L **D**

● A finely proportioned house with more than its full share of charm. The brick ve-neer exterior contrasts pleasingly with the narrow horizontal siding of the oversized attached two-car garage. Perhaps the focal point of the exterior is the recessed front entrance with its double Colonial styled doors. The secondary service entrance through the garage to the kitchen area is a handy feature. Study the plan. It features three bedrooms, two full baths, living room with fireplace, front kitchen with an eating area, formal dining room, plenty of storage potential plus a basement for ad-ditional storage or perhaps to be devel-oped as a recreational area.

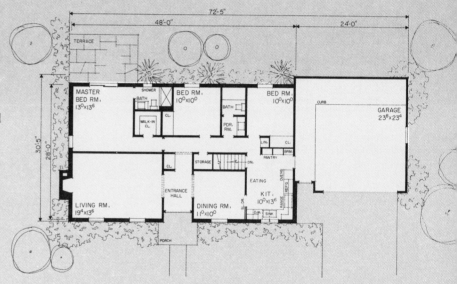

Design V11190
Square Footage: 1,232

● Build this L-shaped house on your lot with the garage door facing the street, or with the front entry door facing the street. Whichever orientation you choose, and you should take into consideration lot re-striction and any particular view you might want to enjoy from the living areas, you will find the floor plan a very fine one. The center entrance hall features twin coat closets, a slate floor and an at-tractive six foot high room divider. This built-in unit has a planter on top with storage space below which is accessible from the living room.

Design V11107
Square Footage: 1,416

L **D**

● A smart looking traditional adaptation which, because of its perfectly rectangular shape, will be most economical to build. The low-pitched roof has a wide overhang which accentuates its low-slung qualities. The attached two-car garage is oversized to permit the location of extra bulk storage space. Further, its access to the house is through the handy separate laundry area. This house will function as either a four bedroom home, or as one that has three bedrooms, plus a quiet study. Features include a fireplace in the living room, built-in china cabinet in the breakfast room, sizable vanity in the main baths and more.

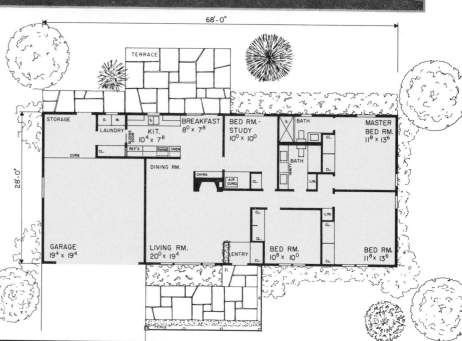

Design V11803
Square Footage: 1,434

● The texture of brick enhances the beauty of this pleasing traditional home. The center entrance with its double doors is protected by the covered porch. The end living room will be free of annoying cross-room traffic. A centered fireplace wall with end book shelves is an outstanding feature of this area. The separate dining room is ideally located between the living room and kitchen which allows for its maximum use.

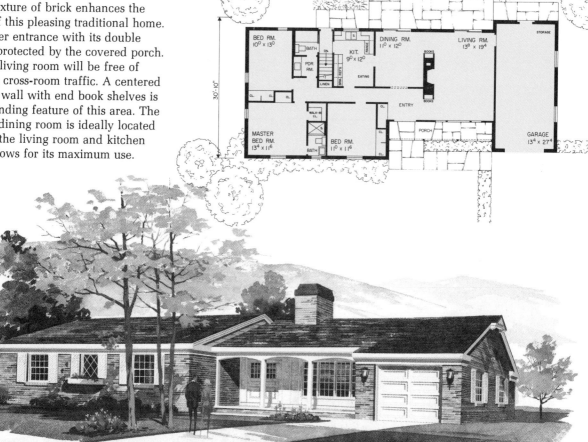

Design V11374
Square Footage: 1,248

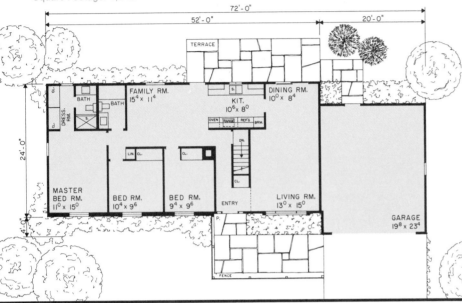

● A low-pitched, overhanging roof that hugs the ground and gives an impression that belies the actual dimensions of the home is a feature of this design. Board and batten siding, stone veneer, muntined windows and paneled shutters are all earmarks of Early American styling. Planning is open and pleasant; the living area leads to the dining space and through sliding glass doors to the outdoor terrace; the in-line kitchen leads to the all-purpose family room.

OPTIONAL NO BASEMENT PLAN

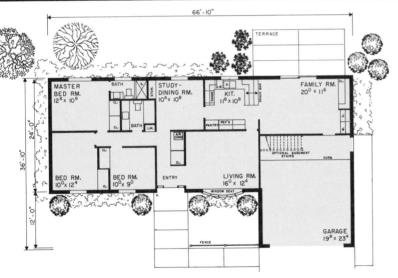

Design V11367
Square Footage: 1,432

● Brick veneer, a projecting two-car garage with a gabled end, wood shutters, attractive window treatment, paneled front door and a wood fence with lamp post are among the features that make the exterior of this traditional house so charming. The formal living room with all that blank wall space for effective furniture placement, is just the right size for quiet conversation. The family room will be the hub of the informal activities with a snack bar and pass-thru to the kitchen. Adjacent to the kitchen is a room which may function as a study, sewing room, TV room or formal dining room. Note the two full baths and stall shower.

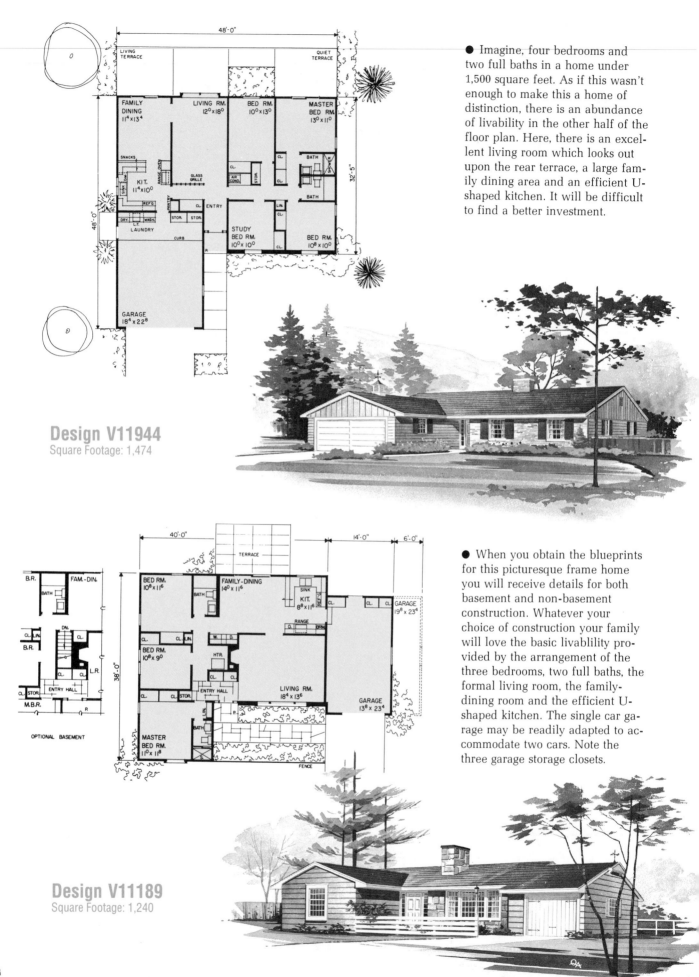

Design V11944
Square Footage: 1,474

● Imagine, four bedrooms and two full baths in a home under 1,500 square feet. As if this wasn't enough to make this a home of distinction, there is an abundance of livability in the other half of the floor plan. Here, there is an excellent living room which looks out upon the rear terrace, a large family dining area and an efficient U-shaped kitchen. It will be difficult to find a better investment.

Design V11189
Square Footage: 1,240

● When you obtain the blueprints for this picturesque frame home you will receive details for both basement and non-basement construction. Whatever your choice of construction your family will love the basic livablility provided by the arrangement of the three bedrooms, two full baths, the formal living room, the family-dining room and the efficient U-shaped kitchen. The single car garage may be readily adapted to accommodate two cars. Note the three garage storage closets.

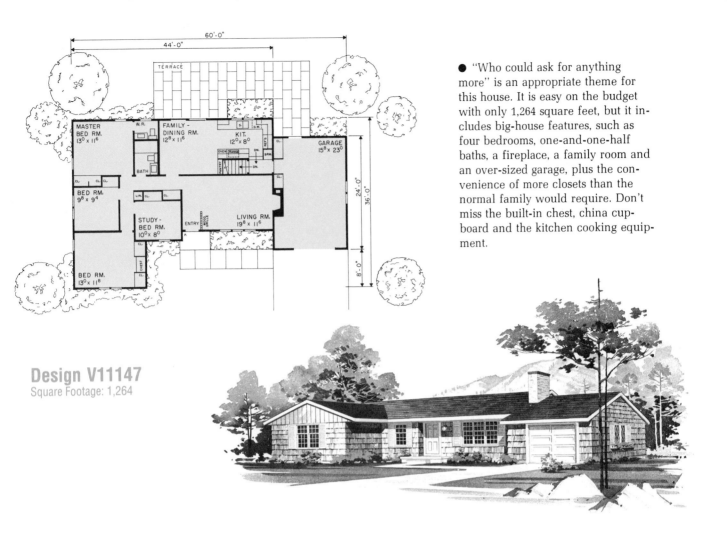

Design V11147
Square Footage: 1,264

● "Who could ask for anything more" is an appropriate theme for this house. It is easy on the budget with only 1,264 square feet, but it includes big-house features, such as four bedrooms, one-and-one-half baths, a fireplace, a family room and an over-sized garage, plus the convenience of more closets than the normal family would require. Don't miss the built-in chest, china cupboard and the kitchen cooking equipment.

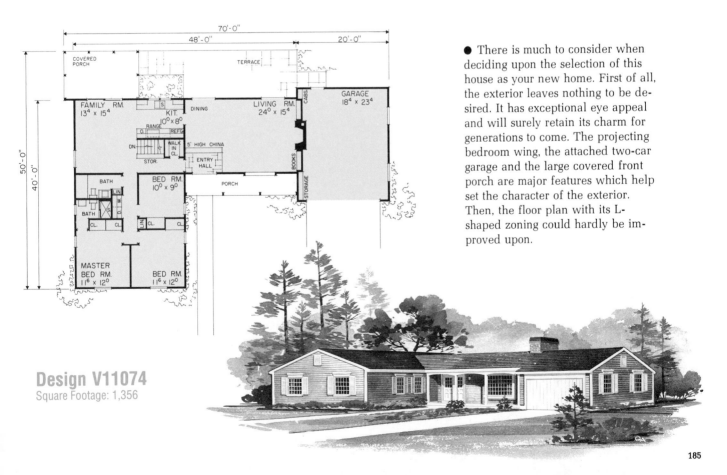

Design V11074
Square Footage: 1,356

● There is much to consider when deciding upon the selection of this house as your new home. First of all, the exterior leaves nothing to be desired. It has exceptional eye appeal and will surely retain its charm for generations to come. The projecting bedroom wing, the attached two-car garage and the large covered front porch are major features which help set the character of the exterior. Then, the floor plan with its L-shaped zoning could hardly be improved upon.

Design V13211
Square Footage: 1,344

● This is a captivating version of the three bedroom, two-bath L-shaped home. Notice that spacious living-dining area with the many windows to the side plus a view of the rear terrace from the dining room. The living room also has a fireplace for added appeal. The breakfast room also will enjoy the rear terrace and includes such features as a pantry, china cabinet and storage closet. The kitchen is an efficient work center with nearby adjacent basement stairs. The basement could be developed into an informal recreation area.

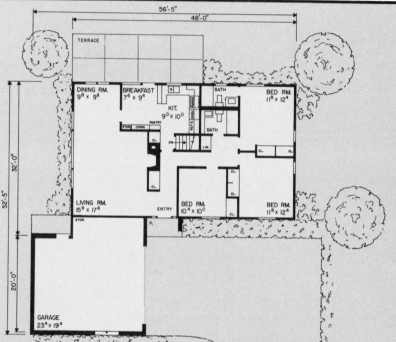

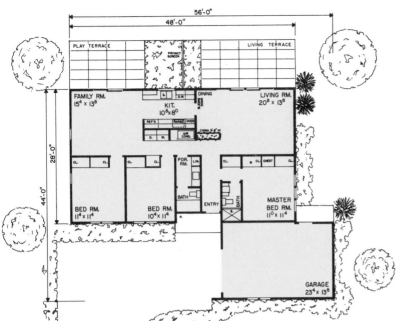

Design V11188
Square Footage: 1,326

● A charming, traditionally styled, L-shaped home which can be built most economically. Constructed on a concrete slab, the house itself forms a perfect rectangle, thus assuring the most efficient use of materials. The center entrance routes traffic to the various areas of this plan most conveniently. Compact, yet spacious. The three bedrooms are sizable and enjoy their privacy. The entire breadth of the rear experiences the delightful feeling of openness.

Design V12122
Square Footage: 1,248

● An ideal home for a family of modest size with a modest budget. This charming frame house can be built most economically. The main portion of the house is a perfect 52 x 24 foot rectangle. The projecting two-car garage with its cupola and traditionally sloped roof, adds immeasurably to the exterior appeal. The double front doors are sheltered by the covered porch. Inside, there is a wealth of livability. Two full baths, located back-to-back for plumbing economy, service the three bedrooms.

OPTIONAL BASEMENT PLAN

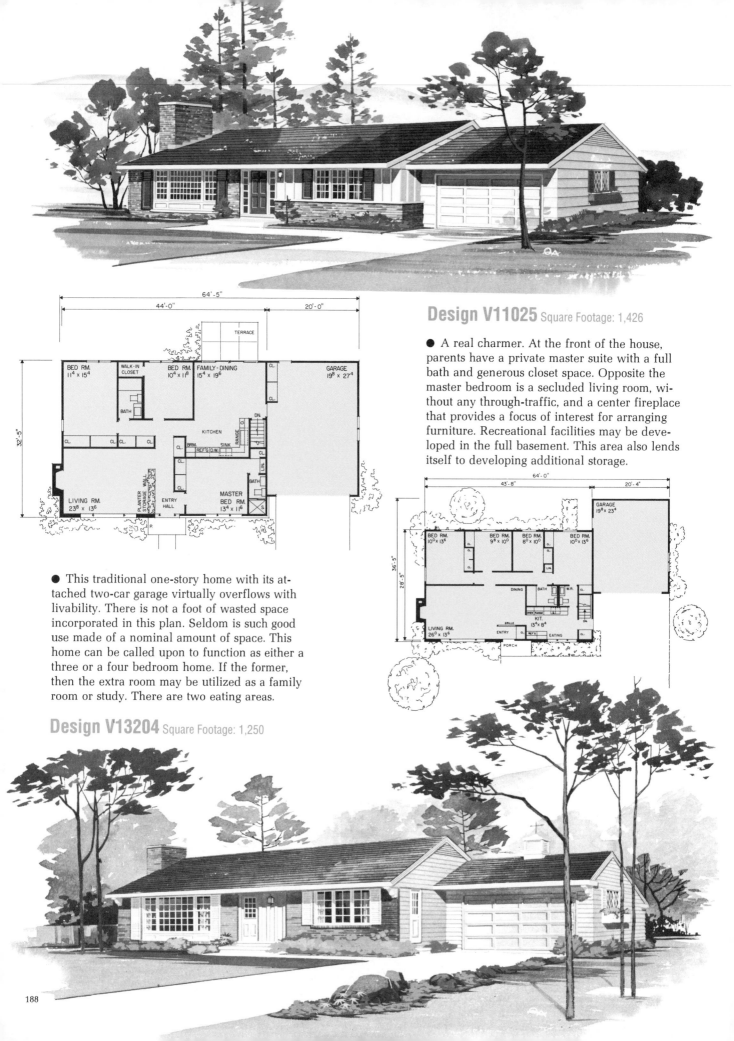

Design V11025 Square Footage: 1,426

● A real charmer. At the front of the house, parents have a private master suite with a full bath and generous closet space. Opposite the master bedroom is a secluded living room, without any through-traffic, and a center fireplace that provides a focus of interest for arranging furniture. Recreational facilities may be developed in the full basement. This area also lends itself to developing additional storage.

● This traditional one-story home with its attached two-car garage virtually overflows with livability. There is not a foot of wasted space incorporated in this plan. Seldom is such good use made of a nominal amount of space. This home can be called upon to function as either a three or a four bedroom home. If the former, then the extra room may be utilized as a family room or study. There are two eating areas.

Design V13204 Square Footage: 1,250

Design V11024
Square Footage: 1,252

● "Charming", is but one of the many words that could be chosen to describe this traditional home. While essentially a frame house, the front exterior features natural quarried stone. Below the overhanging roof, the windows and door treatment is most pleasing. The board fence with its lamp post completes a delightful picture. Highlighting the interior is the living room with its raised hearth fireplace.

● With the kitchen in this strategic location, the homemaker does not have to go through half of the house in order to get to the front door. The second bath with its stall shower is convenient to the third bedroom, the family area and the outdoor terrace. The main bath has a delightful built-in vanity. And how about the living room which has a large picture window and an attractive fireplace? Note storage closet.

Design V11197
Square Footage: 1,232

Design V11075

Square Footage: 1,232

L D

● This picturesque traditional one-story home has much to offer the young family. Because of its rectangular shape and its predominantly frame exterior, construction costs will be economical. Passing through the front entrance, visitors will be surprised to find so much livability in only 1,232 square feet. Consider these features: spacious formal living and dining area; two full baths; efficient kitchen; and large, rear family room. In addition there is the full basement for further recreational facilities and bulk storage. The attached garage is extra long to accommodate the storage of garden equipment, lawn furniture, bicycles, etc.

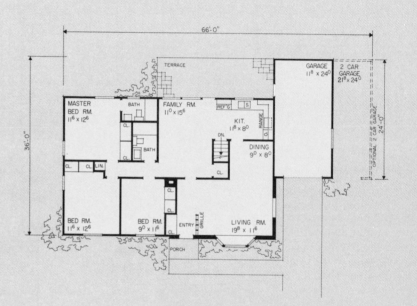

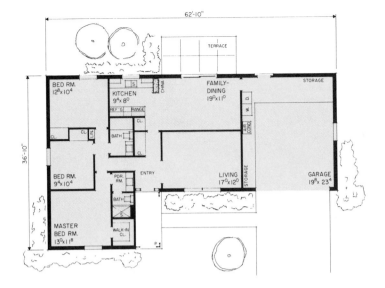

Design V11366
Square Footage: 1,280

● The extension of the main roof, along with the use of ornamental iron, vertical siding and glass side lites flanking the paneled door, all contribute to a delightful and inviting front entrance to this L-shaped design. There is much to recommend this design—from the attached two-car garage to the walk-in closet of the master bedroom. Don't overlook the compartmented master bath with its stall shower and powder room; the built-in china cabinet with an attractive planter above or the two closets right in the center of the house.

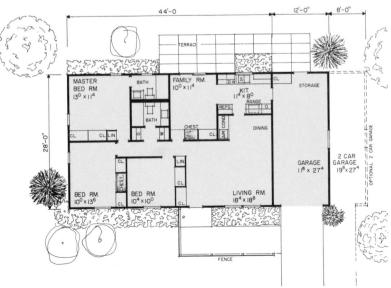

Design V11191
Square Footage: 1,232

L D

● A careful study of the floor plan for this cozy appearing traditional home reveals a fine combination of features which add tremendously to convenient living. For instance, observe the wardrobe and storage facilities of the bedroom area. A built-in chest in the one bedroom and also one in the family room. Then, notice the economical plumbing of the two full back-to-back baths. Positively a great money saving feature for today and in the future. Further, don't overlook the location of the washer and dryer which have cupboards above the units themselves. Observe storage facilities. Optional two-car garage is available if necessary.

191

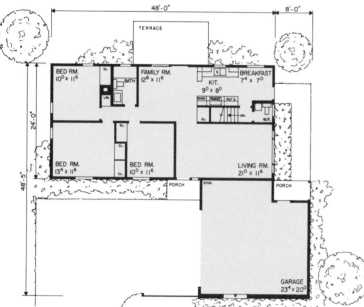

Design V13208
Square Footage: 1,152

● This appealing traditional, L-shaped home has much to offer those in search of a moderately sized home which can be built within the confines of a relatively small budget. First of all, consider the charm of the exterior. Surely this will be one of the most appealing houses on the street. And little wonder. Its proportion and architectural detailing are excellent. The shutters, the window treatment, the roof lines, the planter and the fence and lamp post are all captivating features.

Design V11373
Square Footage: 1,200

D

● A traditional L-shaped home with an attractive recessed front entrance which leads into a floor plan where traffic patterns are most efficient. It is possible to go from one room to any other without needlessly walking through a third room. The daily household chores will be easily dispatched. The U-shaped kitchen has an abundance of cupboard and counter space, plus a pass-thru to the snack bar in the family room. The washer and dryer location is handy.

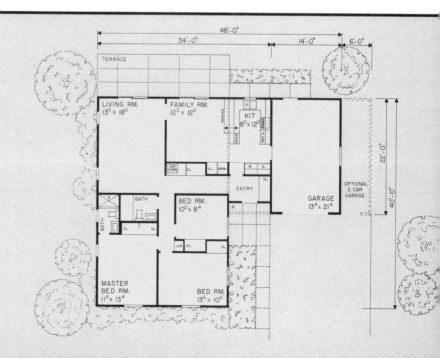

Design V11058
Square Footage: 1,200

● When you build this charming L-shaped traditionally designed home don't leave out the wood fence and lamp post. These are just the features needed to complete the picture. A porch shelters the front door which leads to the centered entry flanked by the formal living room and the informal family room. The kitchen is but a step from the separate dining room. The laundry equipment, the extra wash room and heater location are all grouped together.

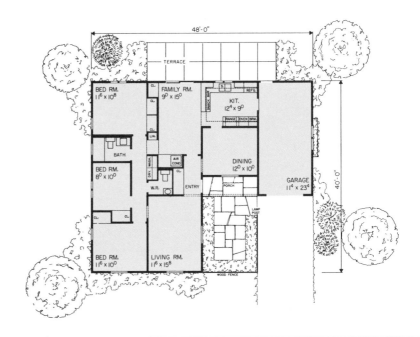

Design V12570
Square Footage: 1,176

L **D**

● This attractive Tudor offers a study which could double ideally as a guest room, sewing room or even serve as the TV room. The living area is a spacious L-shaped zone for formal living and dining. The efficient kitchen is handy to the front door and overlooks the front yard. It features a convenient breakfast nook for those informal meals. Handy to the entry from the garage and the yard are the stairs to the basement. Don't overlook the attractive front porch.

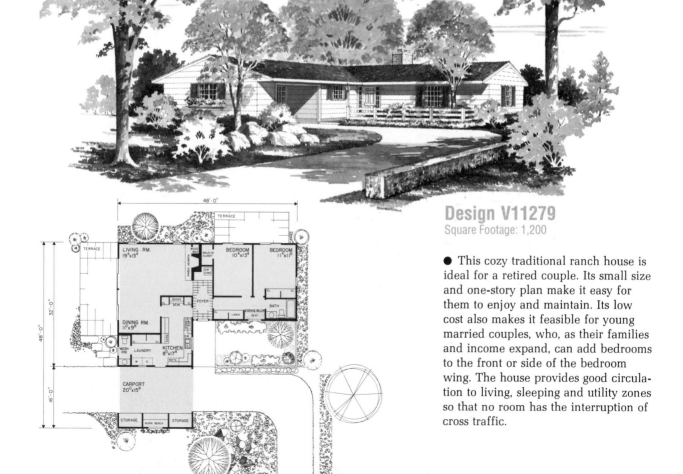

Design V11279
Square Footage: 1,200

● This cozy traditional ranch house is ideal for a retired couple. Its small size and one-story plan make it easy for them to enjoy and maintain. Its low cost also makes it feasible for young married couples, who, as their families and income expand, can add bedrooms to the front or side of the bedroom wing. The house provides good circulation to living, sleeping and utility zones so that no room has the interruption of cross traffic.

Design V12607
Square Footage: 1,208

L **D**

● Here is an English Tudor retirement cottage with two sizable bedrooms, a full bath, plus an extra wash room. The living and dining areas are spacious and overlook both front and rear yards. Sliding glass doors in both these areas lead to the outdoor terrace. Note the fireplace in the living room. In addition to the formal dining area with its built-in china cabinet, there is a delightful breakfast eating alcove in the kitchen. The U-shaped work area is wonderfully efficient. The laundry is around the corner. Blueprints include optional basement details.

OPTIONAL BASEMENT

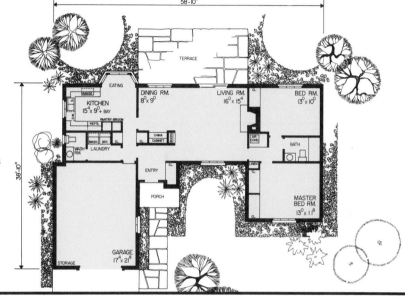

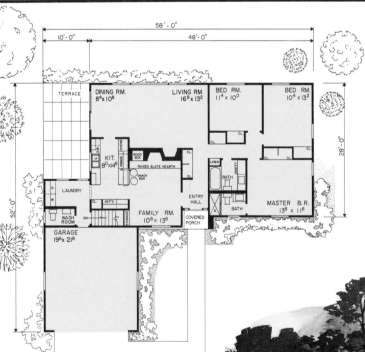

● Picturesque and practical are two words to aptly describe the merits of this fine L-shaped traditional home. The delightful proportion and the appealing details help create the charming image. The floor plan is a particularly well-planned one. In less than 1,500 square feet there are three bedrooms, 2½ baths, a family room, a 25 foot formal living and dining area, a strategically located kitchen, a first floor laundry and a basement. Other noteworthy features include the two fireplaces, the wood box, sliding glass doors to side terrace and excellent storage facilities throughout.

Design V11094
Square Footage: 1,484

Design V11297
Square Footage: 1,034

● The U-shape of this appealing home qualifies it for a narrow building site. The efficiency of the floor plan recommends it for convenient living during the retirement years. The charm of the exterior surely makes it a prize-winner. The attractive wood fence and its lamp post complete the enclosure of the flower court—a delightful setting for the walk to the covered front entrance. The work area is outstanding. There is the laundry with closet space, an extra wash room and a fine kitchen with eating space.

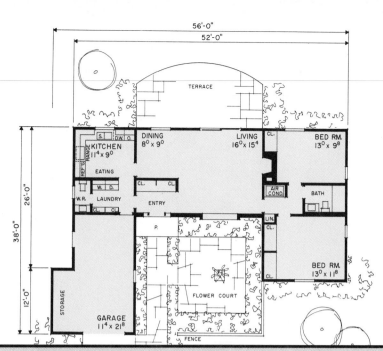

Design V11309
Square Footage: 1,100

● Here is a real low-cost charmer. Delightful proportion and an effective use of materials characterize this Colonial version. Vertical boards and battens, a touch of stone and pleasing window treatment catch the eye. The compact, economical plan offers spacious formal living and dining areas plus a family room. The kitchen is strategically located—it overlooks the rear yard and is but a few steps from the outdoor terrace. The attached garage has a large storage and utility area to the rear.

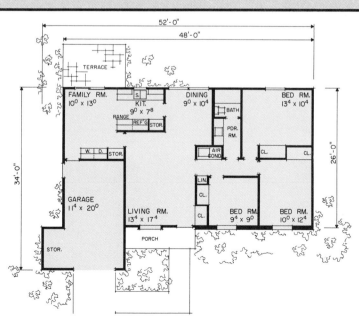

Design V11364
Square Footage: 1,142

D

● The family working within the confines of a restricted building budget will find this eye-catching traditional ranch home the solution to its housing needs. The brick exterior with its recessed front entrance, wood shutters, bowed window, attached garage and wood fence is charming, indeed. The living room is free of cross-room traffic and lends itself to effective and flexible furniture placement. The master bedroom has its own private bath with stall shower, while the main bath features a built-in vanity and adjacent linen storage.

Design V13213
Square Footage: 1,060

● It would be difficult to find a design with more livability built into its 1,060 square feet. There are features galore. Make a list.

Design V11399
Square Footage: 1,040

● A real winner which will surely satisfy the restricted building budget, while returning a tremendous amount in the way of convenient living and pride of ownership.

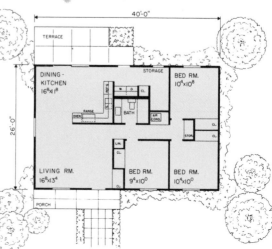

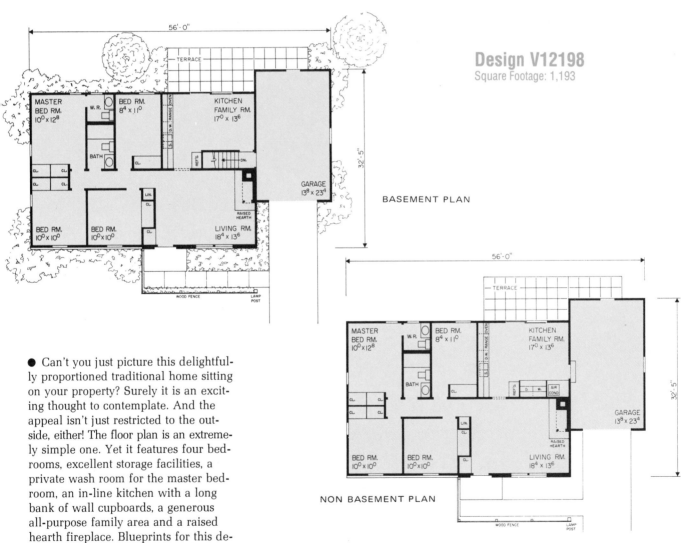

Design V12198
Square Footage: 1,193

BASEMENT PLAN

56'-0"

32'-5"

TERRACE

MASTER BED RM. 10⁰ x 12⁸

W. R.

BED RM. 8⁴ x 11⁰

BATH

CL. CL. CL. CL.

KITCHEN FAMILY RM. 17⁰ x 13⁶

S.I. D.W. RANGE OVEN

REF'G. DN.

CL.

LIN. CL.

CL.

BED RM. 10⁰ x 10⁰

BED RM. 10⁰ x 10⁰

LIVING RM. 18⁴ x 13⁶

RAISED HEARTH

GARAGE 13⁸ x 23⁴

WOOD FENCE

LAMP POST

NON BASEMENT PLAN

56'-0"

32'-5"

TERRACE

MASTER BED RM. 10⁰ x 12⁸

W. R.

BED RM. 8⁴ x 11⁰

BATH

CL. CL. CL. CL.

KITCHEN FAMILY RM. 17⁰ x 13⁶

S.I. D.W. RANGE OVEN

REF'G. D. W. AIR COND.

CL.

LIN. CL.

CL.

BED RM. 10⁰ x 10⁰

BED RM. 10⁰ x 10⁰

LIVING RM. 18⁴ x 13⁶

RAISED HEARTH

GARAGE 13⁸ x 23⁴

WOOD FENCE

LAMP POST

● Can't you just picture this delightfully proportioned traditional home sitting on your property? Surely it is an exciting thought to contemplate. And the appeal isn't just restricted to the outside, either! The floor plan is an extremely simple one. Yet it features four bedrooms, excellent storage facilities, a private wash room for the master bedroom, an in-line kitchen with a long bank of wall cupboards, a generous all-purpose family area and a raised hearth fireplace. Blueprints for this design include both basement and nonbasement details for construction.

Design V11311 Square Footage: 1,050

L D

● Delightful design and effective, flexible planning comes in little packages, too. This fine traditional exterior with its covered front entrance features an alternate basement plan. Note how the non-basement layout provides a family room and mud room, while the basement option shows kitchen eating and dining room. Sensible planning.

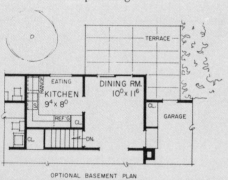

OPTIONAL BASEMENT PLAN

TERRACE

KITCHEN
9⁰ x 8⁰

EATING

RANGE

DINING RM.
10⁰ x 11⁶

REF'G

CL.

DN.

CL.

GARAGE

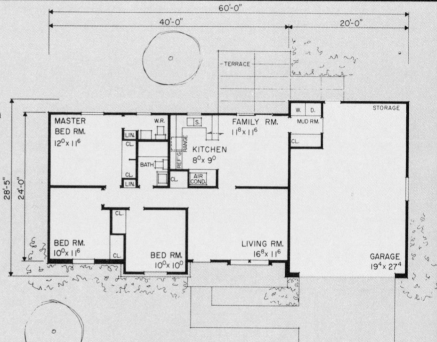

60'-0"

40'-0"

20'-0"

TERRACE

28'-5"

24'-0"

MASTER
BED RM.
12⁰ x 11⁶

LIN.
CL.

W.R.

CL.
LIN.

BATH

REF'G
RANGE

S.

KITCHEN
8⁰ x 9⁰

AIR COND.

FAMILY RM.
11⁸ x 11⁶

W. D.

MUD RM.

STORAGE

CL.

BED RM.
10⁰ x 11⁶

CL.

CL.

BED RM.
10⁰ x 10⁰

LIVING RM.
16⁸ x 11⁶

GARAGE
19⁴ x 27⁴

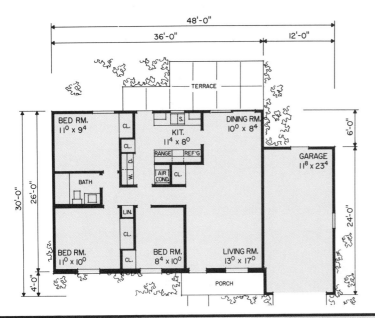

Design V11531
Square Footage: 936

● This is but another example of delightful custom design applied to a small home. The detailing of the windows and the door, plus the effective use of siding and brick contribute to the charm. The attached garage helps make the house appear even bigger than it really is. The front-to-rear living/dining area opens onto the rear terrace through sliding glass doors. The washer and dryer with wall cabinets above complete the efficient work center area. Observe the extra kitchen closet.

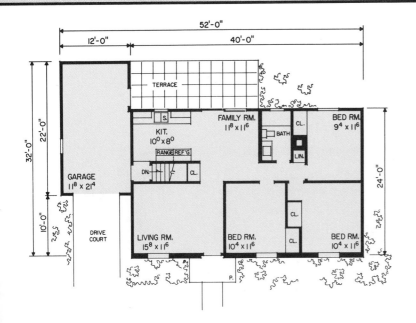

Design V11522
Square Footage: 960

● Certainly a home to make its occupants proud. The front exterior is all brick veneer, while the remainder of the house and garage is horizontal siding. The slightly overhanging roof, the wood shutters and the carriage lights flanking the front door are among the features that will surely catch the eyes of the passerby. The living room has excellent wall space for furniture placement. The family room, the full basement and the attached garage are other features. Don't miss the sliding glass doors.

Design V12153
Square Footage: 960

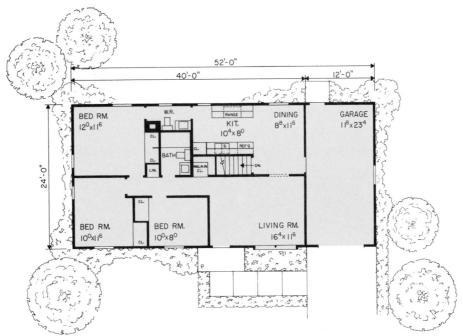

● If you can't make up your mind as to which of the delightful traditional exteriors you like best on the opposing page, you need not decide now. The blueprints you receive show details for the construction of all three front exteriors. However, before you order, decide whether you wish your next home to have a basement or not. If you prefer the basement plan order Design V12153 above. Should your preference be for a non-basement plan you should order blueprints for Design V12154 below. Whatever your choice, you'll forever love the charm of its exterior and the comfort and convenience of the interior. The three bedrooms will serve your family ideally.

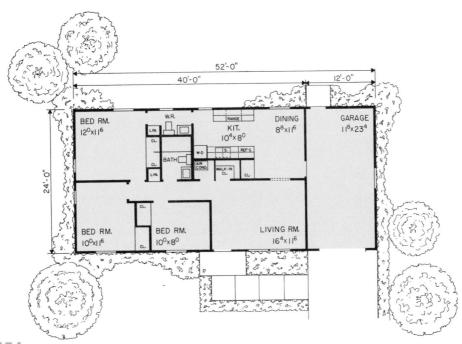

Design V12154
Square Footage: 960

203

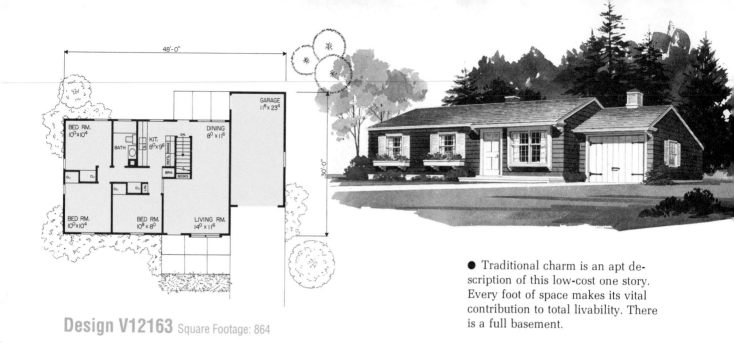

Design V12163 Square Footage: 864

● Traditional charm is an apt description of this low-cost one story. Every foot of space makes its vital contribution to total livability. There is a full basement.

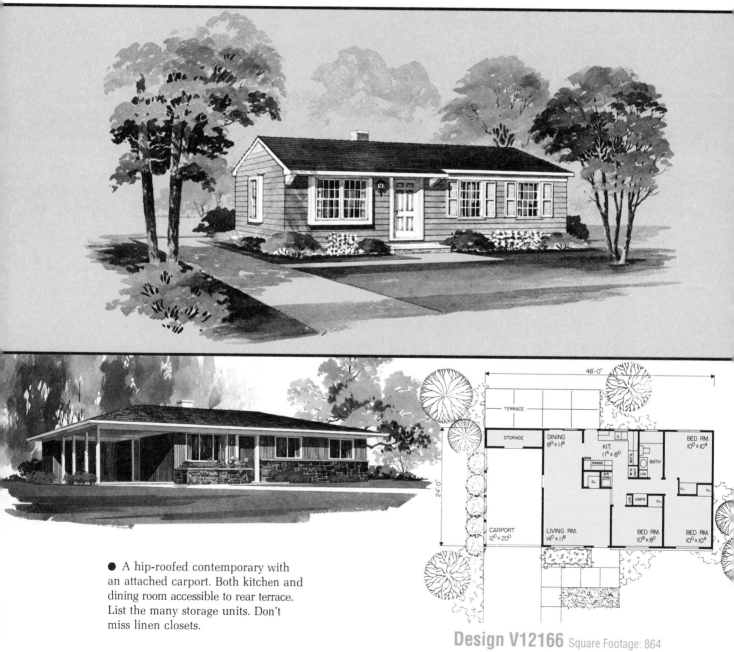

● A hip-roofed contemporary with an attached carport. Both kitchen and dining room accessible to rear terrace. List the many storage units. Don't miss linen closets.

Design V12166 Square Footage: 864

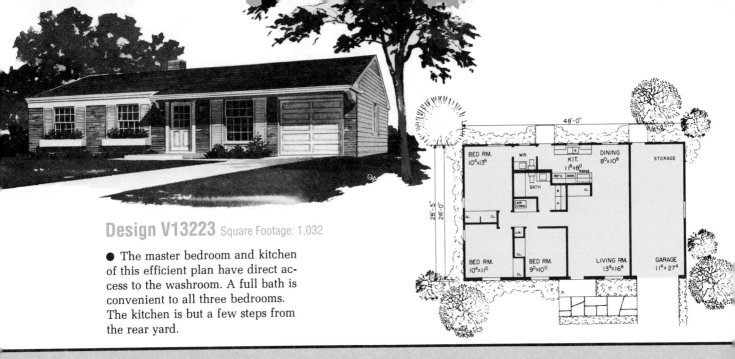

Design V13223 Square Footage: 1,032

● The master bedroom and kitchen
of this efficient plan have direct access to the washroom. A full bath is
convenient to all three bedrooms.
The kitchen is but a few steps from
the rear yard.

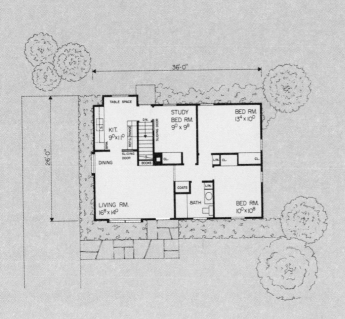

Design V12165 Square Footage: 880

● Whether called upon to function as
a two or a three bedroom home, this
attractive design will serve its occupants ideally for many years. There
are two eating areas.

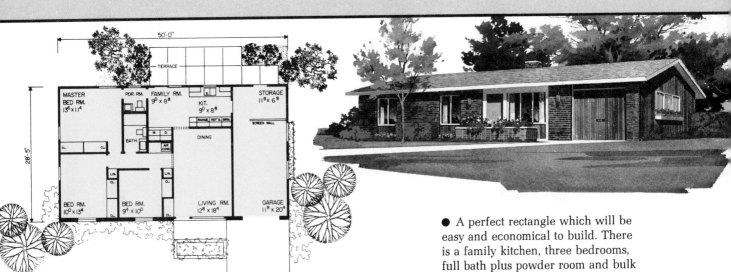

● A perfect rectangle which will be
easy and economical to build. There
is a family kitchen, three bedrooms,
full bath plus powder room and bulk
storage area in the garage.

Design V12159 Square Footage: 1,077

Design V11187
Square Footage: 1,120

● A lovely ranch with everything for a growing family. The large front living room is highlighted by a corridor kitchen and family room to the rear. Note the closet space in the master bedroom and both children's rooms. A rear terrace with family room access adds outdoor livability.

● A cozy plan, but just right for a small family or empty nesters. An ample living room/dining room area leads the way to a rear kitchen overlooking a terrace. Two full baths serve three bedrooms — one a master bedroom. Multi-paned windows with quaint shutters add a touch of charm to the design.

Design V11113
Square Footage: 1,008

L D

● Here are three optional front exteriors which can be built with either the basement plan, V12160, or the non-basement plan, V12161. Whichever number you order, the blueprints will include details for all three optional front elevations. It is interesting to observe the variations in the two floor plans. Don't miss the extra storage facilities. Notice the location of the stacked washer and dryer in the non-basement plan.

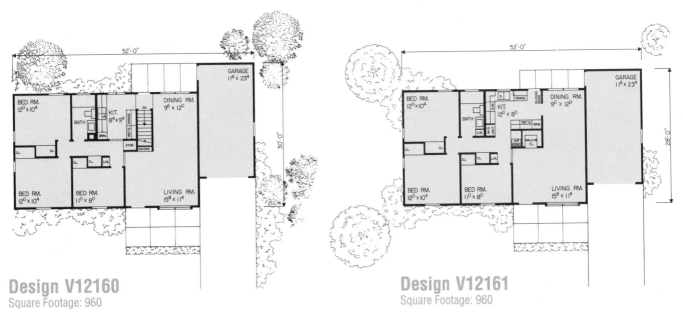

Design V12160
Square Footage: 960

Design V12161
Square Footage: 960

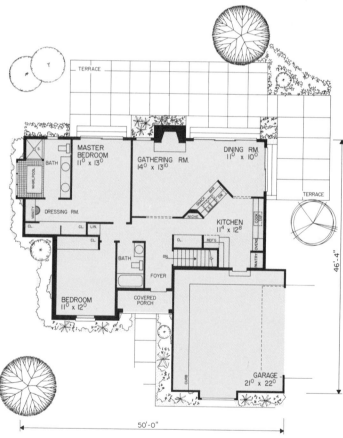

ALTERNATE KITCHEN PLAN

Design V12911
Square Footage: 1,233

● A low budget retirement house can be a neighborhood showplace, too. Exquisite proportion, fine detailing, projecting wings, and interesting roof lines help provide the appeal of this modest one-story. Each of the bedrooms has excellent wall space and wardrobe storage potential. The master

bath features a vanity, twin lavatories, stall shower, plus a whirlpool. Another full bath is strategically located to service the second bedroom as well as other areas of the house. Open planning results in a spacious living-dining area with fireplace and access to the outdoor terraces. This design offers a

choice between two kitchen layouts. Which do you prefer? The one which functions informally with the gathering room, or its more formal counterpart? Each layout has all the amenities to assure a pleasant and efficient workday. Don't miss the basement for the development of additional livability.

CONTEMPORARY DESIGNS UNDER 2000 Sq. Ft. . . .

offer a refreshing and exciting break from the many other so-called "high-styled" traditional exteriors. Their simple, straightforward, unclut-tered appearance makes contemporary exteriors a favorite of many. The houses in this section exemplify the fact that distinctive, yet practi-cal, contemporary design can come in modest packages. Whether simple rectangles, modified L-shapes, or irregular configurations, their floor plans can deliver interesting and convenient living patterns. Whether their exteriors have a low, ground-hugging profile, a geometric shape, or an angular appearance they can capture the eye of the most casual passer-by in a most pleasing fashion.

● This is most certainly an outstanding contemporary design. Study the exteri-or carefully before your journey to in-spect the floor plan. The vertical lines are carried from the siding to the paned windows to the garage door. The front entry is recessed so the over-hanging roof creates a covered porch.

Note the planter court with privacy wall. The floor plan is just as outstand-ing. The rear gathering room has a sloped ceiling, raised hearth fireplace, sliding glass doors to the terrace and a snack bar with pass-thru to the kitch-en. In addition to the gathering room, there is the living room/study. This

room could be utilized in a variety of ways depending on your family's choice. The formal dining room is convenient to the U-shaped kitchen. Three bed-rooms and two closely located baths are in the sleeping wing. This plan in-cludes details for the construction of an optional basement.

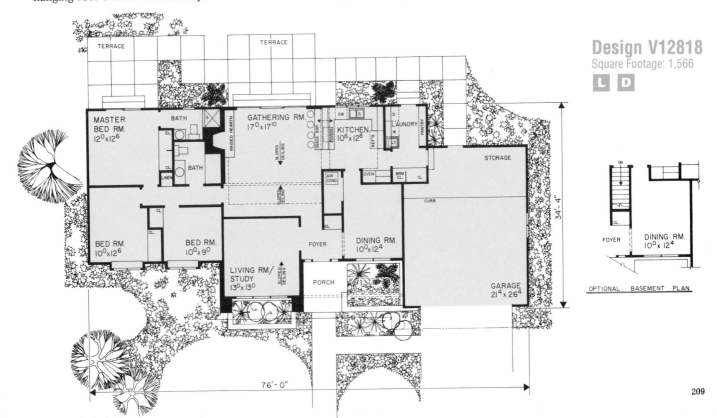

Design V12818
Square Footage: 1,566

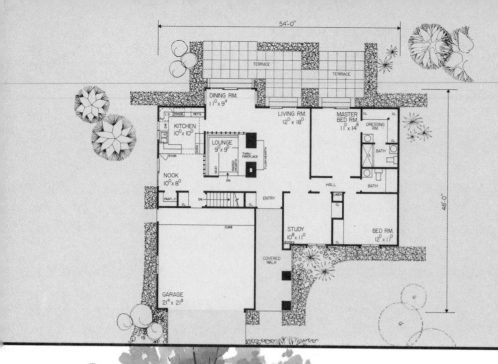

Design V12703
Square Footage: 1,445

D

● This modified, hip-roofed contemporary design will be the answer for those who want something both practical, yet different, inside and out. The covered front walk sets the stage for entering a modest sized home with tremendous livability. The focal point will be the pleasant conversation lounge. It is sunken, partially open to the other living areas and shares the enjoyment of the thru-fireplace with the living room. There are two bedrooms, two full baths and a study. The kitchen is outstanding.

Design V12753
Square Footage: 1,539

D

● In this day and age of expensive building sites, projecting the attached garage from the front line of the house makes a lot of economic sense. It also lends itself to interesting roof lines and plan configurations. Here, a pleasing covered walkway to the front door results. A privacy wall adds an extra measure of design appeal and provides a sheltered terrace for the study/bedroom. You'll seldom find more livability in 1,539 square feet. Imagine, three bedrooms, two baths, a spacious living/dining area and a family room.

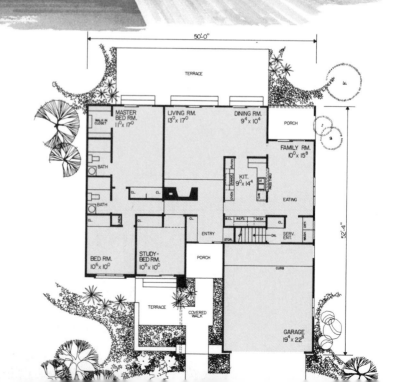

Design V12744
Square Footage: 1,381

● Here is a practical and an attractive contemporary home for that narrow building site. It is designed for efficiency with the small family or retired couple in mind. Sloping ceilings foster an extra measure of spaciousness. In addition to the master bedroom, there is the study that can also serve as the second bedroom or as an occasional guest room. The single bath is compartmented and its dual access allows it to serve living and sleeping areas more than adequately. Note raised hearth fireplace, snack bar, U-shaped kitchen, laundry, two terraces, etc.

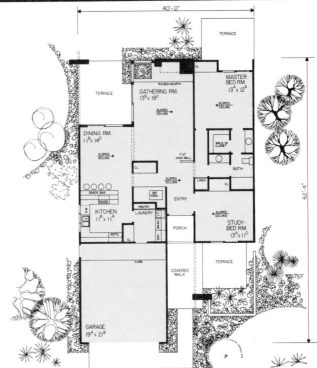

Design V12892
Square Footage: 1,623

● What a striking contemporary! It houses an efficient floor plan with many outstanding features. The foyer has a sloped ceiling and an open staircase to the basement. To the right of the foyer is the work center. Note the snack bar, laundry and covered dining porch, along with the step-saving kitchen. Both the gathering and dining rooms overlook the backyard. Each of the three bedrooms has access to an outdoor area. Now, just think of the potential use of the second floor loft. Its 160 square feet of livability could be used as a den, sewing room, lounge or any of many other activities. It overlooks the gathering room and front foyer and has two large skylights.

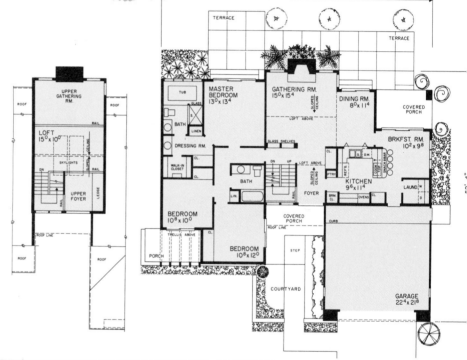

Design V12809
Square Footage: 1,551

● One-story living can be very rewarding and this contemporary home will be just that. Study the indoor-outdoor living relationships which are offered in the back of the plan. Sliding glass doors are in each of the rear rooms leading to the terrace. The formal dining room has a second set of doors to the porch. Many enjoyable hours will be spent here in the hot tub. A sloped ceiling with skylights is above the hot tub area. Back to the interior, there is a large gathering room. It, too, has a sloped ceiling which will add to its spacious appearance. The interior kitchen is conveniently located between the formal and informal dining areas. Two, or optional three, bedrooms are ready to serve the small family.

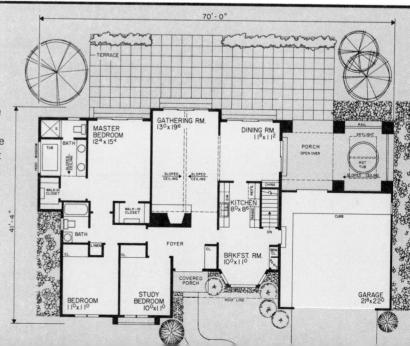

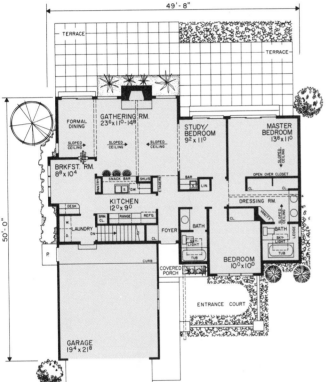

TERRACE

TERRACE

49'-8"

50'-0"

FORMAL DINING

GATHERING RM.
23⁶ x 11⁰-14⁸

SLOPED CEILING

SLOPED CEILING

SLOPED CEILING

STUDY/ BEDROOM
9² x 11⁰

MASTER BEDROOM
13⁶ x 11⁰

SLOPED CEILING

BRKFST. RM.
8⁸ x 10⁴

SNACK BAR

SHLVS.

BAR

LIN

OPEN OVER CLOSET

PANTRY

S.

DW.

CL.

CL.

KITCHEN
12⁰ x 9⁰

DESK

DRESSING RM.

BRM. CL.

RANGE

REFG.

W.

LAUNDRY

DN

FOYER

BATH

SKY LIGHT

SLOPED CEILING

BATH

LEDGE

VANITY

D.

CL.

CL.

SKY LIGHT

TUB

LEDGE

VANITY

TUB

P

CURB

BEDROOM
10⁰ x 10⁰

COVERED PORCH

GARAGE
19⁴ x 21⁸

ENTRANCE COURT

Design V12864
Square Footage: 1,387

L **D**

● Projecting the garage to the front of a house is very economical in two ways. One, it reduces the required lot size for building (in this case the overall width is under 50 feet). And, two, it will protect the interior from street noise and unfavorable winds. Many other characteristics about this design deserve mention, too. The entrance court and covered porch are a delightful way to enter this home. Upon entering, the foyer will take you to the various areas. The interior kitchen has an adjacent breakfast room and a snack bar on the gathering room side. Here, one will enjoy a sloped ceiling and a fireplace. A study with a wet bar is adjacent. If need be, adjust the plan and make the study the third bedroom. Sliding glass doors in the study and master bedroom open to the terrace.

213

Design V12330
Square Footage: 1,854

● The masonry masses of this home's exterior are pleasing. While the blueprints call for the use of stone, you may wish to substitute brick veneer. Sloping ceiling and plenty of glass will assure the living area of a fine feeling of spaciousness. The covered porches enhance the enjoyment of outdoor living. Two baths serve the three bedroom sleeping area.

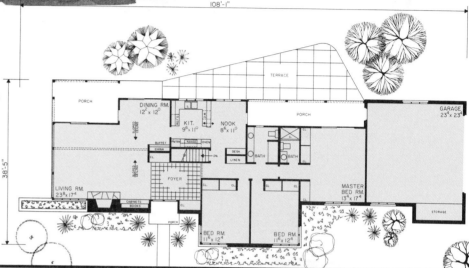

Design V13163
Square Footage: 1,552

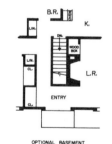

OPTIONAL BASEMENT

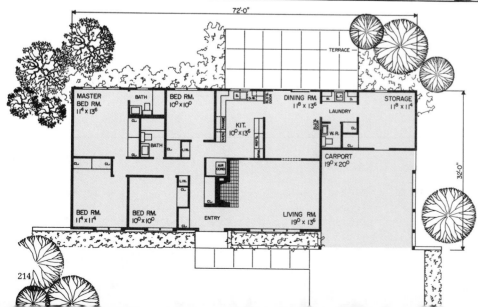

● Four bedrooms and two full baths will very adequately serve the growing family occupying this appealing contemporary. Its perfectly rectangular shape means economical construction. Note the attractive built-in planter adjacent to the front door. The large storage area behind the carport will solve any storage problems. Laundry and wash room are strategically located to serve the family.

Design V11021
Square Footage: 1,432

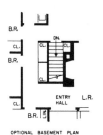

OPTIONAL BASEMENT PLAN

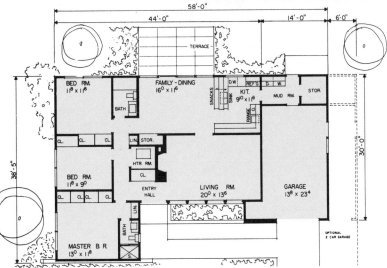

● Behind the double front doors of this straight-forward, contemporary design there is a heap of living to be enjoyed. The large living room with its dramatic glass wall and attractive fireplace will never fail to elicit comments of delight. The master bedroom has a whole wall of wardrobe closets and a private bath. Another two bedrooms and a bath easily serve the family.

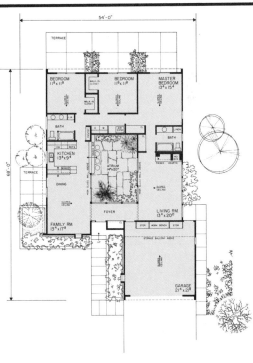

Design V12182
Square Footage: 1,558

● What a great new dimension in living is represented by this unique contemporary design! Each of the major zones comprise a separate unit which, along with the garage, clusters around the atrium. High sloped ceilings and plenty of glass areas assure a feeling of spaciousness. The quiet living room will enjoy its privacy, while activities in the informal family room will be great fun functioning with the kitchen. A snack bar opens the kitchen to the atrium. The view, above right, shows portions of snack bar and the front entry looking through the glass wall. There are two full baths strategically located to service all areas conveniently. Storage facilities are excellent, indeed. Don't miss the storage potential found in the garage. There is a work bench and storage balcony above.

Design V12702
Square Footage: 1,636

● A rear living room with a sloping ceiling, built-in bookcases, a raised hearth fireplace and sliding glass doors to the rear living terrace highlight this design. If desired, bi-fold doors permit this room to function with the adjacent study. An open railing next to the stairs to the basement recreation area fosters additional spaciousness. The kitchen has plenty of cabinet and cupboard space. It features informal eating space and is but a step or two from the separate dining room. Note side dining terrace. Each of the three rooms in the sleeping wing has direct access to outdoor living. The master bedroom highlights a huge walk-in wardrobe closet, dressing room with built-in vanity and private bath with large towel storage closet. Projecting the two-car garage with its twin doors to the front not only contributes to an interesting exterior, but reduces the size of the building site required for this home.

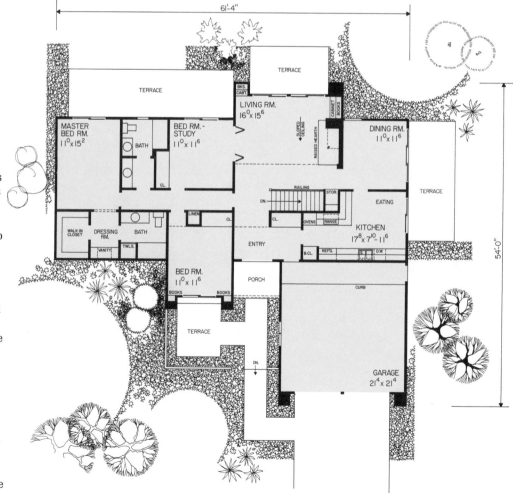

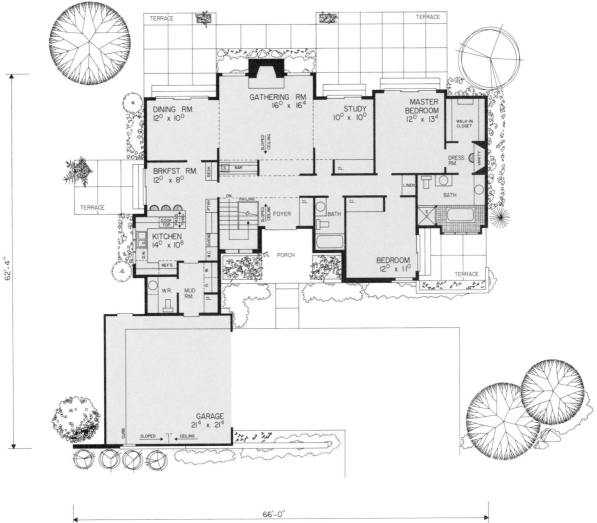

TERRACE

TERRACE

DINING RM.
12⁰ x 10⁰

GATHERING RM.
16⁰ x 16⁴

STUDY
10⁰ x 10⁰

MASTER BEDROOM
12⁰ x 13⁴

WALK-IN CLOSET

SLOPED CEILING

BAR

DESK

CL.

DRESS. RM.

VANITY

BRKFST. RM.
12⁰ x 8⁰

LINEN

BATH

COOK TOP

PTRY

DN. RAILING

SLOPED CEILING

FOYER

CL.

BATH

CL.

KITCHEN
14⁰ x 10⁸

B.C. OVEN

DW

REF'G

PORCH

BEDROOM
12⁰ x 11⁰

TERRACE

TERRACE

W.R.

MUD RM.

CL.

GARAGE
21⁴ x 21⁴

CURB

SLOPED CEILING

62'-4"

66'-0"

Design V12918
Square Footage: 1,693

D

● Alternating use of stone and wood gives a textured look to this striking Contemporary home with wide overhanging roof lines and built-in planter box. The design is just as exciting on the inside with two bedrooms, including a master suite, a study (or optional third bedroom), rear gathering room with fireplace and sloped ceiling, rear dining room, and efficient U-shaped kitchen with pass-thru to an adjoining breakfast room. A mud room and washroom are located between kitchen and spacious two-car garage. Includes plans for optional basement.

Design V11917
Square Footage: 1,728

● Imagine your family living in this appealing one-story home. Think of how your living habits will adjust to the delightful patterns offered here. Flexibility is the byword; for there are two living areas — the front, formal living room and the rear, informal family room. There are two dining areas — the dining room overlooking the front yard and the breakfast room looking out upon the rear yard. There are outstanding bath facilities — a full bath for the master bedroom and one that will be handy to the living areas as a powder room. Then there is the extra wash room just where you need it — handy to the kitchen, the basement and the outdoors.

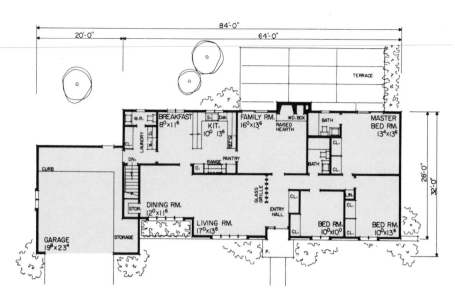

Design V11891
Square Footage: 1,986

● There is much more to a house than just its exterior. And while the appeal of this home would be difficult to beat, it is the living potential of the interior that gives this design such a high ranking. The sunken living room with its adjacent dining room is highlighted by the attractive fireplace, the raised planter and the distinctive glass panels.

A raised hearth fireplace, snack bar and sliding glass doors which open to the outdoor deck are features of the family room. The work center area is efficient. It has plenty of storage space and a laundry area.

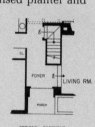

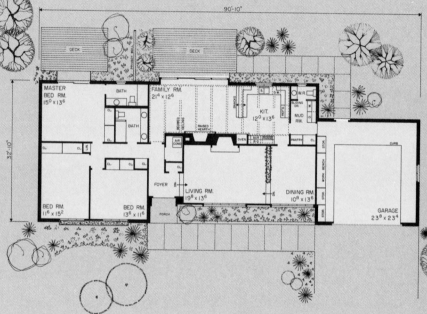

Design V11396
Square Footage: 1,664

● Three bedrooms, 2½ baths, a formal dining area, a fine family room and an attached two-car garage are among the highlights of this frame home. The living-dining area is delightfully spacious with the fireplace wall, having book shelves at each end, functioning as a practical area divider. The many storage units found in this home will be a topic of conversion. The cabinets above the strategically located washer and dryer, the family room storage wall and walk-in closet and the garage facilities are particularly noteworthy. Blueprints show how to build this house with and without a basement.

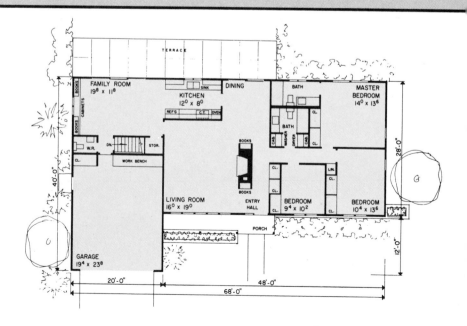

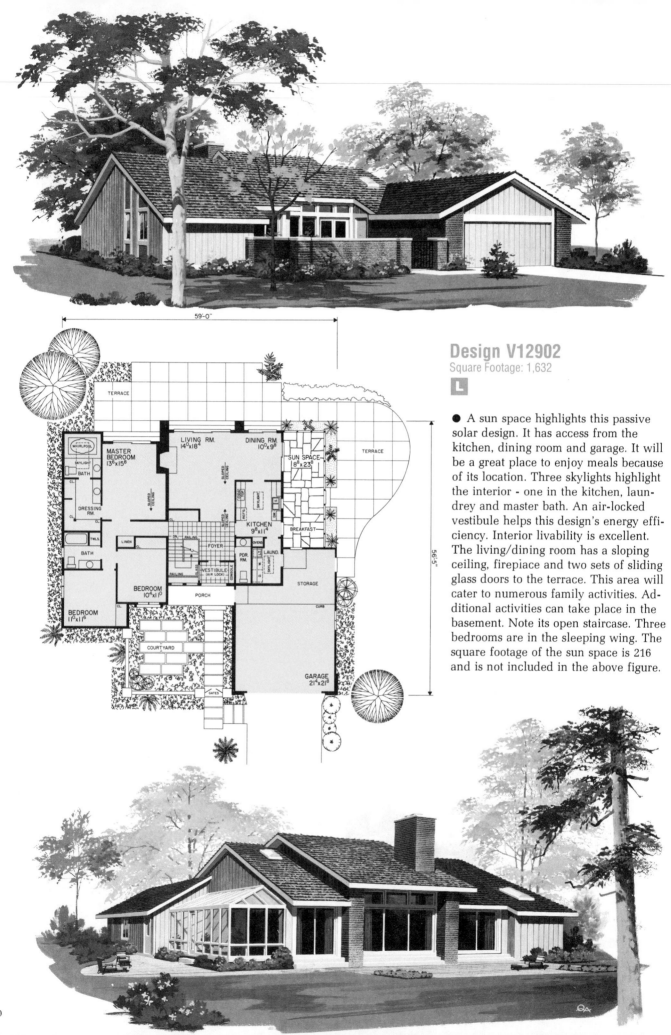

Design V12902
Square Footage: 1,632

L

● A sun space highlights this passive solar design. It has access from the kitchen, dining room and garage. It will be a great place to enjoy meals because of its location. Three skylights highlight the interior - one in the kitchen, laundrey and master bath. An air-locked vestibule helps this design's energy efficiency. Interior livability is excellent. The living/dining room has a sloping ceiling, firepiace and two sets of sliding glass doors to the terrace. This area will cater to numerous family activities. Additional activities can take place in the basement. Note its open staircase. Three bedrooms are in the sleeping wing. The square footage of the sun space is 216 and is not included in the above figure.

Design V12886
Square Footage: 1,733

● This one-story house is attractive with its contemporary exterior. It has many excellent features to keep you and your family happy for many years. For example, notice the spacious gathering room with sliding glass doors that allow easy access to the greenhouse. Another exciting feature of this room is that you will receive an abundance of sunshine through the clerestory windows. Also, this plan offers you two nice sized bedrooms. The master suite is not only roomy but also unique because through both the bedroom and the bath you can enter a greenhouse with a hot tub. The hot tub will be greatly appreciated after a long, hard day at work. Don't forget to note the breakfast room with access to the terrace. You will enjoy the efficient kitchen that will make preparing meals a breeze. A greenhouse window here is charming. An appealing, open staircase leads to the basement. The square footages of the greenhouses are 394 and are not included in the above figure.

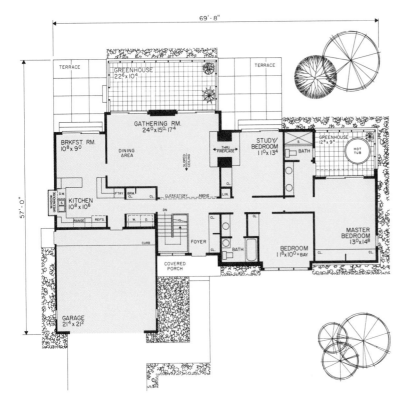

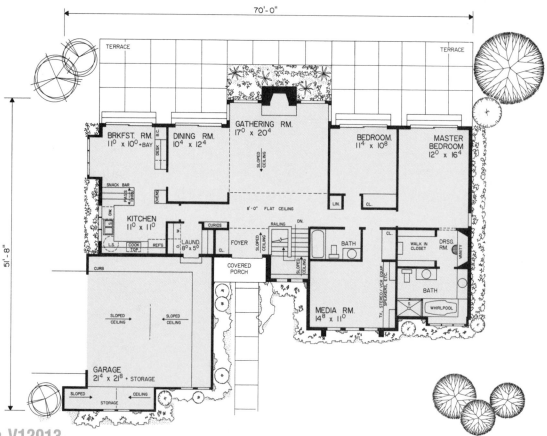

Design V12913
Square Footage: 1,835

D

● This smart design features multi-gabled ends, varied roof lines, and vertical windows. It also offers efficient zoning by room functions and plenty of modern comforts for Contemporary family lifestyle. A covered porch leads through a foyer to a large central gathering room with fireplace, sloped ceiling, and its own special view of a rear terrace. A modern kitchen with snack bar has a pass-thru to a breakfast room with view of the terrace. There's also an adjacent dining room. A media room isolated along with bedrooms from the rest of the house offers a quiet private area for listening to stereos or VCRs. A master bedroom suite includes its own whirlpool. A large garage includes extra storage.

Design V12917
Square Footage: 1,813

● Here's an attractive design with many of today's most-asked-for features: gathering room with fireplace, separate formal dining room, roomy kitchen with equally spacious breakfast area, and three bedrooms, including a master suite with huge walk-in closet and two private vanities. One other plus: a great-to-stretch-out-on terrace leading to the backyard.

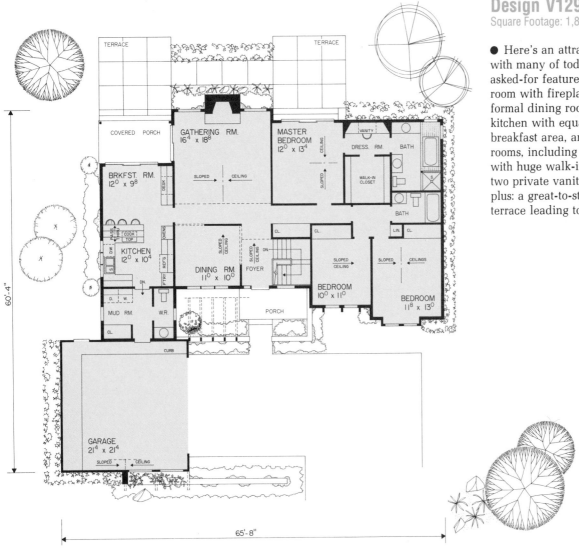

Design V12795
Square Footage: 1,952

● This three-bedroom design leaves no room for improvement. Any size family will find it difficult to surpass the fine qualities that this home offers. Begin with the exterior. This fine contemporary design has open trellis work above the front, covered private court. This area is sheltered by a privacy wall extending from the projecting garage. Inside, the floor plan will be just as breathtaking. Begin at the foyer and choose a direction. To the right is the sleeping wing equipped with three bedrooms and two baths. Straight ahead from the foyer is the gathering room with thru-fireplace to the dining room. To the right is the work center. This area includes a breakfast room, a U-shaped kitchen and laundry.

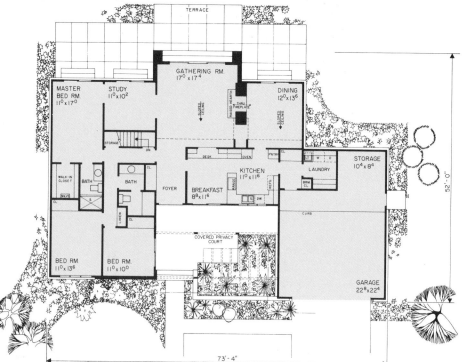

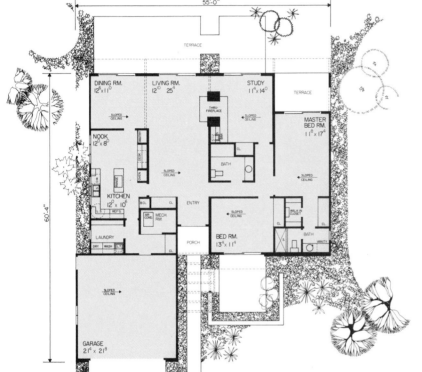

Design V12754
Square Footage: 1,844

● This really is a most dramatic and refreshing contemporary home. The slope of its wide overhanging roofs is carried right indoors to provide an extra measure of spaciousness. The U-shaped privacy wall of the front entrance area provides an appealing outdoor living spot accessible from the front bedroom. The rectangular floor plan will be economical to build. Notice the efficient use of space and how it all makes its contribution to outstanding livability. The small family will find its living patterns delightful, indeed. Two bedrooms and two full baths comprise the sleeping zone. The open planning of the L-shaped living and dining rooms is most desirable. The through-fireplace is just a great room divider. The kitchen and breakfast nook function well together. There is laundry and mechanical room nearby.

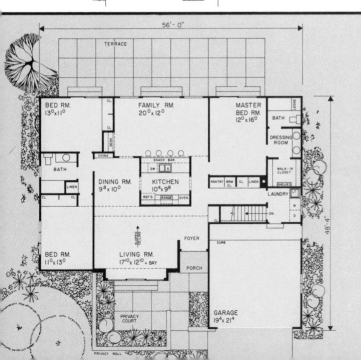

Design V12796
Square Footage: 1,828

● This home features a front living room with sloped ceiling and sliding glass doors which lead to a front private court. What a delightful way to introduce this design. This bi-nuclear design has a great deal to offer. First — the children's and parent's sleeping quarters are on opposite ends of this house to assure the utmost in privacy. Each area has its own full bath. The interior kitchen is a great idea. It frees up valuable wall space for the living areas exclusive use. There is a snack bar in the kitchen/family room for those very informal meals. Also, a planning desk is in the family room. The dining room is conveniently located near the kitchen plus it has a built-in china cabinet. The laundry area has plenty of storage closets plus the stairs to the basement. This home will surely be a welcome addition to any setting.

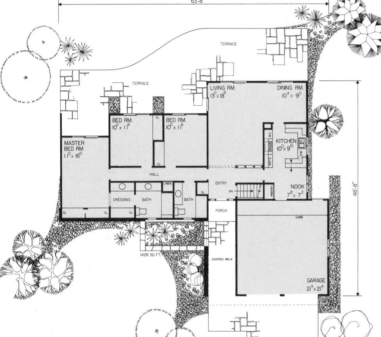

Design V12591
Square Footage: 1,428

● Good times and easy work! There's an efficient kitchen with lots of work space and a large storage pantry. Plus a separate breakfast nook to make casual meals convenient and pleasant. This home creates its own peaceful enviroment! It's especially pleasing to people who love the outdoors.

Design V12797
Square Footage: 1,791

● The exterior appeal of this delightful one-story is sure to catch the attention of all who pass by. The overhanging roof adds an extra measure of shading along with the privacy wall which shelters the front court and entry. The floor plan also will be outstanding to include both leisure and formal activities. The gathering room has a sloped ceiling, sliding glass door to rear terrace and a thru-fireplace to the family room. This room also has access to the terrace and it includes the informal eating area. A pass-thru from the U-shaped kitchen to the eating area makes serving a breeze. Formal dining can be done in the front dining room. The laundry area is adjacent to the kitchen and garage and houses a washroom. Peace and quiet can be achieved in the study. The sleeping zone consists of three bedrooms and two full back-to-back baths. Additional space will be found in the basement.

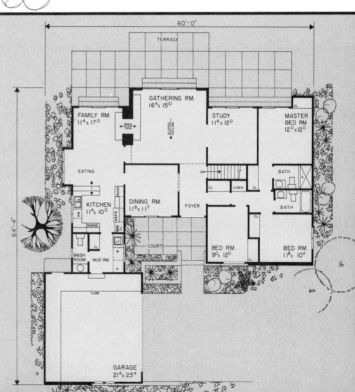

226

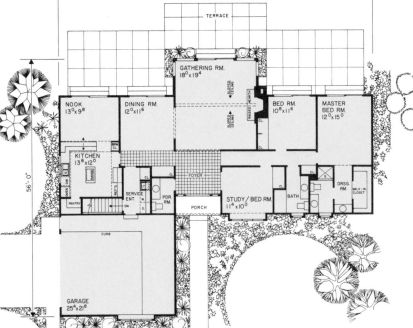

Design V12792
Square Footage: 1,944

● Indoor-outdoor living hardly could be improved upon in this contemporary design. All of the rear rooms have sliding glass doors to the large terrace. Divide the terrace in three parts and the nook and dining room have access to a dining terrace, the gathering room to a living terrace and two bedrooms to a lounging terrace. A delightful way to bring the outdoor view inside. Other fine features include the efficient kitchen which has plenty of storage space and an island range, a first floor laundry with stairs to the basement and a powder room adjacent to the front door.

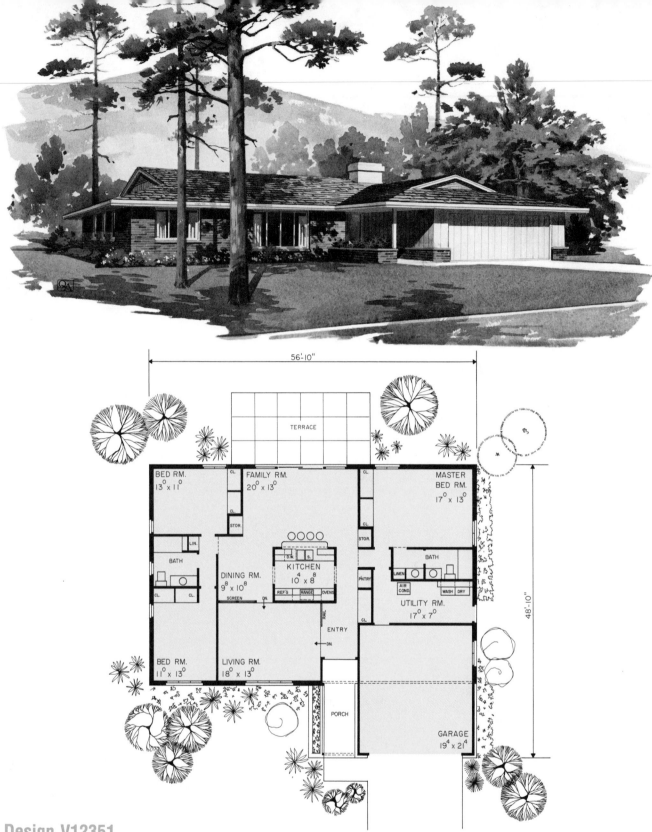

Design V12351
Square Footage: 1,862

D

● The extension of the wide over-hanging roof of this distinctive home provides shelter for the walkway to the front door. A raised brick planter adds appeal to the outstanding exterior design. The living patterns offered by this plan are delightfully different, yet ex-tremely practical. Notice the separation of the master bedroom from the other two bedrooms. While assuring an extra measure of quiet privacy for the parents, this master bedroom location may be ideal for a live-in-relative. Locating the kitchen in the middle of the plan frees up valuable outside wall space and leads to interesting planning. The front living room is sunken for dramatic appeal and need not have any cross-room traffic. The utility room houses the laundry and the heating and cooling equipment.

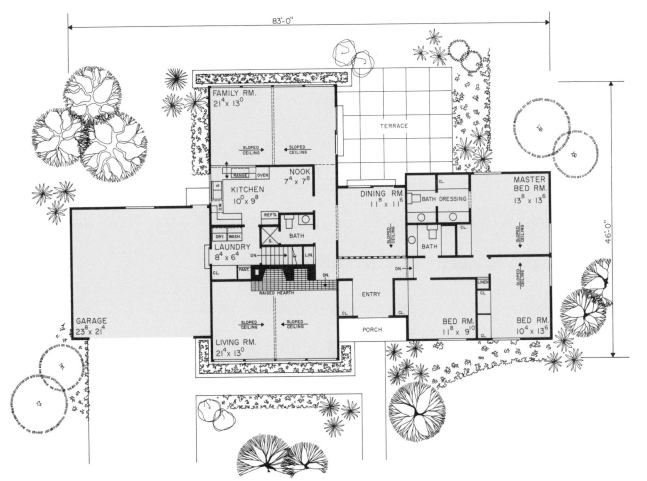

Floor plan labels:

FAMILY RM. 21⁴ x 13⁰
TERRACE
NOOK 7⁴ x 7⁸
KITCHEN 10⁰ x 9⁸
RANGE OVEN
REF'G.
DINING RM. 11⁸ x 11⁶
BATH DRESSING
CL.
MASTER BED RM. 13⁸ x 13⁶
SLOPED CEILING
DRY. WASH.
BATH
LAUNDRY 8⁴ x 6⁴
BATH
CL.
PANT.
LIN
DN.
DN.
RAISED HEARTH
ENTRY
DN.
LINEN
CL.
GARAGE 23⁸ x 21⁴
SLOPED CEILING
SLOPED CEILING
LIVING RM. 21⁴ x 13⁰
PORCH
BED RM. 11⁸ x 9¹⁰
BED RM. 10⁴ x 13⁶
83'-0"
46'-0"

Design V12363
Square Footage: 1,978

● You will have a lot of fun deciding what you like best about this home with its eye-catching glass-gabled living room and wrap-around raised planter. A covered porch shelters the double front doors. Projecting to the rear is a family room identical in size with the formal living room. Between these two rooms there are features galore. There is the efficient kitchen with pass-thru and informal eating space. Then, there is the laundry with a closet, pantry and the basement stairs nearby. Also, a full bath featuring a stall shower. The dining room has a sloped ceiling and an appealing, open vertical divider which acts as screening from the entry. The three bedroom, two bath sleeping zone is sunken. The raised hearth fireplace in the living room has an adjacent wood box.

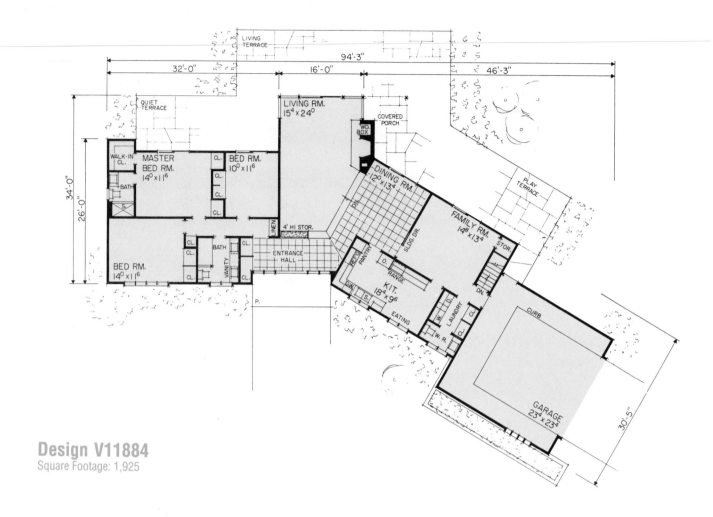

Design V11884
Square Footage: 1,925

● If you are searching for something with an air of distinction both inside and out then search no more. You could hardly improve upon what this home has to offer. You will forever be proud of the impressive hip-roof, angular facade. Its interest will give it an identity all its own. As for the interior, your everyday living patterns will be a delight, indeed. And little wonder, clever zoning and a fine feeling of spaciousness set the stage. As you stand in the entrance hall, you look across the tip of a four foot high planter into the sunken living room. Having an expanse of floor space, the wall of windows and the raised hearth fireplace, the view will be dramatic. Notice covered porch, play terrace and quiet terrace which will provide great outdoor enjoyment.

● Here is a relatively low-cost home with a majority of the features found in today's high priced homes. The three-bedroom sleeping area highlights two full baths. The living area is a huge room of approximately 25 feet in depth zoned for both formal living and dining activities. The kitchen is extremely well-planned and includes a built-in desk and pantry. The family room has a snack bar and sliding glass doors to the terrace. Blueprints include optional basement details.

Design V11357
Square Footage: 1,258

FAMILY RM.
12⁰ x 15⁰

KIT.
10⁸ x 8⁰

SNACKS

RANGE

S.

D.W. REF'G

PANTRY

DESK

DN.

OPTIONAL BASEMENT PLAN

56'-5"

TERRACE

FAMILY RM.
12⁰ x 15⁰

DINING
10⁰ x 8⁶

MASTER BED RM.
13⁴ x 10⁴

KIT.
10⁸ x 8⁰

SNACKS

RANGE

S.

D.W. REF'G

PANTRY

DESK

BATH

BATH

AIR COND.

LIN.

CL. CL.

CL.

CL.

D. W.

36'-5"

26'-5"

LIVING RM.
13⁴ x 16⁸

BED RM.
9⁴ x 9⁰

BED RM.
10⁰ x 12⁴

CL.

GARAGE
19⁴ x 20⁰

Design V11129
Square Footage: 1,904

● Study this floor plan with care, for there is much to recommend it to the large family. The living room and separate dining area look out upon the rear yard. Sliding glass doors permit the dining area to function with the terrace — a delightful indoor-outdoor living feature. An appealing two-way fireplace may be enjoyed from both the living and dining areas. The efficient U-shaped kitchen overlooks the front yard and is but a few steps from the entry hall as well as the service entrance and garage.

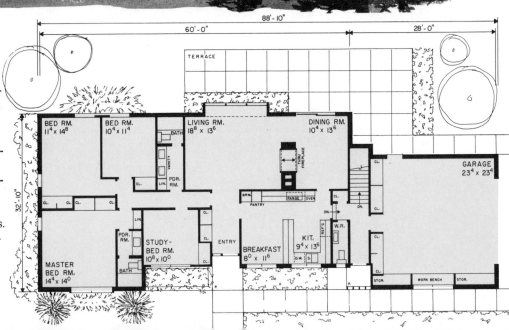

88'- 10"

60'-0"

28'-0"

TERRACE

BED RM.
11⁴ x 14⁸

BED RM.
10⁴ x 11⁴

LIVING RM.
18⁸ x 13⁶

DINING RM.
10⁴ x 13⁶

GARAGE
23⁴ x 23⁴

BATH

VANITY

PDR. RM.

THRU FIREPLACE

32'-10"

CL. CL. CL.

CL.

LIN.

BRM.

RANGE OVEN

PANTRY

DN.

DN.

REF'G

W.R.

CL.

MASTER BED RM.
14⁴ x 14⁰

PDR. RM.

STUDY-BED RM.
10⁸ x 10⁰

ENTRY

BREAKFAST
8⁰ x 11⁶

KIT.
9⁴ x 13⁶

BATH

LIN.

CL.

D.W.

STOR.

WORK BENCH

STOR.

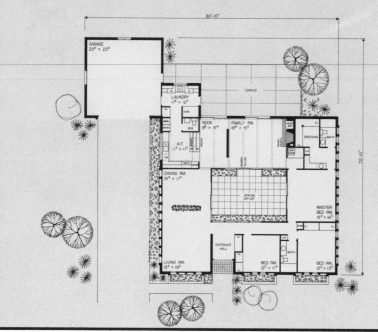

Design V12298
Square Footage: 2,489 (Excluding Atrium)

● If you've ever wanted to enjoy outdoor living indoors, this distinctive and refreshing design comes
close to providing that opportunity. All the tremendous
livability offered in the basic rectangular plan is
wrapped in around a breathtaking 24 x 16 foot atrium
which is open to the sky. Sliding glass doors provide
direct access to this unique area from the family room,
the dining and the master bedroom. Also noteworthy is
the functioning of other areas such as: the living and
dining rooms; the kitchen and laundry; the master bedroom and its dressing/bath area. The two front bedrooms are serviced by a second full bath. That's a four
foot, six inch high planter with storage below separating the living and dining rooms. This will be just a
great area for formal entertaining.

Design V11283
Square Footage: 1,904 (Excluding Atrium)

● Here is a unique home whose livable
area is basically a perfect square. Completely adaptable to a narrow building
site, the presence of the atrium permits
the enjoyment of private outdoor living
"indoors". Sliding glass doors open onto
this delightful atrium with its attractive
planting areas.

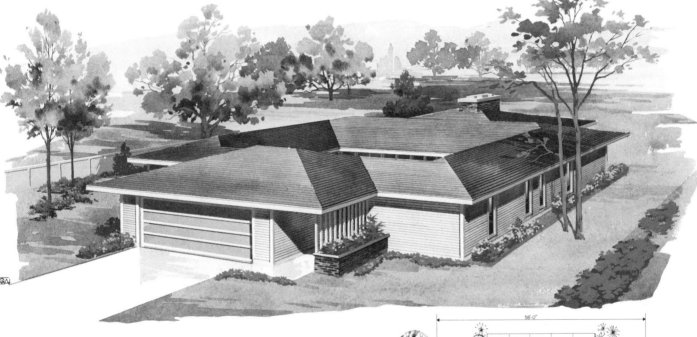

Design V12383
Square Footage: 1,984

● Design your home around an atrium and you will enjoy living patterns unlike any you have experienced in the past. This interior area is assured complete outdoor privacy. Five sets of sliding glass doors enhance the accessibility of this unique area. With the two-car garage projecting from the front of the house, this design will not require a large piece of property. Worthy of particular note is the separation of the master bedroom from the other three bedrooms - a fine feature to assure peace and quiet. Side-by-side are the formal and informal living rooms. Both function with the rear terrace. Separating the two rooms is the thru-fireplace and double access wood box.

233

Design V13203
Square Footage: 1,291

● The degree to which your family's living patterns will be efficient will depend upon the soundness of the basic floor plan. Here is an exceptionally practical arrangment for a medium sized home. Traffic patterns will be most flexible. The work area is strategically located close to the front door and it will function ideally with both the indoor and outdoor informal living areas. The master bath will serve the living room and the sleeping area. The second bath will serve the work area, the family room and third bedroom. Note stall shower.

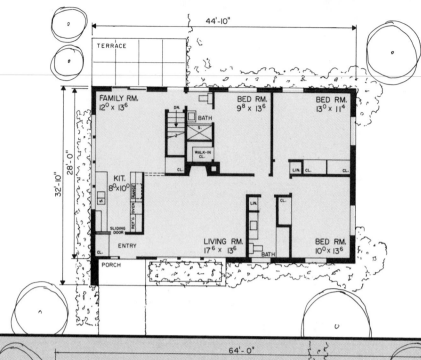

Design V13212
Square Footage: 1,493

● Imagine ushering your first visitors through the front door of your new home. After you have placed their coats in the big closet in the front entry, you will show them your three sizable bedrooms and the two full baths. Next, you will take them through the separate dining area, the efficient kitchen and into the large family room with its wall of built-in storage units. Your visitors will comment about the sliding glass doors which open onto the terrace from the family room.

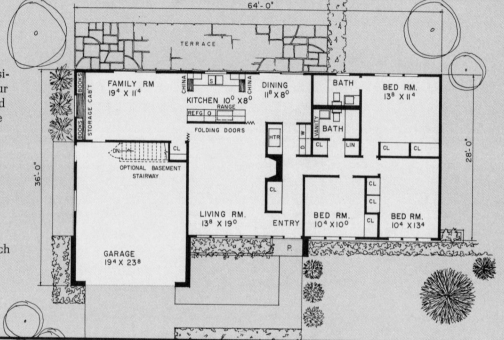

Design V11072
Square Footage: 1,232

● Low-pitched overhanging roof, vertical siding and patterned masonry screen wall create a charming exterior for this house. A fireplace divides the living room from the entry hall. Seven-foot high cabinets separate the kitchen from the living/dining area. The dining area opens through sliding glass doors to a private covered porch and the rear terrace. The informal area is enhanced by a wall of windows overlooking the terrace and a three-foot high built-in planter. For recreation and bulk storage there is a full basement.

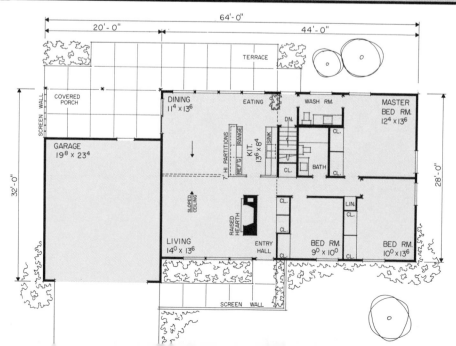

235

Design V11281
Square Footage: 1,190

● Whatever you call it, contemporary or traditional, or even transitional, the prudent incorporation of newer with old design features results in a pleasant facade. The window and door detailing is obviously from an early era; while the low-pitched roof and the carport are features of relatively more recent vintage. Inside, there is an efficient plan which lends itself to the activities of the small family. As a home for a retired couple, or a young newlywed couple, this will be a fine investment. Certainly it will not require a big, expensive piece of property. The plan offers two full baths, three bedrooms, an excellent L-shaped kitchen, 23-foot living and dining area and a basement. Note side terrace.

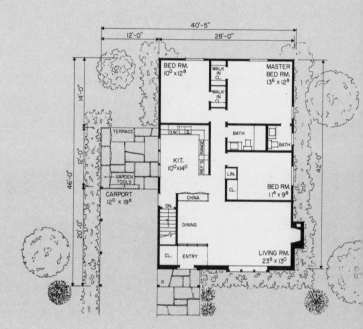

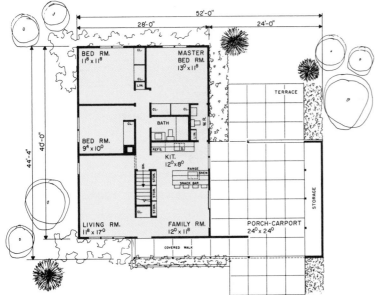

Design V13195
Square Footage: 1,120

● This 28 x 40 foot rectangle is a fine example of how delightful and refreshing contemporary design can become. Though simple in basic construction and floor planning, this home has an abundance of exterior appeal and interior livability. Observe the low-pitched, wide overhanging roof, the attached 24 foot square covered porch/carport, the effective glass area and vertical siding, plus the raised planter. The center entrance is flanked by the formal living room and the informal, all-purpose family room. A snack bar is accessible from the kitchen. Sliding glass doors lead to the outdoor living area. In addition to the main bath there is an extra wash room handy to both the master bedroom and the kitchen.

Design V12755
Square Footage: 1,200

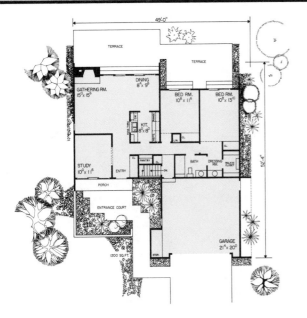

● Here is truly an outstanding, low-cost design created to return all the pride of ownership and livability a small family or retired couple would ask of a new home. The living/dining area measures a spacious 23 feet. It has a fireplace and two sets of sliding glass doors leading to the large rear terrace. The two bedrooms also have access to this terrace. The kitchen is a real step-saver and has a pantry nearby. The study, which has sliding glass doors to the front porch, will function as that extra all-purpose room. Use it for sewing, guests, writing or reading or just plain napping. The basement offers the possibility for the development of additional recreation space. Note the storage area at the side of the garage. Many years of enjoyable living will surely be obtained in this home designed in the contemporary fashion.

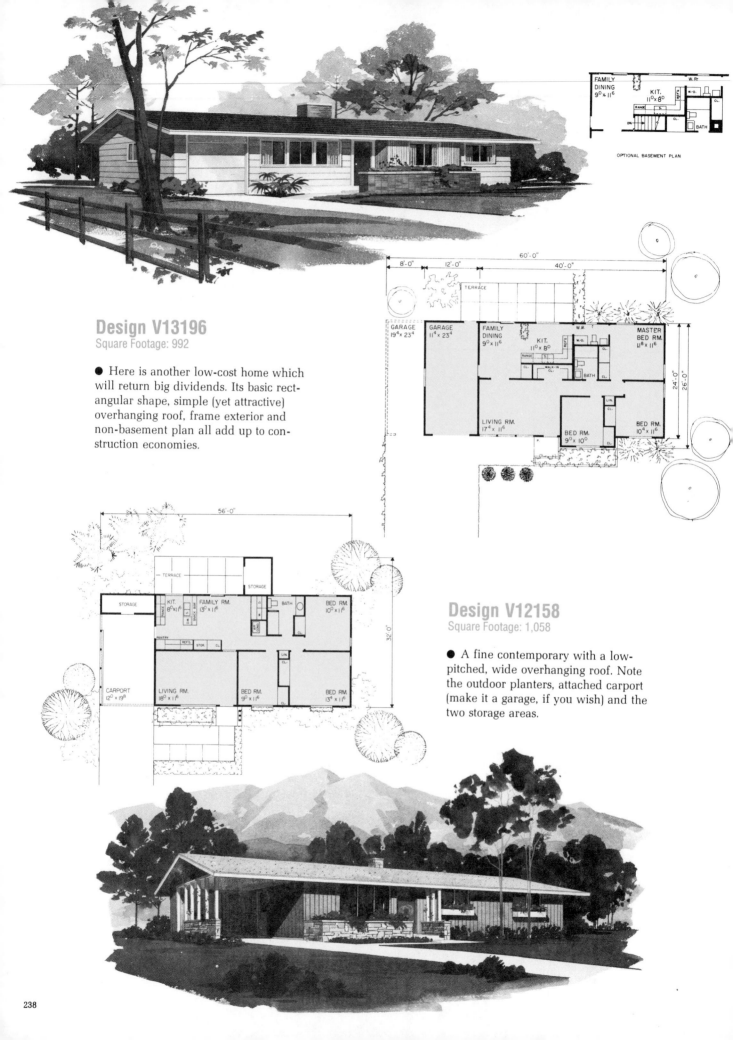

OPTIONAL BASEMENT PLAN

FAMILY DINING 9⁰ x 11⁶
KIT. 11⁰ x 8⁰
W. R.
W-D.
CL.
RANGE
REF'S.
S.
ON.
CL.
BATH

Design V13196
Square Footage: 992

● Here is another low-cost home which will return big dividends. Its basic rectangular shape, simple (yet attractive) overhanging roof, frame exterior and non-basement plan all add up to construction economies.

Design V12158
Square Footage: 1,058

● A fine contemporary with a low-pitched, wide overhanging roof. Note the outdoor planters, attached carport (make it a garage, if you wish) and the two storage areas.

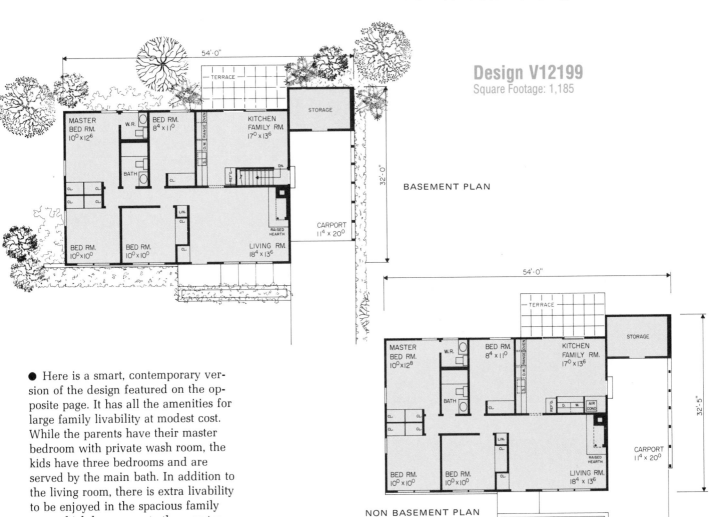

Design V12199
Square Footage: 1,185

BASEMENT PLAN

NON BASEMENT PLAN

● Here is a smart, contemporary version of the design featured on the opposite page. It has all the amenities for large family livability at modest cost. While the parents have their master bedroom with private wash room, the kids have three bedrooms and are served by the main bath. In addition to the living room, there is extra livability to be enjoyed in the spacious family area which has access to the rear terrace. Don't miss all those closets or the bulk storage room of the carport. Blueprints include optional basement and non-basement details.

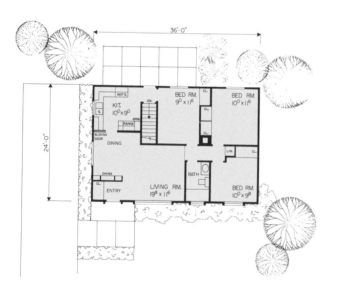

Design V12167
Square Footage: 864

● This 36' x 24' contemporary rectangle will be economical to build whether you construct the basement design at left, V12167, or the non-basement version below, V12168.

Design V12168
Square Footage: 864

● This non-basement design features a storage room and a laundry area with cupboards above the washer and dryer. Notice the kitchen eating space.

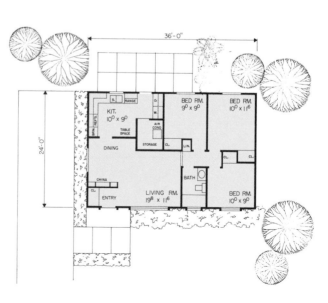

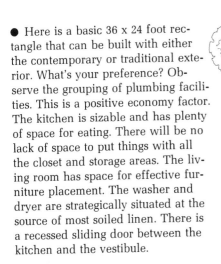

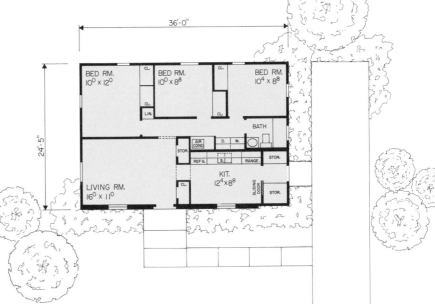

36'-0"

24'-5"

BED RM.
10⁰ x 12⁰

BED RM.
10⁰ x 8⁸

BED RM.
10⁴ x 8⁸

CL.

CL.

CL.

CL.

LIN.

BATH

AIR COND

D.

W.

STOR.

REF G.

S.

RANGE

STOR.

LIVING RM.
16⁰ x 11⁰

CL.

KIT.
12⁴ x 8⁸

SLIDING DOOR

STOR.

● Here is a basic 36 x 24 foot rectangle that can be built with either the contemporary or traditional exterior. What's your preference? Observe the grouping of plumbing facilities. This is a positive economy factor. The kitchen is sizable and has plenty of space for eating. There will be no lack of space to put things with all the closet and storage areas. The living room has space for effective furniture placement. The washer and dryer are strategically situated at the source of most soiled linen. There is a recessed sliding door between the kitchen and the vestibule.

Design V12822

First Floor: 1,363 square feet
Second Floor: 351 square feet
Total: 1,714 square feet

● Here is a truly unique house whose interior was designed with the current decade's economies, lifestyles and demographics in mind. While functioning as a one-story home, the second floor provides an extra measure of livability when required. Note the two optional layouts. The second floor may serve as a lounge, studio or hobby area overlooking the great room. Or, it may be built to function as a complete private guest room. It would be a great place for the visiting grandchildren. Don't miss the outdoor balcony. In addition, this two-story section adds to the dramatic appeal of both the exterior and the interior. Within only 1,363 square feet, this contemporary delivers refreshing and outstanding living patterns for those who are buying their first home, those who have raised their family and are looking for a smaller home and those in search of a retirement home. The center entrance routes traffic effectively to the great room. The adjacent covered porch will provide an ideal spot for warm weather, outdoor dining. The sleeping area may consist of one bedroom and a study, or two bedrooms. Each room functions with the sheltered wood deck - a perfect location for a hot tub.

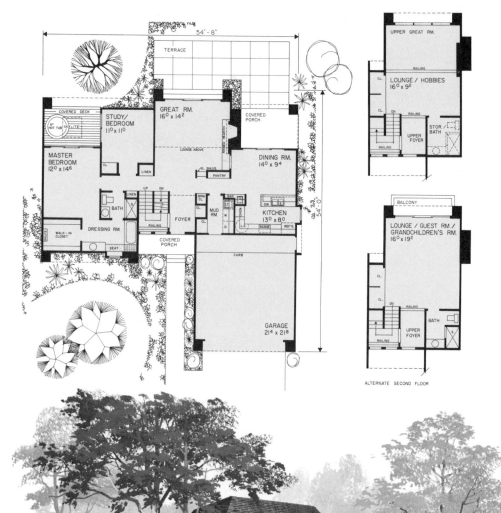

Design V12821

First Floor: 1,363 square feet
Second Floor: 351 square feet
Total: 1,714 square feet

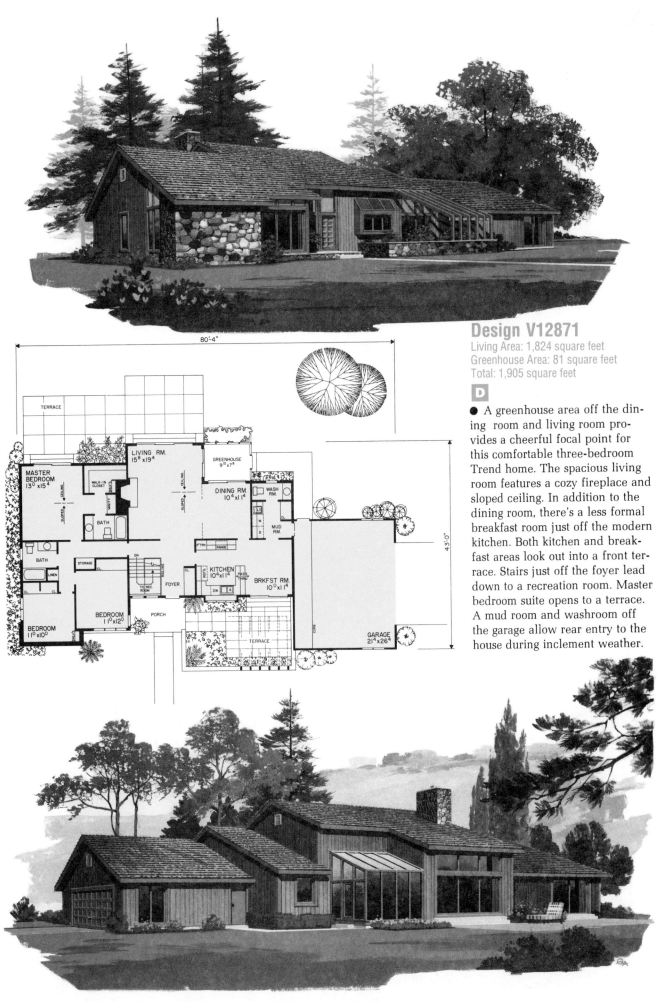

80'-4"

TERRACE

MASTER BEDROOM
13⁰ x15⁴

WALK-IN CLOSET

VANITY

LIVING RM.
15⁸ x19⁴

SLOPED CEILING

GREENHOUSE
9¹⁰ x7⁸

DINING RM.
10⁴ x11⁴

WASH RM.

BATH

MUD RM.

BATH

LINEN

STORAGE

CL

DN

TO REC. ROOM

FOYER

P'TRY.

RANGE

KITCHEN
10⁴ x11⁴

PASS THRU

BRKFST RM.
10⁰ x11⁴

BEDROOM
11⁰ x12⁰

PORCH

TERRACE

GARAGE
21⁴ x26⁴

BEDROOM
11⁰ x10⁰

43'-0"

Design V12871

Living Area: 1,824 square feet
Greenhouse Area: 81 square feet
Total: 1,905 square feet

D

● A greenhouse area off the dining room and living room provides a cheerful focal point for this comfortable three-bedroom Trend home. The spacious living room features a cozy fireplace and sloped ceiling. In addition to the dining room, there's a less formal breakfast room just off the modern kitchen. Both kitchen and breakfast areas look out into a front terrace. Stairs just off the foyer lead down to a recreation room. Master bedroom suite opens to a terrace. A mud room and washroom off the garage allow rear entry to the house during inclement weather.

Design V13330

First Floor: 1,394 square feet
Second Floor: 320 square feet
Total: 1,714 square feet

● Outdoor living and open floor planning are highlights of this moderately sized plan. Amenities include a private hot tub on a wooden deck that is accessible via sliding glass doors in both bedrooms, and a two-story gathering room. An optional second-floor plan allows for a full 503 square feet of space with a balcony.

CONTEMPORARY DESIGNS OVER 2000 Sq. Ft. . . .

can offer a delightful change of pace for your new home planning program. The unique individuality of many contemporary exteriors is refreshing, indeed. The clean, simple lines of the contemporary house offer a break from the past. The lack of adornment is preferred by many. Interesting new shapes not only lead to dramatic exteriors, but to unusual floor plans which deliver exciting living patterns. Open planning, sunken living areas, open stairwells, sloping ceilings, skylights, large and prudently placed glass areas and indoor planting areas all make significant contributions to the enjoyment of contemporary living. And, of course new materials and equipment make their contribution, too.

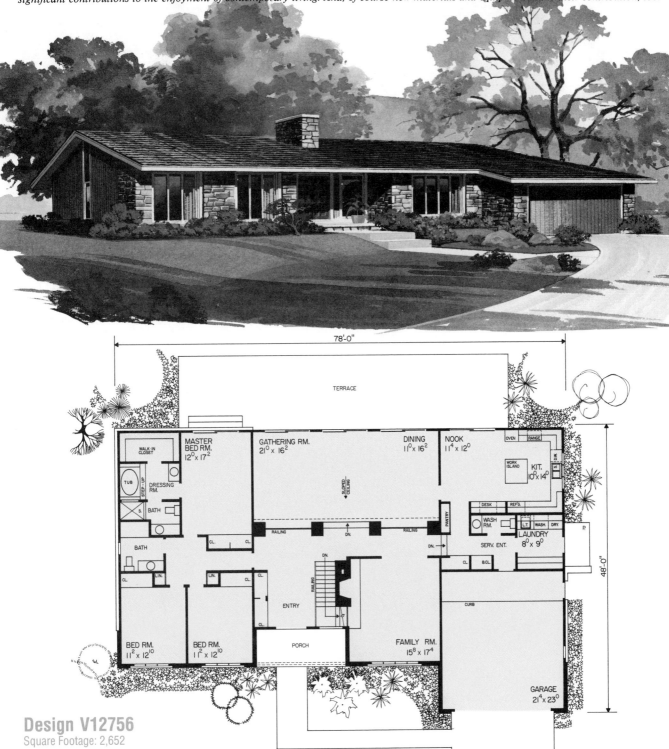

Design V12756
Square Footage: 2,652

L D

● This one-story, contemporary design is bound to serve your family well. It will assure the best in contemporary living with its many fine features. Notice the bath with tub and stall shower, dressing room and walk-in closet featured with the master bedroom. Two more family bedrooms are adjacent. The sunken gathering room/dining room is highlighted by the sloped ceiling and sliding glass doors to the large, rear terrace. This formal area is a full 32' x 16'. Imagine the great furniture placement that can be done in this area. In addition to the gathering room, there is an informal family room with a fireplace. You will enjoy the efficient kitchen and get much use out of the work island, pantry and built-in desk. Note the service entrance with washroom and laundry.

Clutter Room, Media Room To The Fore

● Something new? Something new, indeed!! Here is the introduction of two rooms which will make a wonderful contribution to family living. The clutter room is strategically placed between the kitchen and garage. It is the nerve center of the work area. It houses the laundry, provides space for sewing, has a large sorting table, and even plenty of space for the family's tool bench. A handy potting area is next to the laundry tray. Adjacent to

the clutter room, and a significant part of the planning of this whole zone, are the pantry and freezer with their nearby counter space. These facilities surely will expedite the unloading of groceries from the car and their convenient storing. Wardrobe and broom closets, plus washroom complete the outstanding utility of this area. The location of the clutter room with all its fine cabinet and counter space means that the often numerous family projects

can be on-going. This room is ideally isolated from the family's daily living patterns. The media room may be thought of as the family's entertainment center. While this is the room for the large or small TV, the home movies, the stereo and VCR equipment, it will serve as the library or study. It would be ideal as the family's home office with its computer equipment. Your family will decide just how it will utilize this outstanding area.

Design V12915 Square Footage: 2,758

L D

● The features of this appealing contemporary design go far beyond the clutter and media rooms. The country kitchen is spacious and caters to the family's informal living and dining activities. While it overlooks the rear yard it is just a step from the delightful greenhouse. Many happy hours will be spent here enjoying to the fullest the outdoors from within. The size of the greenhouse is 8'x18' and contains 149 sq. ft. not included in the square foot-

age quoted above. The formal living and dining areas feature spacious open planning. Sloping ceiling in the living room, plus the sliding glass doors to the outdoor terrace enhance the cheerfulness of this area. The foyer is large and routes traffic efficiently to all areas. Guest coat closets and a powder room are handy. The sleeping zone is well-planned. Two children's bedrooms have fine wall space, good wardrobe facilities and a full bath.

The master bedroom is exceptional. It is large enough to accommodate a sitting area and has access to the terrace. Two walk-in closets, a vanity area with lavatory and a compartmented bath are noteworthy features. Observe the stall shower in addition to the dramatic whirlpool installation. The floor plan below is identical with that on the opposite page and shows one of many possible ways to arrange furniture.

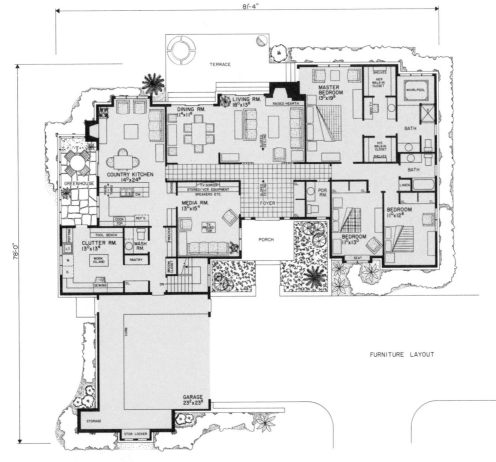

FURNITURE LAYOUT

Design V12857
Square Footage: 2,982

L

● Imagine yourself occupying this home! Study the outstanding master bedroom. You will be forever pleased by its many features. It has "his" and "her" baths each with a large walk-in closet, sliding glass doors to a private, side terrace (a great place to enjoy a morning cup of coffee) and an adjacent study. Notice that the two family bedrooms are separated from the master bedroom. This allows for total privacy both for the parents and the children. Continue to observe this plan. You will have no problem at all entertaining in the gathering room. Your party can flow to the adjacent balcony on a warm summer evening. The work center has been designed in an orderly fashion. The U-shaped kitchen utilizes the triangular work pattern, said to be the most efficient. Only a few steps away, you will be in the breakfast room, formal dining room, laundry or washroom. Take your time and study every last detail in this home plan.

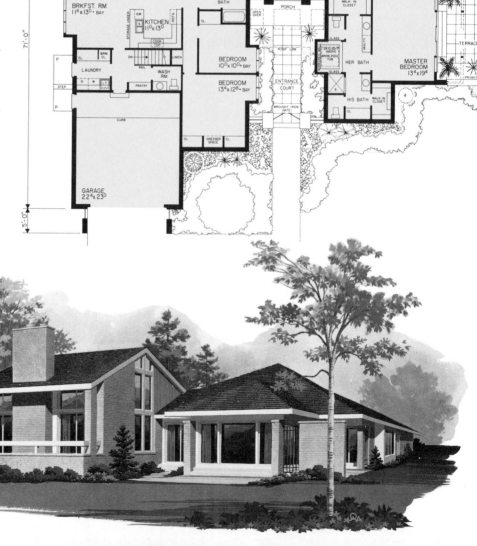

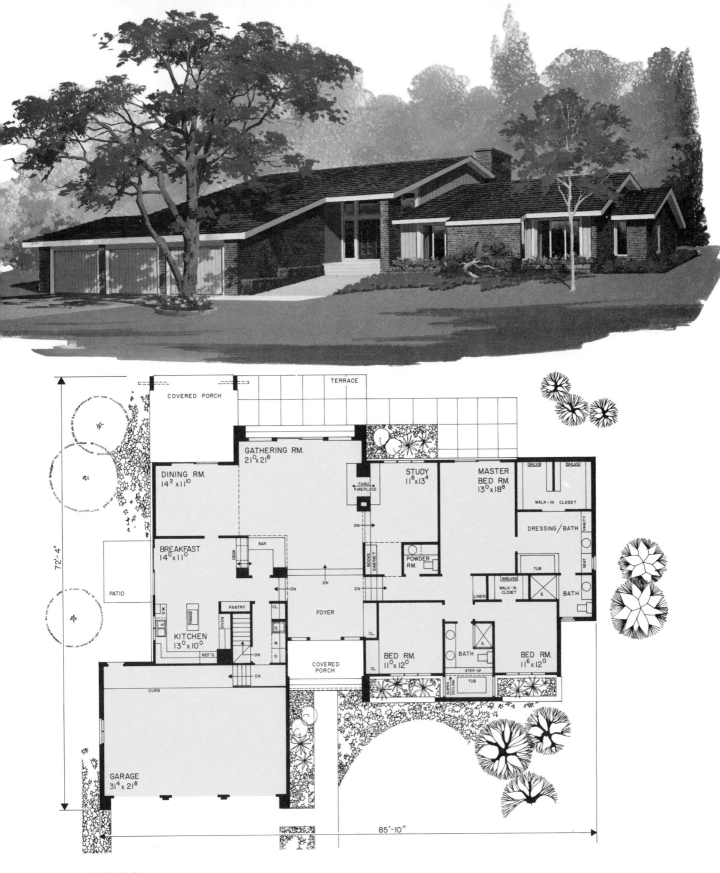

Design V12789 Square Footage: 2,732

L D

● An attached three car garage! What a fantastic feature of this three bedroom contemporary design. And there's more. As one walks up the steps to the covered porch and through the double front doors the charm of this design will be overwhelming. Inside, a large foyer greets all visitors and leads them to each of the three areas, each down a few steps. The living area has a large gathering room with fireplace and a study adjacent on one side and the formal dining room on the other. The work center has an efficient kitchen with island range, breakfast room, laundry and built-in desk and bar. Then there is the sleeping area. Note the raised tub with sloped ceiling.

Design V13560
Square Footage: 2,189

● Simplicity is the key to the stylish good
looks of this home's facade. A walled garden
entry and large window areas appeal to
outdoor enthusiasts. Inside, the kitchen forms
the hub of the plan. It opens directly off the
foyer and contains an island counter and
a work counter with eating space on the living
area side. A sloped ceiling, fireplace, and sliding glass doors to a rear terrace are highlights
in living area. The master bedroom also sports
sliding glass doors to the terrace. Its dressing
area is enhanced with double walk-in closets
and lavatories. A whirlpool tub and seated
shower are additional amenities. Two family
bedrooms are found on the opposite side of the
house. They share a full bath with twin
lavatories.

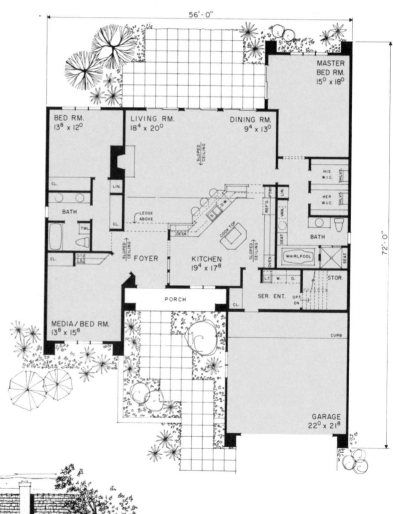

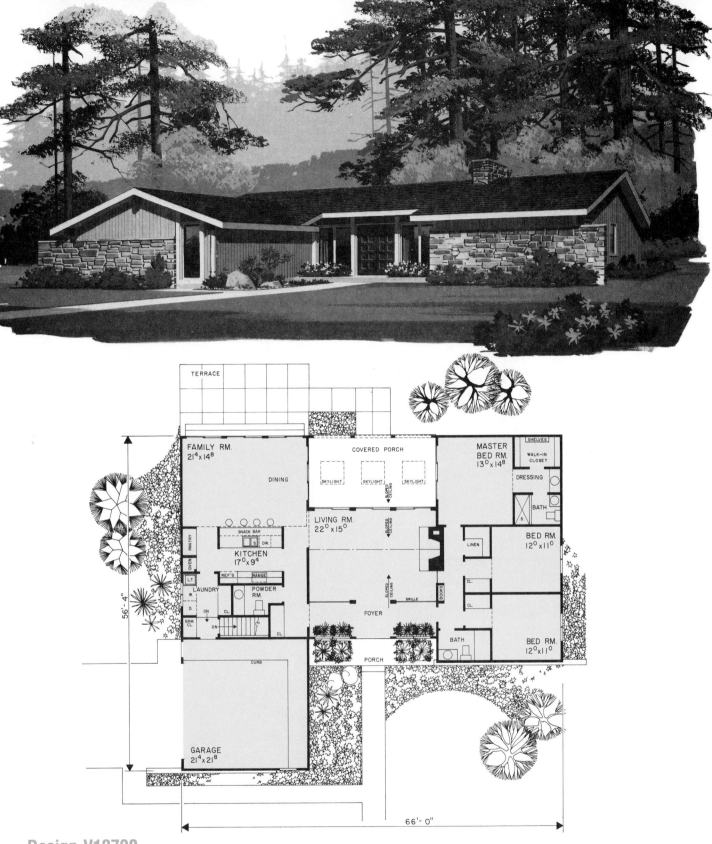

Design V12790
Square Footage: 2,075

● Enter this comtemporary hip-roofed home through the double front doors and immediately view the sloped-ceilinged living room with fireplace. This room will be a sheer delight when it comes to formal entertaining. It has easy access to the kitchen and also a powder room nearby. The work area will be convenient. The kitchen has an island work center with snack bar. The laundry is adjacent to the service entrance and stairs leading to the basement. This area is planned to be a real "step saver". The sleeping wing consists of two family bedrooms, bath and master bedroom suite. Maybe the most attractive feature of this design is the rear covered porch with skylights above. It is accessible by way of sliding glass doors in the family/dining area, living room and master bedroom.

Design V12866
Square Footage: 2,371

● An extra living unit has been built into the design of this home. It would make an excellent "mother-in-law" suite. Should you choose not to develop this area as indicated, maybe you might use it as two more bedrooms, a guest suite or even as hobby and game rooms. Whatever its final use, it will complement the rest of this home. The main house also deserves mention. The focal point will be the large gathering room. Its features include a skylight, sloped ceiling, centered fireplace flanked on both sides by sliding glass doors and adjacent is a dining room on one side, study on the other. The work center is clustered together. Three bedrooms and two baths make up the private area. Note the outdoor areas: court with privacy wall, two covered porches and a large terrace.

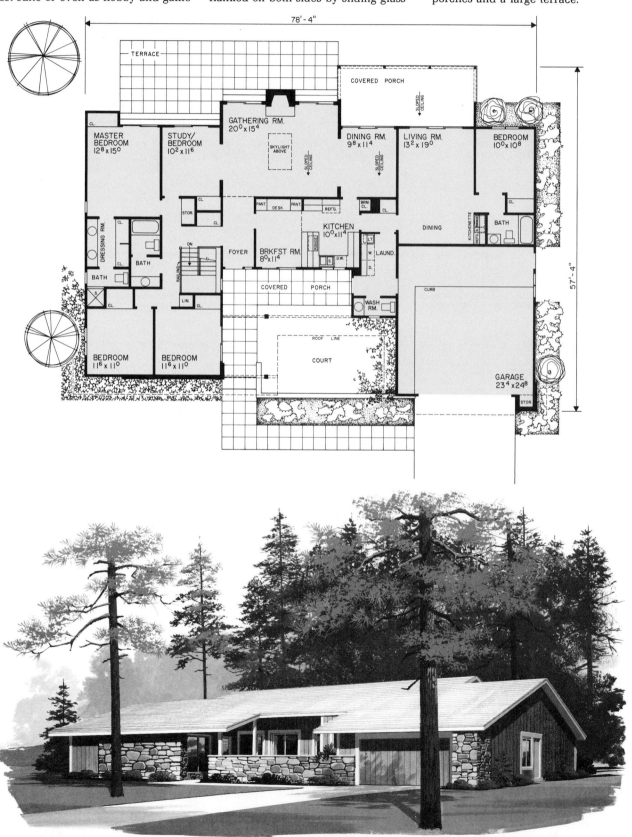

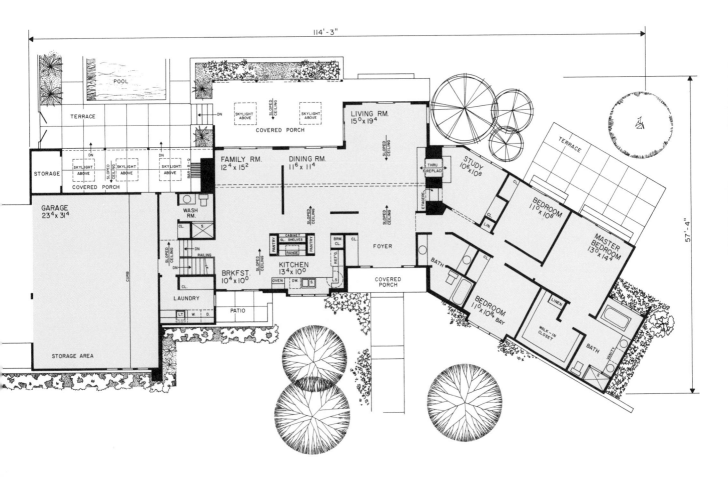

POOL

TERRACE

STORAGE

GARAGE
23⁴ x 31⁴

STORAGE AREA

COVERED PORCH

SKYLIGHT ABOVE SLOPED CEILING SKYLIGHT ABOVE

WASH RM.

BRKFST.
10⁴ x 10⁰

LAUNDRY

PATIO

SKYLIGHT ABOVE SLOPED CEILING SKYLIGHT ABOVE

COVERED PORCH

FAMILY RM.
12⁴ x 15²

DINING RM.
11⁶ x 11⁴

KITCHEN
13⁴ x 10⁰

LIVING RM.
15⁰ x 19⁴

FOYER

COVERED PORCH

THRU FIREPLACE

STUDY
10⁶ x 10⁸

BATH

BEDROOM
11⁰ x 10⁴ BAY

TERRACE

BEDROOM
11⁰ x 10⁸

MASTER BEDROOM
13⁰ x 14⁴

WALK-IN CLOSET

LINEN

BATH

114'-3"

57'-4"

Design V12819
Square Footage: 2,459

D

● Indoor-outdoor living will be enjoyed to the fullest in this rambling one-story contemporary plan. Each of the rear rooms in this design, excluding the study, has access to a terrace or porch. Even the front breakfast room has access to a private dining patio. The covered porch off the living areas, family, dining and living rooms, has a sloped ceiling and skylights. A built-in barbecue unit and a storage room will be found on the second covered porch.

Inside, the plan offers exceptional living patterns for various activities. Notice the thru-fireplace that the living room shares with the study. A built-in etagere is nearby. The three-car garage has an extra storage area.

Design V12730
Square Footage: 2,490

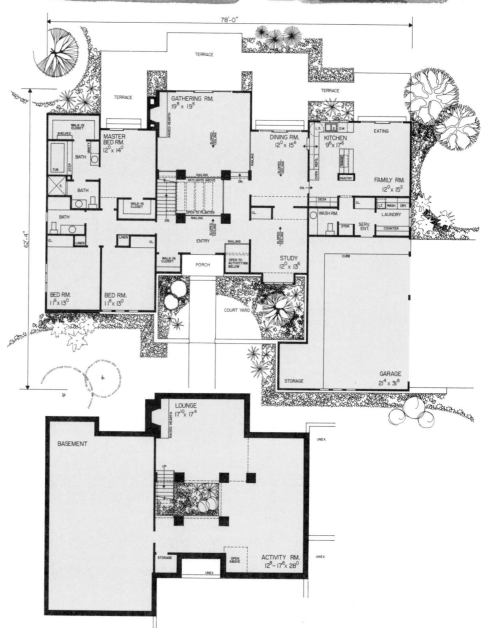

● Here is a basic one-story home that is really loaded with livability on the first floor and has a bonus of an extra 1,086 sq. ft. of planned livability on a lower level. What makes this so livable is that the first floor adjacent to the stairs leading below is open and forms a balcony looking down into a dramatic planting area. The first floor traffic patterns flow around this impressive and distinctive feature. In addition to the gathering room, study and family room, there is the lounge and activity room. Notice the second balcony open to the activity room below. The master bedroom is outstanding with two baths and two walk-in closets. The attached three-car garage has a bulk storage area and is accessible through the service area.

Design V13357
Square Footage: 2,913

L **D**

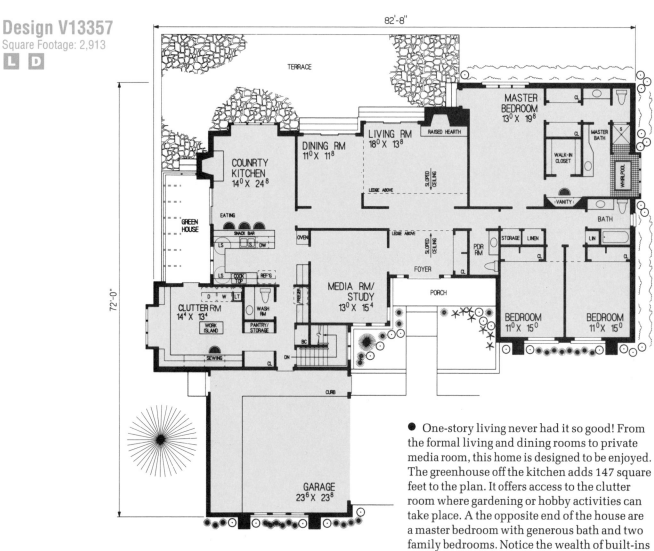

82'-8"

72'-0"

TERRACE

MASTER BEDROOM
13⁰ X 19⁸

MASTER BATH

WALK-IN CLOSET

WHIRL POOL

VANITY

BATH

LIVING RM
18⁰ X 13⁸

RAISED HEARTH

SLOPED CEILING

LEDGE ABOVE

DINING RM
11⁰ X 11⁸

COUNRTY KITCHEN
14⁰ X 24⁸

EATING

SNACK BAR

GREEN HOUSE

LS   DW

LS   COOK TOP   REF'G

OVEN

LEDGE ABOVE

SLOPED CEILING

PDR RM

STORAGE   LINEN

LIN

FOYER

PORCH

CLUTTER RM
14⁴ X 13⁴

D W LT

WASH RM

PANTRY/ STORAGE

WORK ISLAND

SEWING

FREEZ

BC

MEDIA RM/ STUDY
13⁰ X 15⁴

DN

BEDROOM
11⁰ X 15⁰

BEDROOM
11⁰ X 15⁰

CURB

GARAGE
23⁸ X 23⁸

● One-story living never had it so good! From the formal living and dining rooms to private media room, this home is designed to be enjoyed. The greenhouse off the kitchen adds 147 square feet to the plan. It offers access to the clutter room where gardening or hobby activities can take place. A the opposite end of the house are a master bedroom with generous bath and two family bedrooms. Notice the wealth of built-ins throughout the house.

Design V13319
Square Footage: 2,274

● This attractive bungalow design separates the master suite from family bedrooms and puts casual living to the back in a family room. The formal living and dining areas are centrally located and have access to a rear terrace, as does the master suite. The kitchen sits between formal and informal living areas. The two family bedrooms are found to the front of the plan. A home office or study opens off the front foyer and the master suite.

CUSTOMIZABLE

Custom Alterations? See page 381 for customizing this plan to your specifications.

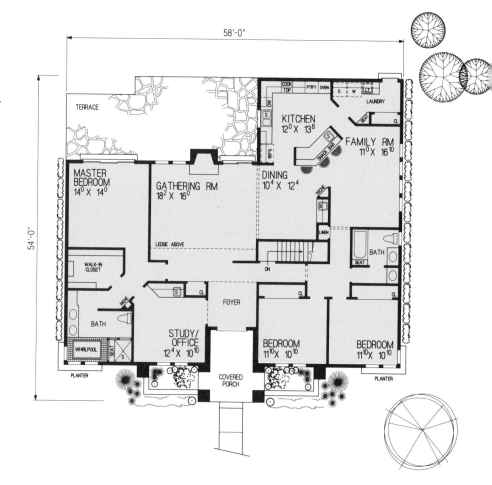

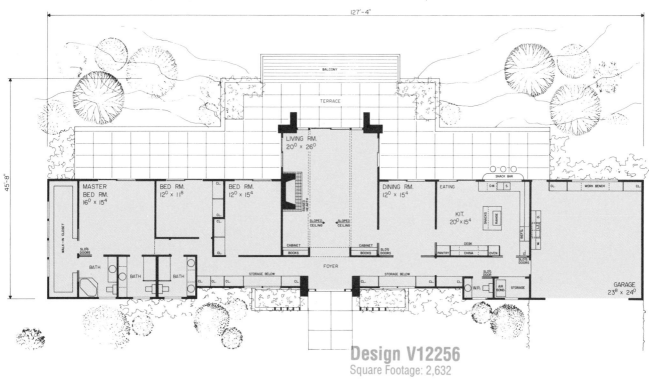

Design V12256
Square Footage: 2,632

● A dream home for those with young ideas. A refreshing, contemporary exterior with a unique, highly individualized interior. What are your favorite features.

127'-4"

45'-8"

BALCONY

TERRACE

LIVING RM.
20⁰ x 26⁰

MASTER
BED RM.
16⁰ x 15⁴

BED RM.
12⁰ x 11⁸

BED RM.
12⁰ x 15⁴

DINING RM.
12⁰ x 15⁴

EATING

SNACK BAR

WALK-IN CLOSET

SLD'G DOORS

SLOPED CEILING

SLOPED CEILING

KIT.
20⁰ x 15⁴

SNACKS RANGE

REF'L

WORK BENCH

CL.

CL.

BATH

BATH

BATH

CABINET BOOKS

CABINET BOOKS

SLD'G DOORS

PANTRY

CHINA

OVEN

DESK

SLD'G DOORS

FOYER

STORAGE BELOW

STORAGE BELOW

W.R.

AIR COND.

STORAGE

GARAGE
23⁸ x 24⁰

257

Design V13368

Square Footage: 2,722

L **D**

● Roof lines are the key to the interesting exterior of this design. Their configuration allow for sloped ceilings in the gathering room and large foyer. The master bedroom suite has a huge walk-in closet, garden whirlpool and separate shower. Two family bedrooms share a full bath. One of these bedrooms could be used as a media room with pass-through wet bar. Note the large kitchen with conversation bay and the wide terrace to the rear.

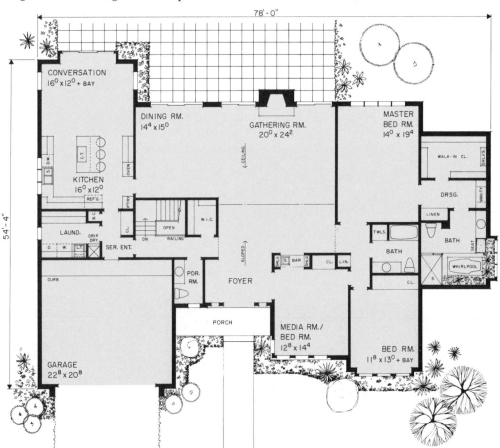

78'-0"

54'-4"

CONVERSATION
16⁰ x 12⁰ + BAY

DINING RM.
14⁴ x 15⁰

GATHERING RM.
20⁰ x 24²

MASTER
BED RM.
14⁰ x 19⁴

WALK-IN CL.

SHLVS.

KITCHEN
16⁰ x 12⁰

OVEN

C.T.

REF'G.

DRSG.

VANITY

LINEN

LAUND.

DRIP
DRY

D. W.

SER. ENT.

CL.

P'TRY.

OPEN
DN   RAILING

W.I.C.

CEILING

TWLS.

BATH

LINEN

BATH

SEAT

CURB

S. BAR

SHLVS.

CL. LIN.

SLOPED

WHIRLPOOL

CL.

S.

PDR.
RM.

FOYER

GARAGE
22⁸ x 20⁸

PORCH

MEDIA RM./
BED RM.
12⁸ x 14⁴

BED RM.
11⁸ x 13⁰ + BAY

258

Design V12304
Square Footage: 2,313

● What an appealing home! And what a list of reasons why it is so eye-catching. First of all, there is the irregular shape and the low-pitched, wide-over-hanging roof. Then, there is the interesting use of exterior materials, including vertical glass window treatment. Further, there are the raised planters flanking the porch of the recessed entrance. Inside, the traffic patterns are excellent. Among the focal points is the 33 foot, beam ceilinged living area. This will surely be fun to plan and furnish for the family's living and dining pursuits. Among other highlights is the layout of the laundry-kitchen-nook area. The extra washroom is strategically located. The sleeping wing has much to offer with its privacy, its convenient bath facilities, and its fine storage.

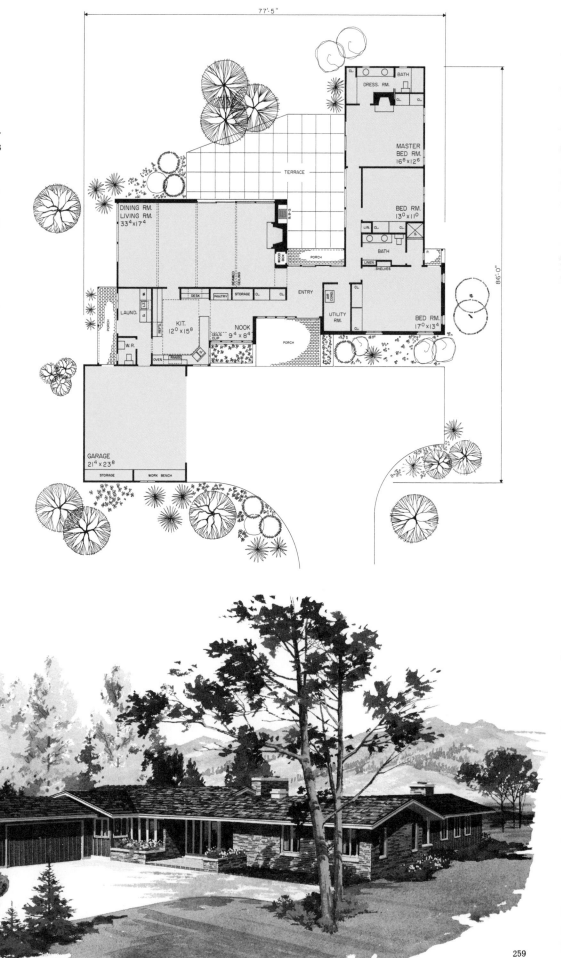

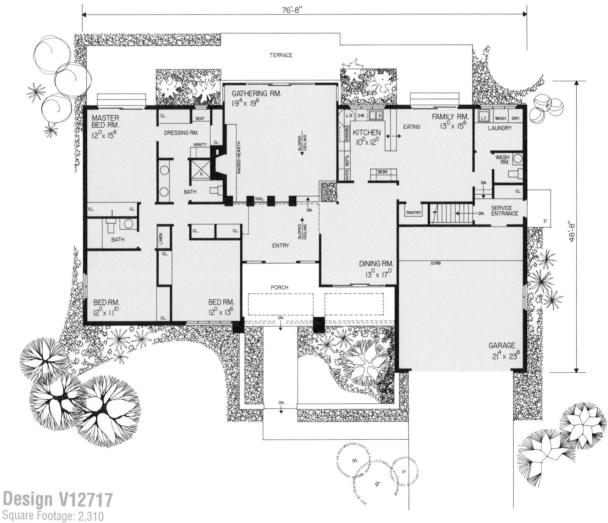

Labels within floor plan:

76'-8"

TERRACE

GATHERING RM.
19⁴ x 19⁶

FAMILY RM.
13⁰ x 15⁶

MASTER BED RM.
12⁰ x 15⁶

CL. SEAT

DRESSING RM.

KITCHEN
10⁰ x 12⁰

EATING

L.S. D.W.

RANGE

OVEN REFG.

LT. WASH. DRY.

LAUNDRY

VANITY CL.

RAISED HEARTH

SLOPED CEILING

WASH. RM.

BATH

DN. CL.

BATH

RAIL

DN.

SERVICE ENTRANCE

PANTRY

DN.

P.

LINEN CL.

CL. CL.

SLOPED CEILING

ENTRY

48'-8"

CL.

CL.

BED RM.
12⁰ x 11¹⁰

BED RM.
12⁰ x 13⁶

PORCH

DINING RM.
13⁰ x 17⁰

CURB

GARAGE
21⁴ x 23⁸

DN.

DN.

Design V12717
Square Footage: 2,310

● Great for family life! There's a spacious family room for casual activities. And a "work efficient" kitchen that features a built-in desk and appliances, a large pantry plus a pass-through to the family room for added convenience. A first floor laundry, too, with adjacent washroom and stairs to the basement. Want glamour? There's a sloped ceiling in the entry hall plus a delightful "over the railing" view of the sunken gathering room. And the gathering room itself! More than 19' by 19' . . . with a sloped ceiling, raised hearth fireplace and sliding glass doors to the rear terrace. A 13' by 17' formal dining room, too. The curb area in the garage is convenient.

CUSTOMIZABLE

Custom Alterations? See page 381 for customizing this plan to your specifications.

59'-0"

TERRACE

STUDY
12⁶ x 16⁰

GATHERING RM.
16⁶ x 16⁰

COVERED PORCH

MASTER BEDROOM
14⁰ x 16⁰

SLOPED CEILING

SLOPED CEILING

DINING RM.
11⁸ x 10⁸

CL.

LINEN

BAR

DRESSING RM.

WALK-IN CLOSET

BATH

SLOPED CEILING

RAILING

DN.

DESK

TERRACE

BRKFST. RM.
11⁸ x 10⁸

CL.

VANITY

BATH

SEAT

WHIRLPOOL

CL.

FOYER

CURIOS

CL.

OVENS

PTRY

PASS THRU

KITCHEN
11⁸ x 10⁰

LAUND.

W

D

REF'G

COOK TOP

DW

S

BEDROOM
12⁴ x 12⁶

COVERED PORCH

Design V12930
Square Footage: 2,032

COURTYARD

SKYLIGHT

SLOPED

CEILING

CURB

GARAGE
21⁴ x 21⁴

62'-0"

● The clean lines of this L-shaped contemporary are enhanced by the interesting, wide overhanging roof planes. Horizontal and vertical siding compliment one another. The low privacy fence adds interest as it forms a delightful front courtyard adjacent to the covered walkway to the front door.

Here's a floor plan made to order for the active small family or empty-nesters. Sloping ceilings and fine glass areas foster a spacious interior. The master bedroom has an outstanding dressing room and bath layout. The guest room has its own full bath. Note how this bath can function as a handy

powder room. A favorite room will be the study with its fireplace and two sets of sliding glass doors. Don't miss the open-planned gathering and dining rooms, or the kitchen/laundry area. The breakfast room has its own terrace. Notice the rear covered porch. Fine indoor-outdoor relationships.

Design V13408
Square Footage: 2,940

● Interesting angles make for interesting rooms. The sleeping zone features two large bedrooms with unique shapes and a master suite with spectacular bath. A laundry placed nearby is both convenient and economical, located adjacent to a full bath. The central kitchen offers a desk and built-in breakfast table. Meals can also be enjoyed in the adjacent eating area, formal dining room with stepped ceiling, or outside on the rear patio. A planter and glass block wall separate the living room and family room, which is warmed by a fireplace.

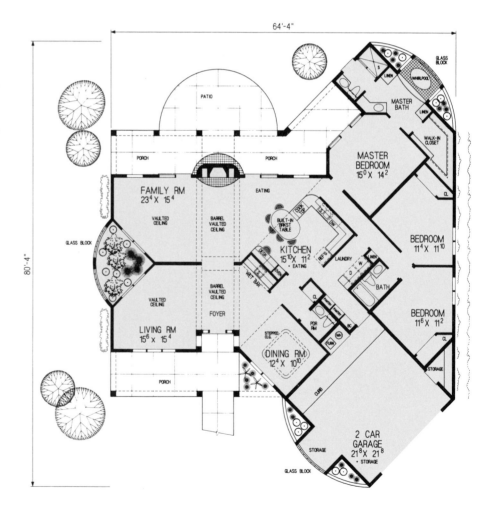

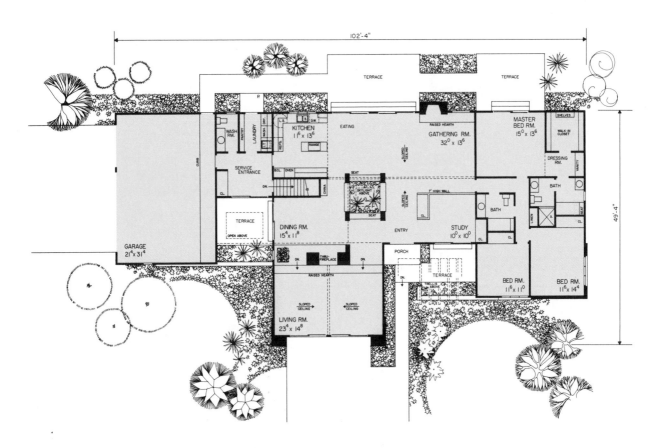

Design V12745
Square Footage: 2,890

● Just imagine the fun everyone will have living in this contemporary home with its frame exterior and accents of stone veneer (make it brick, if you prefer). The living areas revolve around the dramatic atrium-type planting area flooded with natural light from the skylight above. The formal living room is sunken and has a thru-fireplace to the dining room. Also a large gathering room with a second raised hearth fireplace, sloped ceiling, sliding glass doors to a rear terrace and informal eating area. Observe the sloping ceilings, the laundry with pantry, the wash room and the study. Master bedroom has a stall shower, a tub with seat, a vanity and two lavatories.

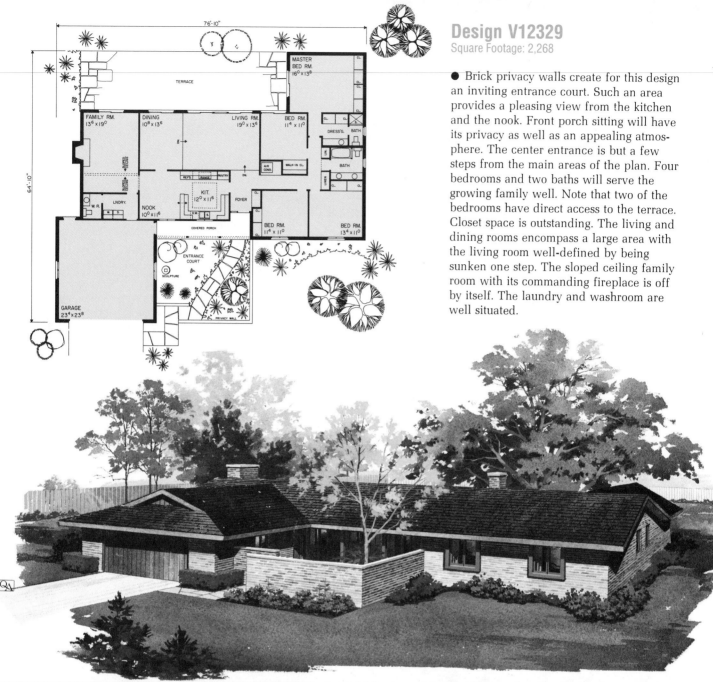

Design V12329
Square Footage: 2,268

● Brick privacy walls create for this design an inviting entrance court. Such an area provides a pleasing view from the kitchen and the nook. Front porch sitting will have its privacy as well as an appealing atmosphere. The center entrance is but a few steps from the main areas of the plan. Four bedrooms and two baths will serve the growing family well. Note that two of the bedrooms have direct access to the terrace. Closet space is outstanding. The living and dining rooms encompass a large area with the living room well-defined by being sunken one step. The sloped ceiling family room with its commanding fireplace is off by itself. The laundry and washroom are well situated.

Design V12529
Square Footage: 2,326

● The front entrance court with its plant areas and surrounding accents of colorful quarried stone (make it brick, if you prefer), provides a delightful introduction to this interesting contemporary home. The spacious entry hall leads directly to a generous L-shaped living and dining area. Sliding glass doors provide direct access to the outdoor terrace. An efficient, interior kitchen will be fun in which to work. It could hardly be more strategically located — merely a step or two from the formal dining area, the breakfast nook, and the family room. Although this home has a basement, there is a convenient first floor laundry and an extra washroom. The four bedroom sleeping wing has two full baths. Two of the rooms have access to the outdoor terraces. Notice garage storage.

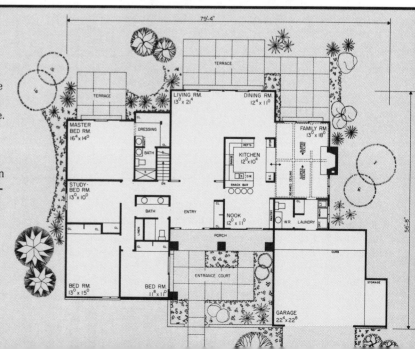

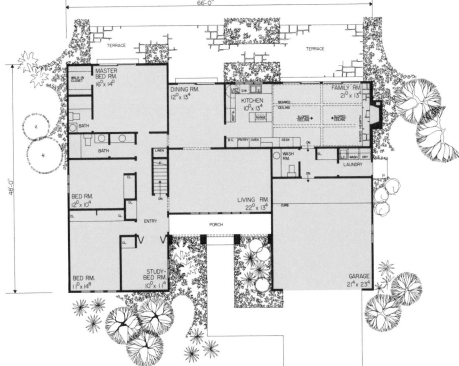

Design V12532
Square Footage: 2,112

● Here is a refreshing, modified U-shaped contemporary that is long on both looks and livability. The board and batten exterior creates simple lines which are complimented by the low-pitched roof with its wide overhang and exposed rafters. The appeal of the front court is enhanced by the massive stone columns at the edge of the covered porch. A study of the floor plan reveals interestingly different and practical living patterns. The location of the entry hall represents a fine conservation of space for the living areas. The L-shaped formal living-dining zone has access to both front and rear yards. The informal living area is a true family kitchen. Its open planning produces a spacious and cheerful area. Note sloping, beamed ceiling, raised hearth fireplace and sliding glass doors.

Design V12793
Square Footage: 2,065

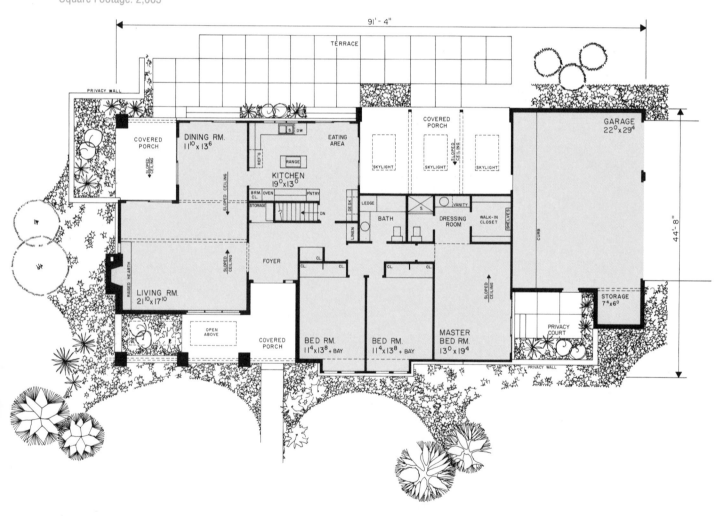

TERRACE

91'- 4"

44'- 8"

PRIVACY WALL

COVERED PORCH

DINING RM.
11¹⁰ x 13⁶

EATING AREA

COVERED PORCH

GARAGE
22⁰ x 29⁴

SKYLIGHT   SKYLIGHT   SKYLIGHT

SLOPED CEILING

KITCHEN
19⁰ x 13⁰

RANGE

BRM. OVEN CL.

STORAGE

PNTRY

DN

LEDGE   DESK   LINEN

BATH

VANITY

DRESSING ROOM

WALK-IN CLOSET

SHELVES

CURB

STORAGE
7⁴ x 6⁰

SLOPED CEILING

FOYER

CL.   CL.   CL.   CL.   CL.

RAISED HEARTH

LIVING RM.
21⁰ x 17¹⁰

OPEN ABOVE

COVERED PORCH

BED RM.
11⁴ x 13⁸ + BAY

BED RM.
11⁴ x 13⁸ + BAY

MASTER BED RM.
13⁰ x 19⁴

SLOPED CEILING

PRIVACY COURT

PRIVACY WALL

● Privacy will be enjoyed in this home both inside and out. The indoor-outdoor living relationships offered in this plan are outstanding. A covered porch at the entrance. A privacy court off the master bedroom divided from the front yard with a privacy wall. A covered porch serving both the living and dining rooms through sliding glass doors. Also utilizing a privacy wall. Another covered porch off the kitchen eating area. This one is the largest and has skylights above. Also a large rear terrace. The kitchen is efficient with eating space available, an island range and built-in desk. Storage space is abundant. Note storage area in the garage and its overall size. Three front bedrooms. Raised hearth fireplace in the living room.

Design V12303
Square Footage: 2,330

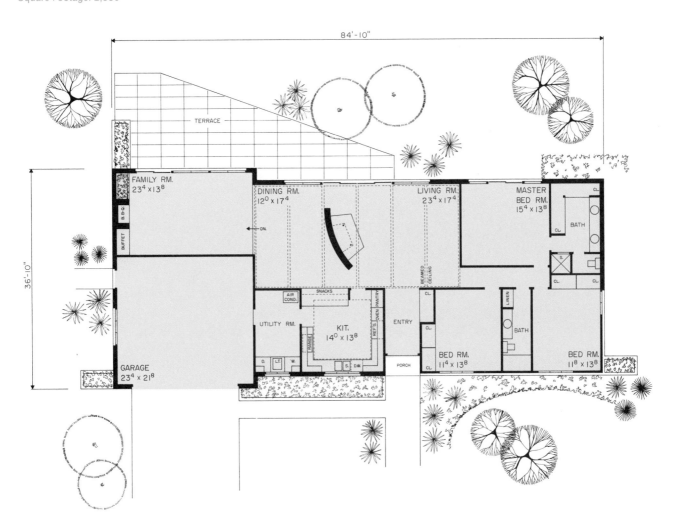

● This hip-roof ranch home has a basic floor plan that is the favorite of many. The reasons for its popularity are, of course, easy to detect. The simple rectangular shape means relatively economical construction. The living areas are large and are located to the rear to function through sliding glass doors with the terrace. The front kitchen is popular because of its view of approaching callers and its proximity to the front entry. The big utility room serves as a practical buffer between the garage and the kitchen.

Worthy of particular note is the efficiency of the kitchen, the stylish living room fireplace, the beamed ceiling, the sunken family room with its wall of built-ins (make that a music wall if you wish). Observe the snack bar and the fine master bath.

Design V12523
Square Footage: 2,055

● For those who like refreshing contemporary lines, this design will rate at the top. The wide overhanging roof, the brick masses, the glass areas, the raised planters, and the covered front entrance highlight the facade. As for the interior, all the elements are present to assure fine living patterns. Consider the room relationships and how they function with one another. Note how they relate to the outdoors.

Design V11820
Square Footage: 2,730

● Whatever the location, snugly tucked in among the hills or impressively oriented on the flatlands - this trim hip-roof ranch home will be fun to own. Here is a gracious exterior whose floor plan has "everything". Traffic patterns are excellent. The zoning of the sleeping wing, as well as the formal and informal living areas, is outstanding. Indoor-outdoor living relationships are most practical and convenient.

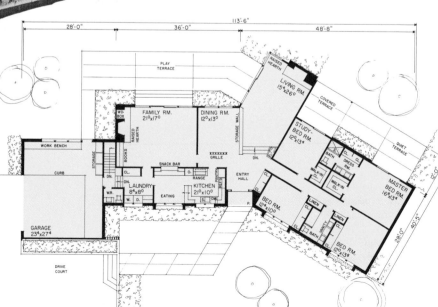

Design V12359
Square Footage: 2,078

● The low-pitched, wide-overhanging roof with its exposed beams, acts as a visor for the projecting living room. This will be an exceedingly pleasant room with its sunken floor, sloped ceiling, large glass area, and raised hearth fireplace. At the rear of this living rectangle is the family room. Between these two living areas is the efficient kitchen with its adjacent eating area. The utility room and its laundry equipment is nearby, as is the powder room. A separate dining room acts as the connecting link to the bedroom zone. Note the master bedroom with its dressing room, twin lavatories and two closets.

Design V12506
Square Footage: 2,851

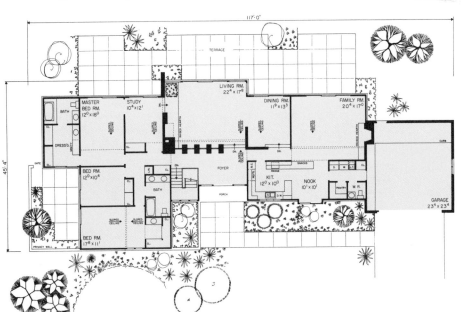

● Here is a home that is sure to add an extra measure of fun to your family's living patterns. The exterior is extremely pleasing with the use of paned glass windows, the hipped roof and the double front doors. The initial impact of the interior begins dramatically in the large foyer. The ceiling is sloped, while straight ahead one views the sunken living room. Impressive are the masonry columns with a railing between each. The stairwell to the partial basement is open and has a view of the outdoor planter. The sleeping area consists of three bedrooms, baths and a study (or fourth bedroom if you prefer). Two raised hearth fireplaces, pantry, washroom and more. List your favorite features.

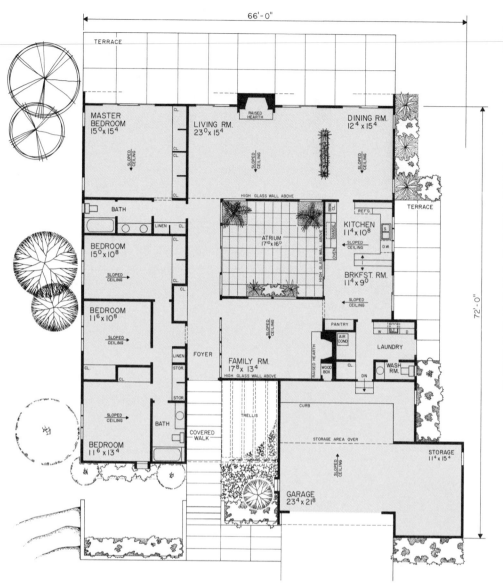

66'-0"

TERRACE

MASTER BEDROOM
15⁰ x 15⁴

LIVING RM.
23⁰ x 15⁴

RAISED HEARTH

DINING RM.
12⁴ x 15⁴

SLOPED CEILING

BATH

LINEN CL.

BEDROOM
15⁰ x 10⁸

SLOPED CEILING

HIGH GLASS WALL ABOVE

ATRIUM
17¹⁰ x 16⁰

HIGH GLASS WALL ABOVE

TERRACE

REF'G.

KITCHEN
11⁴ x 10⁸

OVEN

SLOPED CEILING

D.W.

BEDROOM
11⁶ x 10⁸

SLOPED CEILING

BRKFST. RM.
11⁴ x 9⁰

SLOPED CEILING

FOYER

FAMILY RM.
17⁸ x 13⁴

HIGH GLASS WALL ABOVE

SLOPED CEILING

PANTRY

AIR. COND

WOOD BOX

LAUNDRY

W D

LINEN

STOR.

CL.

WASH RM.

DN

STOR.

BATH

BEDROOM
11⁶ x 13⁴

SLOPED CEILING

COVERED WALK

TRELLIS

CURB

STORAGE AREA OVER

SLOPED CEILING

STORAGE
11⁴ x 15⁴

GARAGE
23⁴ x 21⁸

72'-0"

Design V12135
Square Footage: 2,495 (Excluding Atriur

● For those seeking a new experience in home ownership. The pro-
occupants of this contemporary ho
will forever be thrilled at their ch
of such a distinguished exterior ar
such a practical and exciting floor
plan. The variety of shed roof pla
contrast dramatically with the sim
plicity of the vertical siding. Insid
there is a feeling of spaciousness r
sulting from the sloping ceilings. T
uniqueness of this design is furthe
enhanced by the atrium. Open to t
sky, this outdoor area, indoors, ca
enjoyed from all parts of the hous
The sleeping zone has four bedrooms, two baths and plenty of clo
ets. The informal living zone has a
fine kitchen and breakfast room. T
formal zone consists of a large livi
dining area with fireplace.

BRKFST. RM.

FAM. RM.

PANTRY

W. D

LAUNDRY

WOOD BOX

DN

DN

W. R

GARAGE

CURB

OPTIONAL PARTIAL BASEMENT

270

SOLAR ORIENTED DESIGNS . . .

exist in almost limitless sizes, shapes and types. Most houses can be made more, or less, solar oriented by proper planning of room locations in relation to the siting of the structure on a piece of property. Selection of a floor plan with an array of windows that will face the north in the winter can hardly be recommended. Better to choose either a different plan or site. However, the designs in this section offer a study of the many alternatives to planning a more solar oriented house. Note the atriums, greenhouses, sunspaces, garden rooms, underground and berm houses and even the solar panels that are presented for your consideration.

Design V12832

Square Footage: 2,805 (Excluding Atrium)

D

● The advantage of passive solar heating is a significant highlight of this contemporary design. The huge skylight over the atrium provides shelter during inclement weather, while permitting the enjoyment of plenty of natural light to the atrium below and surrounding areas. Whether open to the sky, or sheltered by a glass or translucent covering, the atrium becomes a cheerful spot and provides an abundance of natural light to its adjacent rooms. The stone floor will absorb an abundance of heat from the sun during the day and permit circulation of warm air to other areas at night. During the summer, shades afford protection from the sun without sacrificing the abundance of natural light and the feeling of spaciousness. Sloping ceilings highlight each of the major rooms, three bedrooms, formal living and dining and study. The conversation area between the two formal areas will really be something to talk about. The broad expanses of roof can accommodate solar panels should an active system be desired to supplement the passive features of this design.

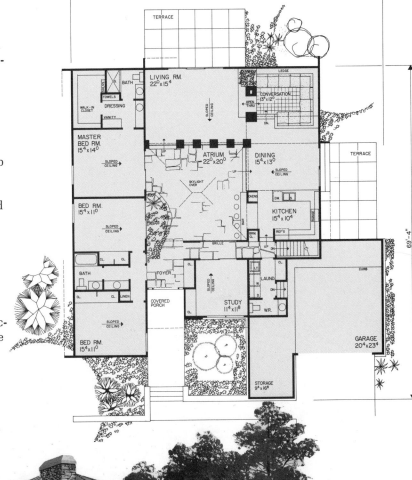

A Sunspace Spa Highlights this Trend House

● Contemporary in exterior styling, this house is energy oriented. It calls for 2 x 6 exterior wall construction with placement on a north facing lot. Traffic flows through the interior of this plan by way of the foyer. Not only is the foyer useful, but it is dramatic with its sloped ceiling and second floor balcony and skylight above. Excellent living areas are throughout. A spacious, sunken living room is to the left of the foyer. It shares a thru-fireplace, faced with fieldstone, with the study. Sloped ceilings are in both of these rooms. Informal activities can take place in the family room. It, too, has a fireplace and is adjacent to the work center. Two of the bedrooms are on the second floor with a lounge overlooking the gathering room below. The master bedroom is on the first floor. A generous amount of closet space with mirrored doors will enhance its appearance. Study the spacious master bath with all of its many features. Its direct access to the sunspace spa. will be appreciated.

Design V12900

First Floor: 2,332 square feet
Second Floor: 953 square feet
Total: 3,285 square feet

● Passive solar benefits will be acquired from the spa. It transmits light and heat to the other parts of the house. Heat stored during the day, by the stone floor, will be circulated at night by mechanical means. Shades may be used to control the amount of heat gain. This spa provides a large area where various activities can be done at the same time. Note the bar, whirlpool and exercise area. It will be a cheerful and spacious family recreation area. There are 551 square feet in the sunspace spa which are not included in the above totals.

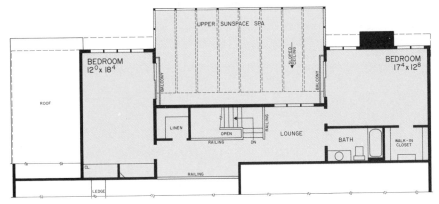

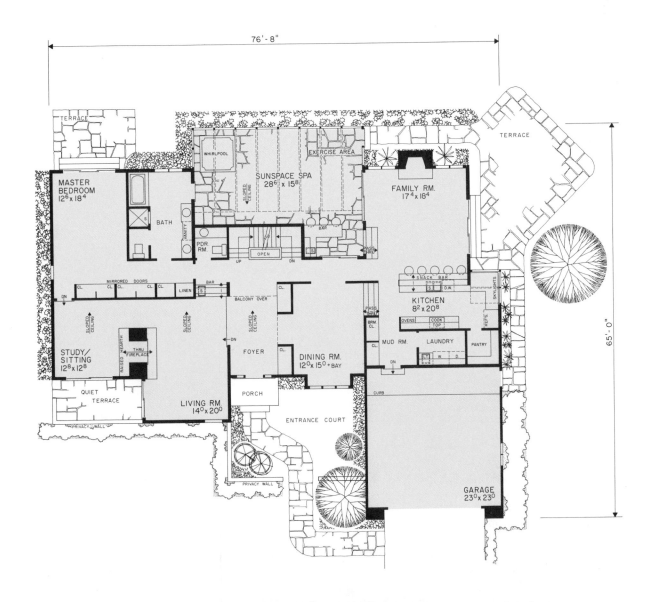

Design V12858
Square Footage: 2,231

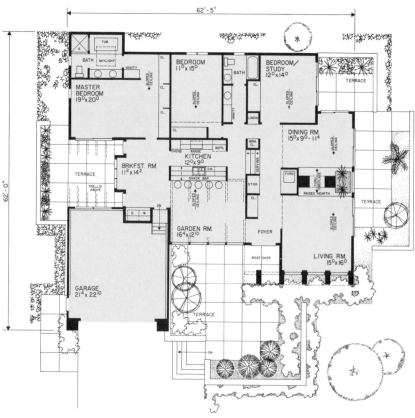

● This sun oriented design was created to face the south. By doing so, it has minimal northern exposure. It has been designed primarily for the more temperate U.S. latitudes using 2 x 6 wall construction. The morning sun will brighten the living and dining rooms, along with the adjacent terrace. Sun enters the garden room by way of the glass roof and walls. In the winter, the solar heat gain from the garden room should provide relief from high energy bills. Solar shades allow you to adjust the amount of light that you want to enter in the warmer months. Interior planning deserves mention, too. The work center is efficient. The kitchen has a snack bar on the garden room side and a serving counter to the dining room. The breakfast room with laundry area is also convenient to the kitchen. Three bedrooms are on the northern wall. The master bedroom has a large tub and a separate shower with a four foot square skylight above. When this design is oriented toward the sun, it should prove to be energy efficient and a joy to live in.

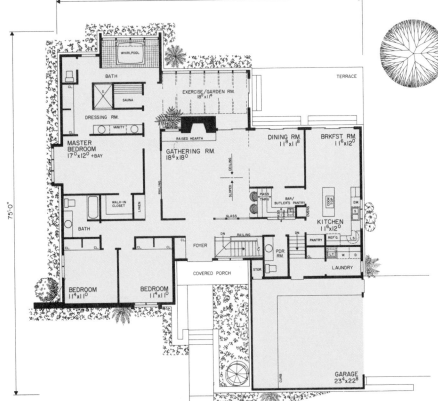

64'-8"

75'-0"

WHIRLPOOL

BATH

EXERCISE/GARDEN RM.
18⁰x11⁰

TERRACE

SAUNA

DRESSING RM.

VANITY

DINING RM.
11⁸x11⁸

BRKFST RM.
11⁶x12⁰

MASTER BEDROOM
17⁰x12⁰+BAY

RAISED HEARTH

GATHERING RM.
18⁶x18⁰

SLOPED CEILING

RAILING

CL

WALK-IN CLOSET

LINEN

PASS THRU

BAR/BUTLER'S PANTRY

COOK TOP

OVENS

DW

BATH

GLASS

KITCHEN
11⁶x12⁰

DN   RAILING

FOYER

DN

PANTRY

REF'G.

L.S.

BEDROOM
11⁴x11⁰

BEDROOM
11⁴x11⁰

CL

CL

PDR. RM.

CL

LT   W   D

COVERED PORCH

STOR.

LAUNDRY

CARB

GARAGE
23⁴x22⁸

Design V12873
Square Footage: 2,838

● This modern three-bedroom home incorporates many of the Contemporary features so popular today. A large gathering room with cozy raised-hearth fireplace and sloped ceiling is central focus and centrally located. Adjacent to the gathering room is a dining room that adjoins a bar or butler's pantry. This handy service area also has pass-thru entry to the central gathering room. Just off the pantry is a large modern kitchen with central cook-top island and adjoining breakfast room. The master bedroom suite is especially luxurious with its own sauna, whirlpool, dressing room, bay window, and adjoining exercise room. This adjacent exercise room could double as a lovely garden room. It's located just off the back terrace. There's even a powder room for guests in front, and a covered porch to keep visitors dry. A laundry is conveniently located off the spacious two-car garage. Note the large view glass off the rear exercise/garden room. This is a comfortable and modern home, indeed.

Design V12882
Square Footage: 2,832

● This contemporary, one-story design should be oriented on a west-facing site if it is built in the northern regions of the country. The result will be minimal exposure to the cold northern winds during the winter. Study the north side of this plan. There is only one small window and it will be protected by the privacy wall. This means that the rooms on the opposite side of the house will have the desirable southern exposure. A westerly exposure for the living room will be most beneficial in many areas of the country. This plan reflects interesting living patterns and excellent indoor/outdoor relationships. Wide overhanging roofs, skylights, glass gables, vented walkways, wind-buffering privacy fences and 2x6 construction are among this design's energy oriented features.

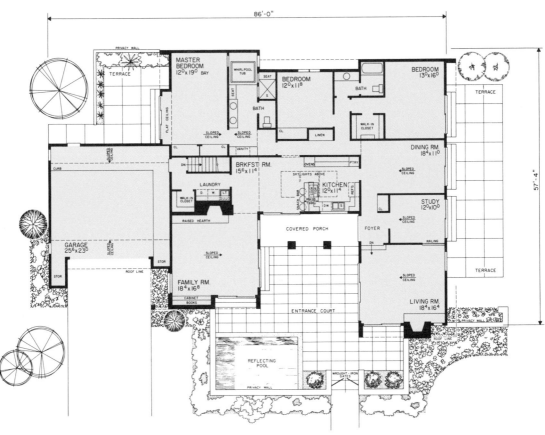

Design V12881
Square Footage: 2,770

● Energy-efficiency will be obtained in this unique, contemporary design. This plan has been designed for a south facing lot in the temperate zones. There is minimal window exposure on the north side of the house so the interior will be protected. The eastern side of the plan, on the other hand, will allow the morning sunlight to enter. As the sun travels from east to west, the various rooms will have light through windows, sliding glass doors or skylights. The garage acts as a buffer against the hot afternoon sun. The living areas are oriented to the front of the plan. They will benefit from the southern exposure during the cooler months. During the summer months, this area will be shielded from the high, hot summer sun by the overhanging roof. If you plan to build in the south, this house would be ideal for a north facing site. This results in a minimum amount of hot sun for the living areas and a maximum amount of protection from the sun on the rear, southern side of the house.

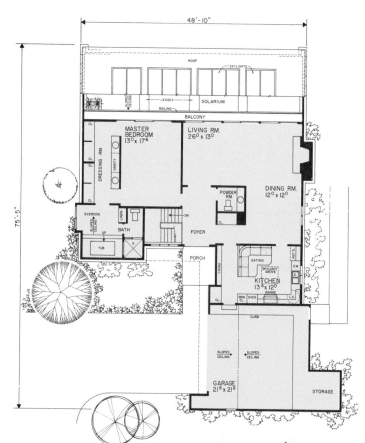

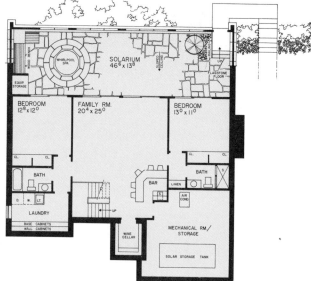

Design V12835 Main Level: 1,626 square feet
Lower Level: 2,038 square feet; Total: 3,664 square feet

● Passive solar techniques with the help of an active solar component - they can work together or the active solar component can act as a back-up system - heat and cool this striking contemporary design. The lower level solarium is the primary passive element. It admits sunlight during the day for direct-gain heating. The warmth, which was absorbed into the thermal floor, is then radiated into the structure at night. The earth berms on the three sides of the lower level help keep out the winter cold and summer heat. The active system uses collector panels to gather the sun's heat. The heat is transferred via a water pipe system to the lower level storage tank where it is circulated throughout the house by a heat exchanger. Note that where active solar collectors are a design OPTION, which they are in all of our active/passive designs, they must be contracted locally. The collector area must be tailored to the climate and sun angles that characterize your building location.

Design V12830 Main Level: 1,795 square feet; Lower Level: 1,546 square feet; Total: 3,341 square feet

● Outstanding contemporary design! This home has been created with the advantages of passive solar heating in mind. For optimum energy savings, this delightful design combines passive solar devices, the solarium, with optional active collectors. Included with the purchase of this design are four plot plans to assure that the solar collectors will face the south. The garage in each plan acts as a buffer against cold northern winds. Schematic details for solar application also are included. Along with being energy-efficient, this design has excellent living patterns. Three bedrooms, the master bedroom on the main level and two others on the lower level at each side of the solarium. The living area of the main level will be able to enjoy the delightful view of the solarium and sunken garden.

58'-4"

73'-4"

SUNKEN GARDEN

ROOF

GLASS GLASS GLASS GLASS

ROOF

STUDY
12⁰ x 16⁴

OPEN TO
SOLARIUM BELOW

DINING RM.
12⁰ x 12⁰

GATHERING RM.
16⁰ x 16⁰

MASTER
BED RM.
12⁰ x 18⁰

BATH

KITCHEN
12⁰ x 9⁶

WALK-IN
CLOSET

VESTIBULE
(AIR LOCK)

LAUND.

BRKFST. RM.
9⁸ x 11⁶

WALK-IN
CLOSET

DRESSING

BATH

SEAT   LEDGE

COVERED
PORCH

COVERED
PORCH

GARAGE
22⁰ x 25⁴

STORAGE
9' x 7⁰

SUNKEN GARDEN

BED RM.
11⁶ x 14²

BED RM.
11⁶ x 14²

SOLARIUM
16⁰ x 11⁴
BALCONY ABOVE

LOUNGE
16⁰ x 16⁰

LINEN   CL.

CL.   LINEN

BATH

BATH

AIR
COND.

SUMMER KITCHEN
11⁸ x 5⁰

BASEMENT / MECHANICAL
(SOLAR EQUIPMENT)

UP

ACTIVITIES RM.
24⁴ x 10¹⁰

279

Design V12827

Upper Level: 1,618 square feet
Lower Level: 1,458 square feet
Total: 3,076 square feet

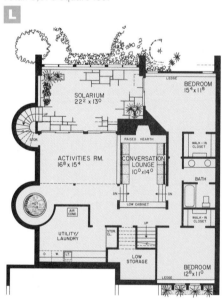

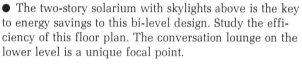

● The two-story solarium with skylights above is the key to energy savings to this bi-level design. Study the efficiency of this floor plan. The conversation lounge on the lower level is a unique focal point.

Design V12884 First Floor: 1,855 square feet
Second Floor: 837 square feet; Total: 2,692 square feet

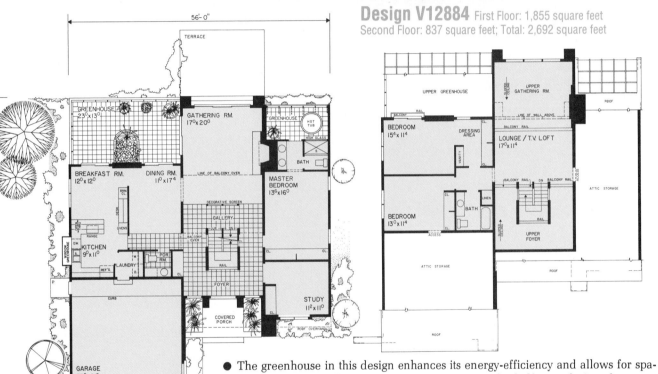

56'-0"

TERRACE

GREENHOUSE 23⁰ x 13⁰

GATHERING RM. 17⁰ x 20⁰

GREENHOUSE

HOT TUB

HIGH GLASS

BATH

BREAKFAST RM. 12⁰ x 12⁰

DINING RM. 11⁰ x 17⁴

LINE OF BALCONY OVER

MASTER BEDROOM 13⁶ x 16⁰

DECORATIVE SCREEN

GALLERY

KITCHEN 9⁰ x 11⁰

RANGE

OVENS

BALCONY OVER

LAUNDRY

PDR. RM.

RAIL

CL.

CL.

FOYER

GARAGE 23⁶ x 21⁶

CURB

COVERED PORCH

STUDY 11² x 11⁰

ROOF OVERHANG

ROOF OVERHANG

UPPER GREENHOUSE

UPPER GATHERING RM.

ROOF

BALCONY RAIL

LINE OF WALL ABOVE

BEDROOM 15⁴ x 11⁴

DRESSING AREA

VANITY

LOUNGE / T.V. LOFT 17⁰ x 11⁴

BALCONY RAIL

CL.

CL.

CL.

BALCONY RAIL

ON

BALCONY RAIL

ATTIC STORAGE

BEDROOM 13⁰ x 11⁴

CL.

BATH

LINEN

CL.

ACCESS

UPPER FOYER

ATTIC STORAGE

ROOF

● The greenhouse in this design enhances its energy-efficiency and allows for spacious and interesting living patterns. Being a one-and-a-half story design, the second floor could be developed at a later date when the space is needed. The greenhouses add an additional 418 sq. ft. to the above quoted figures.

281

● Earth shelters the interior of this house from both the cold of the winter and the heat of the summer. This three bedroom design has passive solar capabilities. The sun room, south facing for light, has a stone floor which will absorb heat. When needed, the heat will be circulated to the interior by opening the sliding glass doors or by mechanical means. Entrance to this home will be obtained through the vestibule or the garage. Both have a western exposure. A large, centrally located, skylight creates an open feeling and lights up the interior of this plan where the formal and informal living areas are located. The sun room contains 425 sq. ft. not included in total to the right.

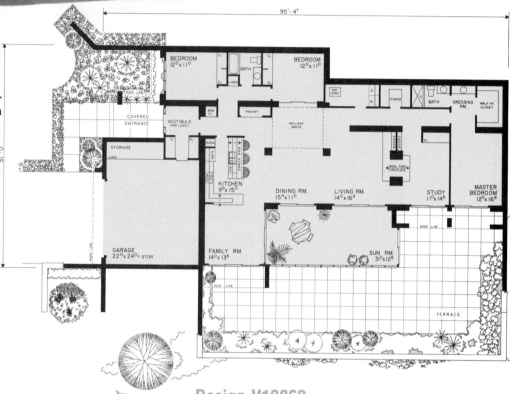

Design V12862
Square Footage: 2,808

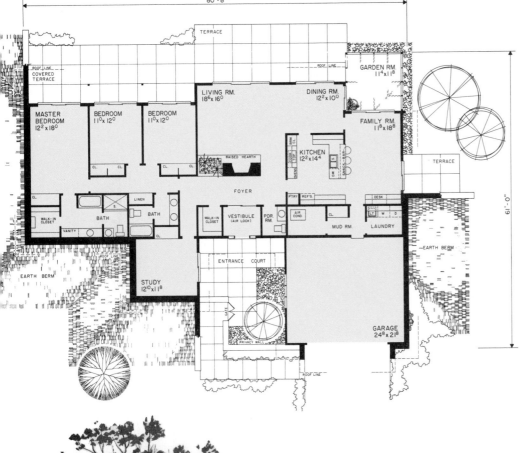

Design V12903
Square Footage: 2,555

● Earth berms on the sides of this house help it achieve energy-efficiency. The maximum amount of light enters this home by way of the many glass areas on the southern exposure. Every room in this plan, except the study, has the benefit of the southern sun. A garden room, tucked between the family and dining rooms, can be used for passive solar capabilities. A front privacy wall and the entrance court will shield the interior from the harsh northern winds. The air-locked vestibule also will be an energy saver. Summer heat gain will be reduced by the wide overhanging roof. The occupants of this home will appreciate the excellent interior planning. Garden room contains 144 sq. ft. not included in above total.

Design V12860
Square Footage: 2,240

● Here is truly a unique home to satisfy your family's desires for something appealing and refreshing. This three bedroom home is also, the very embodiment of what's new and efficient in planning and technology. This is an excellent example of outstanding coordination of house structure, site, interior livability and the sun. Orienting this earth sheltered house toward the south assures a warm, bright and cheerful interior. Major contributions to energy-efficiency result from the earth covered roof, the absence of northern wall exposure and the lack of windows on either end of the house. This means a retention of heat in the winter and cool air in the summer. An effective use of skylights provide the important extra measure of natural light to the interior. Sliding glass doors in the living and dining rooms also help bring the light to the indoors. This earth sheltered house makes no sacrifice of good planning and excellent, all 'round livability. The section is cut through the living room and the skylit hall looking toward the bedrooms.

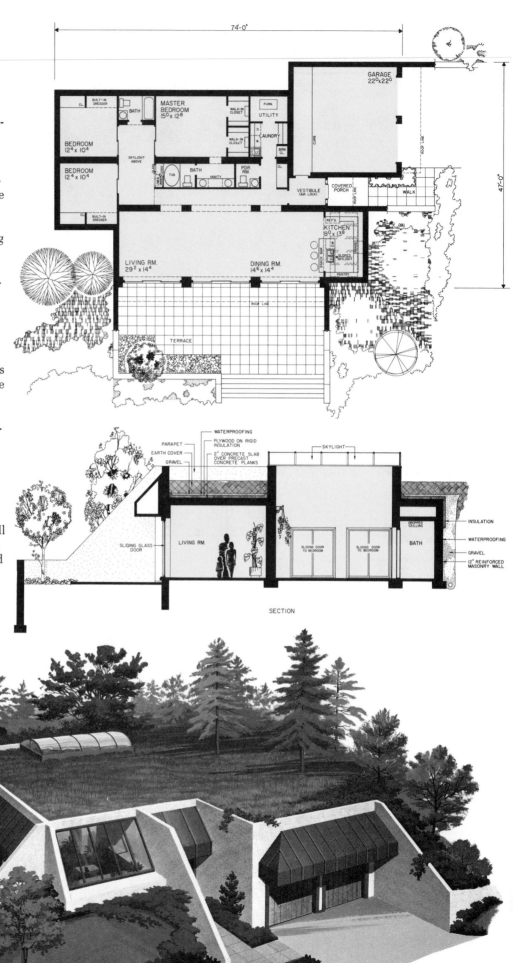

SECTION

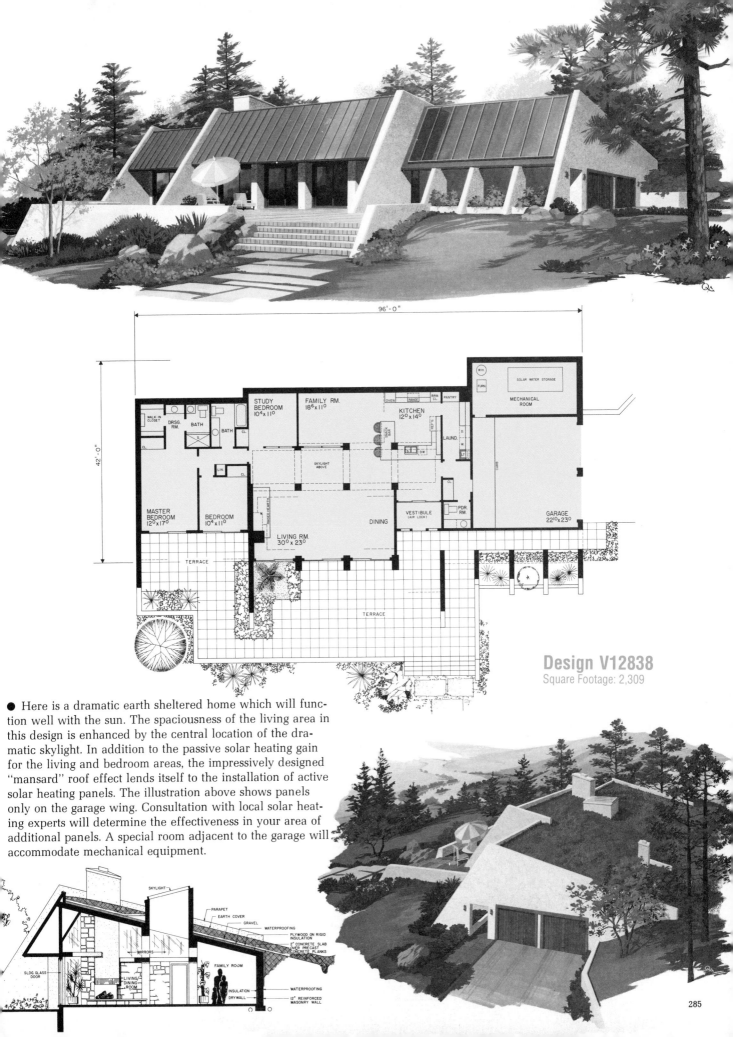

96'-0"

42'-0"

WALK-IN CLOSET

DRSG. RM.

BATH

BATH

CL

S

CL

STUDY BEDROOM
10⁴ x 11⁰

FAMILY RM.
18⁶ x 11⁰

OVEN RANGE

BRM CL

PANTRY

KITCHEN
12⁰ x 14⁰

SOLAR WATER STORAGE

W.H.

FURN.

MECHANICAL ROOM

REF'G

LAUND.

D.

W.

LIN.

CL

SKYLIGHT ABOVE

MASTER BEDROOM
12⁰ x 17⁰

BEDROOM
10⁴ x 11⁰

RAISED HEARTH

LIVING RM.
30⁰ x 23⁰

DINING

VESTIBULE
(AIR LOCK)

PDR. RM.

GARAGE
22¹⁰ x 23⁰

TERRACE

TERRACE

Design V12838
Square Footage: 2,309

● Here is a dramatic earth sheltered home which will function well with the sun. The spaciousness of the living area in this design is enhanced by the central location of the dramatic skylight. In addition to the passive solar heating gain for the living and bedroom areas, the impressively designed "mansard" roof effect lends itself to the installation of active solar heating panels. The illustration above shows panels only on the garage wing. Consultation with local solar heating experts will determine the effectiveness in your area of additional panels. A special room adjacent to the garage will accommodate mechanical equipment.

SKYLIGHT

PARAPET

EARTH COVER

GRAVEL

WATERPROOFING

PLYWOOD ON RIGID INSULATION

2" CONCRETE SLAB OVER PRECAST CONCRETE PLANKS

MIRRORS

FAMILY ROOM

SLDG. GLASS DOOR

LIVING DINING ROOM

INSULATION

WATERPROOFING

DRYWALL

12" REINFORCED MASONRY WALL

Design V12861
Square Footage: 2,499

● Berming the earth against the walls of a structure prove to be very energy efficient. The earth protects the interior from the cold of the winter and the heat of the summer. Interior lighting will come from the large skylight over the garden room. Every room will benefit from this exposed area. The garden room will function as a multi-purpose area for the entire family. The living/dining room will receive light from two areas, the garden room and the wall of sliding glass doors to the outside. Family living will be served by the efficient floor plan. Three bedrooms and two full baths are clustered together. The kitchen is adjacent to the air-locked vestibule where the laundry and utility rooms are housed. The section is cut through the dining, garden and master bedroom facing the kitchen.

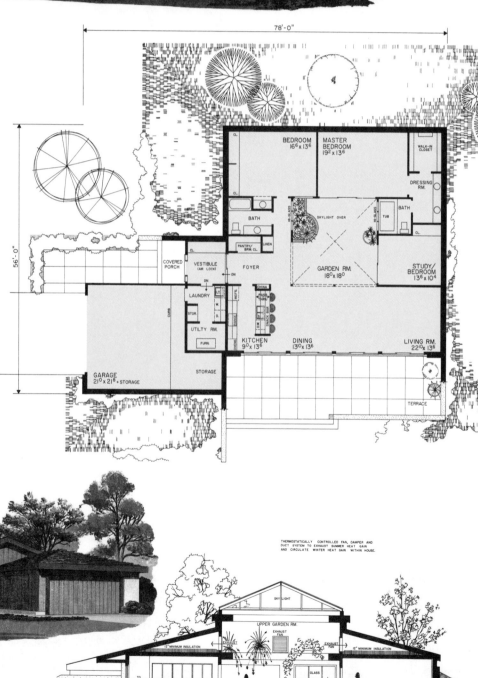

SECTION

● Earth berms are banked against all four exterior walls of this design to effectively reduce heating and cooling demands. The berming is cost-efficient during both hot and cold seasons. In the winter, berming reduces heat loss through the exterior walls and shields the structure from cold winds. It helps keep warm air out during the summer. The two most dramatic interior highlights are the atrium and thru-fireplace. Topped with a large skylight, the atrium floods the interior with natural light. Shades are used to cover the atrium in the summer to prevent solar heat gain. Three bedrooms are featured in this plan and they each open via sliding glass doors to the atrium. This would eliminate any feeling of being closed in. An island with range and oven is featured in the kitchen. Informal dining will be enjoyed at the snack bar. The family/dining room can house those more formal dining occasions. The section at the right is cut through the study, atrium and rear bedroom looking toward master bedroom.

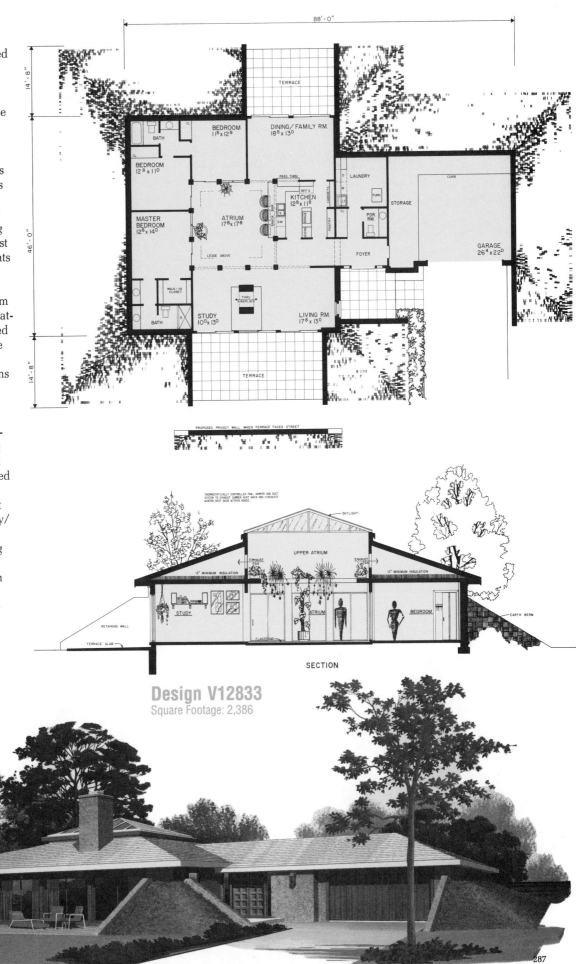

Design V12833
Square Footage: 2,386

Design V12863
Square Footage: 2,955

● Livability is outstanding in this earth-shelter design. Each of the three bedrooms has access to the terrace, along with the gathering and dining rooms. All of the sliding glass doors, along with the atrium, will brighten the interior nicely. The atrium will be enjoyed from the lounge, kitchen and gathering/dining rooms. Efficient work space will be found in the kitchen. It has easy access to the atrium and dining room.

OPTIONAL EXTERIORS & PLANS . . . *as highlighted*

in this section offer a fine study in the interchangeability of varying exterior styles on a given floor plan. Occasionally one's enthusiasm for a favorite floor plan may not be matched by a similar feeling about that plan's exterior styling. Further, within one's family, members may differ about their style preferences. Here are a variety of floor plans which offer an excellent opportunity to observe how (with minor modifications) that particular plan can have differently styled exteriors. As you study these plans which range in size from 1344-1880 sq. ft. note the fine proportion and detailing of the Traditional, Contemporary, Tudor and French exteriors.

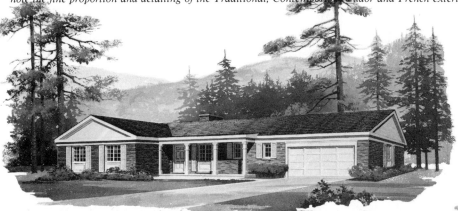

● Here is a unique series of designs with three charming exterior adaptations — Southern Colonial, Western Ranch, French Provincial - and two distinctive floor plans. Each plan has a different design number and is less than 1,600 square feet.

● If yours is a preference for the floor plan featuring the 26 foot keeping room, you should order blueprints for Design V12611. Of course, the details for each of the three delightful exteriors will be included. On the other hand, should the plan with the living,- dining and family rooms be your favorite, order blueprints for Design V12612 and get details for all three exteriors.

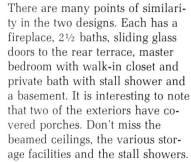

There are many points of similarity in the two designs. Each has a fireplace, 2½ baths, sliding glass doors to the rear terrace, master bedroom with walk-in closet and private bath with stall shower and a basement. It is interesting to note that two of the exteriors have covered porches. Don't miss the beamed ceilings, the various storage facilities and the stall showers.

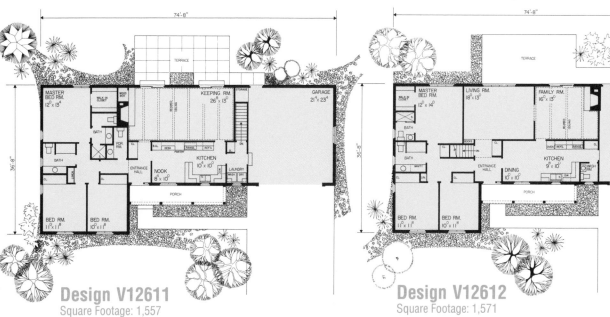

Design V12611
Square Footage: 1,557

Ⓛ Ⓓ

Design V12612
Square Footage: 1,571

Ⓛ Ⓓ

Design V12802
Square Footage: 1,729

L D

● The three exteriors shown at the left house the same, efficiently planned one-story floor plan shown below. Be sure to notice the design variations in the window placement and roof pitch. The Tudor design to the left is delightful. Half-timbered stucco and brick comprise the facade of this English Tudor variation of the plan. Note authentic bay window in the front bedroom.

Design V12803
Square Footage: 1,679

L D

● Housed in varying facades, this floor plan is very efficient. The front foyer leads to each of the living areas. The sleeping area of two, or optional three, bedrooms is ready to serve the family. Then there is the gathering room. This room is highlighted by its size, 16 x 20 feet. A contemporary mix of fieldstone and vertical wood siding characterizes this exterior. The absence of columns or posts gives a modern look to the covered porch.

Design V12804
Square Footage: 1,674

L D

● Stuccoed arches, multi-paned windows and a gracefully sloped roof accent the exterior of this Spanish-inspired design. Like the other two designs, the interior kitchen will efficiently serve the dining room, covered dining porch and breakfast room with great ease. Blueprints for all three designs include details for an optional non-basement plan.

CUSTOMIZABLE
Custom Alterations? See page 381 for customizing this plan to your specifications.

OPTIONAL NON-BASEMENT

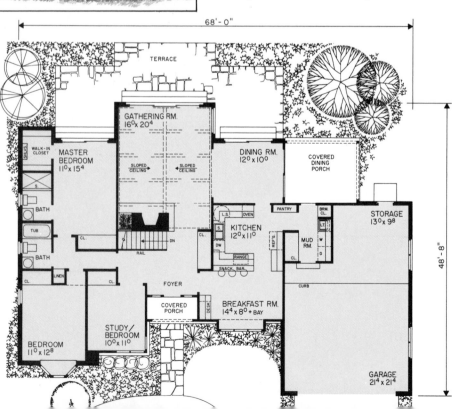

Design V12805
Square Footage: 1,547

L D

● Three completely different exterior facades share one compact, practical and economical floor plan. The major design variations are roof pitch, window placement and garage openings. Each design will hold its own when comparing the three exteriors. The design to the right is a romantic stone-and-shingle cottage design. This design, along with the other two designs presented here, is outstanding.

Design V12806
Square Footage: 1,584

L D

● Even though these exteriors are different in their styling and have a few design variations, their floor plans are identical. Each will provide the family with a livable plan. In this brick and half-timbered stucco Tudor version, the living-dining room expands across the rear of the plan and has direct access to the covered porch. Notice the built-in planter adjacent to the open staircase leading to the basement.

Design V12807
Square Footage: 1,576

L D

● Along with the living-dining areas of the other two plans, this sleek contemporary styled home's breakfast room also will have a view of the covered porch. A desk, snack bar and mud room housing the laundry facilities are near the U-shaped kitchen. Clustering these work areas together is very convenient. The master bedroom has a private bath.

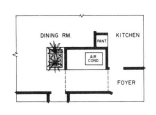

OPTIONAL NON-BASEMENT

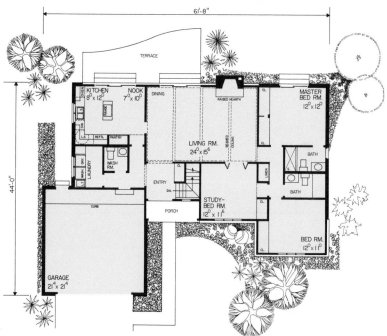

Design V12565
Square Footage: 1,540

L **D**

● This modest sized floor plan has much to offer in the way of livability. It may function as either a two or three bedroom home. The living room is huge and features a fine, raised hearth fireplace. The open stairway to the basement is handy and will lead to what may be developed as the recreation area. In addition to the two full baths, there is an extra wash room. Adjacent is the laundry room and the service entrance from the garage. The blueprints you order for this design will show details for each of the three delightful elevations above. Which is your favorite? The Tudor, the Colonial or the Contemporary?

Design V12505
Square Footage: 1,366

L **D**

● This design offers you a choice of three distinctively different exteriors. Which is your favorite? Blueprints show details for all three optional elevations. A study of the floor plan reveals a fine measure of livability. In less than 1,400 square feet there are features galore. An excellent return on your construction dollar. In addition to the two eating areas and the open planning of the gathering room, the indoor-outdoor relationships are of great interest. The basement may be developed for recreational activities. Be sure to note the storage potential, particularly the linen closet, the pantry, the china cabinet and the broom closet.

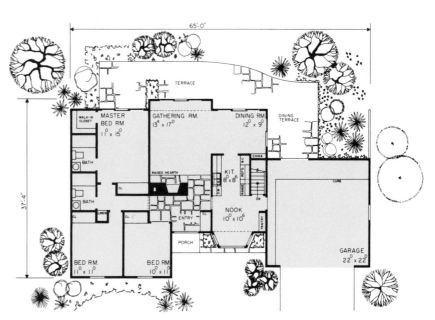

Design V11305
Square Footage: 1,382

D

● Order blueprints for any one of the three exteriors shown on these two pages and you will receive details for building this outstanding floor plan at the right. You'll find the appeal of these exteriors difficult to beat. As for the plan, in less than 1,400 square feet there are three bedrooms, two full baths, a separate dining room, a formal living room, a fine kitchen overlooking the rear yard and an informal family room. In addition, there is the attached two-car garage. Note the location of the stairs when this plan is built with a basement. Each of the exteriors is predominantly brick - the front of Design V11305 (above) features both stone and vertical boards and battens with brick on the other three sides. Observe the double front doors of the French design, V11382 (below) and the Contemporary design, V11383 (bottom). Study the window treatment.

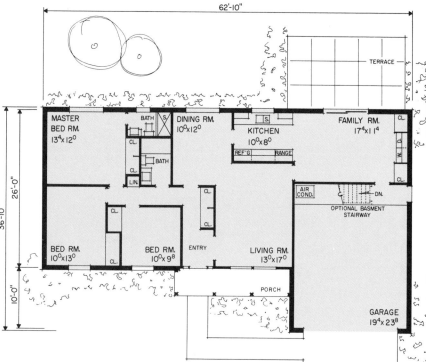

Design V11382
Square Footage: 1,382

D

Design V11383
Square Footage: 1,382

D

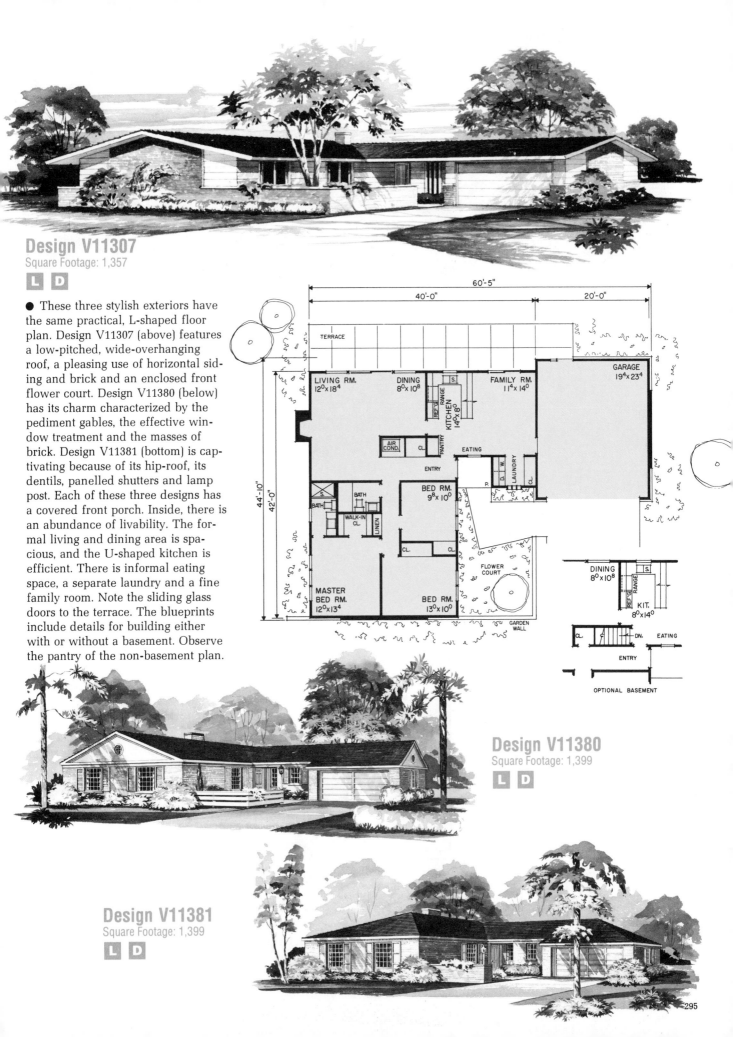

Design V11307
Square Footage: 1,357

L **D**

● These three stylish exteriors have the same practical, L-shaped floor plan. Design V11307 (above) features a low-pitched, wide-overhanging roof, a pleasing use of horizontal siding and brick and an enclosed front flower court. Design V11380 (below) has its charm characterized by the pediment gables, the effective window treatment and the masses of brick. Design V11381 (bottom) is captivating because of its hip-roof, its dentils, panelled shutters and lamp post. Each of these three designs has a covered front porch. Inside, there is an abundance of livability. The formal living and dining area is spacious, and the U-shaped kitchen is efficient. There is informal eating space, a separate laundry and a fine family room. Note the sliding glass doors to the terrace. The blueprints include details for building either with or without a basement. Observe the pantry of the non-basement plan.

60'-5"

40'-0"

20'-0"

44'-10"

42'-0"

TERRACE

LIVING RM.
12⁰x18⁴

DINING
8⁰x10⁸

KITCHEN
14⁴x8⁰

REF'G
RANGE
S.

FAMILY RM.
11⁴x14⁰

GARAGE
19⁴x23⁴

AIR COND.

CL.

PANTRY

EATING

ENTRY

P.

D. W.

LAUNDRY

CL.

BATH

BATH

S.

WALK-IN CL.

LINEN

BED RM.
9⁸x10⁰

CL.

CL.

FLOWER COURT

MASTER BED RM.
12⁰x13⁴

BED RM.
13⁰x10⁰

GARDEN WALL

DINING
8⁰x10⁸

REF'G
RANGE
S.

KIT.
8⁰x14⁰

CL.

DN.

EATING

ENTRY

OPTIONAL BASEMENT

Design V11380
Square Footage: 1,399

L **D**

Design V11381
Square Footage: 1,399

L **D**

Design V11938
Square Footage: 1,428

● An efficient plan designed to fit each of the three delightful exteriors above. You can reserve your choice of exterior until you receive the blueprints. Each set you order contains the details for the construction of all three. Note the differences in exterior materials, window treatment, car storage facilities and roof lines. Observe the beamed ceiling, all purpose family room and the kitchen eating space. There is a lot of living in 1,428 square feet.

Design V11323
Square Footage: 1,344

L D

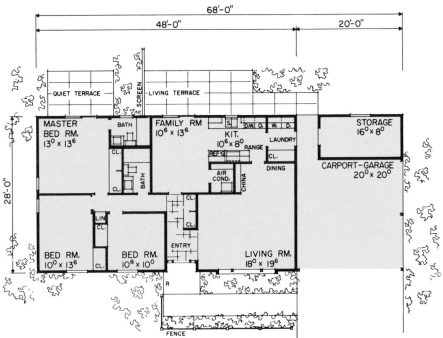

68'-0"

48'-0"   20'-0"

28'-0"

QUIET TERRACE   SCREEN   LIVING TERRACE

MASTER BED RM. 13⁰ x 13⁶   BATH   FAMILY RM 10⁶ x 13⁶   KIT. 10⁶ x 8⁰   LAUNDRY   STORAGE 16⁰ x 8⁰

CL.   REF'G   RANGE   CL.   DINING   CARPORT-GARAGE 20⁰ x 20⁰

CL.   BATH   AIR COND.   CHINA

LIN CL.   CL.

BED RM. 10⁰ x 13⁶   BED RM. 10⁸ x 10⁰   ENTRY   LIVING RM. 18⁰ x 19⁶

CL.   CL.

R

FENCE

● Incorporated in the set of blueprints for this design are details for building each of the three charming, traditional exteriors. Each of the three alternate exteriors has a distinction all its own. A study of the floor plan reveals fine livability. There are two full baths, a fine family room, an efficient work center, a formal dining area, bulk storage facilities and sliding glass doors to the quiet and living terraces. Laundry is strategically located near the kitchen.

Three Distinctively Styled Exteriors . . .

Design V12705
Square Footage: 1,746

L **D**

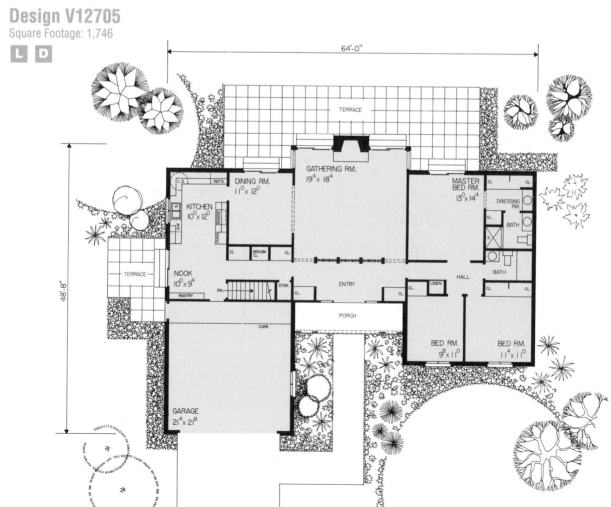

64'-0"

48'-8"

TERRACE

GATHERING RM.
19⁴ x 18⁴

DINING RM.
11⁰ x 12⁰

KITCHEN
10⁰ x 12⁰

REF'G.

RANGE

OVEN

DW

BROOM CL.

CL.

CL.

MASTER BED RM.
13⁰ x 14⁴

CL.

DRESSING RM.

CL.

BATH

BATH

TERRACE

NOOK
10⁰ x 9⁴

PANTRY

DN

STOR.

CL.

ENTRY

CL.

LINEN

HALL

CL.

CL.

CURB

PORCH

BED RM.
9⁸ x 11⁰

BED RM.
11⁴ x 11⁰

GARAGE
21⁴ x 21⁸

Design V12706
Square Footage: 1,746

L D

... One Practical, Efficient Floor Plan

● Three different exteriors! But inside it's all the same livable house. Begin with the impressive entry hall . . . more than 19' long and offering double entry to the gathering room. Now the gathering room which is notable for its size and design. Notice how the fireplace is flanked by sliding glass doors leading to the terrace! That's unusual.

There's a formal dining room, too! The right spot for special birthday dinners as well as supper parties for friends. And an efficient kitchen that makes meal preparation easy whatever the occasion. Look for a built-in range and oven here . . . plus a bright dining nook with sliding doors to a second terrace. Three large bedrooms! All

located to give family members the utmost privacy. Including a master suite with a private dressing room, bath and a sliding glass door opening onto the main terrace. For blueprints of the hip-roof French adaptation on the opposite page order V12705. For the Contemporary version order V12706. The Colonial order V12704.

Design V12704
Square Footage: 1,746

L D

Design V11389
Square Footage: 1,488

D

● Your choice of exterior goes with this outstanding floor plan. If your tastes include a liking for French Provincial, Design V11389, above, will provide a lifetime of satisfaction. On the other hand, should you prefer the simple straightforward lines of comtemporary design, the exterior for Design V11387, below, will be your favorite. For those who enjoy the warmth of Colonial adaptations, the charming exterior for Design V11388, bottom, will be perfect. Of interest, is a comparison of these three exteriors. Observe the varying design treatment of the windows, the double front doors, the garage doors and the roof lines. Don't miss other architectural details. Study each exterior and the floor plan carefully. Three charming designs you won't want to miss.

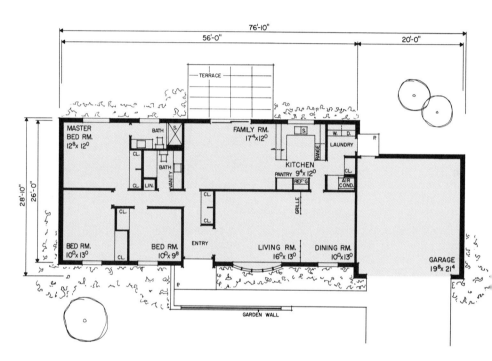

Design V11387
Square Footage: 1,488

D

Design V11388
Square Footage: 1,488

D

Design V11864
Square Footage: 1,598

D

● What's your favorite exterior? The one above which has a distinctive colonial appearance, or that below with its sleek contemporary look? Maybe you prefer the more formal hip-roof exterior (bottom) with its French feeling. Whatever your choice, you'll know your next home will be one that is delightfully proportioned and is sure to be among the most attractive in the neighborhood. It is interesting to note that each exterior highlights an effective use of wood siding and stone (or brick, as in the case of Design V11866). The floor plan features three bedrooms, 2½ baths, a formal living and dining room, a snack bar and a mud room. The master bedroom of the contemporary design has its window located in the left side elevation wall.

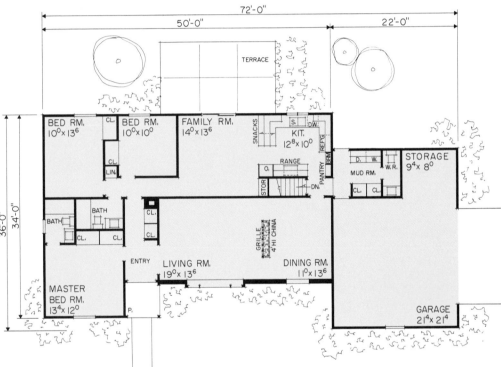

Design V11865
Square Footage: 1,598

D

Design V11866
Square Footage: 1,598

D

Design V12810
3-Bedroom Plan
Square Footage: 1,536

Design V12814
4-Bedroom Plan
Square Footage: 1,536

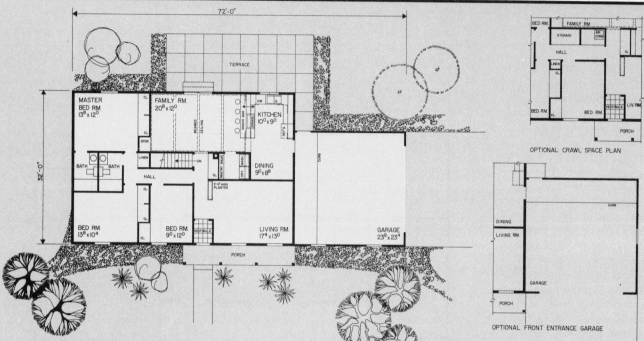

● 2 x 6 stud wall construction front and center! The designs on these two pages are particularly energy-efficient minded. All exterior walls employ the use of the larger size stud (in preference to the traditional 2 x 4 stud) to permit the installation of extra thick insulation. The high cornice design also allows for more ceiling insulation. In addition to the insulation factor, 2 x 6 studs are practical from an economic standpoint. According to many experts, the use of 2 x 6's spaced 24 inches O.C. results in the need for less lumber and saves construction time. However, the energy-efficient features of this series do not end with the basic framing members. Efficiency begins right at the front door where the vestibule acts as an airlock restricting the flow of cold air to the interior. The basic rectangular shape of the house spells efficiency. No complicated and costly construction here. Yet, there has been no sacrifice of delightful exterior appeal. Efficiency and economy are also embodied in such features as back-to-back plumbing, centrally located furnace, minimal window and door openings and, most important of all - size.

Design V12811
3-Bedroom Plan
Square Footage: 1,581

Design V12815
4-Bedroom Plan
Square Footage: 1,581

Design V12812
3-Bedroom Plan
Square Footage: 1,581

Design V12816
4-Bedroom Plan
Square Footage: 1,581

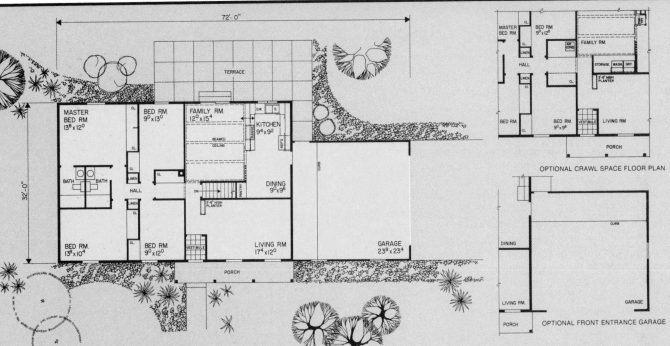

72'-0"

TERRACE

MASTER BED RM. 13⁸ x 12⁰

BED RM. 9⁰ x 13⁰

FAMILY RM. 12⁰ x 15⁴

KITCHEN 9⁴ x 9²

BEAMED CEILING

BATH   BATH

HALL

LINEN

DINING 9⁰ x 9⁶

3'-6" HIGH PLANTER

PANTRY

32'-0"

BED RM. 13⁸ x 10⁴

BED RM. 9⁰ x 12⁰

VESTIBULE

LIVING RM. 17⁴ x 12⁰

GARAGE 23⁸ x 23⁴

PORCH

CURB

MASTER BED RM.

BED RM. 9⁰ x 12⁰

FAMILY RM.

HALL

LINEN   AIR COND.   STORAGE WASH. DRY.

LINEN   CL.   3'-6" HIGH PLANTER

BED RM.   BED RM. 9⁰ x 9⁸   VESTIBULE   LIVING RM.

PORCH

OPTIONAL CRAWL SPACE FLOOR PLAN

DINING   CURB

LIVING RM.   GARAGE

PORCH

OPTIONAL FRONT ENTRANCE GARAGE

● Within 1,536 square feet there is outstanding livability and a huge variety of options from which to choose. For instance, of the four stylish exteriors, which is your favorite? The cozy, front porch Farmhouse adaptation; the pleasing Southern Colonial version, the French creation, or the rugged Western facade? Further, do you prefer a three or a four bedroom floor plan? With or without a basement? Front or side-opening garage? If you wish to order blueprints for the hip-roofed design with three bedrooms, specify Design V12812; for the four bedroom option specify V12816. To order blueprints for the three bedroom Southern Colonial, request Design V12811; for the four bedroom model, ask for Design V12815, etc. All blueprints include the optional non-basement and front opening garage details. Whatever the version you select, you and your family will enjoy the beamed ceiling of the family room, the efficient, U-shaped kitchen, the dining area, the traffic-free living room and the fine storage facilities. Truly a fine design series created to give each home buyer the maximum amount of choice and flexibility.

Design V12813
3-Bedroom Plan
Square Footage: 1,536

Design V12817
4-Bedroom Plan
Square Footage: 1,536

Design V12824
Square Footage: 1,550

● Low-maintenance and economy in building are the outstanding exterior features of this sharp one-story design. It is sheathed in long-lasting cedar siding and trimmed with stone for an eye-appealing facade. Entrance to this home takes you through a charming garden courtyard then a covered walk to the front porch. The garage extending from the front of the house serves two purposes; to reduce lot size and to buffer the interior of the house from street noise. Sliding glass doors are featured in each of the main rooms for easy access to the outdoors. A sun porch is tucked between the study and gathering rooms. Optional non-basement details are included with the purchase of this design.

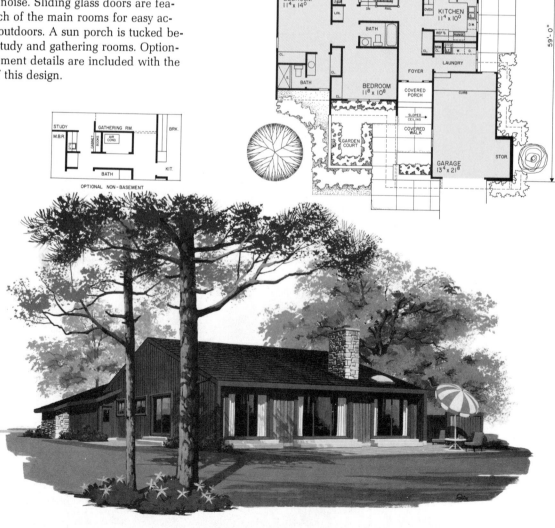

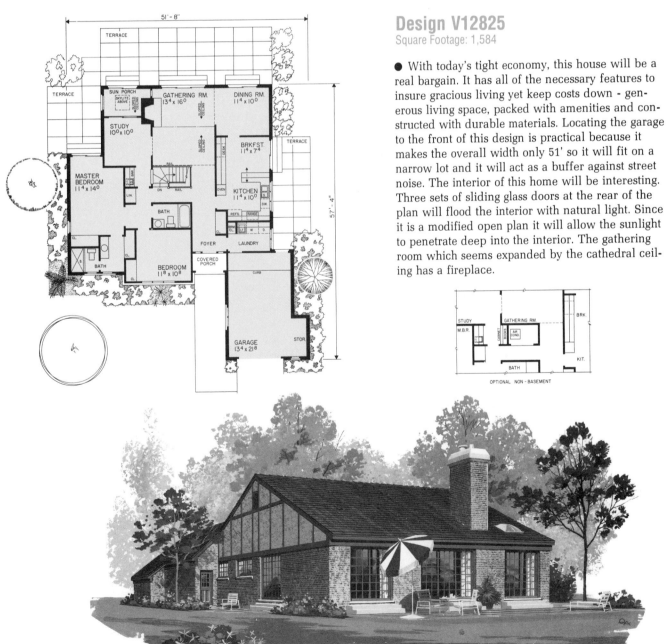

Design V12825
Square Footage: 1,584

● With today's tight economy, this house will be a real bargain. It has all of the necessary features to insure gracious living yet keep costs down - generous living space, packed with amenities and constructed with durable materials. Locating the garage to the front of this design is practical because it makes the overall width only 51' so it will fit on a narrow lot and it will act as a buffer against street noise. The interior of this home will be interesting. Three sets of sliding glass doors at the rear of the plan will flood the interior with natural light. Since it is a modified open plan it will allow the sunlight to penetrate deep into the interior. The gathering room which seems expanded by the cathedral ceiling has a fireplace.

Design V11322 Square Footage: 1,478

D

Design V11321
Square Footage: 1,478

D

Design V11320
Square Footage: 1,478

D

72'-0"

20'-0" 52'-0"

8'-0"

24'-0"

28'-0"

TERRACE

PORCH

GARAGE
19⁸ x 23⁴

DINING RM.
10⁰ x 12⁴

KIT.
16⁰ x 12⁰

REF'G. S DW

BRM. RANGE
O.

STORAGE

CL.

EATING

DN.
S

LIN.

BATH

BATH

CL.

CL.

MASTER
BED RM.
13⁴ x 13⁶

CL.

LIVING RM.
19⁴ x 15⁰

ENTRY

R

BED RM.
10⁸ x 10⁴

CL.

CL.

CL.

CL.

BED RM.
10⁰ x 13⁶

● Three totally different front elevations have the same basic floor plan layout. There is a separate set of blueprints for each attractive front exterior. The economically built plan, because of its simplicity, is outstanding.

Design V11352 Square Footage: 1,592

Design V11351
Square Footage: 1,592

Design V11350
Square Footage: 1,592

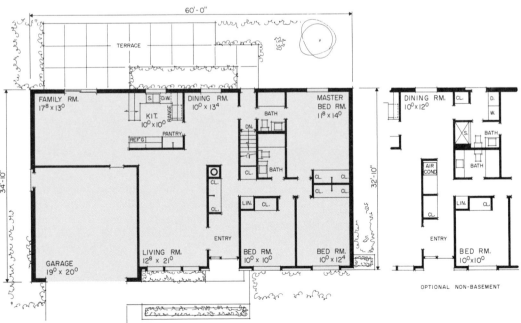

● When you order blueprints for the exterior that appeals to you the most, you'll receive details for building with or without a basement. Note the family room and the arrangements of the two full baths.

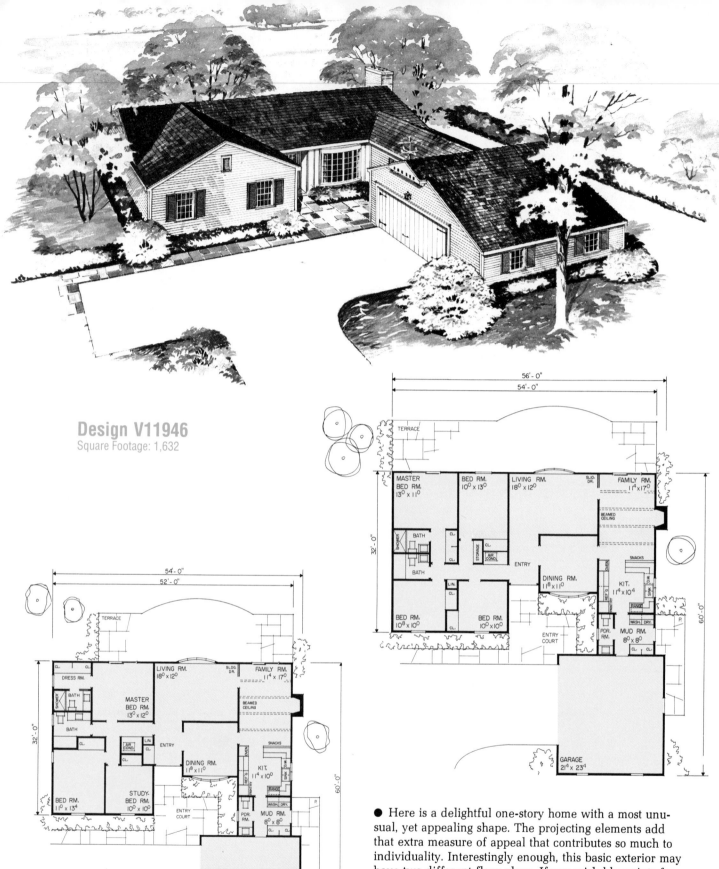

Design V11946
Square Footage: 1,632

Design V11945
Square Footage: 1,568

● Here is a delightful one-story home with a most unusual, yet appealing shape. The projecting elements add that extra measure of appeal that contributes so much to individuality. Interestingly enough, this basic exterior may have two different floor plans. If you wish blueprints for the three bedroom home order Design V11945: for four bedroom blueprints, order Design V11946. Whichever you select, you will enjoy the efficiency of the remainder of the plan. There are formal living and dining rooms, an informal family room with a beamed ceiling, a U-shaped kitchen and a strategically placed mud room with an adjacent powder room for easy convenience.

Design V11947
Square Footage: 1,764

● When it comes to housing your family, if you are among the contemporary-minded, you'll want to give this L-shaped design a second, then even a third, or fourth, look. It is available as either a three or four bedroom home. If you desire the three bedroom, 58 foot wide design order blueprints for V11947; for the four bedroom, 62 foot wide design, order V11948. Inside, you will note a continuation of the contemporary theme with sloping ceilings, exposed beams and a practical 42 inch high storage divider between the living and dining rooms. Don't miss the mud rooms.

Design V11948
Square Footage: 1,876

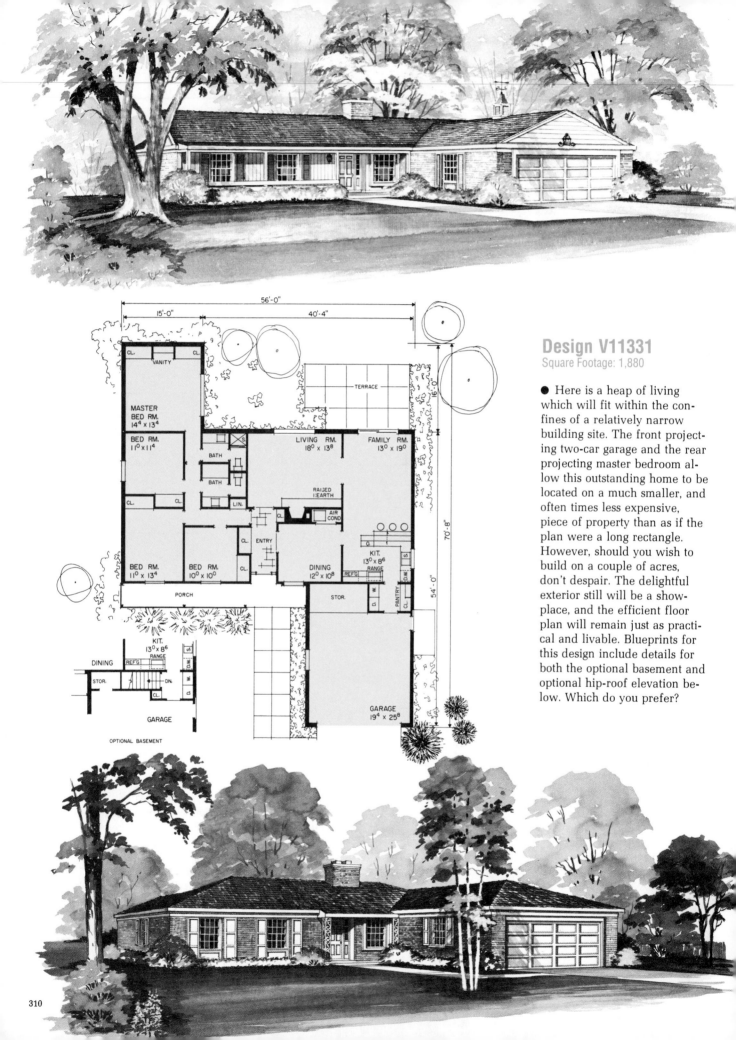

Design V11331
Square Footage: 1,880

● Here is a heap of living which will fit within the confines of a relatively narrow building site. The front projecting two-car garage and the rear projecting master bedroom allow this outstanding home to be located on a much smaller, and often times less expensive, piece of property than as if the plan were a long rectangle. However, should you wish to build on a couple of acres, don't despair. The delightful exterior still will be a showplace, and the efficient floor plan will remain just as practical and livable. Blueprints for this design include details for both the optional basement and optional hip-roof elevation below. Which do you prefer?

56'-0"
15'-0" 40'-4"
16'-0"
70'-8"
54'-0"

CL. VANITY CL.
MASTER BED RM. 14⁴ x 13⁴
BED RM. 11⁰ x 11⁴
BATH
BATH
CL. CL. LIN.
BED RM. 11⁰ x 13⁴ BED RM. 10⁰ x 10⁰
CL. ENTRY CL.
PORCH

TERRACE
LIVING RM. 18⁰ x 13⁸
FAMILY RM. 13⁰ x 19⁰
RAISED HEARTH AIR COND
DINING 12⁰ x 10⁸
KIT. 13⁰ x 8⁶ RANGE
REF'G D.W. PANTRY CL.
STOR.

GARAGE 19⁴ x 25⁸

KIT. 13⁰ x 8⁶ RANGE S
DINING REF'G D.W.
STOR. DN. D W
CL.
GARAGE
OPTIONAL BASEMENT

Design V13373
Square Footage: 1,378
L D

Design V13374
Square Footage: 1,378
L D

Design V13375
Square Footage: 1,378
L D

● This charmingly compact plan has three facades from which to choose: Greek Revival (V13373), Tudor (V13374) or Southwestern (V13375). The interior plan contains a large living room/dining room combination, a media room, a U-shaped kitchen with breakfast room and two bedrooms. If the extra space is needed, the media room could serve as a third bedroom. Note the terrace to the rear of the plan off the dining room and the sloped ceilings throughout.

46'-0"

STOR.

DINING RM.
9⁰ x 12⁰

LIVING RM.
14⁶ x 13⁴

SLOPED CEILING

BATH

MASTER BED RM.
12⁰ x 13⁸ + BAY

SLOPED CEILING

W.I.C.

POR.

DN

B.C. DESK

CL.

BAR/CL.

S

LIN.

BATH

32'-0"

REF'G.

KIT.
10⁰ x 14⁸

RANGE

CL.

SLOPED CEILING

SLOPED CEILING

SLOPED CEILING

CL.

SLOPED CEILING

D.W. S

BRKFST.
8⁰ x 14⁸

FOYER

MEDIA/B.R.
10⁰ x 11⁰

BED RM.
11⁸ x 9⁰ + BAY

POSSIBLE GARAGE

PORCH

6'-0"

Design V12941
Square Footage: 1,842

D

● Here is a basic floor plan which goes with each of the differently styled exteriors. The Early American version above is charming, indeed. Horizontal siding, stone, window boxes, a dovecote, a picket fence and a garden court enhance its appeal. Note the covered entrance.

Design V12942
Square Footage: 1,834

D

● The Tudor exterior above will be the favorite of many. Stucco, simulated timber work and diamond-lite windows set its unique character. Each of the delightful exteriors features eye-catching roof lines. Inside, there is an outstanding plan to cater to the living patterns of the small family, empty nesters, or retirees.

Design V12943
Square Footage: 1,834

D

● The Contemporary optional exterior above features vertical siding and a wide-overhanging roof with exposed rafter ends. The foyer is spacious with sloped ceiling and a dramatic open staircase to the basement recreation area. Other ceilings in the house are also sloped. The breakfast, dining and media rooms are highlights, along with the laundry, the efficient kitchen, the snack bar and the master bath.

BONUS LIVABILITY . . .

for future expansion can result by allowing for the development of a second level of livability. Each of the following designs delivers complete one-story living and gives the appearance of being a one-story house. However, with the development of what would be unused attic space, additional sleeping facilities can be gained. These houses can be of minimal, or expanded, square footage on the first floor. Later as family size grows, or financial constraints lessen, the total livability can be considerably increased. Note the examples of how bonus space may be developed on a lower level. The basements of many one-story homes can be exposed to provide this bonus livability.

Design V12563
First Floor: 1,500 square feet
Second Floor: 690 square feet
Total: 2,190 square feet

L

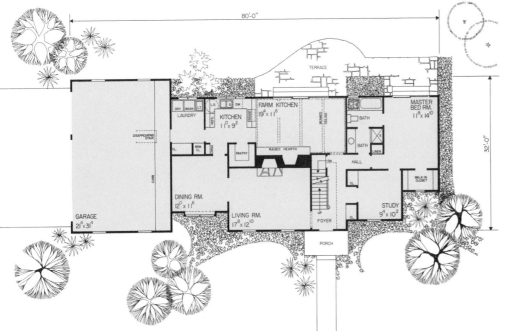

● This charming Cape Cod definitely will capture your heart with its warm appeal. This home offers you and your family a lot of livability. Upon entering this home, to your left, is a nice-sized living room with fireplace. Adjacent is a dining room. An efficient kitchen and a large, farm kitchen eating area with fireplace will be enjoyed by all. A unique feature on this floor is the master bedroom with a full bath and walk-in closet. Also take notice of the first floor laundry, the pantry and a study for all of your favorite books. Note the sliding glass doors in the farm kitchen and master bedroom. Upstairs you'll find two bedrooms, one with a walk-in closet. Also here, a sitting room and a full bath are available. Lastly, this design accommodates a three car garage.

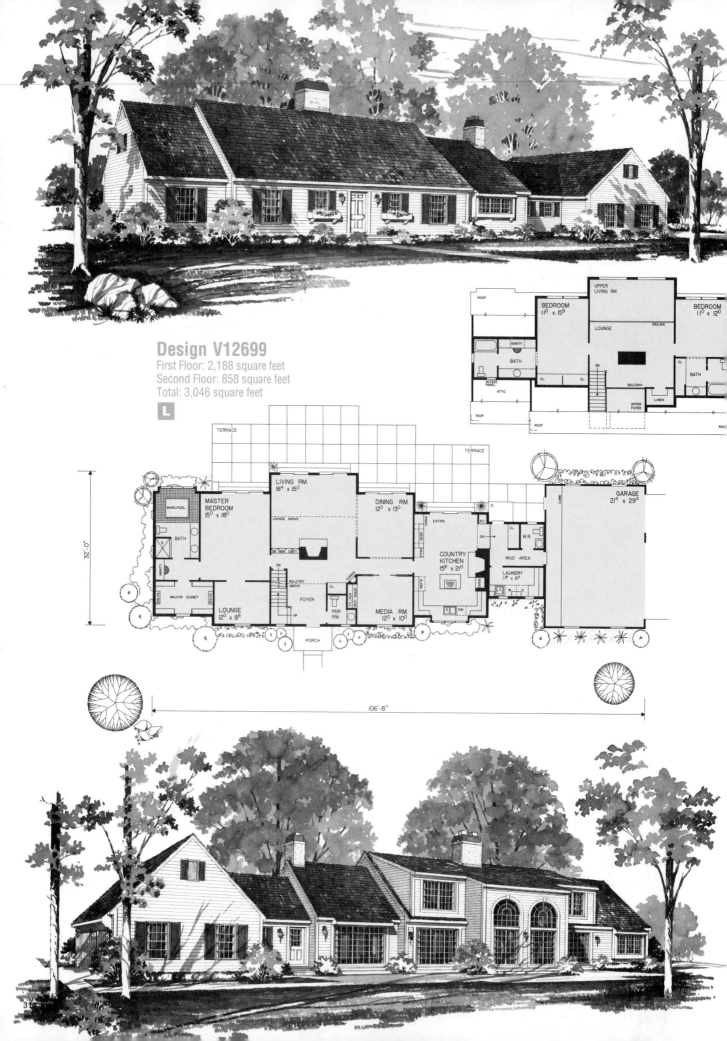

Design V12699

First Floor: 2,188 square feet
Second Floor: 858 square feet
Total: 3,046 square feet

L

Second Floor Plan labels
ROOF
UPPER LIVING RM.
BEDROOM 11⁰ x 15⁸
BEDROOM 11⁰ x 12⁰
LOUNGE
RAILING
VANITY
BATH
BATH
ACCESS PANEL
ATTIC
CL.
CL.
DN.
LINEN
CL.
BALCONY
ROOF
UPPER FOYER
ROOF
ROE

First Floor Plan labels
TERRACE
TERRACE
WHIRLPOOL
MASTER BEDROOM 15⁰ x 18⁰
LIVING RM. 18⁴ x 15⁰
DINING RM. 12⁰ x 13⁰
EATING
GARAGE 21⁴ x 29⁴
BATH
LOUNGE ABOVE
CHINA
DESK
B.Q.
P.
CL.
W.R.
VANITY
36" HIGH CAB'T
COUNTRY KITCHEN 15⁸ x 21⁰
MUD AREA
DN.
BALCONY ABOVE
CL.
REF'G.
OVEN
LAUNDRY 11⁸ x 6⁰
DN.
WALK-IN CLOSET
SHLVS.
SHLVS.
FOYER
T.V. EQUIP.
COOK TOP
W. D.
LOUNGE 12⁰ x 8⁸
UP
PDR. RM.
MEDIA RM. 12⁰ x 10⁰
S. D.W.
PORCH

32'-0"

106'-8"

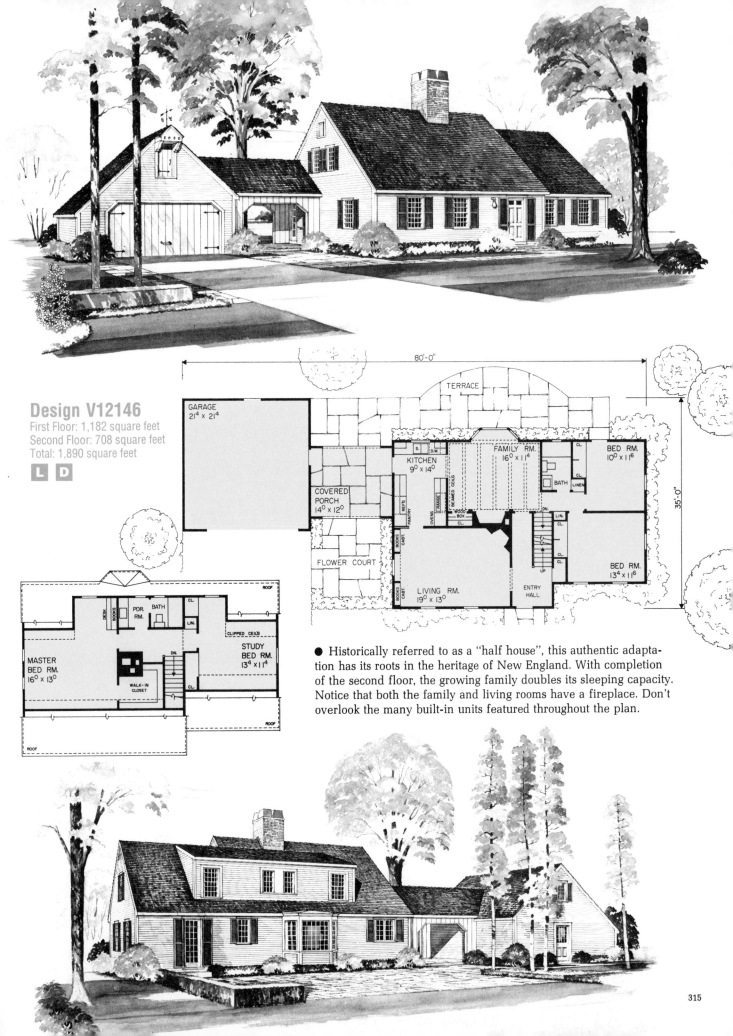

Design V12146
First Floor: 1,182 square feet
Second Floor: 708 square feet
Total: 1,890 square feet

L D

GARAGE 21⁴ x 21⁴

TERRACE

COVERED PORCH 14⁰ x 12⁰

KITCHEN 9⁰ x 14⁰

FAMILY RM. 16⁰ x 11⁴

BED RM. 10⁰ x 11⁶

BATH

LINEN

FLOWER COURT

OVENS

RANGE

WOOD BOX

PANTRY

REFG.

BOOKS CABT.

BOOKS

DN.

CL.

LIN.

CL.

LIVING RM. 19⁰ x 13⁰

UP

ENTRY HALL

BED RM. 13⁴ x 11⁶

80'-0"

35'-0"

DESK

BOOKS

PDR. RM.

BATH

LIN.

CL.

CLIPPED CEILG

ROOF

MASTER BED RM. 16⁰ x 13⁰

WALK-IN CLOSET

DN.

CL.

STUDY BED RM. 13⁴ x 11⁴

ROOF

ROOF

● Historically referred to as a "half house", this authentic adaptation has its roots in the heritage of New England. With completion of the second floor, the growing family doubles its sleeping capacity. Notice that both the family and living rooms have a fireplace. Don't overlook the many built-in units featured throughout the plan.

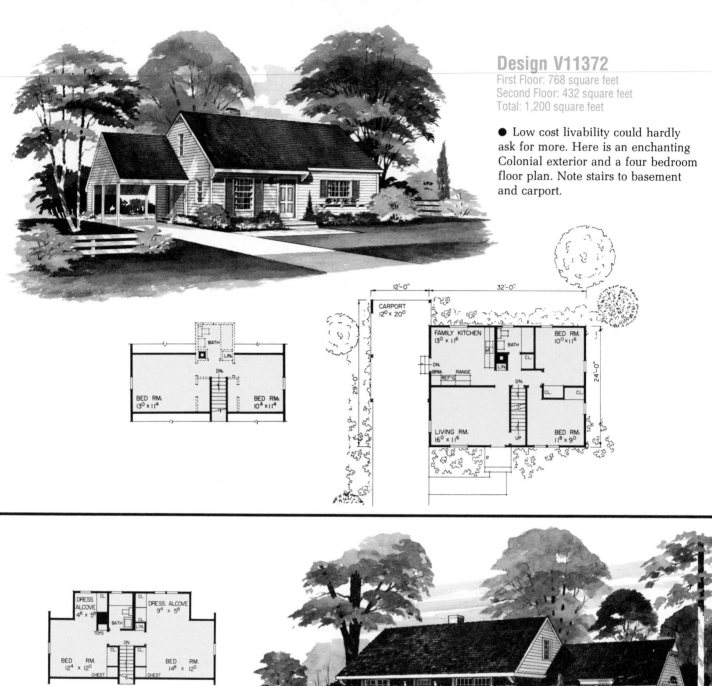

Design V11372

First Floor: 768 square feet
Second Floor: 432 square feet
Total: 1,200 square feet

● Low cost livability could hardly ask for more. Here is an enchanting Colonial exterior and a four bedroom floor plan. Note stairs to basement and carport.

CARPORT
12⁰ x 20⁰

FAMILY KITCHEN
13⁰ x 11⁶

BATH

BED RM.
10⁰ x 11⁶

BROM. RANGE
REF'G

LIN.

CL.

DN.

CL.   CL.

LIVING RM.
16⁰ x 11⁶

UP

BED RM.
11⁸ x 9⁰

12'-0"   32'-0"

29'-0"

24'-0"

BATH   LIN.

DN.

BED RM.
13⁰ x 11⁴

BED RM.
10⁴ x 11⁴

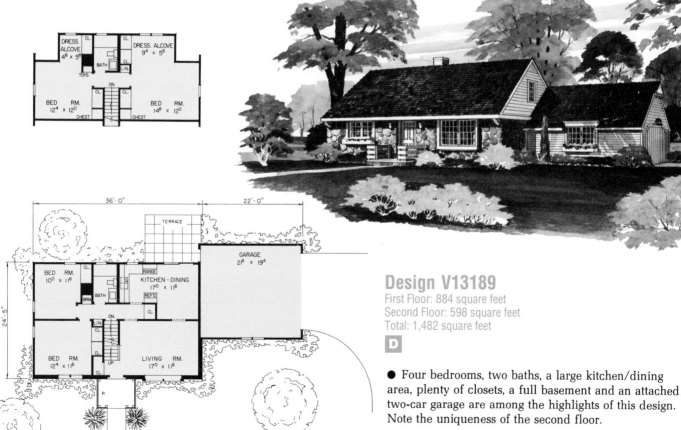

DRESS. ALCOVE
4⁸ x 5⁸

DRESS. ALCOVE
9⁴ x 5⁸

BATH   CL.
TOYS   LIN

CL.

DN.   CL.

BED RM.
12⁴ x 12⁰

BED RM.
14⁸ x 12⁰

CHEST   CHEST

Design V13189

First Floor: 884 square feet
Second Floor: 598 square feet
Total: 1,482 square feet

D

● Four bedrooms, two baths, a large kitchen/dining area, plenty of closets, a full basement and an attached two-car garage are among the highlights of this design. Note the uniqueness of the second floor.

TERRACE

GARAGE
21⁸ x 19⁴

BED RM.
10⁰ x 11⁶

CL.

RANGE

KITCHEN - DINING
17⁰ x 11⁶

BATH
BRM.

REF'G

CL.

LIN.
CL.

DN.

CL.

BED RM.
12⁴ x 11⁶

UP

LIVING RM.
17⁰ x 11⁶

CL.

P.

36'-0"   22'-0"

24'-5"

Design V11394

First Floor: 832 square feet
Second Floor: 512 square feet
Total: 1,344 square feet

L D

● The growing family with a restricted building budget will find this a great investment - a convenient living floor plan inside an attractively designed facade.

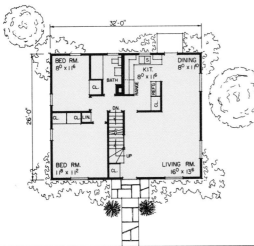

Design V12510

First Floor: 1,191 square feet
Second Floor: 533 square feet
Total: 1,724 square feet

L D

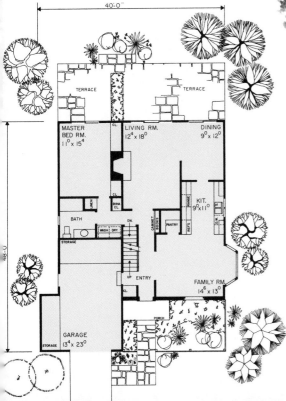

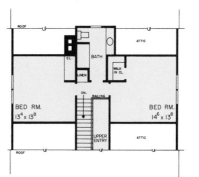

● The pleasant in-line kitchen is flanked by a separate dining room and a family room. The master bedroom is on the first floor with two more bedrooms upstairs.

● If symmetry means any-
thing, this pleasant house
has it. The projecting wings
of the sleeping zone and the
garage are virtually identical.
However, the appeal of this
charmer does not end with
its symmetrical beauty.
There is a world of livability
to be fostered by this home.

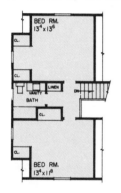

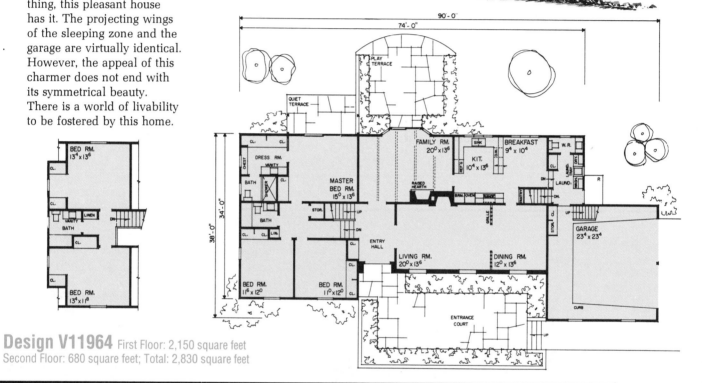

Design V11964 First Floor: 2,150 square feet
Second Floor: 680 square feet; Total: 2,830 square feet

Design V11794 First Floor: 2,122 square feet
Second Floor: 802 square feet; Total: 2,924 square feet

● The inviting warmth of this delightful
home catches the eye of even the most casual observer. Imagine, four big bedrooms!
Formal and informal living can be enjoyed
throughout this charming plan. A private,
formal dining room is available for those
very special occasions.

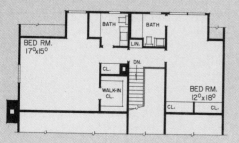

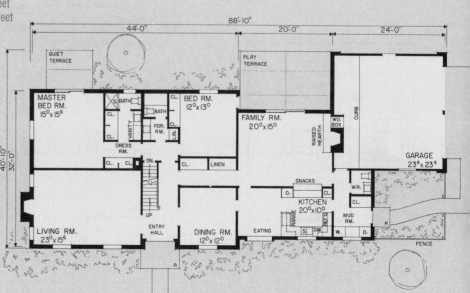

Floor Plan

First floor dimensions: 70'-0", 62'-0", 26'-0", 34'-0", 48'-0"

TERRACE

FAMILY RM.
13⁴ x 18⁰
BEAMED CEILING
SLID. DR.

DINING RM.
11⁰ x 12⁶
OVEN REF'G.
PANTRY DESK

LIVING RM.
18⁸ x 13⁶
BATH

MASTER BED RM.
12⁰ x 13⁶
WALK-IN CL.

BED RM.
11⁴ x 13⁶
CL.

RAISED HEARTH
WOOD BOX
LAUND.
LAUND. TRAY
WASH DRY.
W.R.
CL.

KIT.
10⁰ x 12⁶
SINK D.W.
SLID. DR.
BREAKFAST
8⁰ x 11⁶

ENTRY
UP
DN.
CL. CL.

BATH
LIN. CL. CL.
DN.
VANITY
BATH
WALK-IN CL.
LIN.

PORCH

GARAGE
21⁴ x 21⁸

PORCH

BED RM.
11⁶ x 10⁴

BED RM.
11⁶ x 12⁰

BED RM.
11⁴ x 11⁴

Design V11967
First Floor: 1,804 square feet
Second Floor: 496 square feet
Total: 2,300 square feet

● You'll always want that first impression your guests get of your new home to be a lasting one. There will be much that will linger in the memories of most of your visitors after their visit to this home. Of course, the impressive exterior will long be remembered. And little wonder with its distinctive projecting garage and bedroom wing, its recessed front porch, its horizontal siding and its interesting roof lines. Inside, there is much to behold. The presence of five bedrooms and three full baths will not be forgotten soon. Formal and informal areas will serve every family occasion.

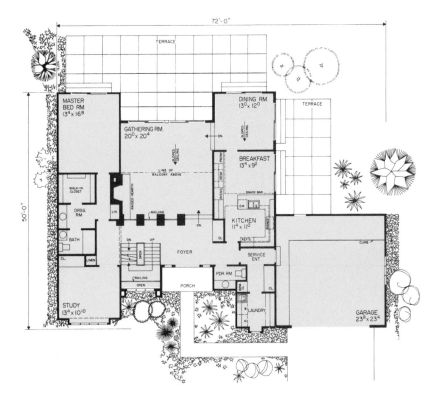

Design V12780

First Floor: 2,006 square feet
Second Floor: 718 square feet
Total: 2,724 square feet

● This 1½-story contemporary has more fine features than one can imagine. The livability is outstanding and can be appreciated by the whole family. A two-story gathering room is reached from the entry foyer and has a sloped ceiling, raised hearth fireplace, and sliding glass doors to the rear terrace. The formal dining room, also with sloped ceiling, is located nicely between the gathering room and well-planned kitchen/nook. A master suite is complemented by a front study on this floor and two bedrooms and a full bath upstairs. Note the fine indoor-outdoor living relationships.

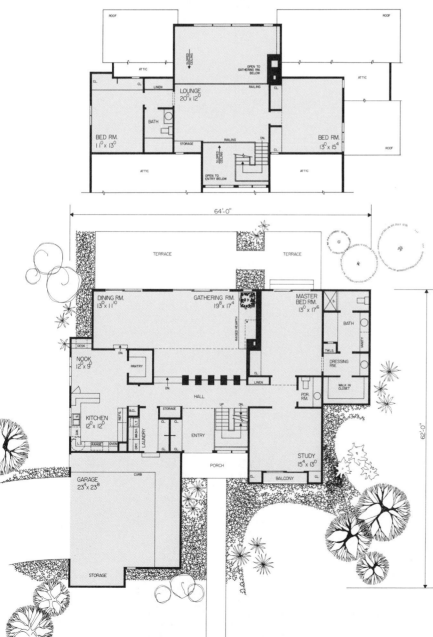

ROOF
ATTIC
CL.
CL.
LINEN
LOUNGE
20⁰ x 12⁶
OPEN TO
GATHERING RM.
BELOW
SLOPED
CEILING
RAILING
CL.
ROOF
ATTIC

BATH
BED RM.
11⁰ x 13⁰
STORAGE
RAILING
DN.
BED RM.
13⁰ x 15⁴
ROOF

ATTIC
SLOPED
CEILING
OPEN TO
ENTRY BELOW
ATTIC

64'-0"

TERRACE
TERRACE

DINING RM.
13⁰ x 11¹⁰
GATHERING RM.
19⁸ x 17⁴
MASTER
BED RM.
13⁰ x 17⁶

DESK
BATH
TWLS.
VANITY

DN.
NOOK
12⁰ x 9
PANTRY
DRESSING
RM.

DN.
LINEN
WALK IN
CLOSET

KITCHEN
12⁰ x 12⁰
STORAGE
HALL
UP
DN.
PDR.
RM.

RANGE OVEN
LAUNDRY
CL.
CL.
ENTRY

GARAGE
23⁰ x 23⁸
CURB
STORAGE
PORCH
BALCONY
STUDY
15⁴ x 13⁰

62'-0"

Design V12708

First Floor: 2,108 square feet
Second Floor: 824 square feet
Total: 2,932 square feet

D

● Here is a one-and-a-half
story home whose exterior is
distinctive. It has a contemporary feeling, yet it retains some
of the fine design features and
proportions of traditional
exteriors. Inside the appealing
double front doors there is liva-
ability galore. The sunken
rear living-dining area is delightfully spacious and is looked down into from the second
floor lounge. The open end
fireplace, with its raised hearth
and planter, is another focal
point. The master bedroom
features a fine compartmented
bath with both shower and tub.
The study is just a couple steps
away. The U-shaped kitchen is
outstanding. Notice the pantry
and laundry. Upstairs provides
children with their own sleeping, studying and TV quarters.
Absolutely a great design! Study
all the fine details closely with
your family.

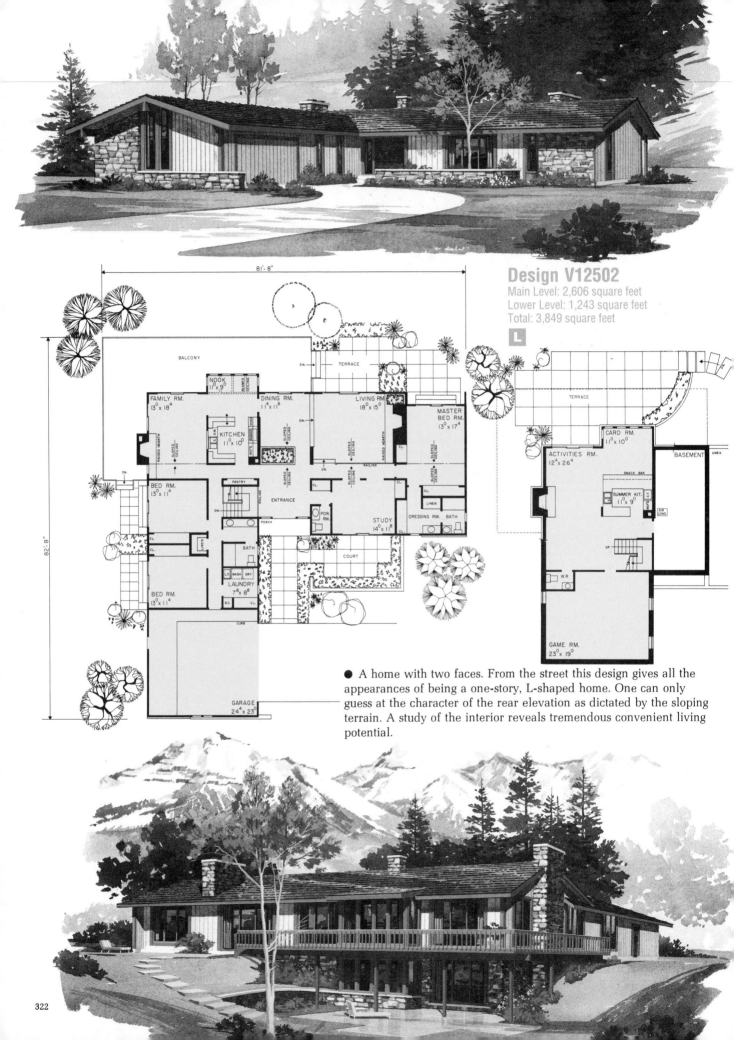

Design V12502

Main Level: 2,606 square feet
Lower Level: 1,243 square feet
Total: 3,849 square feet

L

81'- 8"

82'- 8"

BALCONY

TERRACE

NOOK
11⁴ x 9⁰

FAMILY RM.
13⁰ x 18⁴

DINING RM.
11⁴ x 11⁶

LIVING RM.
18⁰ x 15⁰

MASTER BED RM.
13⁰ x 17⁴

KITCHEN
11⁰ x 10⁰

RAISED HEARTH

SLOPED CEILING

SLOPED CEILING

RAISED HEARTH

SLOPED CEILING

SLOPED CEILING

SLOPED CEILING

BED RM.
13⁰ x 11⁴

PANTRY

ENTRANCE

CL.

CL.

LINEN

BED RM.
13⁰ x 11⁴

CL.

LINEN

CL.

CL.

DN.

PDR. RM.

PORCH

STUDY
14⁴ x 11⁸

DRESSING RM.

BATH

BATH

COURT

L.T. WASH DRY

LAUNDRY
7⁸ x 8⁸

CURB

GARAGE
24⁴ x 23⁰

TERRACE

CARD RM.
11⁰ x 10⁰

BASEMENT

UNEX.

ACTIVITIES RM.
12⁴ x 26⁴

SNACK BAR

SUMMER KIT.
11⁰ x 9⁰

REF. CT.

AIR COND.

UP

W.R.

GAME RM.
23⁰ x 19⁰

● A home with two faces. From the street this design gives all the appearances of being a one-story, L-shaped home. One can only guess at the character of the rear elevation as dictated by the sloping terrain. A study of the interior reveals tremendous convenient living potential.

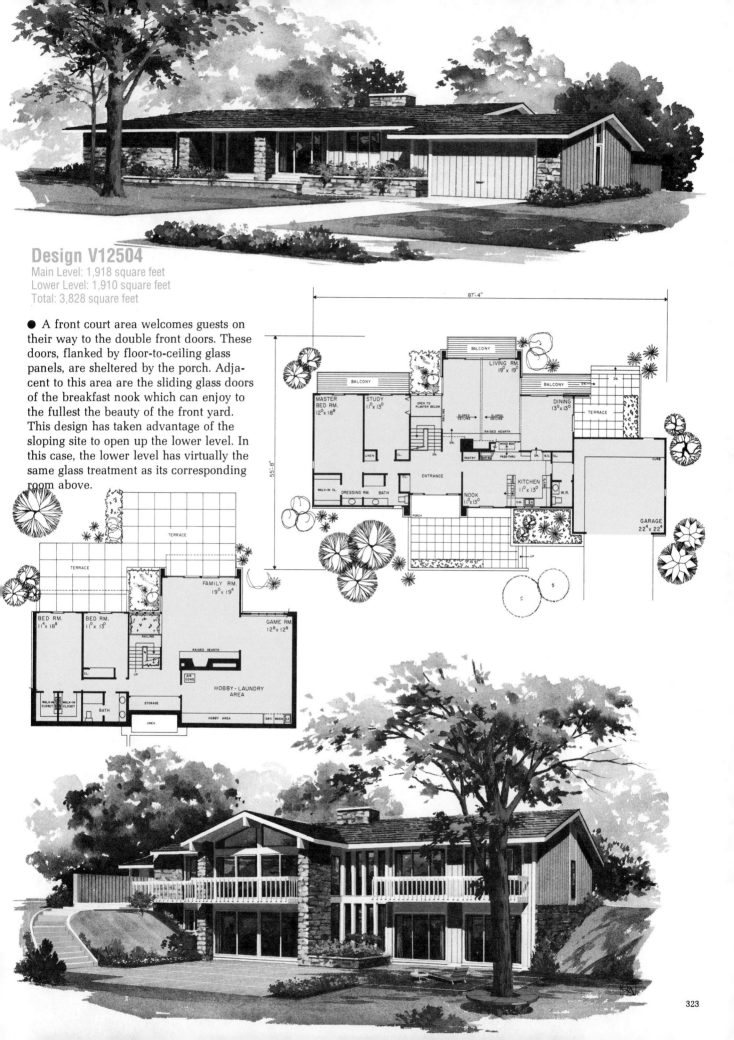

Design V12504

Main Level: 1,918 square feet
Lower Level: 1,910 square feet
Total: 3,828 square feet

● A front court area welcomes guests on their way to the double front doors. These doors, flanked by floor-to-ceiling glass panels, are sheltered by the porch. Adjacent to this area are the sliding glass doors of the breakfast nook which can enjoy to the fullest the beauty of the front yard. This design has taken advantage of the sloping site to open up the lower level. In this case, the lower level has virtually the same glass treatment as its corresponding room above.

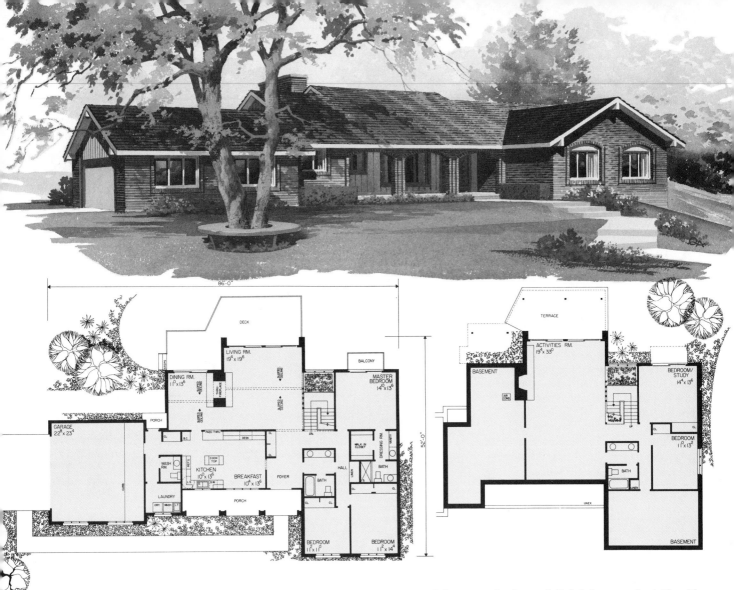

● This hillside home gives all the appearances of being a one-story ranch home; and what a delightful one at that! Should the contours of your property slope to the rear, this plan permits the exposing of the lower level. This results in the activities room and bedroom/study gaining direct access to outdoor living. Certainly a most desirable aspect for active, outdoor family living. The large and growing family will be admirably served with five bedrooms and three baths. An extra washroom and separate laundry add to the convenient living potential.

Design V12549
Main Level: 2,260 square feet
Lower Level: 1,406 square feet
Total: 3,666 square feet

Design V12846 Main Level: 2,341 square feet; Lower Level: 1,380 square feet; Total: 3,721 square feet

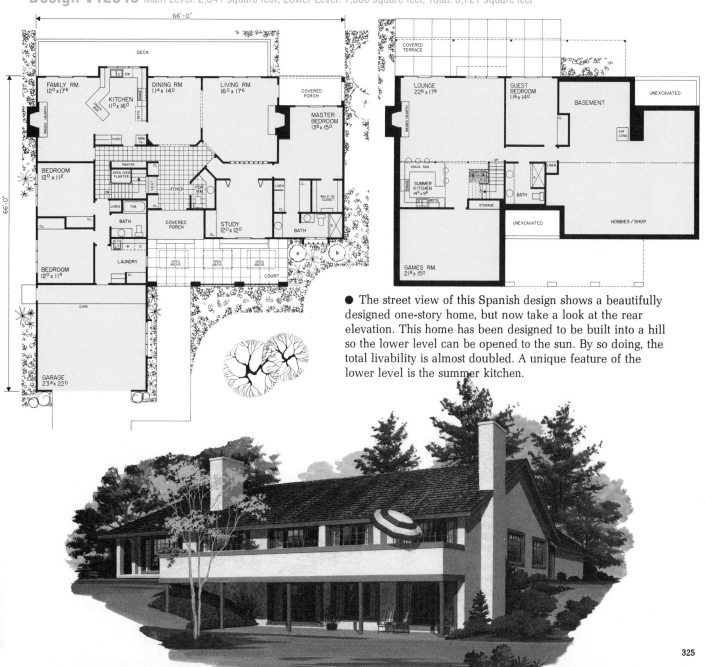

66'-0"

66'-0"

DECK

FAMILY RM.
12⁰ x 17⁶

KITCHEN
11⁰ x 16⁰

SNACK BAR

RAISED HEARTH

DINING RM.
11⁴ x 14⁰

LIVING RM.
16⁰ x 17⁶

COVERED
PORCH

MASTER
BEDROOM
13⁸ x 15⁰

OVEN

BRM
CL.

PANTRY

OPEN OVER
PLANTER

SEAT

BEDROOM
12⁰ x 11²

FOYER

PDR
RM.

LINEN

CL.

WALK-IN
CLOSET

CL.

LINEN

TUB

BATH

COVERED
PORCH

STUDY
12⁰ x 12⁰

BATH

LAUNDRY

OPEN
ABOVE

OPEN
ABOVE

OPEN
ABOVE

BEDROOM
12⁰ x 11⁴

COURT

CURB

GARAGE
23⁴ x 22⁰

COVERED
TERRACE

LOUNGE
22⁶ x 17⁶

GUEST
BEDROOM
11⁶ x 14⁰

BASEMENT

UNEXCAVATED

CL.

RAISED HEARTH

AIR
COND

UP

SNACK BAR

RANGE

SUMMER
KITCHEN
14⁸ x 9⁸

REF'G.

LINEN

BATH

STORAGE

UNEXCAVATED

HOBBIES / SHOP

GAMES RM.
21⁸ x 15⁰

● The street view of this Spanish design shows a beautifully designed one-story home, but now take a look at the rear elevation. This home has been designed to be built into a hill so the lower level can be opened to the sun. By so doing, the total livability is almost doubled. A unique feature of the lower level is the summer kitchen.

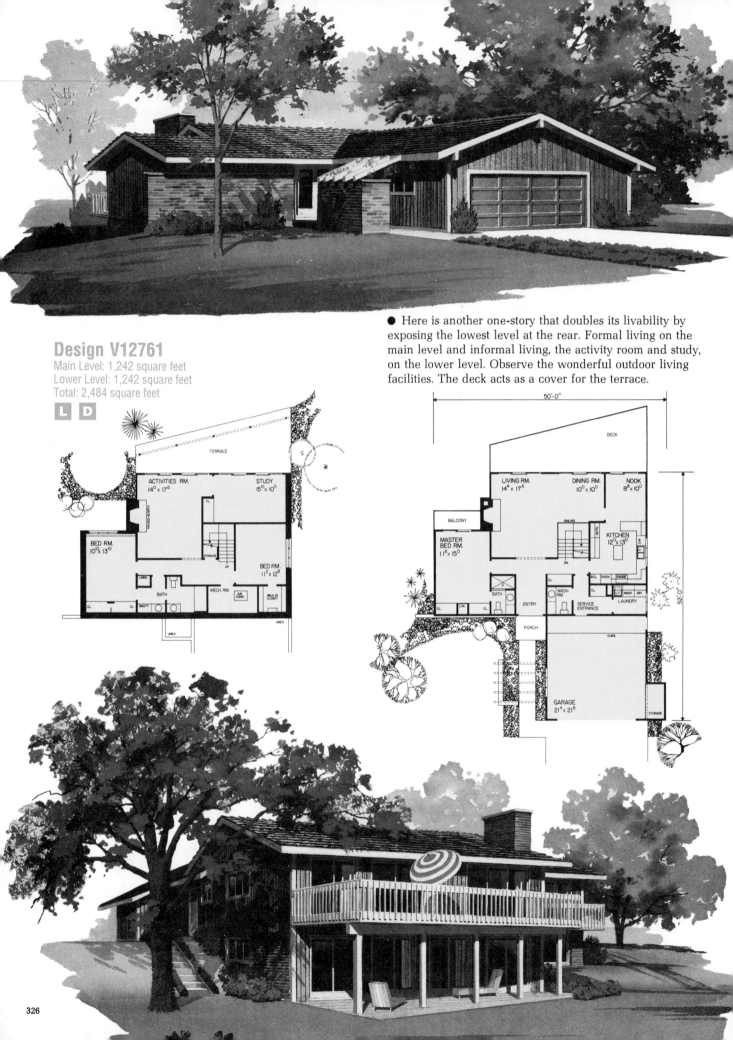

Design V12761

Main Level: 1,242 square feet
Lower Level: 1,242 square feet
Total: 2,484 square feet

L D

● Here is another one-story that doubles its livability by exposing the lowest level at the rear. Formal living on the main level and informal living, the activity room and study, on the lower level. Observe the wonderful outdoor living facilities. The deck acts as a cover for the terrace.

TERRACE

ACTIVITIES RM.
14⁰ x 17⁶

STUDY
15¹⁰ x 10⁰

CL.

RAISED HEARTH

BED RM.
10⁰ x 13¹⁰

STORAGE
UP

LAUN.

BATH

MECH. RM.

AIR COND.

WALK IN CLOSET

BED RM.
11² x 12⁸

VANITY

CL.

CL.

UNEX.

UNEX.

50'-0"

DECK

LIVING RM.
14⁴ x 17⁶

DINING RM.
10⁰ x 10⁰

NOOK
8⁸ x 10⁰

BALCONY

RAILING

REF.

KITCHEN
12⁰ x 13⁰

MASTER BED RM.
11⁸ x 15⁰

DN.

BCL. OVEN RANGE

LT.

CL.

WASH RM.

SERVICE ENTRANCE

LT. WASH DRY.

LAUNDRY

52'-0"

BATH

LIN.

CL.

ENTRY

CL.

PORCH

CURB

GARAGE
21⁴ x 21⁸

STORAGE

Second Floor

BED RM.
13⁶ x 13⁸

BALCONY

BATH

CL

CL

STORAGE

ROOF LINES

BED RM.
19⁶ x 11⁶

ROOF

LINEN

WALK-IN CLOSET

SLOPED CEILING

BEAM

SLOPED CEILING

ATTIC

RAILING

SKYLIGHT ABOVE

DN.

BEAM

RAILING

UPPER GATHERING RM.

LOUNGE
9¹⁰ x 19⁴

CL

SLOPED CEILING

ROOF

BALCONY

UPPER ENT HALL

BED RM./STUDY
11⁸ x 11⁸

CL

ROOF LINE

First Floor

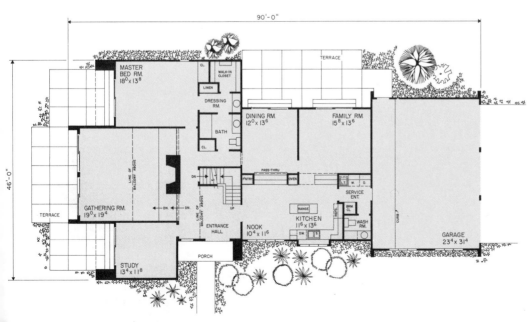

90'-0"

46'-0"

MASTER BED RM.
18⁰ x 13⁸

WALK-IN CLOSET

CL

TERRACE

LINEN

DRESSING RM.

DINING RM.
12⁰ x 13⁶

FAMILY RM.
15⁸ x 13⁶

LINE OF BALCONY ABOVE

BATH

CL

TERRACE

GATHERING RM.
19⁰ x 19⁴

LINE OF BALCONY ABOVE

DN.

DN.

PASS-THRU

OVEN

SERVICE ENT.

CURB

W.
D.

PNTRY

UP

ENTRANCE HALL

RANGE

BRM CL.

WASH RM.

STUDY
13⁴ x 11⁸

NOOK
10⁴ x 11⁶

KITCHEN
11⁶ x 13⁶

DW

REF.

GARAGE
23⁴ x 31⁴

PORCH

Design V12781
First Floor: 2,132 square feet
Second Floor: 1,156 square feet
Total: 3,288 square feet

L D

● This beautifully designed two-story could be con-
sidered a dream house of a
lifetime. The exterior is
sure to catch the eye of
anyone who takes sight of
its unique construction.
The front kitchen features
an island range, adjacent
breakfast nook and pass-
thru to formal dining room.
The master bedroom suite
with its privacy and con-
venience on the first floor
has a spacious walk-in
closet and dressing room.
The side terrace is accessible through sliding glass
doors from the master bedroom, gathering room and
study. The second floor has
three bedrooms and storage
space galore. Also notice
the lounge which has a
sloped ceiling and a sky-
light above. This delightful
area looks down into the
gathering room. The out-
door balconies overlook the
wrap-around terrace. Surely an outstanding trend
house for decades to come.

Design V12488

First Floor: 1,113 square feet
Second Floor: 543 square feet
Total: 1,656 square feet

D

● A cozy cottage for the young at heart! Whether called upon to serve the young, active family as a leisure-time retreat at the lake, or the retired couple as a quiet haven in later years, this charming design will perform well. As a year round second home, the upstairs with its two sizable bedrooms, full bath and lounge area, looking down into the gathering room below, will ideally accommodate the younger generation.

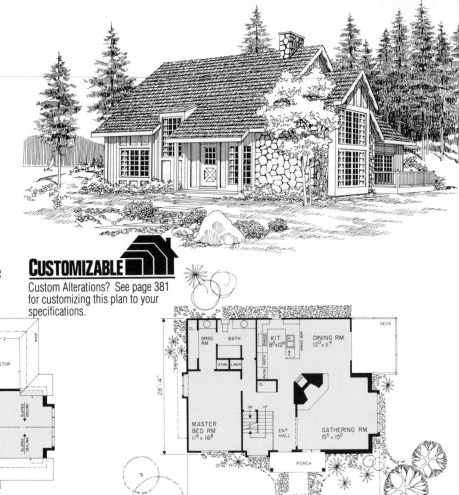

CUSTOMIZABLE

Custom Alterations? See page 381 for customizing this plan to your specifications.

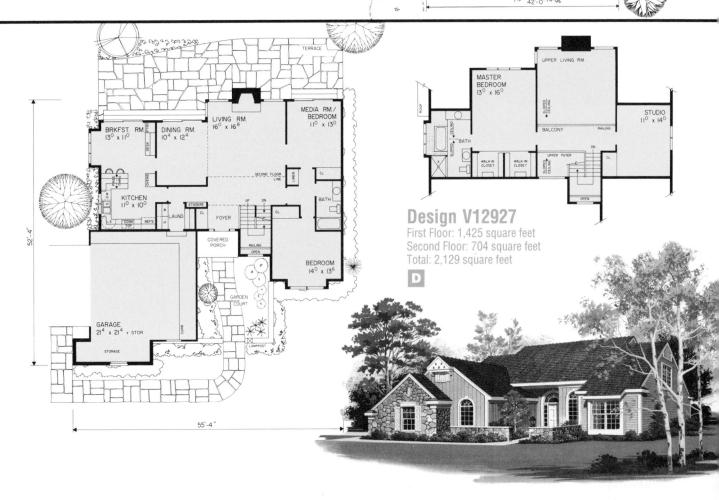

Design V12927

First Floor: 1,425 square feet
Second Floor: 704 square feet
Total: 2,129 square feet

D

BONUS FEATURE — Some Of Our More Popular Plans With More Than One Story . . .

For those who may be as yet undecided on a one-story design and would like to explore other alternatives, we offer this collection. It represents some of our bestselling two-story and multi-level homes to whet the appetite. For an even greater selection, see our other books, Two-Story Homes or Multi-Level and Hillside Homes, which feature a vast array of designs in these categories.

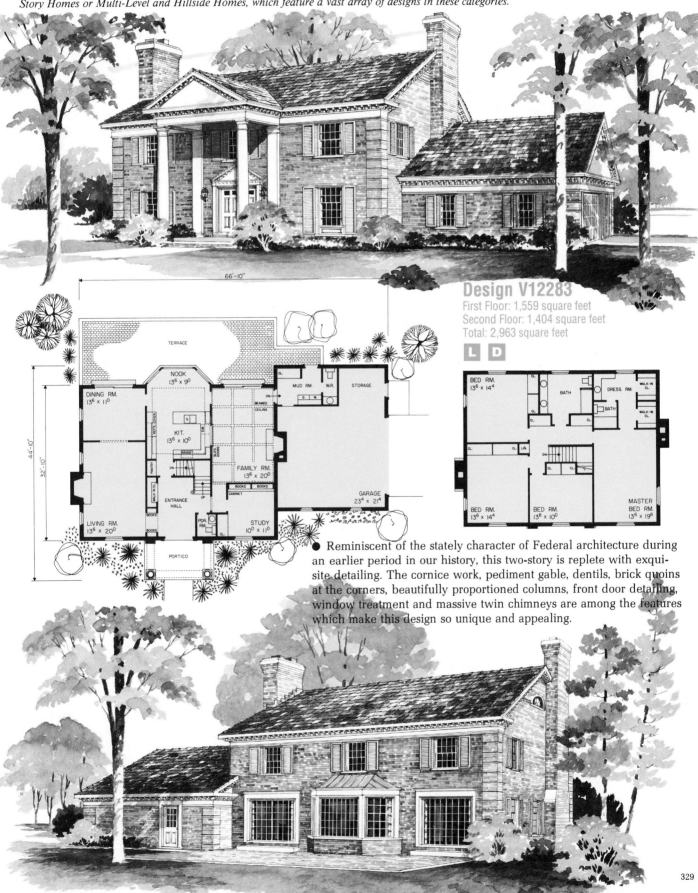

Design V12283

First Floor: 1,559 square feet
Second Floor: 1,404 square feet
Total: 2,963 square feet

L **D**

● Reminiscent of the stately character of Federal architecture during an earlier period in our history, this two-story is replete with exquisite detailing. The cornice work, pediment gable, dentils, brick quoins at the corners, beautifully proportioned columns, front door detailing, window treatment and massive twin chimneys are among the features which make this design so unique and appealing.

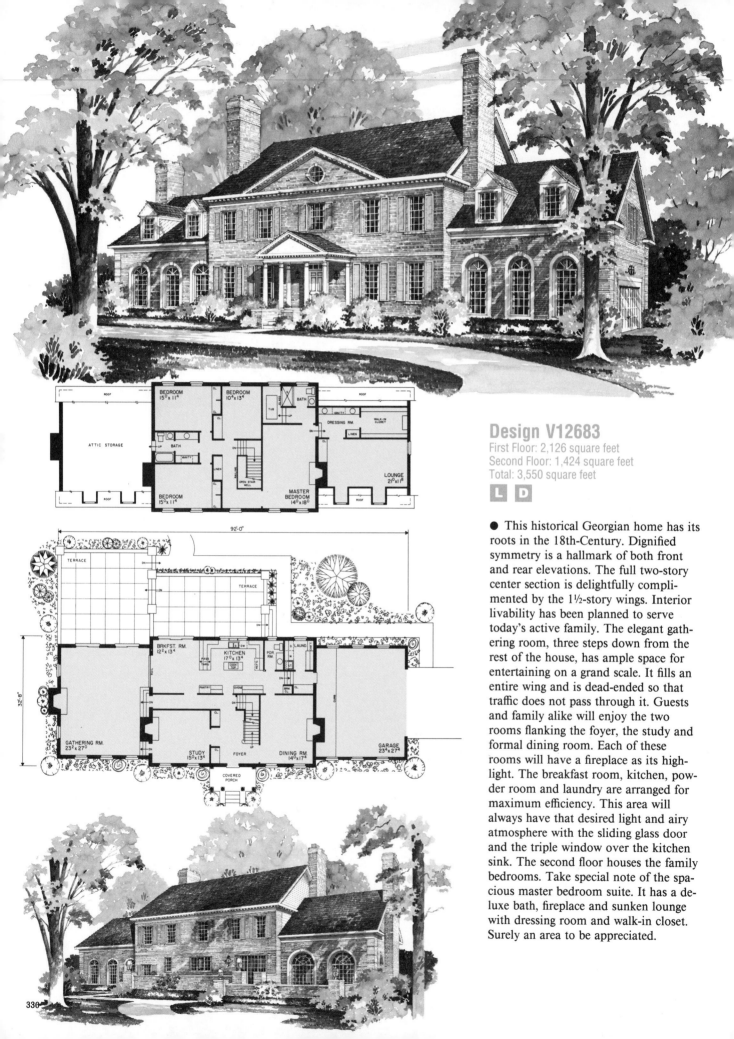

Design V12683

First Floor: 2,126 square feet
Second Floor: 1,424 square feet
Total: 3,550 square feet

L **D**

● This historical Georgian home has its roots in the 18th-Century. Dignified symmetry is a hallmark of both front and rear elevations. The full two-story center section is delightfully complimented by the 1½-story wings. Interior livability has been planned to serve today's active family. The elegant gathering room, three steps down from the rest of the house, has ample space for entertaining on a grand scale. It fills an entire wing and is dead-ended so that traffic does not pass through it. Guests and family alike will enjoy the two rooms flanking the foyer, the study and formal dining room. Each of these rooms will have a fireplace as its highlight. The breakfast room, kitchen, powder room and laundry are arranged for maximum efficiency. This area will always have that desired light and airy atmosphere with the sliding glass door and the triple window over the kitchen sink. The second floor houses the family bedrooms. Take special note of the spacious master bedroom suite. It has a deluxe bath, fireplace and sunken lounge with dressing room and walk-in closet. Surely an area to be appreciated.

Design V12889

First Floor: 2,529 square feet
Second Floor: 1,872 square feet
Total: 4,401 square feet

L D

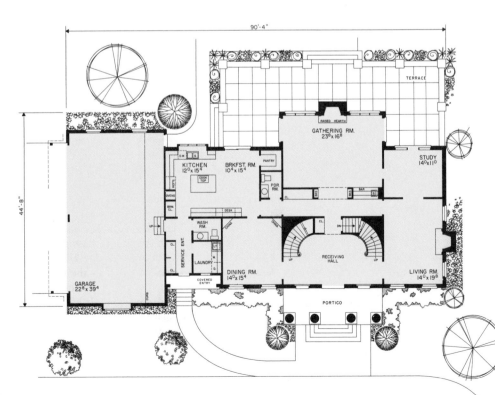

● This is truly classical, Georgian design at its best. Some of the exterior highlights of this two-story include the pediment gable with cornice work and dentils, the beautifully proportioned columns, the front door detailing and the window treatment. These are just some of the features which make this design so unique and appealing. Behind the facade of this design is an equally elegant interior. Imagine greeting your guests in the large receiving hall. It is graced by two curving staircases and opens to the formal living and dining rooms. Beyond the living room is the study. It has access to the rear terrace. Those large, informal occasions for family get-togethers or entertaining will be enjoyed in the spacious gathering room. It has a centered fireplace flanked by windows on each side, access to the terrace and a wet bar. Your appreciation for this room will be never-ending. The work center is efficient: the kitchen with island cook top, breakfast room, washroom, laundry and service entrance. The second floor also is outstanding. Three family bedrooms and two full baths are joined by the feature-filled master bedroom suite. Study this area carefully.

Design V12192

First Floor: 1,884 square feet
Second Floor: 1,521 square feet
Total: 3,405 square feet

L **D**

● This is surely a fine adaptation from the 18th-Century when formality and elegance were by-words. The authentic detailing of this design centers around the fine proportions, the dentils, the window symmetry, the front door and entranceway, the massive chimneys and the masonry work. The rear elevation retains all the grandeur exemplary of exquisite architecture. The appeal of this outstanding home does not end with its exterior elevations. Consider the formal living room with its corner fireplace. Also, the library with its wall of bookshelves and cabinets. Further, the dining room highlights corner china cabinets. Continue to study this elegant plan.

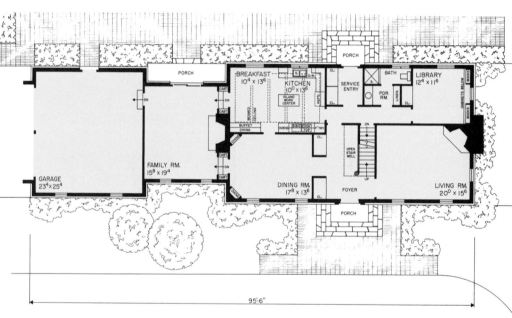

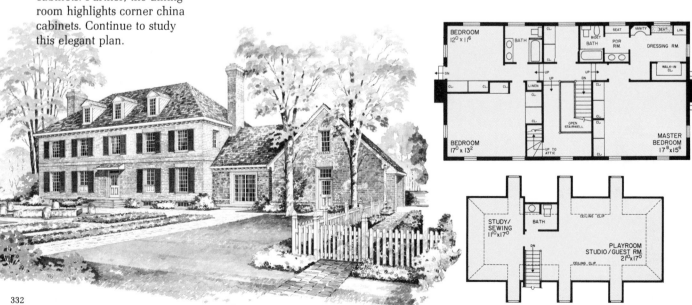

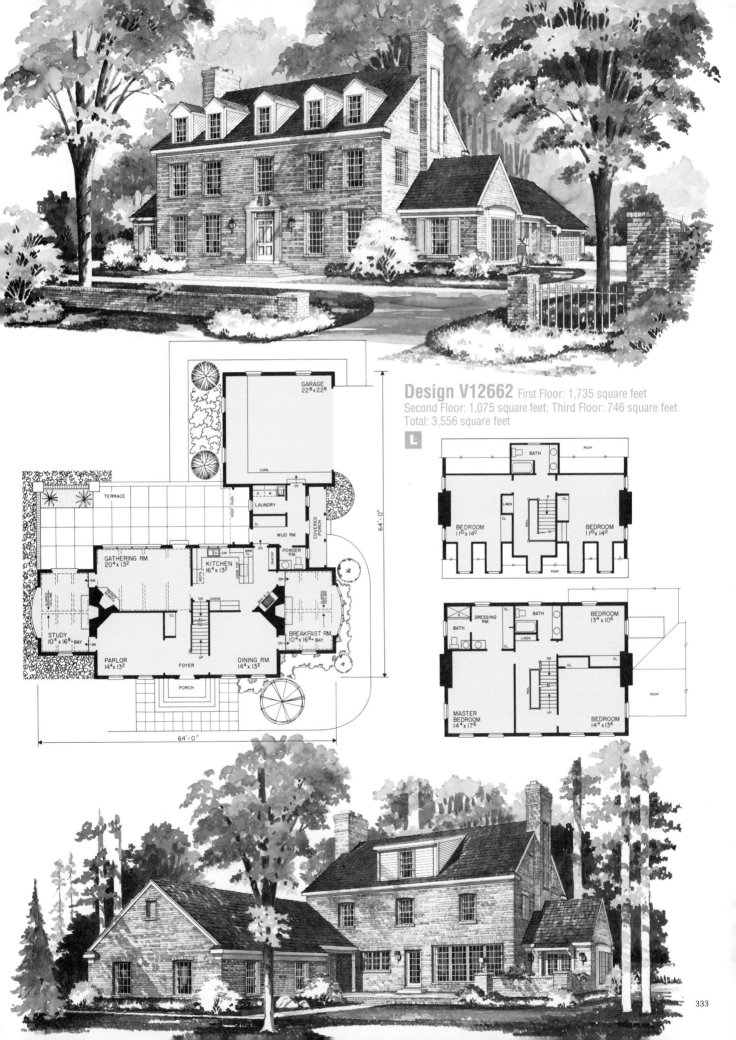

Design V12662 First Floor: 1,735 square feet
Second Floor: 1,075 square feet; Third Floor: 746 square feet
Total: 3,556 square feet

GARAGE 22⁸ x 22⁸

TERRACE

LAUNDRY

MUD RM.

COVERED PORCH

GATHERING RM. 20⁴ x 13²

KITCHEN 16⁴ x 13²

POWDER RM.

PANTRY

STUDY 10⁴ x 16⁸ BAY

BREAKFAST RM. 10⁴ x 16⁸ BAY

OVENS

PARLOR 14⁴ x 13²

FOYER

DINING RM. 14⁴ x 13²

PORCH

64'-0"

64'-0"

BATH

ROOF

BEDROOM 11¹⁰ x 14⁰

LINEN

BEDROOM 11¹⁰ x 14⁰

ROOF

DRESSING RM.

BATH

BATH

LINEN

BEDROOM 13⁴ x 10⁶

MASTER BEDROOM 14⁴ x 17⁶

BEDROOM 14⁴ x 13⁶

ROOF

333

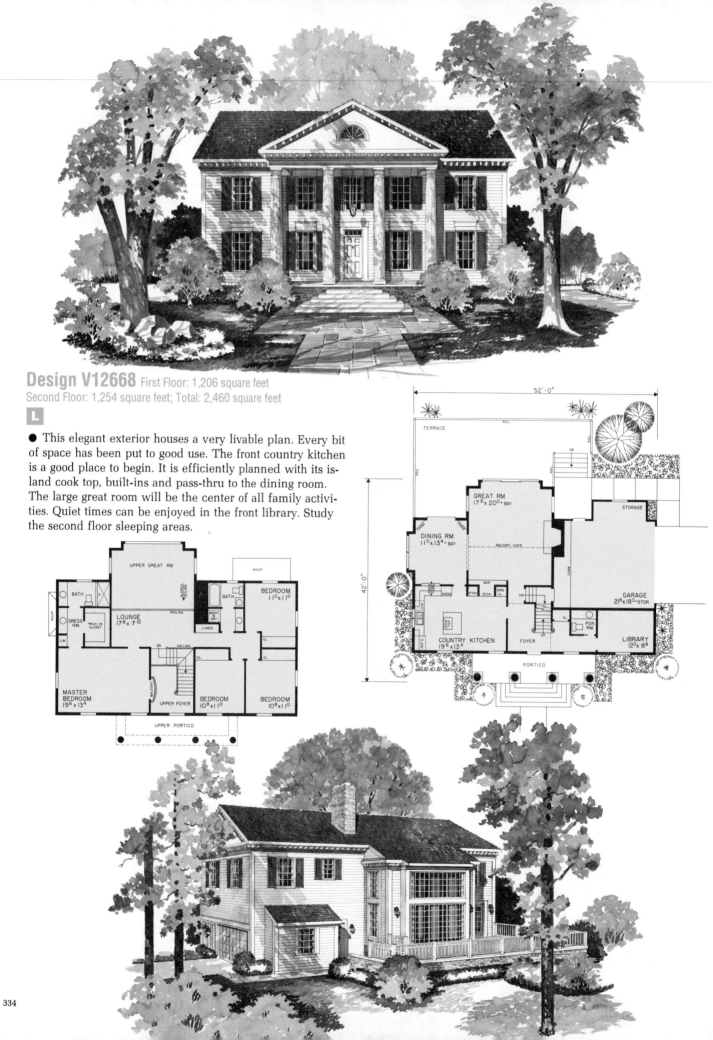

Design V12668 First Floor: 1,206 square feet
Second Floor: 1,254 square feet; Total: 2,460 square feet

L

● This elegant exterior houses a very livable plan. Every bit of space has been put to good use. The front country kitchen is a good place to begin. It is efficiently planned with its island cook top, built-ins and pass-thru to the dining room. The large great room will be the center of all family activities. Quiet times can be enjoyed in the front library. Study the second floor sleeping areas.

Design V12659 First Floor: 1,023 square feet; Second Floor: 1,008 square feet
Third Floor: 476 square feet; Total: 2,507 square feet

L D

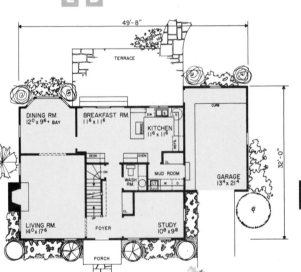

● The facade of this three-storied, pitch-roofed house has a symmetrical placement of windows and a restrained but elegant central entrance. The central hall, or foyer, expands midway through the house to a family kitchen. Off the foyer are two rooms, a living room with fireplace and a study. The windowed third floor attic can be used as a study and studio. Three bedrooms are housed on the second floor.

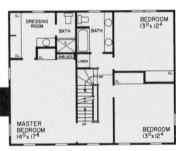

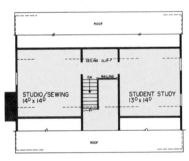

Design V12733 First Floor: 1,177 square feet; Second Floor: 1,003 square feet; Total: 2,180 square feet

L D

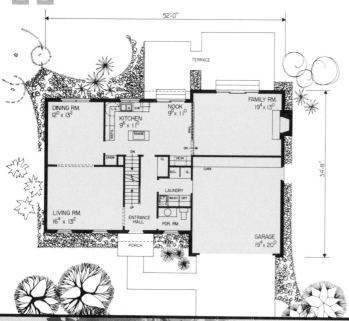

● This is definitely a four bedroom Colonial with charm galore. The kitchen features an island range and other built-ins. All will enjoy the sunken family room with fireplace, which has sliding glass doors leading to the terrace. Also a basement for recreational activities with laundry remaining on first floor for extra convenience.

Design V12585 First Floor: 990 square feet; Second Floor: 1,011 square feet; Total: 2,001 square feet

.L D

● An elegant Colonial! After entering through the front door one can either go directly to the formal area of the living room and dining room or to the informal area which is the front family room with fireplace. The U-shaped kitchen will serve the nook area and is just a step away from the washroom. Upstairs one will find all of the sleeping facilities.

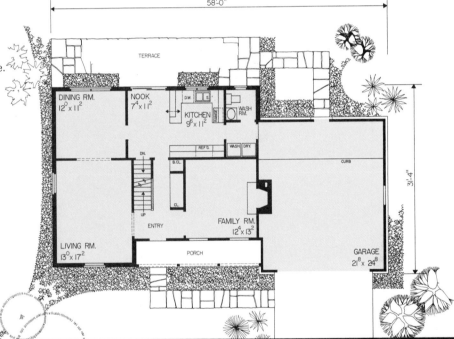

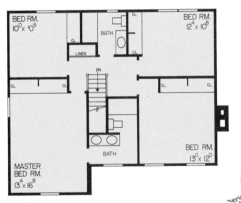

Design V12622

First Floor: 624 square feet
Second Floor: 624 square feet
Total: 1,248 square feet

L D

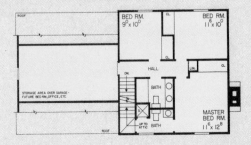

CUSTOMIZABLE
Custom Alterations? See page 381 for customizing this plan to your specifications.

● Appealing design can envelop little packages, too. Here is a charming, Early Colonial adaptation with an attached two-car garage to serve the young family with a modest building budget.

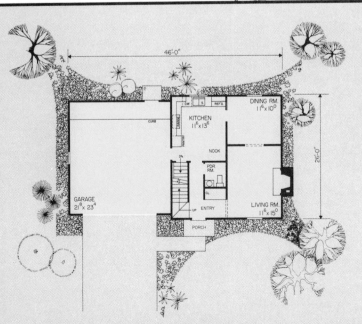

337

Design V11957 First Floor: 1,042 square feet; Second Floor: 780 square feet; Total: 1,822 square feet

L D

● When you order your blueprints for this design you will receive details for the construction of each of the three charming exteriors pictured above. Whichever the exterior you finally decide to build, the floor plan will be essentially the same except the location of the windows. This will be a fine home for the growing family. It will serve well for many years. There are four bedrooms and two full baths (one with a stall shower) upstairs.

Design V11956

First Floor: 990 square feet
Second Floor: 728 square feet
Total: 1,718 square feet

D

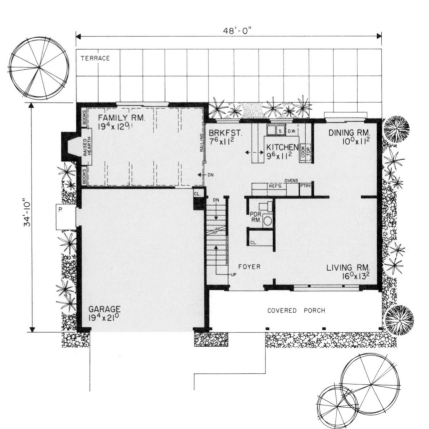

CUSTOMIZABLE

Custom Alterations? See page 381 for customizing this plan to your specifications.

● The blueprints for this home include details for both the three bedroom and four bedroom options. The first floor livability does not change.

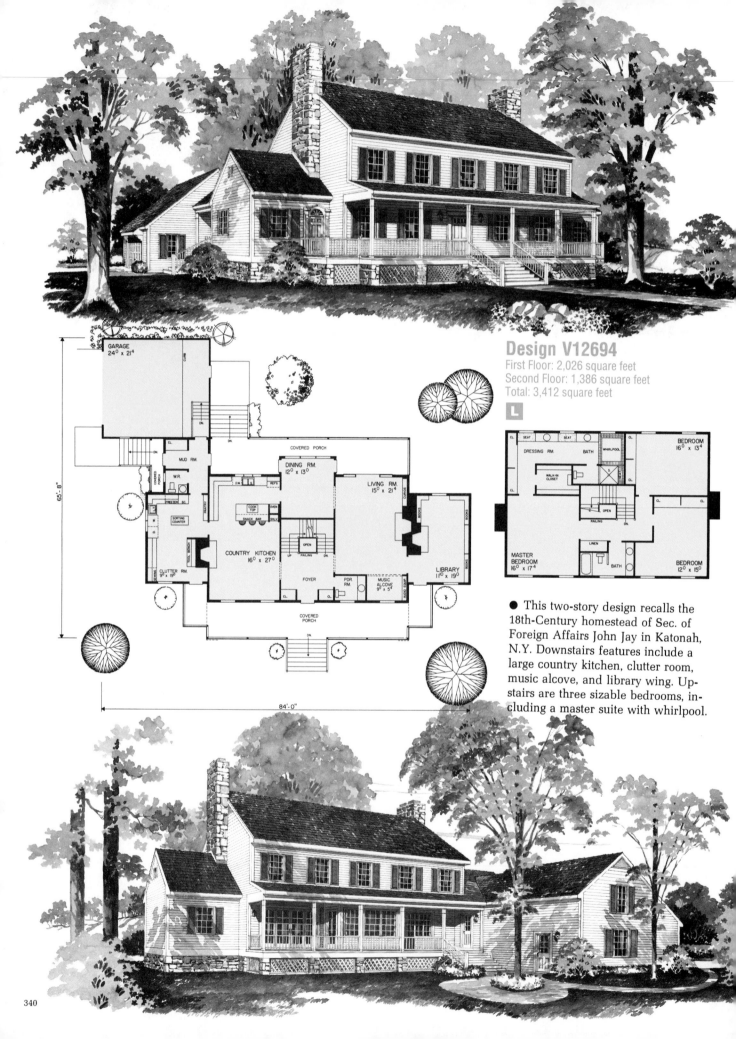

Design V12694

First Floor: 2,026 square feet
Second Floor: 1,386 square feet
Total: 3,412 square feet

L

GARAGE 24⁰ x 21⁴

COVERED PORCH

DN

CL

MUD RM.

DN

W.R.

FREEZER BC

SORTING COUNTER

PANTRY

DW

REF'S.

DINING RM. 12⁰ x 13⁰

LIVING RM. 15⁰ x 21⁴

CURIO

BOOKS

COOK TOP OVEN

SNACK BAR

COUNTRY KITCHEN 16⁰ x 27⁰

OPEN RAILING

UP

DN

CLUTTER RM. 9⁰ x 19⁰

POOL BENCH

OPEN

FOYER

PDR. RM.

MUSIC ALCOVE 9⁰ x 5⁴

AUDIO EQUIP.

LIBRARY 11⁰ x 19⁰

BOOKS

CL

CL

CL

65'-8"

84'-0"

COVERED PORCH

DN

CL SEAT SEAT

DRESSING RM. **BATH** WHIRLPOOL

BEDROOM 16⁰ x 13⁴

WALK-IN CLOSET

CL

OPEN

DN

RAILING

CL CL

LINEN

MASTER BEDROOM 16⁰ x 17⁴

BATH

BEDROOM 12⁰ x 15⁰

● This two-story design recalls the 18th-Century homestead of Sec. of Foreign Affairs John Jay in Katonah, N.Y. Downstairs features include a large country kitchen, clutter room, music alcove, and library wing. Upstairs are three sizable bedrooms, including a master suite with whirlpool.

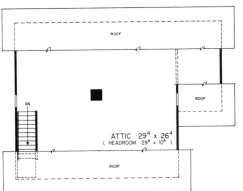

ROOF

ROOF

DN.

ATTIC 29⁴ x 26⁴
(HEADROOM 29⁴ x 10⁴)

ROOF

BEDROOM /
STUDY
11⁰ x 13²

BATH   DRESS. RM.   VANITY

MASTER
BEDROOM
13⁰ x 13²

CL.

CL.

BATH

CL.

DN.

LIN.

CL.   CL.

CL.

BEDROOM
10⁰ x 10⁶

BEDROOM
13⁰ x 10⁶

CL.

UP TO
ATTIC

Design V12774

First Floor: 1,370 square feet
Second Floor: 969 square feet
Total: 2,339 square feet

L D

● Farmhouse adaptation with all the most up-to-date features expected in a new home. Beginning with the formal areas, this design offers pleasures for the entire family. There is the quiet corner living room which has an opening to the sizeable dining room. This room will enjoy plenty of natural light from the delightful bay window overlooking the rear yard. It is also conveniently located with the efficient U-shaped kitchen just a step away. The kitchen features many built-ins with pass-thru to the beamed ceiling nook. Sliding glass doors to the terrace are fine attractions in both the sunken family room and nook. The service entrance to the garage has a storage closet on each side, plus there is a secondary entrance through the laundry area. Recreational activities and hobbies can be pursued in the basement area. Four bedrooms, two baths upstairs.

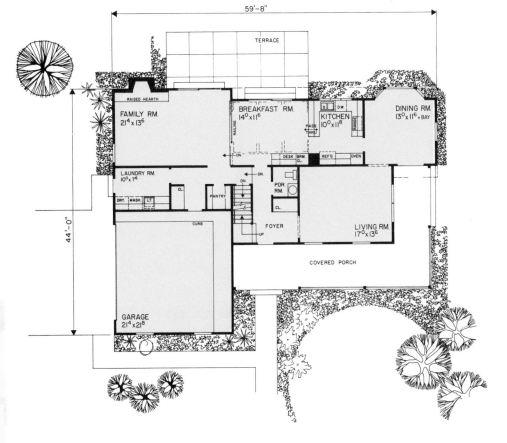

59'-8"

TERRACE

RAISED HEARTH

FAMILY RM.
21⁴ x 13⁶

BREAKFAST RM.
14⁰ x 11⁶

KITCHEN
10⁰ x 11⁸

DINING RM.
13⁰ x 11⁶ + BAY

S.   DW

RANGE

PASS
THRU

RAILING

DN.

44'-0"

LAUNDRY RM.
10⁰ x 7⁶

DESK   BRM.   CL.

REF'G

OVEN

DN.

DRY.   WASH.   LT.

CL.

PANTRY

DN.

PDR.
RM.

CL.

LIVING RM.
17⁰ x 13⁶

CURB

FOYER

UP

GARAGE
21⁴ x 21⁸

COVERED PORCH

CUSTOMIZABLE

Custom Alterations? See page 381 for customizing this plan to your specifications.

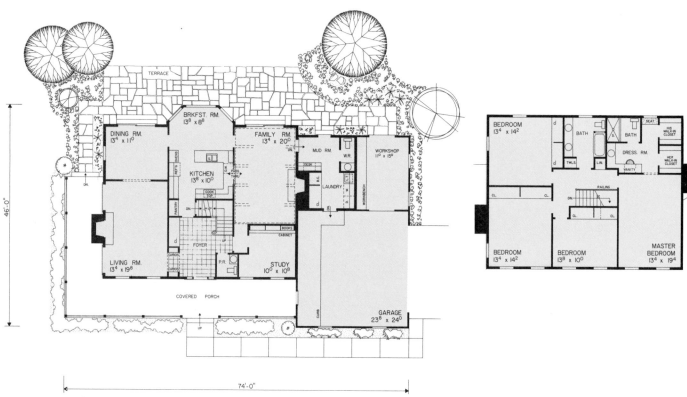

Design V12946

First Floor: 1,590 square feet
Second Floor: 1,344 square feet
Total: 2,934 square feet

L D

● Here's a traditional design that's made for down-home hospitality, the pleasures of casual conversation, and the good grace of pleasant company. The star attractions are the large covered porch and terrace, perfectly relaxing gathering points for family and friends. Inside, though, the design is truly a hard worker; separate living room and family room, each with its own fireplace; formal dining room; large kitchen and breakfast area with bay windows; separate study; workshop with plenty of room to maneuver; mud room; and four bedrooms up, including a master suite. Not to be overlooked are the curio niches, the powder room, the built-in bookshelves, the kitchen pass-thru, the pantry, the planning desk, the workbench, and the stairs to the basement.

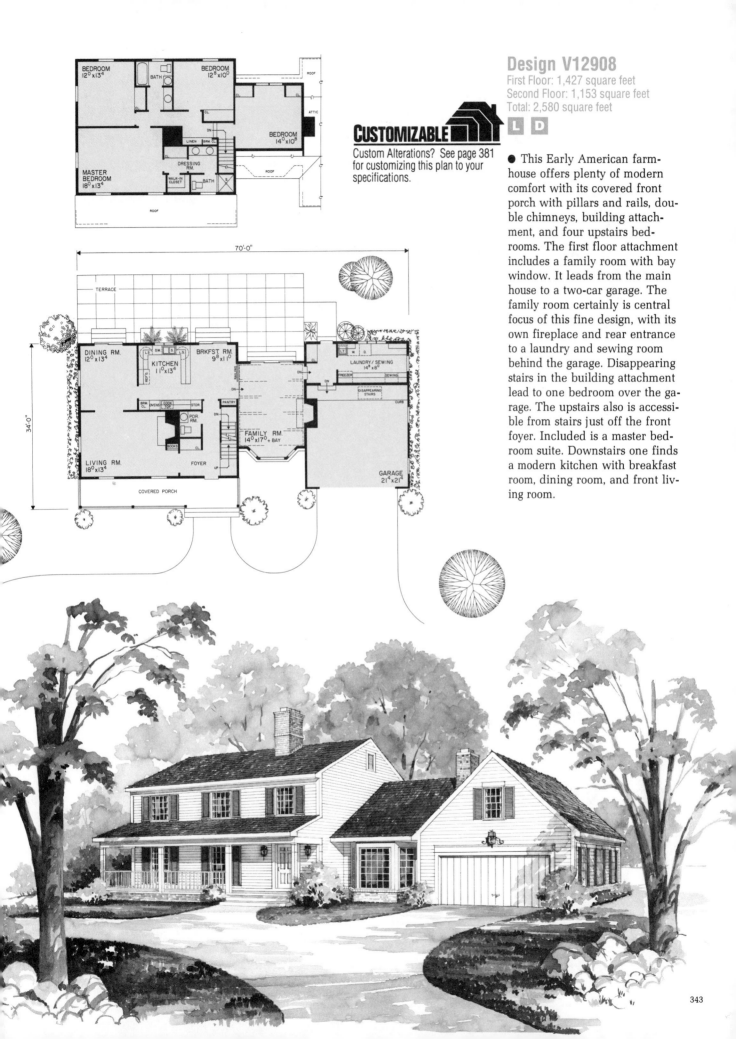

Floor Plans (labels)

Second Floor:
- BEDROOM 12⁰x13⁴ → BEDROOM $12^0 \times 13^4$
- BATH
- CL
- BEDROOM $12^8 \times 10^0$
- CL
- ROOF
- ATTIC
- CL
- BEDROOM $14^0 \times 10^8$
- LINEN
- BRM CL
- DRESSING RM.
- CL
- MASTER BEDROOM $18^0 \times 13^4$
- WALK-IN CLOSET
- BATH
- S
- ROOF
- ROOF

First Floor:
- 70'-0"
- 34'-0"
- TERRACE
- DINING RM. $12^0 \times 13^4$
- KITCHEN $11^0 \times 13^4$
- BRKFST RM. $9^8 \times 11^0$
- REF'S.
- LS
- DW.
- B
- RAILING
- LAUNDRY / SEWING $14^8 \times 8^0$
- CL
- W
- D
- FREEZER
- SEWING
- DN
- DN
- DISAPPEARING STAIRS
- CURB
- BRM CL
- OVENS
- COOK TOP
- STOR.
- PANTRY
- PDR. RM.
- BOOKS
- CL
- DN
- FAMILY RM. $14^0 \times 17^0$ + BAY
- GARAGE $21^4 \times 21^4$
- LIVING RM. $18^0 \times 13^4$
- FOYER
- UP
- COVERED PORCH

Design V12908

First Floor: 1,427 square feet
Second Floor: 1,153 square feet
Total: 2,580 square feet

L D

CUSTOMIZABLE

Custom Alterations? See page 381 for customizing this plan to your specifications.

● This Early American farmhouse offers plenty of modern comfort with its covered front porch with pillars and rails, double chimneys, building attachment, and four upstairs bedrooms. The first floor attachment includes a family room with bay window. It leads from the main house to a two-car garage. The family room certainly is central focus of this fine design, with its own fireplace and rear entrance to a laundry and sewing room behind the garage. Disappearing stairs in the building attachment lead to one bedroom over the garage. The upstairs also is accessible from stairs just off the front foyer. Included is a master bedroom suite. Downstairs one finds a modern kitchen with breakfast room, dining room, and front living room.

343

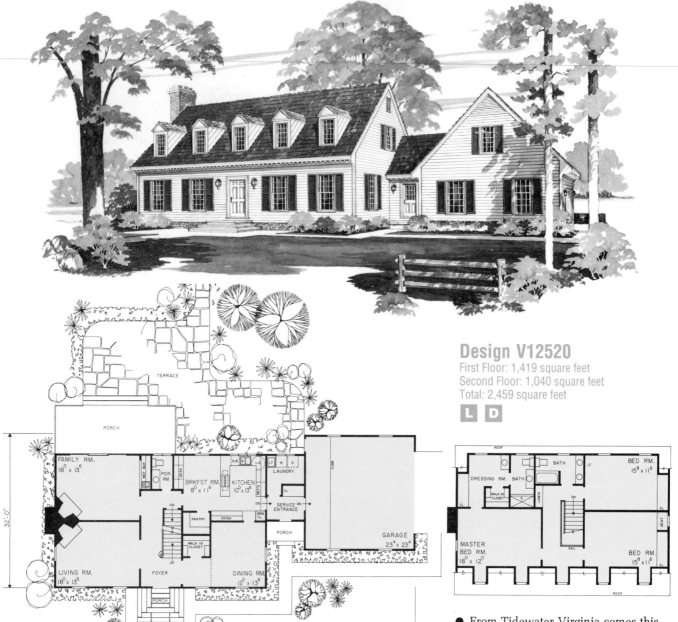

Design V12520

First Floor: 1,419 square feet
Second Floor: 1,040 square feet
Total: 2,459 square feet

L **D**

● From Tidewater Virginia comes this historic adaptation, a positive reminder of the charm of Early American architecture. Note how the center entrance gives birth to fine traffic circulation. List the numerous features.

Design V12776

First Floor: 1,134 square feet
Second Floor: 874 square feet
Total: 2,008 square feet

L D

61'-4"

TERRACE

DINING RM. 11⁴ x 10⁰

KITCHEN 11⁰ x 10⁰

FAMILY RM. 16⁴ x 15⁶

CURB

GARAGE 21⁰ x 21⁴

OVEN RANGE REF'G.

RAISED HEARTH

38'-0"

DN

UP

LIVING RM. 15⁶ x 17⁰

BRM CL

PDR. RM.

ENTRANCE

SERVICE ENTRANCE

LAUNDRY

SEAT

PORCH

WALK-IN CLOSET

BATH

BATH

CL

LINEN

BED RM. 11⁶ x 10⁰

ROOF

MASTER. BED RM. 15⁶ x 13⁴

DN

CL

CL

BED RM. 14⁶ x 10⁰

ROOF

ROOF

Design V12650

First Floor: 1,451 square feet
Second Floor: 1,091 square feet
Total: 2,542 square feet

L D

82'-8"

TERRACE

PORCH

DINING RM. 10⁰ x 13⁶

NOOK 10⁴ x 13⁶

KITCHEN 11⁰ x 13⁶

LAUNDRY

SERVICE ENTRANCE

GARAGE 23⁴ x 21⁰

34'-0"

DESK

OVEN MW

DN

DN

POWDER RM.

PORCH

UP

GATHERING RM. 18⁰ x 25⁴

ENTRANCE

STUDY 12⁰ x 11⁶

PORCH

WALK-IN CLOSET

DRESSING RM.

BATH

BED RM 11⁴ x 10⁰

BATH

SHELVES

MASTER BED RM. 18⁰ x 14⁰

DN

CL

LINEN

SHELVES

BED RM 17⁰ x 12⁶

ROOF

Expanding the Half-House

Design V12682 First Floor (Basic Plan): 976 square feet
First Floor (Expanded Plan): 1,230 square feet
Second Floor (Both Plans): 744 square feet
Total (Basic Plan): 1,720 square feet; Total (Expanded Plan): 1,974 square feet

L D

● Here is an expandable Colonial with a full measure of Cape Cod Charm. For those who wish to build the basic house, there is an abundance of low-budget livability. Twin fireplaces serve the formal living room and the informal country kitchen. Note the spaciousness of both areas. A dining room and powder room are also on the first floor of this basic plan. Upstairs three bedrooms and two full baths.

CUSTOMIZABLE
Custom Alterations? See page 381 for customizing this plan to your specifications.

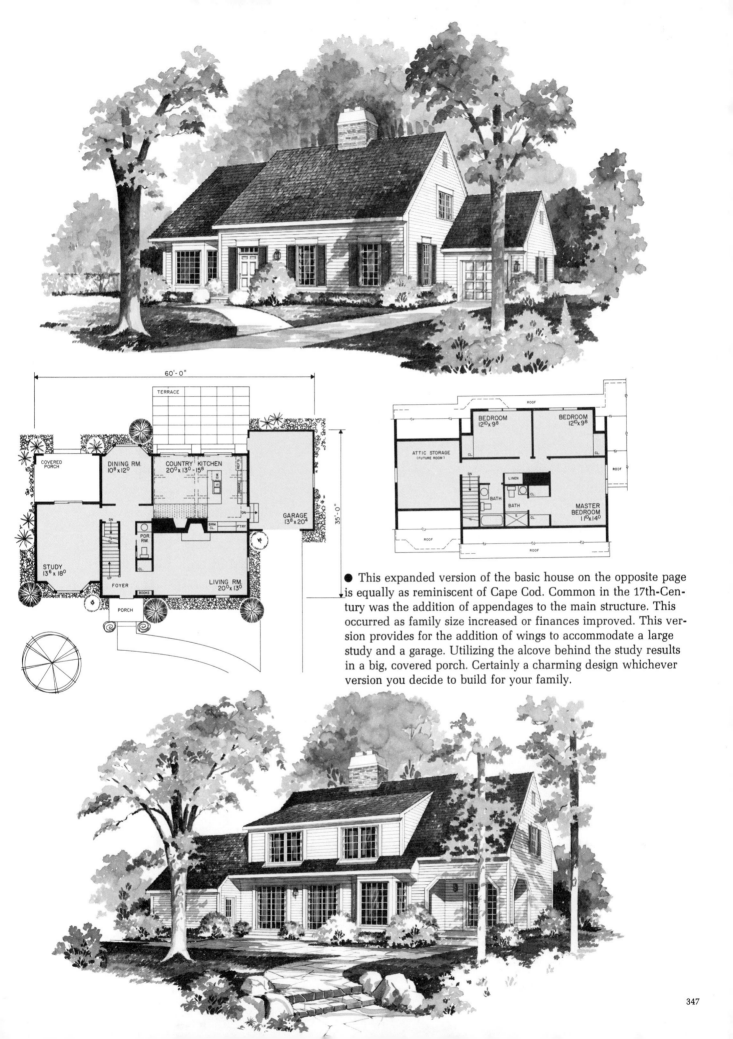

60'-0"

TERRACE

COVERED PORCH

DINING RM.
10⁸ x 12⁰

COUNTRY KITCHEN
20⁰ x 13⁰ - 15⁸

GARAGE
13⁸ x 20⁴

35'-0"

STUDY
13⁶ x 18⁰

DN

UP

PDR. RM.

CL.

BRM CL.

FOYER

BOOKS

LIVING RM.
20⁰ x 13⁰

PORCH

ROOF

BEDROOM
12¹⁰ x 9⁸

BEDROOM
12¹⁰ x 9⁸

ATTIC STORAGE
(FUTURE ROOM)

CL.

ROOF

DN

LINEN

BATH

CL.

BATH

CL.

S.

MASTER BEDROOM
11⁰ x 14⁰

ROOF

ROOF

ROOF

● This expanded version of the basic house on the opposite page is equally as reminiscent of Cape Cod. Common in the 17th-Century was the addition of appendages to the main structure. This occurred as family size increased or finances improved. This version provides for the addition of wings to accommodate a large study and a garage. Utilizing the alcove behind the study results in a big, covered porch. Certainly a charming design whichever version you decide to build for your family.

Design V12657

First Floor: 1,217 square feet
Second Floor: 868 square feet
Total: 2,085 square feet

L

● Deriving its design from the traditional Cape Cod style, this facade features clapboard siding, small-paned windows and a transom-lit entrance flanked by carriage lamps. A central chimney services two fireplaces, one in the country-kitchen and the other in the formal living room which is removed from the disturbing flow of traffic. The master suite is located to the left of the upstairs landing. A full bathroom services two additional bedrooms on the second floor.

Design V12661

First Floor: 1,020 square feet
Second Floor: 777 square feet
Total: 1,797 square feet

L **D**

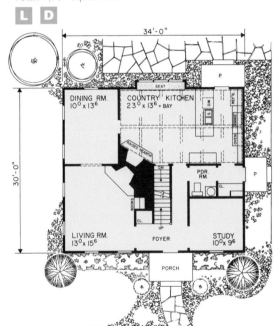

● Any other starter house or retirement home couldn't have more charm than this design. Its compact frame houses a very livable plan. An outstanding feature of the first floor is the large country kitchen. Its fine attractions include a beamed ceiling, raised hearth fireplace, built-in window seat and a door leading to the outdoors. A living room is in the front of the plan and has another fireplace which shares the single chimney. The rear dormered second floor houses the sleeping and bath facilities.

CUSTOMIZABLE

Custom Alterations? See page 381 for customizing this plan to your specifications.

CUSTOMIZABLE
Custom Alterations? See page 381
for customizing this plan to your
specifications.

Design V12855
First Floor: 1,372 square feet
Second Floor: 1,245 square feet
Total: 2,617 square feet

L D

● This elegant Tudor house is perfect for the family who wants to move-up in living area, style and luxury. As you enter this home you will find a large living room with a fireplace on your right. Adjacent, the formal dining room has easy access to both the living room and the kitchen. The kitchen/breakfast room has an open plan and access to the rear terrace. Sunken a few steps, the spacious family room is highlighted with a fireplace and access to the rear, covered porch. Note the optional planning of the garage storage area. Plan this area according to the needs of your family. Upstairs, your family will enjoy three bedrooms and a full bath, along with a spacious master bedroom suite. Truly a house that will bring many years of pleasure to your family.

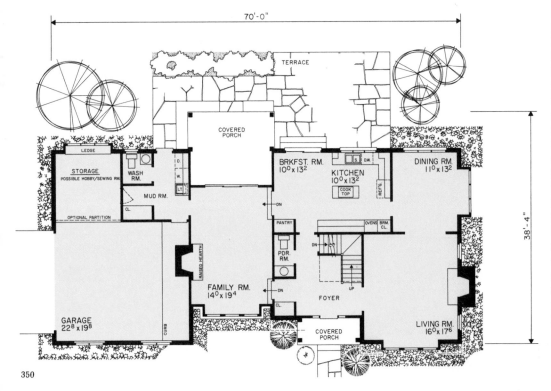

● This Tudor design has many fine features. The exterior is enhanced by front and side bay windows in the family and dining rooms. Along with an outstanding exterior, it also contains a modern and efficient floor plan within its modest proportions. Flanking the entrance foyer is a comfortable living room. The U-shaped kitchen is conveniently located between the dining and breakfast rooms.

Design V12800 First Floor: 999 square feet
Second Floor: 997 square feet; Total: 1,996 square feet

L D

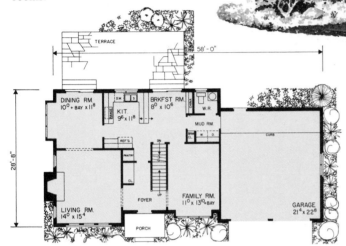

● The charm of old England has been captured in this outstanding one-and-a-half story design. Interior livability will efficiently serve the various needs of all family members. The first floor offers both formal and informal areas along with the work centers. Features include: a wet-bar in the dining room, the kitchen's snack bar, first floor laundry and rear covered porch.

Design V12854 First Floor: 1,261 square feet
Second Floor: 950 square feet; Total: 2,211 square feet

L D

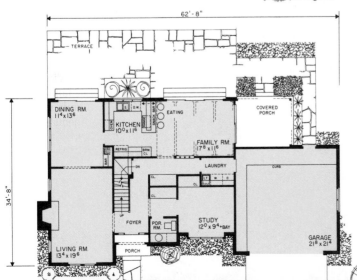

351

Design V12511

Main Level: 1,043 square feet
Upper Level: 703 square feet
Lower Level: 794 square feet
Total: 2,540 square feet

L **D**

Upper Level Floor Plan:

UPPER GATHERING RM.

BALCONY — BALCONY

BED RM.
11⁸ x 13⁸

BUNK RM.
11⁸ x 19⁰

BALCONY — RAILING

CL — CL

BATH — RAILING — DN. — CL — CL

UPPER FOYER

Lower Level Floor Plan:

TERRACE

ACTIVITIES RM.
15⁴ x 18⁴

BUNK RM. OPTIONAL
11⁴ x 15⁸ — BASEMENT

RAISED HEARTH

AIR COND.

BATH — UP — STORAGE CABINETS — CL — LT. WASH. DRY. — UNEX.

Main Level Floor Plan:

40'-4"

52'-0"

GATHERING RM.
15⁴ x 18⁴ — DECK

BALCONY

STUDY-BED RM.
11⁸ x 13⁸

DINING RM.
11⁸ x 11⁸

LINEN — CL — SNACK BAR

BATH — DN. — UP — KITCHEN
11⁸ x 9⁸

FOYER — PANTRY — REF'G — RANGE

CL

PORCH

ENTRANCE COURT — OPEN TRELLIS

STORAGE

CARPORT
11⁸ x 20⁰

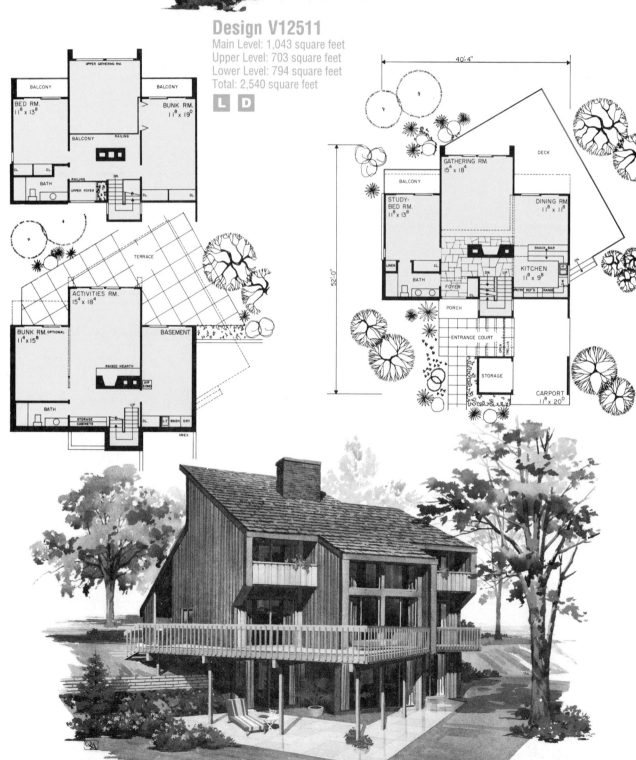

Design V12937 Main Level: 1,096 square feet
Upper Level: 1,115 square feet; Lower Level: 1,104 square feet
Total: 3,315 square feet

L

● This contemporary multi-level home features an extended rear balcony that covers a rear patio, plus a master bedroom suite, complete with whirlpool and raised-hearth pass-thru. Two other bedrooms and a second bath are on the upper level.

Design V12711

First Floor: 975 square feet
Second Floor: 1,024 square feet
Total: 1,999 square feet

L D

CUSTOMIZABLE

Custom Alterations? See page 381 for customizing this plan to your specifications.

● This stunning, contemporary, two-story house will captivate you with its many attractive features. Notice the projecting garage that will reduce the lot size as well as your cost. You will love the roomy kitchen with an adjacent snack bar. Take note of the spacious rear dining and gathering rooms. The fireplace and the view of the outdoors through the sliding glass doors will bring hours of pleasure to you and your family. A nice feature is the study with a handy storage closet. A few steps upstairs and you will be pleasantly surprised at what the master suite offers. Notice the spaciousness of the bedroom and walk-in closet. A dressing room and two vanities also can be found. An attractive feature is the sliding glass doors that lead to a balcony. Two other sizable bedrooms and a full bath are nearby. This home will be admired by all who view it.

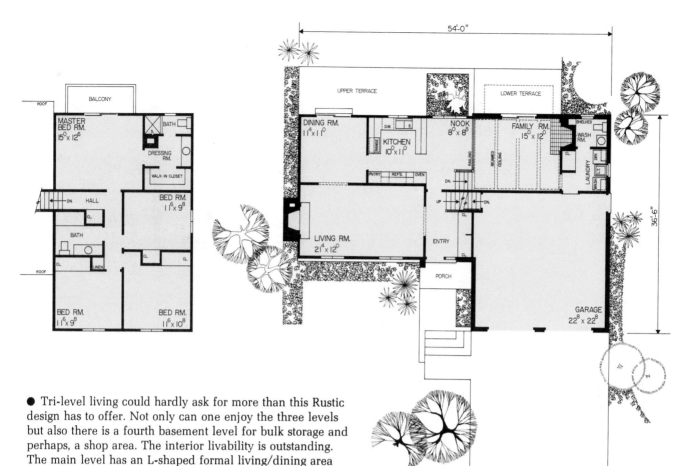

Upper Level (left plan):

ROOF

BALCONY

MASTER BED RM. 15⁰ x 12⁶

BATH

S

DRESSING RM.

WALK-IN CLOSET

DN. HALL CL.

BED RM. 11⁶ x 9⁸

BATH

CL. CL.

LINEN CL.

ROOF

BED RM. 11⁶ x 9⁸

BED RM. 11⁶ x 10⁸

Main Level (right plan):

54'-0"

UPPER TERRACE

LOWER TERRACE

DINING RM. 11⁴ x 11⁰

KITCHEN 10⁰ x 11⁰

D.W.

S.

RANGE

PANTRY REF'G. OVEN

NOOK 8⁰ x 8⁸

FAMILY RM. 15 x 12

SHELVES

WASH RM.

LAUNDRY

WASH DRY

CL.

BEAMED CEILING

RAILING

DN.

UP

DN.

CL.

LIVING RM. 21⁴ x 12⁰

ENTRY

PORCH

GARAGE 22⁸ x 22⁸

36'-6"

● Tri-level living could hardly ask for more than this Rustic design has to offer. Not only can one enjoy the three levels but also there is a fourth basement level for bulk storage and perhaps, a shop area. The interior livability is outstanding. The main level has an L-shaped formal living/dining area with a fireplace in the living room and sliding glass doors in the dining room to the upper terrace, a U-shaped kitchen and an informal eating area. Down a few steps to the lower level is the family room with another fireplace and sliding doors to the lower terrace, a washroom and laundry. The upper level houses all of the sleeping facilities including three bedrooms, bath and master suite.

Design V12608
Main Level: 728 square feet
Upper Level: 874 square feet
Lower Level: 310 square feet
Total: 1,912 square feet

L D

Design V12905 First Floor: 1,342 square feet; Second Floor: 619 square feet; Total: 1,961 square feet

L D

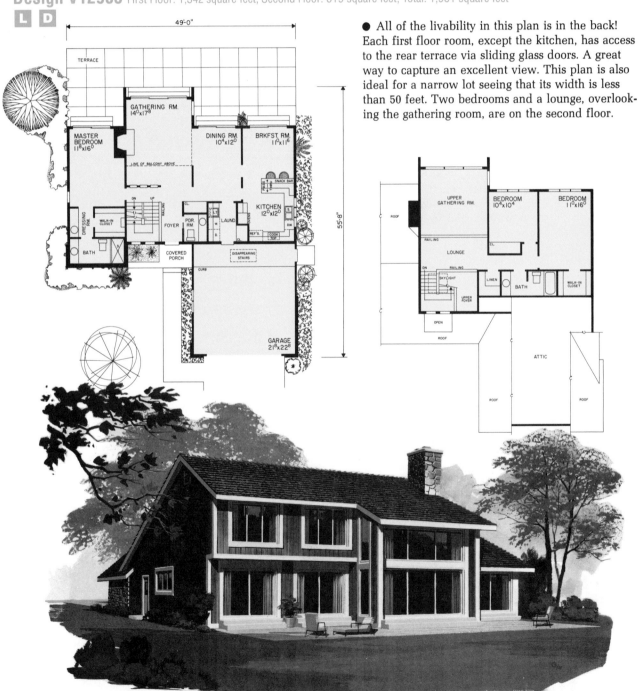

● All of the livability in this plan is in the back! Each first floor room, except the kitchen, has access to the rear terrace via sliding glass doors. A great way to capture an excellent view. This plan is also ideal for a narrow lot seeing that its width is less than 50 feet. Two bedrooms and a lounge, overlooking the gathering room, are on the second floor.

Great Outdoor Projects

No house should go empty-landed for long. If you're searching for just the right structure to fill up those wide open spaces, we've got eight solid choices to show you. Among other exciting plans, you'll find a get-away-from-it-all gazebo that's big enough for small gatherings; a storage shed that does a number on clutter but looks great doing it; a two-dormer studio garage with all the comforts of home and a nice old-timey feel; and a gorgeous little crafts cottage with one very bright touch: an attached sunroom.

Plan V1-G108 is a good, solid gazebo; larger than most, it's better suited to entertaining alfresco. **Plan V1-G106** is no ordinary garage. In fact, it's a model building: room for two cars below and a complete studio apartment on top.

OUTDOOR PROJECTS INDEX & PRICE SCHEDULE

TO ORDER, CALL TOLL FREE 1-800-521-6797, OR SEE PAGE 381.

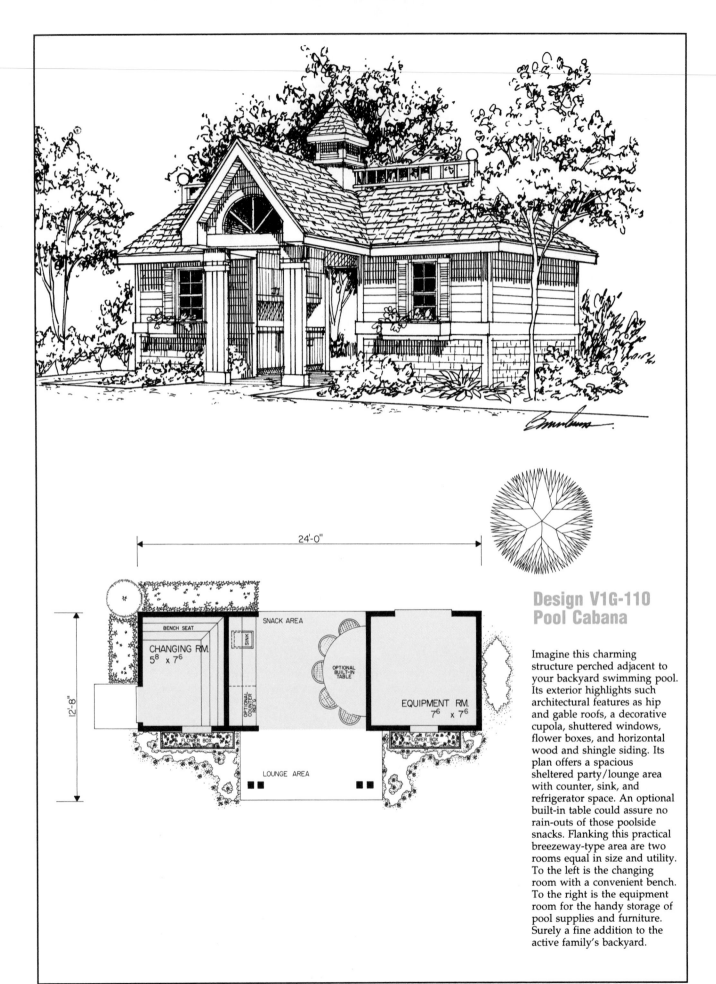

BENCH SEAT

CHANGING RM.
5^8 x 7^6

SNACK AREA

SINK

OPTIONAL
COUNTER
REF'G.

OPTIONAL
BUILT-IN
TABLE

EQUIPMENT RM.
7^6 x 7^6

FLOWER BOX

FLOWER BOX

LOUNGE AREA

24'-0"

12'-8"

Design V1G-110
Pool Cabana

Imagine this charming
structure perched adjacent to
your backyard swimming pool.
Its exterior highlights such
architectural features as hip
and gable roofs, a decorative
cupola, shuttered windows,
flower boxes, and horizontal
wood and shingle siding. Its
plan offers a spacious
sheltered party/lounge area
with counter, sink, and
refrigerator space. An optional
built-in table could assure no
rain-outs of those poolside
snacks. Flanking this practical
breezeway-type area are two
rooms equal in size and utility.
To the left is the changing
room with a convenient bench.
To the right is the equipment
room for the handy storage of
pool supplies and furniture.
Surely a fine addition to the
active family's backyard.

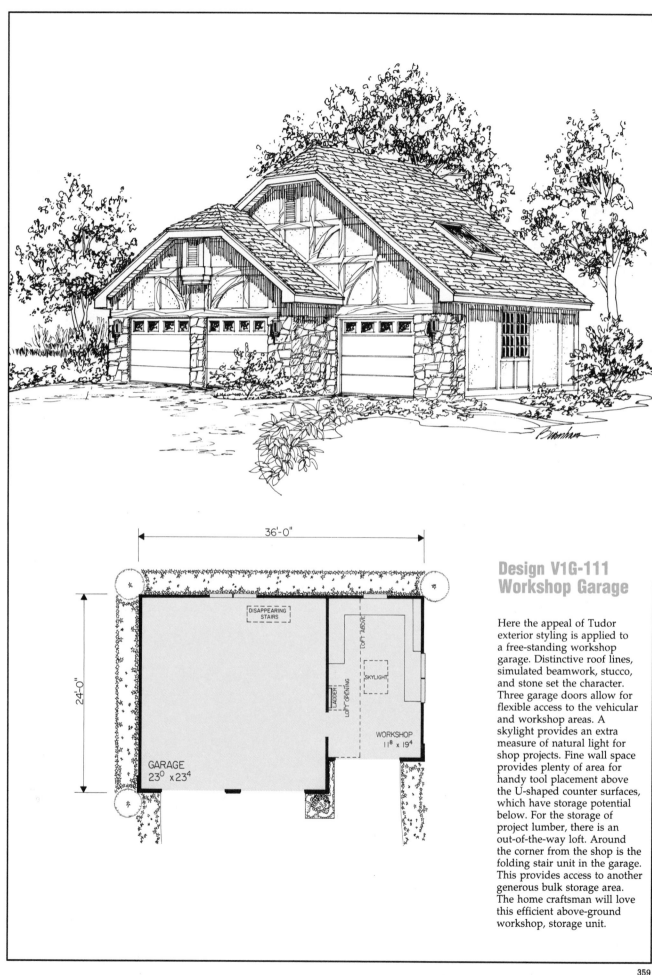

36'-0"

24'-0"

DISAPPEARING STAIRS

LOFT ABOVE

LADDER

LOFT OPENING

SKYLIGHT

WORKSHOP
11⁸ x 19⁴

GARAGE
23⁰ x23⁴

Design V1G-111
Workshop Garage

Here the appeal of Tudor exterior styling is applied to a free-standing workshop garage. Distinctive roof lines, simulated beamwork, stucco, and stone set the character. Three garage doors allow for flexible access to the vehicular and workshop areas. A skylight provides an extra measure of natural light for shop projects. Fine wall space provides plenty of area for handy tool placement above the U-shaped counter surfaces, which have storage potential below. For the storage of project lumber, there is an out-of-the-way loft. Around the corner from the shop is the folding stair unit in the garage. This provides access to another generous bulk storage area. The home craftsman will love this efficient above-ground workshop, storage unit.

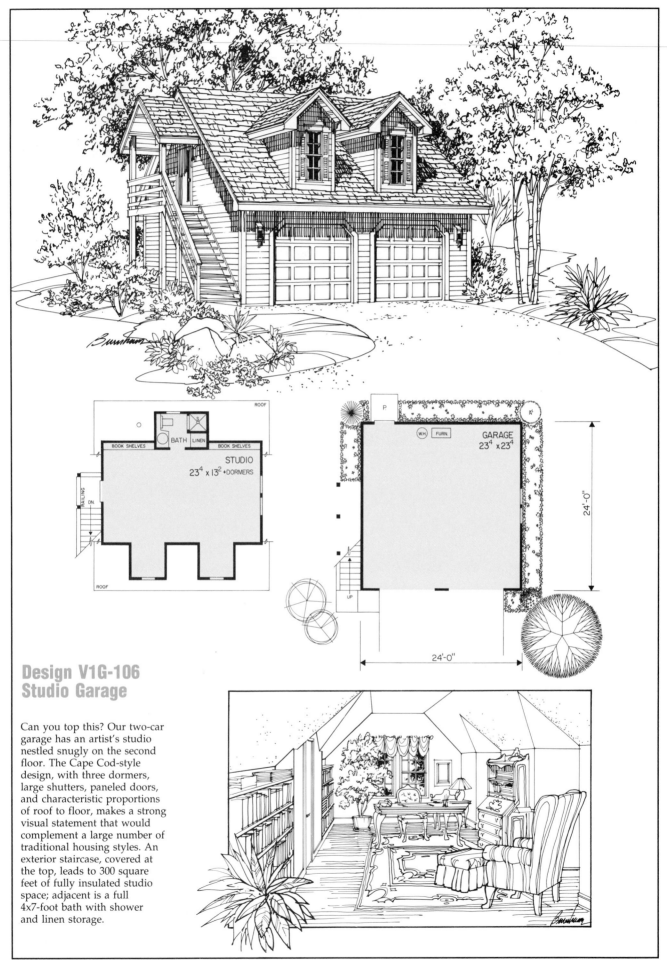

BOOK SHELVES | BATH | LINEN | **BOOK SHELVES**

ROOF

STUDIO
23⁴ x 13² +DORMERS

RAILING

DN.

ROOF

P

W.H. | FURN.

GARAGE
23⁴ x 23⁴

24'-0"

24'-0"

UP

Design V1G-106
Studio Garage

Can you top this? Our two-car garage has an artist's studio nestled snugly on the second floor. The Cape Cod-style design, with three dormers, large shutters, paneled doors, and characteristic proportions of roof to floor, makes a strong visual statement that would complement a large number of traditional housing styles. An exterior staircase, covered at the top, leads to 300 square feet of fully insulated studio space; adjacent is a full 4x7-foot bath with shower and linen storage.

COVERED PATIO
10⁰ x 10⁰

STORAGE AREA

WORKBENCH

12'-0"

12'-0"

Design V1G-107
Storage Shed
with Patio

Here's a hard-working storage shed with a number of bright touches. At 120 square feet, it's bigger than most. Cupola, birdhouse, shutters, and grooved plywood siding add up to a traditional look that complements many popular housing styles—from Cape Cods to Farmhouses. It's a flexible design, too, and could also be a potting shed, lathhouse, or workshop. The nicest feature may well be the covered patio. After you cut the grass, just stash the lawn mower, take a seat, and survey your handiwork.

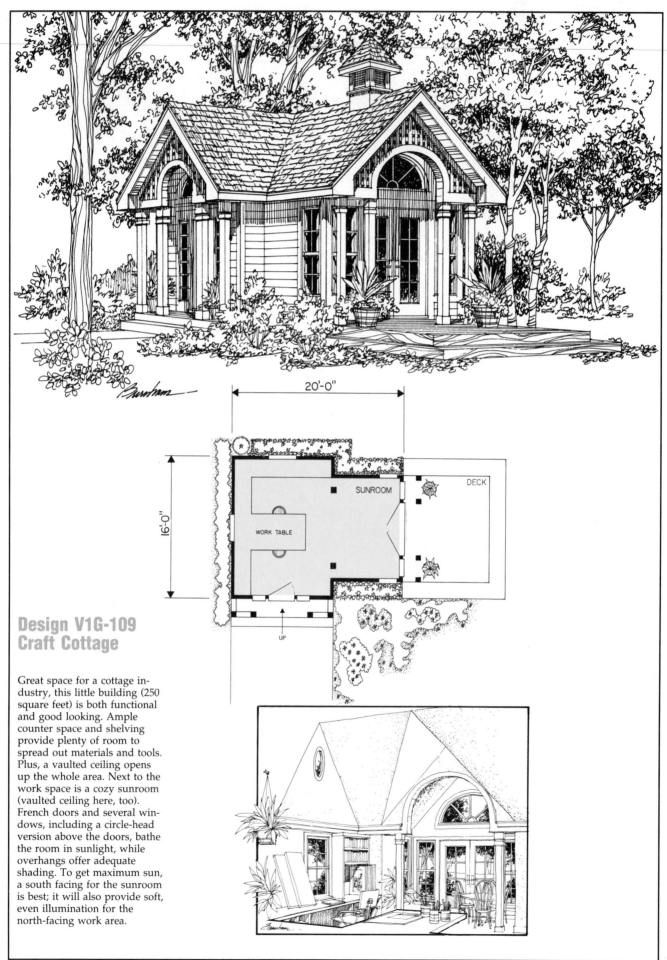

20'-0"

16'-0"

SUNROOM

DECK

WORK TABLE

UP

Design V1G-109
Craft Cottage

Great space for a cottage industry, this little building (250 square feet) is both functional and good looking. Ample counter space and shelving provide plenty of room to spread out materials and tools. Plus, a vaulted ceiling opens up the whole area. Next to the work space is a cozy sunroom (vaulted ceiling here, too). French doors and several windows, including a circle-head version above the doors, bathe the room in sunlight, while overhangs offer adequate shading. To get maximum sun, a south facing for the sunroom is best; it will also provide soft, even illumination for the north-facing work area.

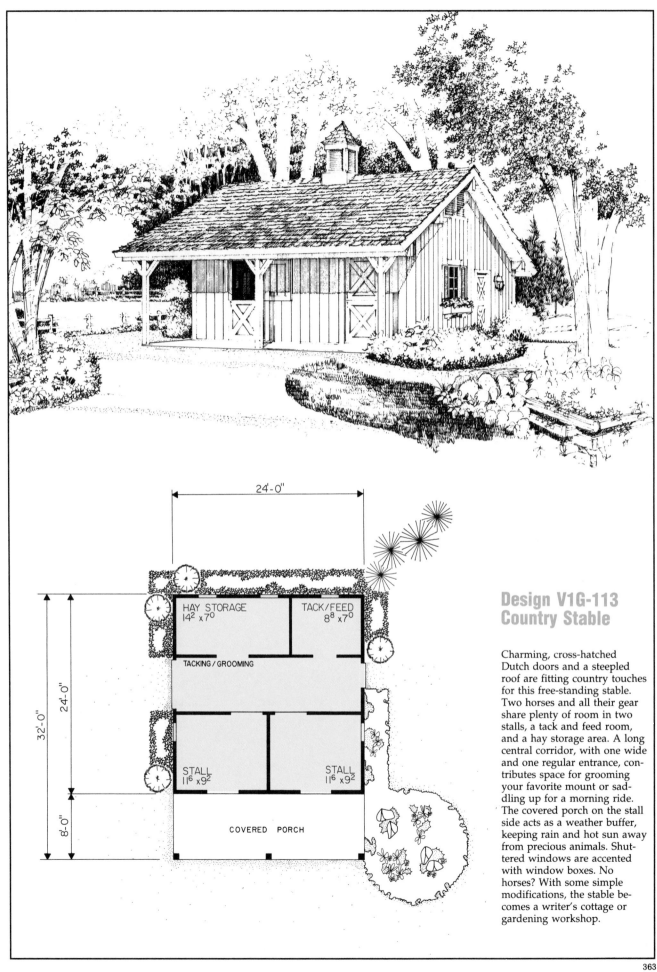

24'-0"

HAY STORAGE
14^2 x 7^0

TACK/FEED
8^8 x 7^0

TACKING / GROOMING

32'-0"
24'-0"

STALL
11^6 x 9^2

STALL
11^6 x 9^2

8'-0"

COVERED PORCH

Design V1G-113
Country Stable

Charming, cross-hatched
Dutch doors and a steepled
roof are fitting country touches
for this free-standing stable.
Two horses and all their gear
share plenty of room in two
stalls, a tack and feed room,
and a hay storage area. A long
central corridor, with one wide
and one regular entrance, contributes space for grooming
your favorite mount or sad-
dling up for a morning ride.
The covered porch on the stall
side acts as a weather buffer,
keeping rain and hot sun away
from precious animals. Shuttered windows are accented
with window boxes. No
horses? With some simple
modifications, the stable becomes a writer's cottage or
gardening workshop.

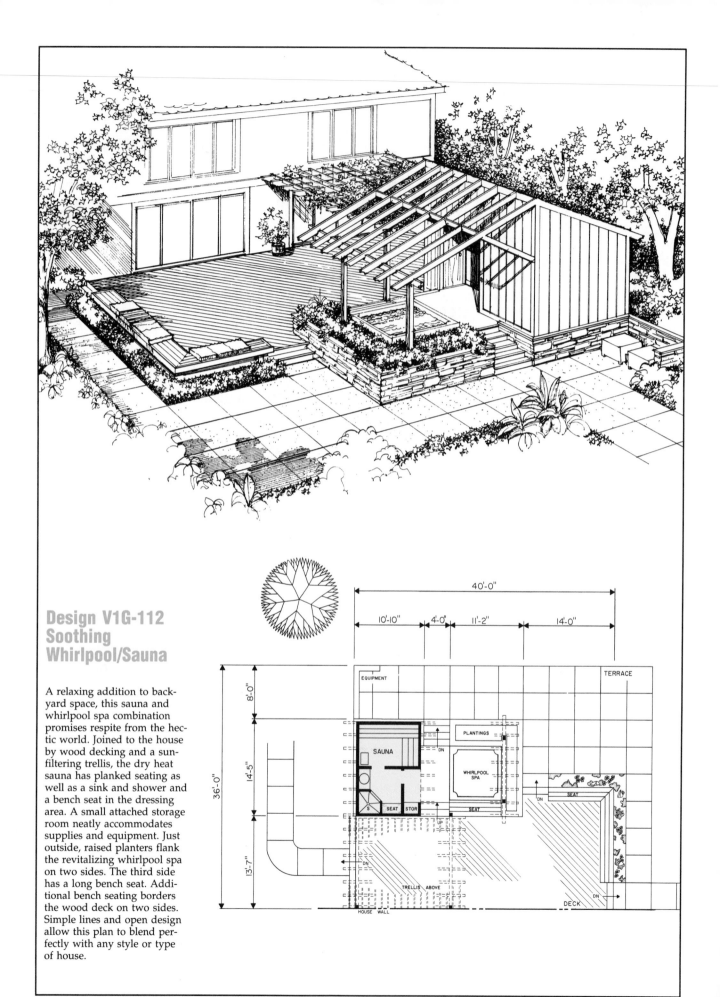

Design V1G-112
Soothing
Whirlpool/Sauna

A relaxing addition to back-yard space, this sauna and whirlpool spa combination promises respite from the hectic world. Joined to the house by wood decking and a sun-filtering trellis, the dry heat sauna has planked seating as well as a sink and shower and a bench seat in the dressing area. A small attached storage room neatly accommodates supplies and equipment. Just outside, raised planters flank the revitalizing whirlpool spa on two sides. The third side has a long bench seat. Additional bench seating borders the wood deck on two sides. Simple lines and open design allow this plan to blend perfectly with any style or type of house.

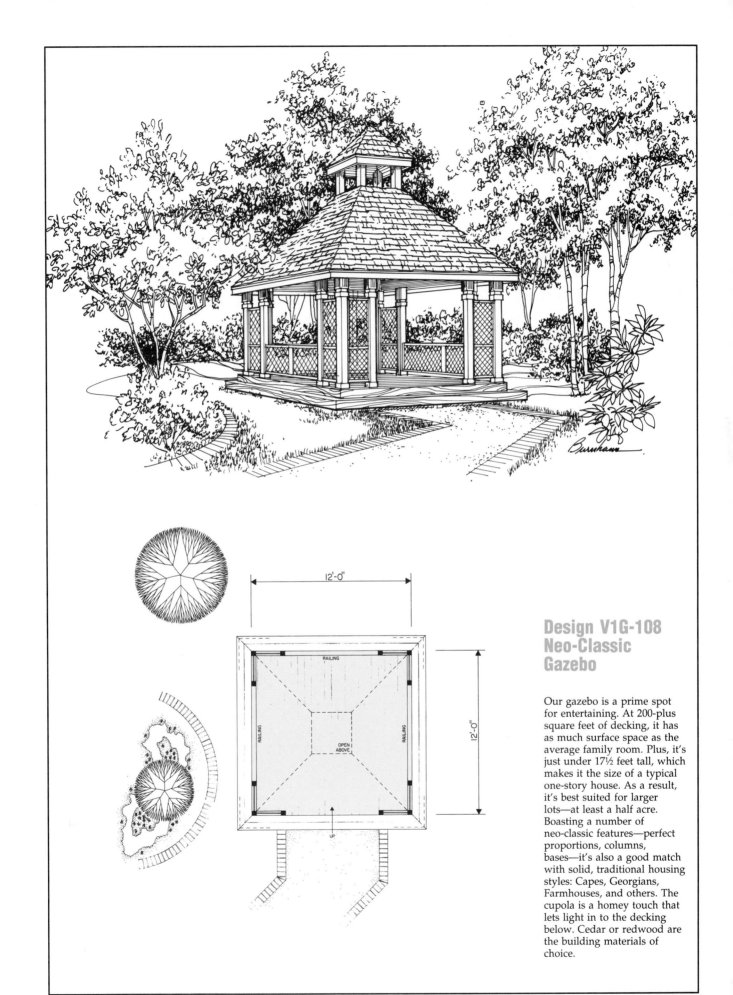

12'-0"

RAILING

RAILING   RAILING

OPEN ABOVE

12'-0"

UP

Design V1G-108 Neo-Classic Gazebo

Our gazebo is a prime spot for entertaining. At 200-plus square feet of decking, it has as much surface space as the average family room. Plus, it's just under 17½ feet tall, which makes it the size of a typical one-story house. As a result, it's best suited for larger lots—at least a half acre. Boasting a number of neo-classic features—perfect proportions, columns, bases—it's also a good match with solid, traditional housing styles: Capes, Georgians, Farmhouses, and others. The cupola is a homey touch that lets light in to the decking below. Cedar or redwood are the building materials of choice.

When You're Ready To Order . . .

Let Us Show You Our Home Blueprint Package.

Building a home? Planning a home? Our Blueprint Package contains nearly everything you need to get the job done right, whether you're working on your own or with help from an architect, designer, builder or subcontractors. Each Blueprint Package is the result of many hours of work by licensed architects or professional designers.

QUALITY

Hundreds of hours of painstaking effort have gone into the development of your blueprint set. Each home has been quality-checked by professionals to insure accuracy and buildability.

VALUE

Because we sell in volume, you can buy professional-quality blueprints at a fraction of their development cost. With our plans, your dream home design costs only a few hundred dollars, not the thousands of dollars that custom architects charge.

SERVICE

Once you've chosen your favorite home plan, you'll receive fast efficient service whether you choose to mail your order to us or call us toll free at 1-800-848-2550.

SATISFACTION

Our years of service to satisfied home plan buyers provide us the experience and knowledge that guarantee your satisfaction with our product and performance.

ORDER TOLL FREE 1-800-848-2550

After you've studied our Blueprint Package and Important Extras on the following pages, simply mail the accompanying order form on page 381 or call toll free on our Blueprint Hotline: 1-800-848-2550. We're ready and eager to serve you.

Each set of blueprints is an interrelated collection of floor plans, interior and exterior elevations, dimensions, cross-sections, diagrams and notations showing precisely how your house is to be constructed.

Here's what you get:

Frontal Sheet
This artist's sketch of the exterior of the house, done in realistic perspective, gives you an idea of how the house will look when built and landscaped. Large ink-line floor plans show all levels of the house and provide a quick overview of your new home's livability, as well as a handy reference for studying furniture placement.

Foundation Plan
Drawn to 1/4-inch scale, this sheet shows the complete foundation layout including support

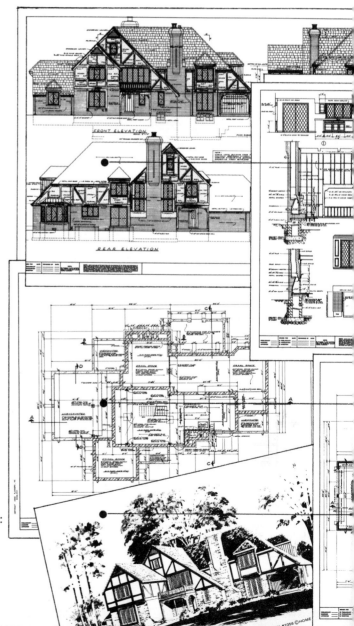

walls, excavated and unexcavated areas, if any, and foundation notes. If slab construction rather than basement, the plan shows footings and details for a monolithic slab. This page, or another in the set, also includes a sample plot plan for locating your house on a building site.

Detailed Floor Plans
Complete in 1/4-inch scale, these plans show the layout of each floor of the house. All rooms and interior spaces are carefully dimensioned and keys are provided for cross-section details given later in the plans. The positions of all electrical outlets and switches are clearly shown.

House Cross-Sections
Large-scale views, normally drawn at 3/8-inch equals 1 foot, show sections or cut-aways of the foundation, interior walls, exterior walls, floors, stairways and roof details. Additional cross-sections are given to show important changes in floor, ceiling or roof heights or the relationship of one level to another. Extremely valuable for construction, these sections show exactly how the various parts of the house fit together.

Interior Elevations
These large-scale drawings show the design and placement of kitchen and bathroom cabinets, laundry areas, fireplaces, bookcases and other built-ins. Little "extras," such as mantelpiece and wainscoting drawings, plus moulding sections, provide details that give your home that custom touch.

Exterior Elevations
Drawings in 1/4-inch scale show the front, rear and sides of your house and give necessary notes on exterior materials and finishes. Particular attention is given to cornice detail, brick and stone accents or other finish items that make your home distinctive.

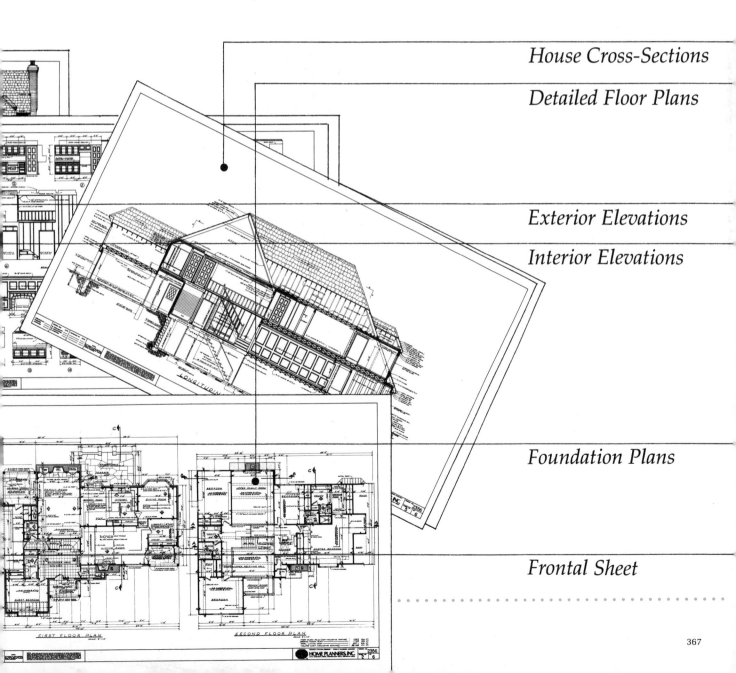

House Cross-Sections

Detailed Floor Plans

Exterior Elevations

Interior Elevations

Foundation Plans

Frontal Sheet

Important Extras To Do The Job Right!

Introducing seven important planning and construction aids developed by our professionals to help you succeed in your home-building project.

To Order, Call Toll Free 1-800-848-2550

To add these important extras to your Blueprint Package, simply indicate your choices on the order form on page 381 or call us Toll Free 1-800-848-2550 and we'll tell you more about these exciting products.

MATERIALS LIST

For many of the designs in our portfolio, we offer a customized materials take-off that is invaluable in planning and estimating the cost of your new home. This comprehensive list outlines the quantity, type and size of material needed to build your house (with the exception of mechanical system items). Included are:

- framing lumber
- roofing and sheet metal
- windows and doors
- exterior sheathing material and trim
- masonry, veneer and fireplace materials
- tile and flooring materials
- kitchen and bath cabinetry
- interior drywall and trim
- rough and finish hardware
- many more items

(Note: Because of differing local codes, building methods, and availability of materials, our Materials Lists do not include mechanical materials. To obtain necessary take-offs and recommendations, consult heating, plumbing and electrical contractors. Materials Lists are not sold separately from the Blueprint Package.)

This handy list helps you or your builder cost out materials and serves as a ready reference sheet when you're compiling bids. It also provides a cross-check against the materials specified by your builder and helps coordinate the substitution of items you may need to meet local codes.

SPECIFICATION OUTLINE

This valuable 16-page document is critical to building your house correctly. Designed to be filled in by you or your builder, this booklet lists 166 stages or items crucial to the building process.

For the layman, it provides a comprehensive review of the construction process and helps in making the specific choices of materials, models and processes. For the builder, it serves as a guide to preparing a building quotation and forms the basis for the construction program.

Designed primarily as a reference for the homeowner, this Specification Outline can become a legally binding document. Once it is filled out and agreed upon by owner and builder, it becomes a complete Project Specification.

When combined with the blueprints, a signed contract and schedule, the Specification Outline becomes a legal document and record for the building of your home. Many home builders find it useful to order two of these outlines—one as a worksheet in formulating the specifications and another to be carefully completed as a legal document.

DETAIL SHEETS

If you want to know more about techniques—and deal more confidently with subcontractors—we offer these remarkably useful detail sheets. Each is an excellent tool that will enhance your understanding of these technical subjects.

Plan-A-Home®

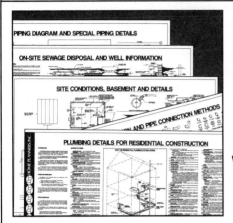

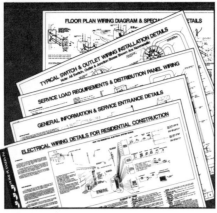

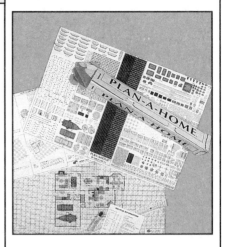

PLUMBING

The Blueprint Package includes locations for all the plumbing fixtures in your new house, including sinks, lavatories, tubs, showers, toilets, laundry trays and water heaters. However, if you want to know more about the complete plumbing system, these 24x36-inch detail sheets will prove very useful. Prepared to meet requirements of the National Plumbing Code, these six fact-filled sheets give general information on pipe schedules, fittings, sump-pump details, water-softener hookups, septic system details and much more. Color-coded sheets include a glossary of terms.

ELECTRICAL

The locations for every electrical switch, plug and outlet are shown in your Blueprint Package. However, these Electrical Details go further to take the mystery out of household electrical systems. Prepared to meet requirements of the National Electrical Code, these comprehensive 24x36-inch drawings come packed with helpful information, including wire sizing, switch-installation schematics, cable-routing details, appliance wattage, door-bell hookups, typical service panel circuitry and much more. Six sheets are bound together and color-coded for easy reference. A glossary of terms is also included.

Plan-A-Home® is an easy-to-use tool that helps you design a new home, arrange furniture in a new or existing home, or plan a remodeling project. Each package contains:

- More than *700 peel-off planning symbols* on a self-stick vinyl sheet, including walls, windows, doors, all types of furniture, kitchen components, bath fixtures and many more. All are made of durable, peel-and-stick vinyl you can use over and over.

- A reusable, transparent, *1/4-inch scale planning grid* made of tough mylar that matches the scale of actual working drawings (1/4 -inch equals 1 foot). This grid provides the basis for house layouts of up to 140x92 feet.

- *Tracing paper* and a protective sheet for copying or transferring your completed plan.

- A *felt-tip pen*, with water-soluble ink that wipes away quickly.

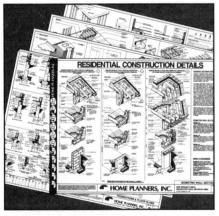

CONSTRUCTION

The Blueprint Package contains everything an experienced builder needs to construct a particular house. However, it doesn't show all the ways that houses can be built, nor does it explain alternate construction methods. To help you understand how your house will be built–and offer additional techniques–this set of drawings depicts the materials and methods used to build foundations, fireplaces, walls, floors and roofs. Where appropriate, the drawings show acceptable alternatives. These six sheets will answer questions for the advanced do-it-yourselfer or home planner.

MECHANICAL

This package contains fundamental principles and useful data that will help you make informed decisions and communicate with subcontractors about heating and cooling systems. The 24 x 36-inch drawings contain instructions and samples that allow you to make simple load calculations and preliminary sizing and costing analysis. Covered are today's most commonly used systems from heat pumps to solar fuel systems. The package is packed full of illustrations and diagrams to help you visualize components and how they relate to one another.

With Plan-A-Home®, you can make basic planning decisions for a new house or make modifications to an existing house. Use with your Blueprint Package to test modifications to rooms or to plan furniture arrangements before you build. Plan-A-Home® lets you lay out areas as large as a 7,500 square foot, six-bedroom, seven-bath house.

ⓓ *The Deck Blueprint Package*

Many of the homes in this book can be enhanced with a professionally designed Deck Plan. Those home plans highlighted with a ⓓ have a matching or corresponding deck plan available which includes a Deck Plan Frontal Sheet, Deck Framing and Floor Plans, Deck Elevations and a Deck Materials List. A Standard Deck Details Package, also available, provides all the how-to information necessary for building *any* deck. Our Complete Deck Building Package contains 1 set of Custom Deck Plans of your choice, plus 1 set of Standard Deck Building Details all for one low price. Our plans and details are carefully prepared in an easy-to-understand format that will guide you through every stage of your deck-building project. See these pages for 25 different Deck layouts to match your favorite house.

SPLIT–LEVEL SUN DECK
Deck Plan D100

BI–LEVEL DECK WITH COVERED DINING
Deck Plan D101

FRESH–AIR CORNER DECK
Deck Plan D102

BACK–YARD EXTENDER DECK
Deck Plan D103

WRAP–AROUND FAMILY DECK
Deck Plan D104

DRAMATIC DECK WITH BARBECUE
Deck Plan D105

SPLIT–PLAN COUNTRY DECK
Deck Plan D106

DECK FOR DINING AND VIEWS
Deck Plan D107

BOLD, ANGLED CORNER DECK
Deck Plan D108

SPECTACULAR "RESORT–STYLE" DECK
Deck Plan D109

TREND–SETTER DECK
Deck Plan D110

TURN–OF–THE–CENTURY DECK
Deck Plan D111

WEEKEND ENTERTAINER DECK
Deck Plan D112

STRIKING "DELTA" DECK
Deck Plan D113

CENTER–VIEW DECK
Deck Plan D114

KITCHEN–EXTENDER DECK
Deck Plan D115

BI–LEVEL RETREAT DECK
Deck Plan D116

SPLIT–LEVEL ACTIVITY DECK
Deck Plan D117

OUTDOOR LIFESTYLE DECK
Deck Plan D118

TRI–LEVEL DECK WITH GRILL
Deck Plan D119

CONTEMPORARY LEISURE DECK
Deck Plan D120

ANGULAR WINGED DECK
Deck Plan D121

DECK FOR A SPLIT–LEVEL HOME
Deck Plan D122

GRACIOUS GARDEN DECK
Deck Plan D123

TERRACED DECK FOR ENTERTAINING
Deck Plan D124

For Deck Plan prices and ordering information, see page 376.

 Or call **Toll Free,**
1-800-848-2550.

◼ *The Landscape Blueprint Package*

For the homes marked with an ◼ in this book, we have created a front-yard landscape plan that matches or is complementary in design to the house plan. These comprehensive blueprint packages include a Frontal Sheet, Plan View, Regionalized Plant & Materials List, a sheet on Planting and Maintaining Your Landscape, Zone Maps and Plant Size and Description Guide. These plans will help you achieve professional results, adding value and enjoyment to your property for years to come. Each set of blueprints is a full 18" x 24" in size with clear, complete instructions and easy-to-read type. See the following pages for 40-different front-yard Landscape Plans to match your favorite house.

Regional Order Map

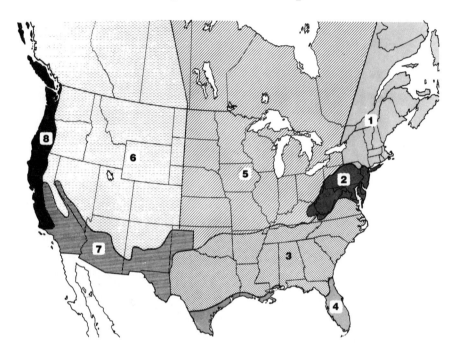

Most of the Landscape Plans shown on these pages are available with a Plant & Materials List adapted by horticultural experts to 8 different regions of the country. Please specify Geographic Region when ordering your plan. See pages 376-379 for prices, ordering information and regional availability.

Region	**1**	Northeast
Region	**2**	Mid-Atlantic
Region	**3**	Deep South
Region	**4**	Florida & Gulf Coast
Region	**5**	Midwest
Region	**6**	Rocky Mountains
Region	**7**	Southern California & Desert Southwest
Region	**8**	Northern California & Pacific Northwest

CAPE COD TRADITIONAL
Landscape Plan L200

WILLIAMSBURG CAPE
Landscape Plan L201

CAPE COD COTTAGE
Landscape Plan L202

GAMBREL–ROOF COLONIAL
Landscape Plan L203

CENTER–HALL COLONIAL
Landscape Plan L204

CLASSIC NEW ENGLAND COLONIAL
Landscape Plan L205

SOUTHERN COLONIAL
Landscape Plan L206

COUNTRY–STYLE FARMHOUSE
Landscape Plan L207

PENNSYLVANIA STONE FARMHOUSE
Landscape Plan L208

RAISED–PORCH FARMHOUSE
Landscape Plan L209

NEW ENGLAND BARN–STYLE HOUSE
Landscape Plan L210

NEW ENGLAND COUNTRY HOUSE
Landscape Plan L211

TRADITIONAL COUNTRY ESTATE
Landscape Plan L212

FRENCH PROVINCIAL ESTATE
Landscape Plan L213

GEORGIAN MANOR
Landscape Plan L214

GRAND–PORTICO GEORGIAN
Landscape Plan L215

BRICK FEDERAL
Landscape Plan L216

COUNTRY FRENCH RAMBLER
Landscape Plan L217

FRENCH MANOR HOUSE
Landscape Plan L218

ELIZABETHAN TUDOR
Landscape Plan L219

TUDOR ONE–STORY
Landscape Plan L220

ENGLISH–STYLE COTTAGE
Landscape Plan L221

MEDIEVAL GARRISON
Landscape Plan L222

QUEEN ANNE VICTORIAN
Landscape Plan L223

GOTHIC VICTORIAN
Landscape Plan L224

BASIC RANCH
Landscape Plan L225

L–SHAPED RANCH
Landscape Plan L226

SPRAWLING RANCH
Landscape Plan L227

TRADITIONAL SPLIT–LEVEL
Landscape Plan L228

SHED–ROOF CONTEMPORARY
Landscape Plan L229

WOOD–SIDED CONTEMPORARY
Landscape Plan L230

HILLSIDE CONTEMPORARY
Landscape Plan L231

FLORIDA RAMBLER
Landscape Plan L232

CALIFORNIA STUCCO
Landscape Plan L233

LOW–GABLE CONTEMPORARY
Landscape Plan L234

NORTHERN BRICK CHATEAU
Landscape Plan L235

MISSION–TILE RANCH
Landscape Plan L236

ADOBE–BLOCK HACIENDA
Landscape Plan L237

COURTYARD PATIO HOME
Landscape Plan L238

CENTER–COURT CONTEMPORARY
Landscape Plan L239

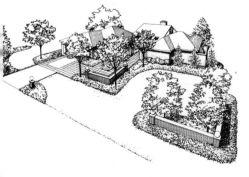

For Landscape Plan prices and ordering information, see page 376.

 Or call **Toll Free,** **1-800-848-2550**.

Price Schedule & Plans Index

House Blueprint Price Schedule
(Prices guaranteed through December 31, 1994)

	1-set Study Package	4-set Building Package	8-set Building Package	1-set Reproducible Sepias
Schedule A	$210	$270	$330	$420
Schedule B	$240	$300	$360	$480
Schedule C	$270	$330	$390	$540
Schedule D	$300	$360	$420	$600
Schedule E	$390	$450	$510	$660

Additional Identical Blueprints in same order.....$50 per set
Reverse Blueprints (mirror image).........................$50 per set
Specification Outlines...$7 each
Materials Lists:
      Schedule A-D..$40
      Schedule E..$50

Deck Plans Price Schedule

CUSTOM DECK PLANS

Price Group	Q	R	S
1 Set Custom Plans	$25	$30	$35

   Additional identical sets:.......................................$10 each
   Reverse sets (mirror image): ....$10 each

STANDARD DECK DETAILS
1 Set Generic Construction Details ....$14.95 each

COMPLETE DECK BUILDING PACKAGE

Price Group	Q	R	S
1 Set Custom Plans 1 Set Standard Deck Details	$35	$40	$45

Landscape Plans Price Schedule

Price Group	X	Y	Z
1 set	$35	$45	$55
3 sets	$50	$60	$70
6 sets	$65	$75	$85

Additional Identical Sets ....$10 each
Reverse Sets (mirror image)................................$10 each

These pages contain all the information you need to price your blueprints. In general the larger and more complicated the house, the more it costs to design and thus the higher the price we must charge for the blueprints. Remember, however, that these prices are far less than you would normally pay for the services of a licensed architect or professional designer.

Custom home designs and related architectural services often cost thousands of dollars, ranging from 5% to 15% of the cost of construction. By ordering our blueprints you are potentially saving enough money to afford a larger house, or to add those "extra" amenities such as a patio, deck, swimming pool or even an upgraded kitchen or luxurious master suite.

Index

To use the Index below, refer to the design number listed in numerical order (a helpful page reference is also given). Note the price index letter and refer to the House Blueprint Price Schedule above for the cost of one, four or eight sets of blueprints or the cost of a reproducible sepia. Additional prices are shown for identical and reverse blueprint sets, as well as a very useful Materials List. Also note in the Index below those plans that have matching or complementary Deck

Plans or Landscape Plans. Refer to the schedules above for prices of these plans. Some of our plans can be customized through our Home Customizer® Service. These plans are indicated below with this symbol: ☏. See page 381 for more information.

To Order: Fill in and send the order form on page 381—or call toll free 1-800-848-2550.

DESIGN	PRICE	PAGE	CUSTOMIZABLE	DECK	DECK PRICE	LANDSCAPE	LANDSCAPE PRICE	REGIONS
V11021	A	215						
V11024	A	189						
V11025	A	188						
V11054	B	55						
V11058	A	193						
V11072	A	234						
V11074	A	185						
V11075	A	190		D114	R	L225	X	1-3,5,6,8
V11091	B	101		D100	Q			
V11094	A	195						
V11100	B	96						
V11102	C	119						
V11107	A	182		D112	R	L225	X	1-3,5,6,8
V11113	A	206		D113	R	L202	X	1-3,5,6,8
V11129	B	231						
V11147	A	185						
V11149	B	120						
V11174	C	128						
V11186	B	105						
V11187	A	206						
V11188	A	187						
V11189	A	184						
V11190	A	180						
V11191	A	191		D114	R	L225	X	1-3,5,6,8
V11193	A	178						
V11197	A	189						
V11201	C	141						
V11222	B	108						
V11228	D	58		D124	S	L217	Y	1-8
V11252	B	104						
V11272	B	52						
V11279	A	194						
V11280	B	99						
V11281	A	236						
V11283	C	232						
V11295	C	142						
V11297	A	196						
V11305	A	294		D106	S			
V11307	A	295		D114	R	L226	X	1-8
V11309	A	196						
V11311	A	200		D114	R	L225	X	1-3,5,6,8
V11316	A	180						
V11317	B	101						
V11320	A	306		D112	R			
V11321	A	306		D112	R			
V11322	A	306		D112	R			

DESIGN	PRICE	PAGE	CUSTOMIZABLE	DECK	DECK PRICE	LANDSCAPE	LANDSCAPE PRICE	REGIONS
V11323	A	297		D117	S	L225	X	1-3,5,6,8
V11325	B	114		D106	S	L225	X	1-3,5,6,8
V11326	B	57						
V11327	A	179						
V11330	B	56						
V11331	B	310						
V11337	B	94						
V11343	B	96				L226	X	1-8
V11345	B	54						
V11346	B	100						
V11350	B	307						
V11351	B	307						
V11352	B	307						
V11357	A	231						
V11362	B	52						
V11364	A	197		D117	S			
V11366	A	191						
V11367	A	183						
V11372	A	316						
V11373	A	192		D113	R			
V11374	A	183						
V11380	A	295		D114	R	L226	X	1-8
V11381	A	295		D114	R	L226	X	1-8
V11382	A	294		D106	S			
V11383	A	294		D106	S			
V11387	A	300		D101	R			
V11388	A	300		D101	R			
V11389	A	300		D101	R			
V11394	A	317		D105	R	L202	X	1-3,5,6,8
V11396	B	218						
V11399	B	198						
V11522	A	201						
V11531	A	201						
V11711	D	176						
V11748	B	114		D117	S			
V11758	B	100						
V11761	C	139		D117	S	L217	Y	1-8
V11784	C	59						
V11786	C	129						
V11787	C	165		D117	S			
V11788	C	121		D101	R	L206	Z	1-6,8
V11794	C	318						
V11797	B	52						
V11803	A	182						
V11820	C	268						
V11829	B	110		D113	R	L226	X	1-8
V11835	B	128		D100	Q	L225	X	1-3,5,6,8
V11851	C	134						
V11864	B	301		D103	R			
V11865	B	301		D103	R			
V11866	B	301		D103	R			
V11872	C	133						
V11884	B	230						
V11886	C	135						
V11890	B	94						
V11891	B	218						
V11892	B	51		D106	S	L225	X	1-3,5,6,8
V11896	B	97						
V11911	D	150						
V11916	D	151						
V11917	B	218						
V11920	B	95		D103	R	L225	X	1-3,5,6,8
V11924	C	134						
V11928	D	168						
V11929	C	132		D117	S			
V11931	C	132						
V11936	D	159						
V11938	A	296						
V11939	A	180		D117	S	L225	X	1-3,5,6,8
V11944	A	184						
V11945	B	308						
V11946	B	308						
V11947	B	309						
V11948	B	309						
V11950	B	118		D100	Q			
V11952	C	145						
V11956	A	339	▲	D117	S			
V11957	A	338		D100	Q	L228	Y	1-8
V11964	C	318						
V11967	B	319						
V11980	B	110						

DESIGN	PRICE	PAGE	CUSTOMIZABLE	DECK	DECK PRICE	LANDSCAPE	LANDSCAPE PRICE	REGIONS
V11989	C	24		D100	Q	L220	Y	1-3,5,6,8
V11993	D	60				L213	Z	1-8
V12122	A	187						
V12129	B	25						
V12134	C	55						
V12135	C	270						
V12142	C	46		D106	S			
V12146	A	315		D114	R	L203	Y	1-3,5,6,8
V12153	A	203		D114	R			
V12154	A	203		D114	R			
V12158	A	238						
V12159	A	205						
V12160	A	207						
V12161	A	207						
V12163	A	204						
V12165	A	205						
V12166	A	204						
V12167	A	240						
V12168	A	240						
V12170	B	26		D101	R	L221	X	1-3,5,6,8
V12181	C	137		D100	Q	L226	X	1-8
V12182	B	215						
V12183	D	153						
V12192	D	332		D117	S	L218	Z	1-6,8
V12194	A	241						
V12198	A	199						
V12199	A	239						
V12200	B	88						
V12204	B	122						
V12206	B	16		D100	Q	L220	Y	1-3,5,6,8
V12208	C	123						
V12209	C	138						
V12212	D	61				L217	Y	1-8
V12220	C	47		D114	R	L217	Y	1-8
V12236	C	63						
V12241	C	41						
V12245	D	30		D100	Q			
V12256	C	257						
V12260	B	122						
V12261	B	99						
V12264	C	138						
V12270	C	140						
V12271	C	141						
V12273	C	35						
V12278	C	40						
V12283	C	329		D114	R	L206	Z	1-6,8
V12286	B	29						
V12298	C	232						
V12303	C	267						
V12304	C	259						
V12316	B	120		D106	S	L225	X	1-3,5,6,8
V12317	D	31						
V12318	B	18		D117	S	L220	Y	1-3,5,6,8
V12329	C	264						
V12330	B	214						
V12342	D	57						
V12343	D	173						
V12351	B	228		D101	R			
V12352	B	127						
V12353	C	126						
V12359	B	269						
V12360	B	111						
V12362	B	127						
V12363	B	229						
V12372	C	42						
V12374	B	29						
V12378	C	24						
V12383	B	233						
V12385	B	33						
V12387	C	32						
V12391	C	43						
V12488	A	328	▲	D102	Q			
V12502	C	322				L212	Z	1-8
V12504	C	323						
V12505	A	293	▲	D113	R	L226	X	1-8
V12506	C	269						
V12510	A	317		D105	R	L200	X	1-3,5,6,8
V12511	B	352		D108	R	L229	Y	1-8
V12515	C	19		D101	R			
V12519	C	148						
V12520	B	344		D105	R	L201	Y	1-3,5,6,8

DESIGN	PRICE	PAGE	CUSTOMIZABLE	DECK	DECK PRICE	LANDSCAPE	LANDSCAPE PRICE	REGIONS
V12908	B	343	●	D117	S	L205	Y	1-3,5,6,8
V12911	A	208						
V12912	B	74						
V12913	B	222		D124	S			
V12915	C	247		D114	R	L212	Z	1-8
V12916	B	124						
V12917	B	223						
V12918	B	217		D124	S			
V12920	D	167		D104	S	L212	Z	1-8
V12921	D	166		D104	S	L212	Z	1-8
V12922	D	69						
V12927	B	328	●	D100	Q			
V12929	B	14						
V12930	B	261	●					
V12931	B	112	●					
V12937	C	253				L229	Y	1-8
V12938	E	169						
V12941	B	312		D112	R			
V12942	B	312		D112	R			
V12943	B	312		D112	R			
V12946	C	342	●	D114	R	L207	Z	1-6,8
V12947	B	102	●					
V12948	B	77	●					
V12949	C	68		D123	S			
V12950	C	66						
V12961	D	39						
V12962	B	15	●					
V12966	D	45						
V12977	D	160				L214	Z	1-3,5,6,8
V12997	D	162						
V13144	B	98						
V13163	B	214						
V13177	B	106						
V13189	A	316		D113	R			
V13195	A	237						
V13196	A	238						
V13203	A	234						
V13204	A	188						
V13208	A	192						
V13211	A	186						
V13212	A	234						
V13213	A	198						
V13223	A	205						
V13314	B	113						
V13315	D	157						
V13319	C	256	●	D112	R	L217	Y	1-8
V13330	A	244						
V13332	B	125						
V13336	B	103						
V13340	B	93						
V13344	D	156						
V13345	B	92	●					
V13346	B	38	●					
V13348	C	131						
V13350	B	107		D115	Q	L205	Y	1-3,5,6,8
V13355	A	178	●	D117	S	L220	Y	1-3,5,6,8
V13357	D	255		D115	Q	L211	Y	1-8
V13368	C	258		D104	S	L220	Y	1-3,5,6,8
V13373	A	311		D110	R	L202	X	1-3,5,6,8
V13374	A	311		D115	Q	L202	X	1-3,5,6,8
V13375	A	311		D115	Q	L202	X	1-3,5,6,8
V13376	B	108						
V13377	C	37						
V13400	C	72	●					
V13401	C	72	●					
V13402	D	73	●					
V13405	D	83	●			L236	Z	3,4,7
V13408	D	262						
V13411	C	80	●					
V13412	B	76	●					
V13415	C	81	●					
V13416	A	70	●					
V13419	B	71	●					
V13421	B	66	●					
V13422	B	79	●					
V13423	C	78	●					
V13430	C	76	●					
V13433	C	84	●			L213	Z	1-8
V13434	D	82	●					
V13436	C	84	●					
V13440	C	67	●	D120	R	L233	Y	3,4,7
V13453	A	5				L238	Y	3,4,7,8
V13460	A	384	●			L200	X	1-3,5,6,8
V13466	B	3	●	D110	R	L207	Z	1-6,8
V13481	B	5	●			L200	X	1-3,5,6,8
V13560	B	250						
V13569	B	5				L204	Y	1-3,5,6,8

Before You Order . . .

Before completing the coupon at right or calling us on our Toll-Free Blueprint Hotline, you may be interested to learn more about our service and products. Here's some information you will find helpful.

Quick Turnaround
We process and ship every blueprint order from our office within 48 hours. On most orders, we do even better. Normally, if we receive your order by 5 p.m. Eastern Time, we'll process it the same day and ship it the following day. Because of this quick turnaround, we won't send a formal notice acknowledging receipt of your order.

Our Exchange Policy
Since blueprints are printed in response to your order, we cannot honor requests for refunds. However, we will exchange your entire first order for an equal number of blueprints at a price of $40 for the first set and $10 for each additional set; $60 total exchange fee for 4 sets; $90 total exchange fee for 8 sets... *plus* the difference in cost if exchanging for a design in a higher price bracket or *less* the difference in cost if exchanging for a design in a lower price bracket. (Sepias are not exchangeable.) All sets from the first order must be returned before the exchange can take place. Please add $8 for postage and handling via ground service; $20 via 2nd Day Air.

About Reverse Blueprints
If you want to build in reverse of the plan as shown, we will include an extra set of reversed blueprints (mirror image) for an additional fee of $50. Although lettering and dimensions appear backward, reverses will be a useful visual aid if you decide to flop the plan. Right-reading reverses of Customizable Plans are available through our Customization Service. Call for more details.

Modifying or Customizing Our Plans
With such a great selection of homes, you are bound to find the one that suits you. However, if you need to make alterations to a design that is customizable, you need only order our Customizer® kit or call our Customization representative at 1-800-322-6797, ext. 800, to get you started (see additional information on next page). It is possible to customize many of our plans that are not part of our Home Customizer® Service.

If you decide to revise plans significantly that are not customizable through our service, we strongly suggest that you order reproducible sepias and consult a licensed architect or professional designer to help you redraw the plans.

Architectural and Engineering Seals
Some cities and states are now requiring that a licensed architect or engineer review and "seal" your blueprints prior to construction. This is often due to local or regional concerns over energy consumption, safety codes, seismic ratings, etc. For this reason, you may find it necessary to consult with a local professional to have your plans reviewed. This can normally be accomplished with minimum delays, for a nominal fee. In some cases, we can seal your plans through our Customization Service. Call for more details.

Compliance with Local Codes and Regulations
At the time of creation, our plans are drawn to specifications published by Building Officials Code Administrators (BOCA), the Southern Standard Building Code, or the Uniform Building Code and are designed to meet or exceed national building standards. Some states, counties and municipalities have their own codes, zoning requirements and building regulations. Before starting construction, consult with local building authorities and make sure you comply with local ordinances and codes, including obtaining any necessary permits or inspections as building progresses. In some cases, minor modifications to your plans by your builder, local architect or designer may be required to meet local conditions and requirements. We may be able to make these changes to Customizable Plans providing you supply all pertinent information from your local building authorities.

Foundation and Exterior Wall Changes
Most of our plans are drawn with either a full or partial basement foundation. Depending upon your specific climate or regional building practices, you may wish to convert this basement to a slab or crawlspace. Most professional contractors and builders can easily adapt your plans to alternate foundation types. Likewise, most can easily convert 2x4 wall construction to 2x6, or vice versa. If you need more guidance on these conversions, our handy Construction Detail Sheets, shown on page 369, describe how such conversions can be made. For Customizable Plans, we can easily provide the necessary changes for you.

How Many Blueprints Do You Need?
A single set of blueprints is sufficient to study a home in greater detail. However, if you are planning to obtain cost estimates from a contractor or subcontractors—or if you are planning to build immediately—you will need more sets. Because additional sets are cheaper when ordered in quantity with the original order, make sure you order enough blueprints to satisfy all requirements. The following checklist will help you determine how many you need:

_____Owner

_____Builder (generally requires at least three sets; one as a legal document, one to use during inspections, and at least one to give to subcontractors)

_____Local Building Department (often requires two sets)

_____Mortgage Lender (usually one set for a conventional loan; three sets for FHA or VA loans)

_____TOTAL NUMBER OF SETS

Toll Free 1-800-848-2550

Normal Office Hours:
8:00 a.m. to 8:00 p.m. Eastern Time
Monday through Friday
Our staff will gladly answer any questions during normal office hours. Our answering service can place orders after hours or on weekends.

If we receive your order by 5:00 p.m. Eastern Time, Monday through Friday, we'll process it the same day and ship it the following business day. When ordering by phone, please have your charge card ready. We'll also ask you for the Order Form Key Number at the bottom of the coupon. Please use our Toll-Free number for blueprint and book orders only.

For Customization orders call 1-800-322-6797, ext. 800.

By FAX: Copy the Order Form on the next page and send it on our International FAX line: 1-602-297-6219.

Canadian Customers
Order Toll-Free 1-800-848-2550
For faster, more economical service, Canadian customers may now call in orders on our Toll-Free line. Or, complete the order form at right adding 30% to all prices, and mail in Canadian funds to:

       Home Plans
       3275 W. Ina Road, Suite 110
       Tucson, AZ 85741

By FAX: Copy the Order Form on the next page and send it on our International FAX line: 1-602-297-6219.

The Home Customizer®

Many of the plans in this book are customizable through our Home Customizer® service. Look for this symbol ⌂ on the pages of home designs. It indicates that the plan on that page is part of The Home Customizer® service.

Some changes to customizable plans that can be made include:

- exterior elevation changes
- kitchen and bath modifications
- roof, wall and foundation changes
- room additions
- and much more!

If the plan you have chosen to build is one of our customizable homes, you can easily order the Home Customizer® kit to start on the path to making your alterations. The kit, priced at only $19.95, may be ordered at the same time you order your blueprint package by calling on our toll-free number or using the order blank at right. Or you can wait until you receive your blueprints, spend some time studying them and then order the kit by phone, FAX or mail. If you then decide to proceed with the customizing service, the $19.95 price of the kit will be refunded to you after your customization order is received. The Home Customizer® kit includes:

- instruction book with examples
- architectural scale
- clear acetate work film
- erasable red marker
- removable correction tape
- ¼" scale furniture cutouts
- 1 set of Customizable Drawings with floor plans and elevations

The service is easy, fast and *affordable*. Because we know and work with our plans and have them available on state-of-the-art computer systems, we can make the changes efficiently at prices much lower than those charged by normal architectural or drafting services. In addition, you'll be getting custom changes directly from a company whose dedication to excellence and long-standing professional experience are well recognized in the industry.

Call now to learn more about how simple it can be to have the *custom home* you've always wanted.

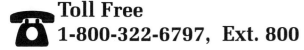

☎ Toll Free
1-800-322-6797, Ext. 800

ORDER FORM

HOME PLANS, 3275 WEST INA ROAD
SUITE 110, TUCSON, ARIZONA 85741

THE BASIC BLUEPRINT PACKAGE
Rush me the following (please refer to the Plans Index and Price Schedule in this section):

_____	Set(s) of blueprints for plan number(s) _____.	$_____
_____	Set(s) of sepias for plan number(s) _____.	$_____
_____	Additional identical blueprints in same order @ $50 per set.	$_____
_____	Reverse blueprints @ $50 per set.	$_____
_____	Home Customizer®Kit(s) for Plan(s)_____ @ $19.95 per kit.	$_____

IMPORTANT EXTRAS
Rush me the following:

_____	Materials List @ $40 Schedule A-D; $50 Schedule E	$_____
_____	Specification Outlines @ $7 each.	$_____
_____	Detail Sets @ $14.95 each; any two for $22.95; any three for $29.95; all four for $39.95 (save $19.85). ❏ Plumbing ❏ Electrical ❏ Construction ❏ Mechanical (These helpful details provide general construction advice and are not specific to any single plan.)	$_____
_____	Set(s) of blueprints for Outdoor Project number(s)_____.	$_____
_____	Plan-A-Home® @ $29.95 each.	$_____

DECK BLUEPRINTS

_____	Set(s) of Deck Plan _____	$_____
_____	Additional identical blueprints in same order @ $10 per set.	$_____
_____	Reverse blueprints @ $10 per set.	$_____
_____	Set of Standard Deck Details @ $14.95 per set.	$_____
_____	Set of Complete Building Package (Best Buy!) Includes Custom Deck Plan _____ (See Index and Price Schedule) Plus Standard Deck Details	$_____

LANDSCAPE BLUEPRINTS

_____	Set(s) of Landscape Plan _____.	$_____
_____	Additional identical blueprints in same order @ $10 per set.	$_____
_____	Reverse blueprints @ $10 per set.	$_____

Please indicate the appropriate region of the country for Plant & Material List. (See Map on page 372): Region _____

SUB-TOTAL — $_____

SALES TAX (Arizona residents add 5% sales tax; Michigan residents add 6% sales tax.) — $_____

POSTAGE AND HANDLING	1-3 sets	4 or more sets	
COMMERCIAL SERVICE (Requires street address - No P.O. Boxes)			
•Ground Service Allow 4-6 days delivery	❏ $6.00	❏ $8.00	$_____
•2nd Day Air Service Allow 2-3 days delivery	❏ $12.00	❏ $20.00	$_____
•Next Day Air Service Allow 1 day delivery	❏ $22.00	❏ $30.00	$_____
POST OFFICE DELIVERY If no street address available. Allow 4-6 days delivery	❏ $8.00	❏ $12.00	$_____
OVERSEAS AIR MAIL DELIVERY Note: All delivery times are from date Blueprint Package is shipped.	❏ $30.00	❏ $50.00	$_____

TOTAL (Sub-total, tax, and postage) — $_____

YOUR ADDRESS (please print)

Name _____

Street _____

City _____State_____Zip _____

Daytime telephone number (_____) _____

FOR CREDIT CARD ORDERS ONLY
Please fill in the information below:

Credit card number _____

Exp. Date: Month/Year _____

Check one ❏ Visa ❏ MasterCard ❏ Discover Card

Signature _____

Please check appropriate box: Order Form Key
   ❏ Licensed Builder-Contractor
   ❏ Home Owner | CHP1BP |

☎ ORDER TOLL FREE
1-800-848-2550

CREATIVE HOMEOWNER PRESS®

How-To Books for...

Quick Guide:
Ceramic Tile
Includes projects on tiling walls, floors, countertops and backsplashes; showers and tub surrounds, fireplaces and wood stoves, steps and stairs.

80 pages   **$7.95**

Quick Guide:
Floors
Focuses on ways of restoring old floors and preparing floors for new surfaces. Includes how to install hardwood floors, carpeting, tiling and more.

80 pages   **$7.95**

Quick Guide:
Decks
Covers every stage from developing a site plan to the final construction. Includes plans for freestanding, attached, or raised decks.

80 pages   **$7.95**

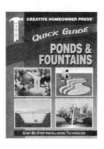

Quick Guide:
Ponds & Fountains
Topics incude: selecting a site, basic materials, formal and natural pools, waterfalls, filtration options, plumbing and electrical requirements, installing a pump, pool maintenance and more.

80 pages   **$7.95**

Quick Guide:
Fences & Gates
Covers site construction and installation for different styles of wood fences, plus chain link and sectional aluminum fences.

80 pages   **$7.95**

Quick Guide:
Interior & Exterior Painting
Topics include both interior and exterior painting projects, preparing surfaces for paint, color selection and design, choosing a finish, surface treatments, painting tools and more.

80 pages   **$7.95**

Quick Guide:
Trim & Molding
Topics include: types of molding and trim, tools needed and how to use them. Projects include decorating with molding and trim, door and window applications, maintenance, repair and more.

80 pages   **$7.95**

Quick Guide:
Storage Sheds
Every facet of planning and construction is covered from design selection to the installation of windows, doors and finishing trim.

80 pages   **$7.95**

Quick Guide:
Patios & Walks
Covers designing the area, selecting materials, creating patterns and using surface textures. Includes techniques for working with stone, concrete and brick.

80 pages   **$7.95**

Quick Guide:
Walls & Ceilings
Covers simple cracks to replacing entire surfaces. Includes surface repair and preparation, painting, wallpapering and tiling.

80 pages   **$7.95**

the Home Planner, Builder & Owner

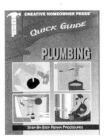

Quick Guide:
Plumbing

Covers all areas of home plumbing including all the techniques necessary for working on sinks, toilets, baths, showers and water heaters.

80 pages   **$7.95**

Quick Guide:
Windows & Doors

Provides complete up-to-date, step-by-step instructions for the installation of original or replacement windows and doors.

80 pages   **$7.95**

Quick Guide:
Small Gasoline Engines

Small gasoline engine powered equipment for the homeowner includes lawnmowers, grass trimmers, hedge trimmers, leaf blowers, chain saws, edgers, snow blowers and more.

80 pages   **$7.95**

Quick Guide:
Wiring

Demonstrates the basics of wiring so the do-it-yourselfer can repair a lamp, replace an outlet, or extend electrical circuits in the home.

80 pages   **$7.95**

Basic Wiring

Learn how to repair a lamp, replace an outlet, extend electrical circuits, install ceiling and attic fans and programmable thermostats. Includes pertinent sections from the National Electrical Code. Over 350 illustrations.

160 pages   **$12.95**

Modern Home Plumbing

Take the guesswork out of plumbing repair and installation for old and new systems. Projects include replacing faucets, unclogging drains, installing a tub, replacing a water heater and much more. 500 illustrations and diagrams.

160 pages   **$12.95**

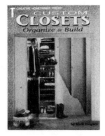

Custom Closets:
Organize & Build

Learn how to build wooden, laminate and coated-wire organizer systems tailor-made to the specific needs of men, women and children. Over 350 illustrations and color photographs.

160 pages   **$9.95**

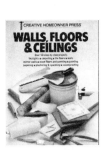

Walls, Floors & Ceilings

Fifty projects to beautify a home's interior. Features many remodeling ideas including installing skylights, recessed lighting, ceiling fans, hardwood floors, and laying wall-to-wall carpet. Over 500 illustrations and color photographs.

160 pages   **$12.95**

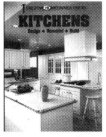

Kitchens
Design, Remodel, Build

Whether tackling a small kitchen project or a major overhaul, this title offers both creative and practical ideas in over 100 step-by-step projects. Over 300 color photographs and line drawings.

176 pages   **$12.95**

Dream Kitchens

The kitchen designs, plans and projects offered in this book can transform an average or dull kitchen into a more functional and beautiful one. 40 step-by-step projects range from replacing cabinets to installing skylights. Over 70 full-color photographs and 300 illustrations.

160 pages   **$9.95**

Place Your Order ...

Decks & Patios
Create additional living space and learn how to beautify an outdoor setting. Includes deck and patio building basics plus projects for overhead covers, benches, outdoor furniture, screens, lighting, barbecues and firepits. Over 350 illustrations and color photographs.
160 pages   **$9.95**

Design, Remodel and Build Your Bathroom
Floor plans are provided for all bathroom shapes and sizes. Instructions for building cabinets, platform and sunken tubs, plumbing repairs, tiling, wiring and more. Over 350 illustrations and color photographs.
160 pages   **$9.95**

Fireplaces
How to build, install, renovate and maintain fireplaces of many types. Discusses the elements of fireplace efficiency and decor. Includes wood stoves, recycling systems, energy conservation, safety and wood use. Over 300 illustrations and color photographs.
128 pages   **$9.95**

Spas & Hot Tubs
Saunas & Home Gyms
How to create the environments in which to exercise, relax, unwind or entertain. Step-by-step instructions will guide you in installing and maintaining a spa, hot tub, sauna or exercise room. Over 300 line drawings and color photographs.
160 pages   **$9.95**

Swimming Pools
A pool will enhance your health and relaxation, as well as add to the beauty and value of your home. Features both inground/above ground and indoor pools. Also included are ponds, cabanas, gazebos, fountains, fences, spas and hot tubs. 400 illustrations and color photos.
160 pages   **$9.95**

Decks
Design and build your dream deck. Parts of a deck and materials used in construction are explained. Features step-by-step instructions on railing and step construction, overhead deck covers and deck maintenance. Outdoor lighting and how to install it is included. Over 400 illustrations and color photographs.
160 pages   **$12.95**

BOOK ORDER FORM
Please Print

SHIP TO:

Name:

Address:

City: State: Zip: Phone Number:
(should there be a problem with your order)

Quantity	Title	CHP #	Price	Cost
	Quick Guide: Ceramic Tile	287730	$ 7.95 ea.	
	Quick Guide: Decks	287720	7.95 ea.	
	Quick Guide: Fences & Gates	287880	7.95 ea.	
	Quick Guide: Floors	287734	7.95 ea.	
	Quick Guide: Ponds & Fountains	287804	7.95 ea.	
	Quick Guide: Interior & Exterior Painting	287784	7.95 ea.	
	Quick Guide: Trim & Molding	287745	7.95 ea.	
	Quick Guide: Patios & Walks	287778	7.95 ea.	
	Quick Guide: Plumbing	287863	7.95 ea.	
	Quick Guide: Small Gasoline Engines	287849	7.95 ea.	
	Quick Guide: Storage Sheds	287815	7.95 ea.	
	Quick Guide: Walls & Ceilings	287792	7.95 ea.	
	Quick Guide: Windows & Doors	287812	7.95 ea.	
	Quick Guide: Wiring	287884	7.95 ea.	
	Basic Wiring	277825	12.95 ea.	
	Custom Closets	277132	9.95 ea.	
	Decks: Design & Build	277174	12.95 ea.	
	Decks & Patios	277100	9.95 ea.	
	Dream Kitchens	277067	9.95 ea.	

Quantity	Title	CHP #	Price	Cost
	Fireplaces	277174	9.95 ea.	
	Kitchens, Design, Remodel, Build	277060	12.95 ea.	
	Modern Home Plumbing	277612	12.95 ea.	
	Spas, Hot Tubs, Saunas, Home Gyms	277845	9.95 ea.	
	Swimming Pools	277850	9.95 ea.	
	Walls, Floors & Ceilings	277694	12.95 ea.	
	Your Bathroom: Design, Remodel, Build	277040	9.95 ea.	

Number of Books Ordered _____   Total for Books _____

Prices subject to change without notice.   NJ residents add 6% tax _____

Sub-total _____

Postage/Handling Charges _____
$2.50 for first book / $1.00 for each additional book

TOTAL _____

Make checks (in U.S. currency only) payable to:
CREATIVE HOMEOWNER PRESS®
P.O. Box 38, 24 Park Way
Upper Saddle River, New Jersey 07458-9960.